The Redistribution Recession

The Redistribution Recession

How Labor Market Distortions
Contracted the Economy

CASEY B. MULLIGAN

OXFORD
UNIVERSITY PRESS

Oxford University Press is a department of the
University of Oxford. It furthers the University's objective
of excellence in research, scholarship, and education
by publishing worldwide

Oxford   New York
Auckland   Cape Town   Dar es Salaam   Hong Kong   Karachi
Kuala Lumpur   Madrid   Melbourne   Mexico City   Nairobi
New Delhi   Shanghai   Taipei   Toronto

With offices in
Argentina   Austria   Brazil   Chile   Czech Republic   France   Greece
Guatemala   Hungary   Italy   Japan   Poland   Portugal   Singapore
South Korea   Switzerland   Thailand   Turkey   Ukraine   Vietnam

Oxford is a registered trade mark of Oxford University Press
in the Uk and certain other countries

Published in the United States of America by
Oxford University Press
198 Madison Avenue, New York, NY 10016

Library of Congress Cataloging-in-Publication Data
Mulligan, Casey B.
The redistribution recession : how labor market distortions contracted the economy / Casey B. Mulligan.
p.   cm.
Includes bibliographical references and index.
ISBN 978-0-19-994221-3 (cloth : alk. paper)   1. Labor market—United States—21st century.
2. Recessions—United States—History—21st century.   3. Income distribution—United States
—History—21st century.   I. Title.
HD5724.M83 2012
331.120973'090511—dc23   2012030181

3 5 7 9 8 6 4 2

Printed in the United States of America
on acid-free paper

To the Mulligan kids: Jack, Marc, John Casey, and Ella!

Contents

Preface

THROUGHOUT MY CAREER as an economist, I have been interested in the mutual feedback between economic activity and public policy. In studying those issues, I began to appreciate not only that taxes matter but also that public finance concepts such as tax distortions help in understanding private sector activity, even in those cases where market outcomes are less than fully efficient for reasons that have nothing to do with public policy. Like millions of other people, I turned my attention to the monthly U.S. economic data releases after Lehman Brothers failed in September 2008, except that in my mind labor market distortions were the way to organize that news. The effort yielded some surprising and unconventional conclusions, and some of the connections with taxation turned out to be as much literal as conceptual.

My essential results require only a few relatively simple economic concepts, and they point to the potential for important contributions to recession economics from fields as diverse as poverty analysis, law, political science, labor, and macroeconomics. Hoping to facilitate entry by these varied experts, I decided to rework my analysis of recent labor market events—much of it previously unpublished—into a book written for social scientists generally interested in why employment fell so much in 2008 and 2009 and has so far failed to recover. The first four chapters introduce economic jargon sparingly, with clear definitions, and leave technical notes to endnotes and appendices, and yet they are able to both identify and quantify (what I think are) the main economic forces affecting the labor market. The second half of the book pushes the argument further and offers tests of key assumptions, but in a style that is more familiar to economics graduate students than to noneconomists. All of the chapters contain the details necessary for a professional economist to replicate my results.

I thank Julia and the rest of my family, Tsega Beyene, and Mekdes Yohannes for helping me dedicate the time needed to write this book. Fernando Alvarez, Gary Becker, John Covell, Bob Dalrymple, Steve Davis, Bill Dougan, Aaron Edlin, Gauti Eggertsson, Christian Ferrada, Joe Jackson, Kyle Herkenhoff, Matt Kahn, Emir Kamenica, Michael Kirker, Elizabeth Lower-Basch, Bruce Meyer, Jeff Miron, Robert Moffitt, Tom Mulligan, Kevin Murphy, Derek Neal, David Neumark, Marcus Nunes, Lee Ohanian, Nicola Pavoni, Tomas Philipson, Yona Rubinstein, Jesse Shapiro, Rob Shimer, Andrei Shleifer, Curtis Simon, Cheryl Sturm, Luke Threinen, Kevin Tsui, Glen Weyl, Paul Willen, more than a dozen anonymous referees, and graduate students, undergraduate students, and seminar participants at the University of Chicago, the Congressional Budget Office, Brown, Clemson, the FDIC, the Federal Reserve Board, Harvard, MIT, the New York Federal Reserve, Tel Aviv University, UC Irvine, UCLA, Wheaton College, Wisconsin, and the World Bank improved this book with their comments on research papers that were the basis for book chapters. Kevin McKenna, Josh Mills, and Catherine Rampell also helped with their comments and suggestions on my posts at economix.blogs.nytimes.com about related topics. I also appreciate the assistance of Sophie Wang, Eric Anderson, Ada Barbosa, and Getfriday's Vishwas; computing support from the National Bureau of Economic Research; the financial support of the George J. Stigler Center for the Study of the Economy and the State; and support from the University of Chicago's Division of Social Sciences during a part-year leave of absence that allowed this book to get started.

Chicago

March 2012

The Redistribution Recession

1

Introduction

I can remember sitting in the Roosevelt Room with Hank Paulson and Ben Bernanke and others, and they said to me that if we don't act boldly, Mr. President, we could be in a depression greater than the Great Depression.

— PRESIDENT GEORGE W. BUSH (December 1, 2008, *ABC News* interview)

AS THE PRESIDENT was warned by his advisers, market economies were dramatically cutting back their labor usage. Between the end of 2007 and the end of 2009, the fraction of Americans with jobs fell 7 percent, and hours worked per capita fell 10 percent. Would the U.S. recession have been deeper if the federal government had not intervened in financial markets and had not enhanced its safety nets for the unemployed and the poor? Or were the labor market declines amplified and prolonged by federal government actions?

The answers to these questions depend on the causes of labor market change. Labor economists prior to the recession often explained market outcomes in terms of "fundamentals" in the labor market itself: worker productivity, the willingness of people to work, labor income taxes, and labor market regulations. But the large labor collapse of 2008–09, and the capital market crashes occurring at about the same time, created and renewed interest in impulses from outside the labor market such as a drop in investment, financial deleveraging, a "liquidity trap," and a lack of consumer confidence.

Although the less proximate impulses have been mentioned for years, less is known about their quantitative importance or exactly how to trace their links to the labor market through a chain of microeconomic reasoning. If we assume for the moment that labor market fundamentals still influence labor market outcomes, but in this recession they were perhaps joined by less proximate impulses, it is helpful to adjust actual labor market outcomes for the fundamentals. This book estimates what would have happened to labor usage and other major economic variables if productivity, the willingness of people to work, labor income tax rates, and labor market regulations had remained constant. The decline in labor usage that remains can be interpreted as the combined influence of remaining impulses such as a lack of consumer confidence, the drop in investment, etc., to the extent that they have an influence separate from the fundamentals.

This kind of residual approach is familiar from labor economics, where it has been used to quantify the effects of, among other things, employer discrimination against women. Because the effects of discrimination are difficult to measure directly, studies have compared labor market outcomes for men and women; estimated the amount of the gender differences that are due to gender differences in education, hours worked, etc.; and then interpreted the differences that remained, if any, as possible evidence of effects of gender discrimination (Blau and Kahn's 2000 study is an example).

When this familiar and conventional methodology is used to gauge the importance of possible causes of the recent recession, the results are surprising and the conclusions are unconventional. The residual labor decline that remains after correcting for labor market fundamentals, and therefore the amount and dynamics of the labor decline that might be attributed to impulses from outside the labor market, is dramatically different from the total labor decline because the labor market fundamentals have by no means been constant since 2007. The federal minimum wage was hiked three times. "Baby boomers"—the large cohorts of people born shortly after World War II—began reaching normal retirement age, but many of them with less wealth than they had anticipated.

A more important, but rarely acknowledged, change in labor market fundamentals has been an increase in marginal labor income tax rates from a variety of sources (by *marginal labor income tax rate* I mean the extra taxes paid, and subsidies forgone, as the result of working, expressed as a ratio to the income from working). Parts of the 2009 "stimulus law" increased the generosity of subsidies such as food stamps for low-income families, and subsidies such as unemployment insurance for people who do not find a job. Congress considered legislation that would raise marginal personal income tax rates and would present Americans with new health benefits to be phased out as a function of income. A large number of homeowners owed more on their mortgage than their house was worth, and both private and public sector renegotiations of the mortgage contracts have served as a large implicit tax on earning during the recession because borrowers can expect their earnings to affect the amount that lenders will forgive (Mulligan 2009a). Renegotiations of business debts (Jermann and Quadrini 2009), consumer loans (Han and Li 2007), student loans, and tax debts present debtors with similar disincentives.

Traditional labor and macroeconomic theory predicts that marginal labor income tax rates and binding minimum wages distort the labor market and thereby reduce aggregate labor usage, reduce aggregate consumer spending and investment, and, in the short term, increase wages, labor productivity, and the usage of factors that can take the place of labor hours. As a result of greater labor productivity, part of the population—those (if any) not subject to the marginal tax rates or minimum wages—actually works more, even while aggregate work hours are less. The size of these effects depends on various factors, the most important of which are (1) the size of the marginal tax rate change or minimum wage distortion, (2) the rate at which the productivity of labor diminishes with the amount of labor, and (3) the degree to which the rewards from working encourage people to work.

Chapter Two examines the national time series for consumer spending, labor usage, productivity, and real wages, showing that their evolution during the recession closely matches the predictions of the marginal tax rate model. Moreover, with the exceptions of manufacturing, residential construction, and perhaps a couple of other industries experiencing obvious declines in relative demand, it appears that usage of production inputs aside from labor hours actually increased, which contradicts the view that labor hours changes were merely a result of output reductions. In this sense, the recession seems to have been caused or amplified by high marginal tax rates, or by other labor market distortions with many of the same effects as high marginal tax rates.

People without jobs or otherwise with low incomes sometimes receive benefits from social safety net programs such as unemployment insurance and food stamps. The benefit receipts are rarely called taxes by laypeople, but economists understand the benefits to have many of the characteristics of marginal tax rates because a program beneficiary loses some or all of the benefits as a consequence of working. Regardless of whether redistribution is achieved by collecting more taxes from families with high incomes, providing more subsidies to families with low incomes, or both, an essential consequence is the same: a reduction in the reward to activities and efforts that raise incomes. Chapter Three of this book measures the amounts of some of the changes in marginal tax rates implicit in social safety net programs, otherwise known as "replacement rates."

With the exception of Medicaid, subsidies flowing to the unemployed and to financially distressed households in the forms of consumer loan forgiveness and government transfers almost tripled after 2007. A minority of that increase is due to an increase in the number of people who would have been eligible for subsidies under prerecession rules, and a majority is the result of

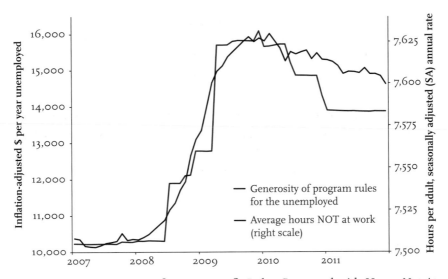

FIGURE 1.1. Government Safety Net Benefit Rules Compared with Hours Not At Work

more than a dozen changes in benefit rules made possible by several new federal and state government statutes. For example, multiple rule changes since 2007 permitted unemployed people to collect benefits longer and gave them bonuses, health subsidies, and tax deductions, to the point that, among persons aged twenty-five and over, unemployed people without government help were actually less common than they were before the recession. Some of the rule changes will eventually expire, but others continue indefinitely.

Figure 1.1 offers a preview of some of the results from Chapters Two and Three. The red series is a monthly index of government safety net eligibility and benefit rules from the perspective of a typical unemployed head of household or spouse. Before the recession began, an unemployed person typically received about $10,000 per year of unemployment, taking into account that some of the unemployed are not eligible for all, or any, of the safety net programs run by the government. Changes in the red series occur only when federal or state governments change the rules for eligibility or benefit amounts in at least one of their safety net programs (Chapter Three has the details of constructing this and other indices), which is why the red series is labeled "program rules for the unemployed." By the end of 2009, program rule changes alone had increased the typical benefit to almost $16,000. By 2011, a few of the new safety net provisions had expired, but still the program rules index remained at about $14,000 per year of unemployment.

The black series in Figure 1.1 shows the recession itself by measuring average hours *not* at work per adult as the difference between total hours in a year and average hours at work. Fewer work hours are higher in the chart, and more work hours are lower. Largely because more people became unemployed, the black series shows that average work hours were about 120 fewer (at an annual rate) at the end of 2009 than they were at the end of 2007; hours not at work rose from 7,509 to 7,627. Growth of 120 hours may seem small on the scale of total daytime and nighttime hours in a year, but it is a shocking 10 percent of the average amount adults were working before the recession began. This book explains and executes additions, adjustments, and variations to the red rules index that are more appropriate for aggregate analysis of the labor market, but even so a comparison of the two series in Figure 1.1 is informative. Both series started to change at about the same time in late 2007 or early 2008. By the end of 2008, both series had achieved about half of their maximum change, which for both occurred in late 2009 or early 2010. They have changed direction since then, although reversal of the safety net rules appears to have occurred sooner and more rapidly.

Economists have observed that higher payments to the unemployed often increase the number of people unemployed and reduce the number of people employed, because the payments serve as marginal tax rates: they take away some of the reward from working. At the same time, we know that a number of the changes in safety net program rules were a reaction—maybe the kind of "bold" action described by President Bush—to the black series and related indicators of the economic situation. The goal of this book is to determine how much of the change in the black hours series is the result of changes in the red program rules index and other marginal tax rate changes since 2007. In other words, the goal is to determine the extent to which changes in the forms of redistribution (as captured by marginal tax rate series, such as the red one in Figure 1.1) caused them, or others in the economy, to have more time away from work (the black series in Figure 1.1) and thereby less time at work.

Unfortunately, I doubt that the goal can be accomplished by staring at the two series in Figure 1.1, or even executing a sophisticated econometric analysis of them attempting to discern which one caused the other, especially once we acknowledge some of the series' omissions and weaknesses (see the chapters that follow). Fortunately, economic history before 2008 provided a number of episodes of productivity and labor hours changes for specific groups, and the nation as a whole, that are informative about the causal effects of financial rewards on labor hours. Economists have often summarized the relevant historical effects in terms of wage elasticities of labor supply and labor demand. Chapters Four and Five show that, for a range of elasticities wide enough to encompass many of the varied interpretations of the historical evidence, safety net replacement rate increases of the size measured in Chapter Three are expected to significantly depress labor usage, consumption, and investment. It is possible, although not necessary, that nearly all of the decline in labor usage can be attributed to rising replacement rates from the social safety net. At the very least, redistribution on the basis of income and employment status was a major factor depressing labor usage, and aggregate labor hours would have fallen a lot less if replacement rates had remained constant.

Many impulses can plausibly reduce work hours, such as changes in productivity, sectoral shifts, and demographic shifts. The more interesting and challenging question is whether these and others are enough, separately or in combination, to reduce aggregate work hours 10 percent in a short period of time, and do so in a way that is quantitatively consistent with the actual changes in the other major economic variables such as consumer spending, productivity, and investment. This book does not just add to the list of plausible though potentially minor impulses, but instead shows that actual safety net expansions and minimum wage hikes were, in combination, enough to explain a majority of the reduction in labor hours since 2007, and many of the other changes in the major economic variables.

Chapters Four and Five contain the book's foremost quantitative analysis and conclusions, but Figure 1.1 already permits an approximate understanding of core quantitative elements of my conclusion that government safety net benefit rule changes were a major factor reducing average work hours. Household studies of labor supply done before the recession suggested that the reduction in the average reward to working that would be required to reduce average work hours by 10 percent would have to be approximately 9 to 25 percent. Figure 1.1 suggests that the reward to working fell by about $5,600 per year between 2007 and the end of 2009, because that is how much extra the average unemployed person was receiving from the safety net as a consequence of program rule changes. For someone capable of earning $36,000 per year (just about the middle of what working nonelderly household heads and spouses earn), that is a 16 percent reduction in the reward to working—in the 9 to 25 percent range needed to explain a large fraction of the actual 10 percent decline in work hours over that time frame. The 16 percent amount from Figure 1.1 is only a back-of-the-envelope calculation, because it does not include taxes, fringe benefits, wealth effects, population aging, safety net programs with no rule changes since 2007, private sector safety nets, hours reductions that do not involve unemployment, the accumulation and returns to capital, minimum wage hikes, and other relevant factors examined in the body of this book, but it is enough to recognize that ignoring the changes in the reward to working induced by the safety net since 2007 is misleading as to what happened in the labor market.

The basic framework of Chapters Two through Five also serves as a theory of which groups would experience lesser reductions in their work hours, and even which groups might have increased work hours since 2007, because the replacement rate changes documented in Chapter Three are not uniform across people. Many of the changes have less impact on marginal tax rates of people who are capable of earning well above the poverty line, less impact on spouses of persons earning above the poverty line, and little impact on the elderly regardless of their income. The replacement rate changes coming from debt discharges are relevant over the entire income distribution but are less relevant for people with positive net worth. Debt-related replacement rate changes are therefore less relevant for the elderly, and for homeowners living in states with housing prices that were more stable prior to the recession. To the degree that the replacement rate changes documented in Chapter Three are a major factor reducing aggregate labor hours, labor hours would increase for the elderly, would decrease more for single people than for married people, would decrease less in regions that had more stable housing prices, and would decrease less (if at all) for persons high in the income distribution. Chapter Six shows that all of these predictions are confirmed with cross-sectional measures of labor hours and earnings changes.

The results in Chapter Five assume that replacement or marginal tax rates had about the same effects during the recession that they did before. However, a group of economists presume that marginal tax rates and other aspects of labor supply do not matter during a recession, even while marginal tax rates normally depress labor usage. In their view, it's either a coincidence or a case of reverse causality that marginal tax rates increased when labor fell, so that the entire labor drop might still be explained by the less proximate impulses. But the question of whether labor supply has different aggregate effects during recessions does not have to be a matter of assumption; it can be examined by measuring labor market outcomes in and around large recession-era changes in labor supply and demand. Chapters Seven and Eight examine such episodes, and uniformly they find that labor supply matters at the margin about the same in 2008, 2009, and 2010 as it did prior to the recession. In doing so, Chapter Eight reviews estimates of the effect of the 2007–2009 federal minimum wage hikes on the amount and composition of employment and compares them to estimates from studies that pre-dated the recession.

As noted above, some of the replacement rate increases can be traced to the collapse of housing prices. By some measures, U.S. average housing prices fell by almost one-third between 2006 and 2009. Prices fell more than 50 percent in Las Vegas and Phoenix, and nearly as much in Detroit, Miami, and much of California. As a result, more than fourteen million home mortgages nationwide were "under water" in early 2009: the amount owed exceeded the market value of the collateral. Chapter Nine investigates some effects of underwater mortgages on foreclosures and the incentives to earn income, and the degree to which those effects are shaped by public policy.

Because much of the decline in labor usage since 2007 was a reaction to the combination of higher marginal tax rates and a higher federal minimum wage, it is important to understand why labor market distortions like these suddenly increased, and to what degree those increases were themselves a response to financial market gyrations and other recession-era events outside the labor market. Some of the answers—such as why President Bush signed a 2007 law that would hike the federal minimum wage three times between 2007 and 2009 or why marginal tax rates would sometimes exceed 100 percent—may lie in politics, which is beyond the scope of this book. Other marginal tax or replacement rate increases may be a desired response by the public and private sectors to a bad situation of uncertainty, as I explore in Chapter Ten. Chapter Eleven concludes with estimates of what would have happened to labor hours if redistribution—marginal tax rates and minimum wages—had remained constant, and it addresses some common misconceptions about the incidence of unemployment and marginal tax rate changes.

2

The Rise of Labor Productivity

A PAYCHECK IS an important reason people devote time to, and exert effort for, working. Businesses willingly pay their employees because the workers help produce goods and services that can be sold to customers. Thus, three important indicators of the state of the labor market are the amount of time worked, the amount produced, and the ratio of production to time worked, known as labor productivity. A few indicators such as these go a long way toward revealing causes of the recession, with some surprising conclusions.

Figure 2.1 displays monthly seasonally adjusted measures of time worked since January 2007.[1] The gray and black series are civilian and nonfarm payroll employment, respectively, measured on the left axis in employees per thousand persons (civilian employment is shifted by thirty persons per thousand in order to be displayed on the same axis with nonfarm payroll employees). The red series is an index of hours worked per person—a product of employees per person and weekly hours worked per employee—measured as the sum of private work hours per person (measured as the all-employees aggregate weekly hours index for all private industries, divided by population) and aggregate public work hours (estimated as public sector employment per person times private work hours per private sector employee).[2]

Although the two employment series are measured differently, their dynamics during the recession are pretty similar, as evidenced in the figure by the close agreement of the gray and black series. To the extent that employment and hours per employee move together, the red hours series has larger percentage changes than the other two series because it is the product of employment and hours per employee. All three series had their steepest declines in late 2008 and early 2009.[3] Neither employment series has had a significant and prolonged increase relative to population between 2007 and the time I am writing (early 2012), and the increase of the hours series since the end of 2009 still leaves hours per capita 8 percent below where it was

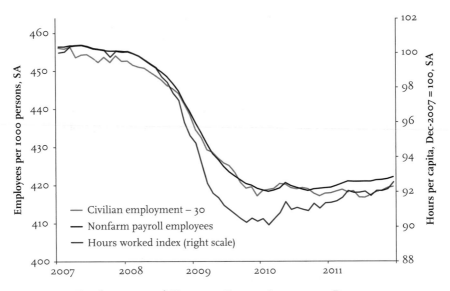

FIGURE 2.1 Employment and Hours per Person, Jan-2007 to Dec-2011

when the recession officially began in December 2007. The purpose of this book is to help explain, in the context of the wider economy, why time worked declined so much, and why time worked has been so slow to recover to prerecession levels, and to offer estimates of how the labor market might have been different with alternative public policies.[4]

A recession is, by definition, a period when the amount of market work declines. A variety of explanations have been offered for previous recessions: adverse productivity shocks (Kydland and Prescott 1982), a surge in the demand for "liquidity" (Friedman and Schwartz (1963); Lucas, (2008)), a collapse in international trade (Crucini and Kahn 1996), and a stock market crash are among them. Do any of these explain the labor decline since 2007? This chapter begins an answer to the question by examining the time series for labor productivity and real hourly wages, and finding that both series are higher now than they were in 2007.

In their studies of prior recessions, economists have closely examined the cyclicality of real wages—that is, whether real wages tend to fall during a recession and rise during an expansion (a pro-cyclical real wage), or instead rise during a recession and fall during expansions (a countercyclical real wage). John Maynard Keynes claimed in his *General Theory* that real wages were countercyclical ("an increase in employment can only occur to the accompaniment of a decline in the rate of real wages"; 2008/1936, 15), although a countercyclical pattern is not readily observed in a number of recessions.[5]

When it comes to the 2008–09 recession, at least, I conclude that real wages and productivity are countercyclical.

High wages and low employment make some sense from an employer's perspective because wages are the main cost of employing a worker. But this raises the question of whether potential workers are all that eager to take the jobs that are available, or instead whether something prevents millions of people eager for work from bidding down wages. My next step adapts some of the labor market ingredients that are common to both "New Keynesian" and "real business cycle" models in order to decompose the labor reductions since 2007 into three types of potential "causes": *labor distortions and labor preferences* that raise productivity and reduce labor, *productivity shocks* that reduce labor and productivity, and *wealth and intertemporal substitution effects* that reduce labor and raise consumption.[6] I conclude that labor fell more than output during the 2008–09 recession, while labor "supply" (defined more rigorously below) shifted in the direction of less labor. Later chapters use this finding to help identify the recession's causes.

Analytically, this chapter's decomposition is most like that of Katz and Murphy (1992), who look at changes over time in the relative amounts and productivity of skilled and unskilled labor in order to determine the relative importance of supply and demand shocks. In terms of substance, this chapter is about the changes over time in the overall *levels* of labor and labor productivity, which raises the possibilities of tax distortions, wealth effects, and intertemporal substitution effects that would be less important for understanding one skill group's changes relative to another. In this regard, my analysis is more like that of Chari, Kehoe, and McGrattan (2007), who also consider capital market fluctuations and total factor productivity. Galí, Gertler, and Lopez-Salido (2007), Mulligan (2002), and Mulligan (2005) are three other papers using the supply-demand decomposition to quantify labor market distortions over time; Hall (1997) uses it to quantify labor preference shifts.

The first section of this chapter displays the basic time series used to make the decomposition: aggregate labor, consumption, and productivity per hour. Four aggregate changes since 2007 help gauge the relative importance of various explanations for the recession and slow recovery. First, in contrast to the patterns of some previous recessions and depressions, output fell significantly less than did labor hours. That is, labor productivity (output per hour) increased. The following section examines the amount of labor productivity change, showing that it is consistent with a fairly constant trend for total factor productivity. This result suggests that the recession and slow recovery cannot primarily be explained by adverse productivity shocks such as interruptions to the production process created by unusually bad weather, strikes, labor immobility, or business sector attempts to economize on raw materials.

Second, as shown in the section on real wage changes, aggregate labor compensation per hour is also significantly greater now than it was before the recession began. This finding suggests that wage-depressing impulses such as sectoral shifts in the direction of capital-intensive sectors, or perceived increases in employment costs (aside from wages themselves), cannot explain much of the recession. However, departures between the wage and productivity series since the middle of 2009 are consistent with some role for wage-depressing factors.

Third, consumption dropped significantly during the recession. As shown in more detail in Chapter Five, this drop contradicts some of the investment collapse models of the recession because at least some of the resources freed up from forgone investment opportunities would have been used for additional consumption.

Fourth, as shown in the section on customer demand and factor substitution, growth accounting suggests that, on average, the use of production inputs other than labor hours actually increased during the recession, when labor hours fell. This factor substitution finding appears to contradict claims that the 2008–09 recession began because people were spending less, and that their low spending forced the businesses serving them to cut output. The spending-impulse theories may be a good description of the declines in manufacturing, residential construction, and perhaps a couple of other industries where all factors of production were used less, but it is difficult to reconcile them with the increased use of nonlabor production factors that happened in the rest of the economy.

The fifth and sixth sections of the chapter bring all of these findings together to explain how they might be symptoms of increases in labor market distortions, akin to marginal tax rate hikes, that occurred during the recession. The amount of the consumption drop helps quantify the amount of the labor market distortion that would be needed to explain what happened in the labor market after 2007. Appendix 2.1 compares these results to analogous calculations for previous recessions.

Quarterly Indicators of Aggregate Economic Quantities

Figure 2.2 displays four quarterly seasonally adjusted indices of real per capita consumption since the beginning of 2007.[7] Two of them are exclusive

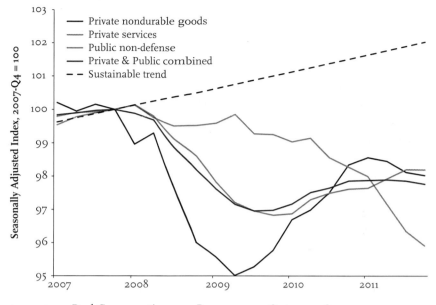

FIGURE 2.2 Real Consumption per Person, 2007-Q1 to 2011-Q4

to the private sector: private nondurable consumption goods and private consumption services. The third (gray) series is public nondefense consumption. The fourth (red) series aggregates the three, chain-weighting by their contributions to total expenditure. My purpose here is to measure current living standards, so purchases of consumer durables are excluded, and nondefense public consumption is combined with the private series (because much of public nondefense consumption is publicly provided health care, schooling, and housing similar to what is provided by the private sector).[8]

The figure also displays a dashed black line to represent a sustainable trend: an estimate of how much total consumption could have increased if the economy had continued to produce and grow as it did prior to the recession.[9] All of the series have declined 4 or 5 percent below the trend and are lower in absolute terms than they were before the recession began. The most rapid deviations from trend occurred in 2008 for the private series, and after early 2009 for the public sector.

Overall, it is clear that per capita consumption dropped—and dropped much less in percentage terms than labor ultimately did (labor per person fell about 10 percent). It appears that most of the 4–5 percent consumption drop below trend occurred in 2008, and since early 2009 consumption has

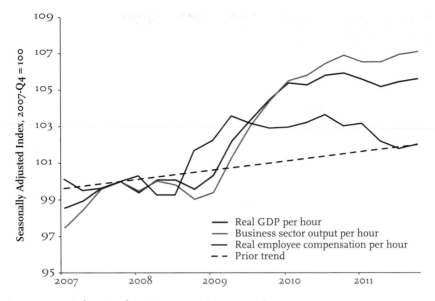

FIGURE 2.3 Labor Productivity, 2007-Q1 to 2011-Q4

resumed something of an upward trend.[10] As shown below, the direction and amounts of the consumption changes are informative as to the recession's causes.

Figure 2.3 displays three quarterly indices of labor productivity: real GDP per hour, business sector output per hour, and real employee compensation per hour. The black dashed line is the prior trend for real GDP per hour of 0.5 percent per year (the same trend shown in Figure 2.2). By the middle of 2009, all three measures were about 3 percent above what they were when the recession began, and therefore well above the prior trend.[11] Four years have passed since the recession began, and labor productivity remains above trend by all three measures.[12]

By definition, labor productivity is the ratio of output to hours worked, so it might seem almost automatic that the ratio would rise when its denominator falls, as it did in 2008 and 2009. However, as we see below, some of the severe recessions or depressions in the past have seen output fall more than hours worked, and therefore labor productivity fell (see also Ohanian 2010). Even in this recession, sectors most obviously depressed by lack of demand had their hours and output fall in roughly equal proportions. The time pattern of labor productivity indicates something about the causes of the recession, as we examine in more detail below.

Movements Along an Aggregate Marginal Productivity Schedule

Goods and services are produced with labor and other factors of production, so it is no surprise that output fell at about the same time that labor did. But this still leaves open the question of whether the usage of other factors of production changes in the same amount, or even in the same direction, as labor did. The aggregate Cobb-Douglas production function helps arrive at an answer. According to that function, and on the basis of the observation that about 70 percent of national income accrues to labor, quarter t's aggregate output per hour y_t depends on the ratio of other inputs A_t to labor n_t, raised to the 0.3 power:[13]

$$y_t \equiv \left(\frac{A_t}{n_t} \right)^{0.3}$$

(2.1)

Holding constant the usage of other factors A_t, each unit reduction in log labor increases log labor productivity by 0.3. This downward-sloping relationship between labor and labor productivity is often called the "aggregate labor productivity schedule." Given the Cobb-Douglas assumption, marginal labor productivity is a constant proportion of the ratio (2.1) of output to hours worked. For this reason, I also refer to the downward-sloping relationship (2.1) as the "aggregate marginal labor productivity schedule."

Changes in the usage or efficiency of other production factors, such as capital accumulation, technical change, and changes in capital utilization, shift the aggregate marginal productivity schedule. Inverting equation (2.1), and using data on output and labor hours, we can calculate the amount of the shift of that schedule, measured in the quantity dimension:

$$\Delta \ln A_t \equiv \Delta \ln n_t + \frac{\Delta \ln y_t}{0.3}$$

(2.2)

where ln denotes natural log and the difference operator Δ denotes changes from a benchmark quarter to quarter t. In other words, the "input residual" $\Delta \ln A_t$ calculated from equation (2.2) is the change in the usage of other factors that must have occurred in order for output to change as much as measured.[14]

Figure 2.4 illustrates how the actual changes in labor productivity from 2007-Q4 through 2011-Q2 can be decomposed using the marginal productivity schedule (2.1). Each data point in the figure graphs the actual values of real GDP per hour and aggregate work hours (the same series as shown in

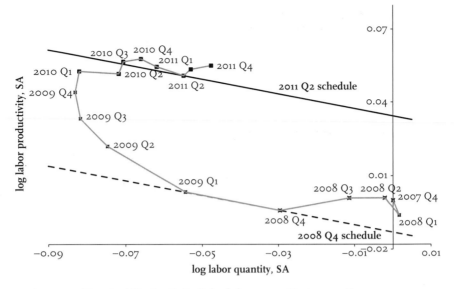

FIGURE 2.4 Marginal Productivity Schedules, 2007 Q4 to 2011 Q2

Figure 2.1), measured on a logarithmic scale with the origin normalized to be 2007-Q4. The points are connected in chronological order.

Two of the points each have a straight line (with slope −0.3) drawn through them representing the marginal productivity schedule (2.1) applicable at those two dates. If (hypothetically) a single marginal productivity schedule applied at each date, then all of the data points would be on the same straight line with slope −0.3. In fact, each date is a different distance from any particular schedule, so the log input residual measures the horizontal distance from a schedule with slope −0.3 passing through the origin and the actual data.

By the end of 2009, labor quantity had declined seven quarters in a row, for a total log labor change of −0.083. Productivity was essentially constant during 2008,[15] but by eight quarters after the recession started, log labor productivity had risen 0.044. The marginal productivity schedule (Figure 2.1) attributes most, but less than all, of the 0.044 increase, namely 0.025, to the reduction in labor that occurred over that time. The other 0.019 of productivity change is attributed to an *increase* in the usage or efficiency of other factors. This finding is an important reason to doubt that a *reduction* in the usage or efficiency of other factors was a significant contributor to the recession.

Normally, the marginal productivity schedule tends to shift up over time; in the eight quarters prior to the recession it shifted up (0.028, or 0.007 per quarter). In this regard, it is perhaps no surprise the marginal productivity

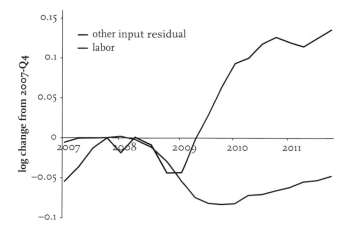

FIGURE 2.5 Labor and Other Inputs, 2007-Q1 to 2011-Q4

schedule also shifted up between the end of 2007 and the end of 2009. For the same reason, it is perhaps unsurprising that the marginal productivity schedule continued to shift up after 2009.

Figure 2.5 displays the quarterly measures of log labor input n_t and log input residual A_t, relative to their values for 2007-Q4. For each quarter, the log input residual is measured as the horizontal distance between the quarter's data point in Figure 2.4 and the marginal productivity schedule passing through the data point for the base quarter (recall equation 2.2). The input residual can be interpreted as the change in nonlabor inputs, or a change in input efficiency, needed to explain the change in output. Given that labor and the residual followed similar patterns during 2008, it seems that labor and nonlabor inputs were falling in about the same proportions during that year. But in 2009 labor continued to fall while the residual quickly surged beyond its prerecession values. The input residual continued to increase during 2010.

Thus, even though labor's path during the beginning of the recession might be explained by a reduction in other inputs, the overall pattern since 2007 has been a significant *increase* in other inputs and a large reduction in labor. The remaining chapters of this book seek to explain why production shifted so suddenly and so dramatically away from labor hours and toward the usage of other inputs.

On Average, Real Wages Did Not Fall

It is possible that aggregate hourly compensation changes do not accurately measure changes in the average person's reward to working, perhaps because of a change in the composition of the workforce that effectively gives more weight in the aggregate to higher-paid workers during recessions than during expansions. For example, employment could drop the most for less-skilled workers (as it has in past recessions; Bils 1985 and Solon, Barsky, and Parker 1994), so that the average compensation (and output per hour) among the employed rises even though none of those employees is compensated more than before the recession. Another possibility is that compensation is fixed for existing workers but dropped during the recession for new hires, and it's the compensation of new hires that allocates labor in the marketplace.

Composition Bias Is Relatively Small

The effect of changes in the composition of the workforce on aggregate hourly earnings and productivity is known as "composition bias," and the size of the bias depends on (1) the percentage change in the size of the workforce and (2) the degree to which persons leaving the workforce or joining the workforce have different hourly wages from the rest of the employees. On the second point, job losses during the recession were certainly not random. Table 2.1 partitions the population by gender, schooling, age, and industry and displays percentage employment rate changes from 2007 to 2009, calculated from the CPS Merged Outgoing Rotation Groups public-use microdata files. In order to help assess the size of the composition bias, the table's righthand column reports each group's average hourly earnings.[16] Some of the composition changes did serve to increase aggregate wage measures: young persons and those with less schooling, who also tend to earn less per hour, had larger employment rate declines. On the other hand, the composition changes by gender tended to reduce aggregate wage measures because the gender with the higher average wage (male) is the one that experienced the larger employment rate decline.

The bottom of the table shows that the construction and manufacturing industries sharply reduced employment. Manufacturing is the larger of the two, and its average hourly wage was somewhat greater than average. Health care is an example of an industry that increased its employment since 2007, and its average hourly earnings were close to the national average. Overall, it appears that changing industry composition did little, if anything, to increase aggregate hourly earnings (see also Bils 1985, 667).

On the basis of age, race, and schooling patterns shown in Table 2.1, and the likely effects of some of the public policy impulses discussed in the following chapters, I suspect that low-wage persons in 2007 were disproportionately represented among those not employed in 2009 (see also Chapter Six), so that

Table 2.1 2007–2009 **Employment Rate Changes by Demographic Group and Industry**

	Employment per Person, % Chg	Earnings Among Those at Work Full-time in 2007, $/hr
By gender		
Men	−7%	21.17
Women	−4%	17.53
Both	−6%	19.60
By schooling		
Less than high school grad	−13%	11.97
High school grad	−8%	15.62
Beyond high school	−4%	23.23
By age		
16–24	−12%	11.77
25–39	−6%	8.85
40–64	−4%	21.83
65–75	3%	19.46
By industry		
Construction	−19%	18.76
Manufacturing	−13%	20.21
Education	0%	21.22
Health care	3%	19.54
Other	−5%	19.35

Note: Each industry employment rate is measured as the ratio of industry employees to total adults.

Source: Author calculations from CPS-MORG microdata.

aggregate wage measures somewhat exaggerate the rate of wage increase and aggregate productivity measures somewhat exaggerate the rate of labor-quality-adjusted productivity growth. Nevertheless, workforce composition did not change enough to be the primary reason aggregate real wage measures increased 3 percent from 2007 to 2009, rather than declining. For the composition bias to be as much as 3 percent, the roughly six million not working in 2009 who were working in 2007 would have had to earn an average of about $5.50.[17] We know instead that the job losses included, for example, educated people and people over age thirty, which are groups of people for whom wages almost always exceed the federal minimum. In fact, a wage of $5.50 would have violated the federal minimum wage for half of 2007, and a number of state minimums for the entire year.[18] Thus, although changing composition alone likely increased aggregate wage and productivity measures between 2007 and 2009, the composition bias on the measured wage change is less than 3 percentage points, and likely much less.[19]

Wage Rates for Marginal Workers

For the purposes of understanding employer incentives to hire and potential employees' incentives to accept work, the wage rate for new hires and other workers with weak attachments to an employer may be more important than the average wage of all employees, and the latter may not evolve in the same way as the former. Nevertheless, my finding that, even after adjustments for composition, the average wage of all employees rose during the recession suggests that the average wage of marginal employees also rose (although perhaps in a different amount) because marginal workers are included in the overall average.

To see this, suppose that a majority of the workforce, whose aggregate hours are L, is paid pursuant to long-term contracts paying X and will be employed under any contingency. The remainder M of the workforce is hired in a spot market at rate w (that is, their wage w is updated to market conditions). Average hourly earnings are:

$$\overline{w} = \frac{M}{L+M} w + \frac{L}{L+M} \frac{X}{L} \tag{2.3}$$

For small changes in w and M, the change in average hourly earnings is:

$$d\overline{w} = \frac{M}{L+M} dw - \left(\frac{X}{L} - w\right) d\left(\frac{M}{L+M}\right) \tag{2.4}$$

The first term on the right is the effect of the marginal workers' average wage change dw on the average change, holding the workforce composition constant. The second term is the composition bias. The change in the composition-bias-adjusted average wage (the combination of the term on the far left and the term on the far right) therefore has the same sign as dw, and the amount of the change is proportional to the marginal workers' share of the workforce.[20] Given my previous conclusion that the composition-bias-adjusted average wage increased over time, the marginal workers' wage rate must have also increased.

Was It Customer Demand? Factor Reduction and Factor Substitution by Industry

A reduction of labor usage during a recession with rising labor productivity is sometimes attributed to employer desires to reduce their production, which in turn derives from a lack of customer demand. If we assume that, as in a number of New Keynesian models (e.g., Woodford 2003), nonlabor inputs are fixed in the short term, then it follows from the diminishing returns to labor that reducing output involves reducing labor by an even greater proportion. The other input residual is constant by assumption.

However, if at least some of the other inputs are adjustable in the short term, then reducing output would involve reducing those inputs too. In this case, the other input residual would decline, and perhaps enough so that labor productivity is constant.[21]

The assumption that inputs other than work hours are constant is convenient for many purposes, but a complete analysis of productivity statistics needs it relaxed because other inputs are subject to some of the same economic forces as work hours (Jorgenson 2009). In particular, an increase in other inputs together with a reduction in labor hours would suggest that employers may have perceived labor to be more expensive, and it would be difficult to reconcile this with the view that labor was cut merely as a means of reducing output.

Particular industries undoubtedly experienced a reduction in demand after 2007. We know, for example, that consumers cut their spending significantly, and one of the best ways to cut spending with minimum short-term impact on living standards is to reduce purchases of durable goods.[22] From the point of view of the manufacturers of those goods, customer demand fell. Residential construction is another industry that experienced reduced demand, as evidenced by the sharp decline in housing prices and increase in vacancy rates. To the degree that production inputs are adjustable, we expect manufacturing and residential construction to reduce their usage of all inputs, and not just work hours.

Table 2.2 displays measures of input and value-added (that is, output minus purchases of materials and services from outside the industry) changes from 2007-Q4 to 2009-Q4 for selected industries. Real value-added declines 0.17 log points in manufacturing, where labor hours fell 0.19 log points. Using formula (2.2), I calculate the other inputs residual change to be −0.15 log points.[23] In other words, the value-added and labor hours data suggest that

Table 2.2 Factor Reduction and Factor Substitution by Industry

| | Log Changes from 2007-Q4 to 2009-Q4 | | | |
| | Factor Reduction Industries | | Factor Substitution Industries | |
	Manufacturing	Residential Construction	Wireless Telecommunications	Business Sector, Excluding Manufacturing and Residential Construction
Real value added or final output	−0.17	−0.42	0.09	−0.03
Labor hours	−0.19	−0.44	−0.15	−0.06
Labor's share, 2007	0.55	0.68	0.15	0.70
Other inputs residual	**−0.15**	**−0.38**	**0.13**	**0.04**
Addendum: capacity utilization	−0.16	NA	NA	NA

Notes: Residential construction refers to home building and all upstream industries, assuming that labor hours in the upstream activities change in the same percentage as home building labor hours do. Labor share for this industry is estimated as the share for all construction.

Final output is measured for the wireless telecommunications industry (as revenue deflated by the price index for consumer cellular services); value-added is measured for all others.

Wireless telecommunications changes are 2007–2009, rather than 2007-Q4 to 2009-Q4.

Sources: BEA, Components of Value Added by Industry as a Percentage of Value Added; Census Bureau, 2009 Services Annual Survey Data: Information Services; BLS, Labor Productivity and Costs: Industry Employment and Hours; Board of Governors of the Federal Reserve System.

the manufacturing industry sharply reduced its usage of other inputs. The last row of the table confirms this prediction with data from the Federal Reserve Board of Governors on capacity utilization in the manufacturing industry,[24] which changed –0.16 log points from 2007-Q4 to 2009-Q4.

The second column of Table 2.2 tells a similar story for the residential construction industry. Real value-added fell 0.42 log points while work hours and other inputs were reduced 0.44 and 0.38 log points, respectively. Thus the manufacturing and residential construction industries reduced their usage of both labor hours and other inputs and did so in about the same amount that they reduced value-added—just as one would expect if those industries had experienced a reduction in demand and were able to adjust the other inputs.

The third column of the table displays results for a familiar industry that experienced growing output and revenues throughout the recession: the mobile telecommunications industry (i.e., the sellers of wireless phone and wireless data services). On an annual basis, the industry's revenues have been increasing every year for many years (U.S. Census Bureau 2011). According to the Federal Communications Commission (2011) and the industry association CTIA (2011), customers' mobile connections increased 12 percent from the end of 2007 to the end of 2009. Nevertheless, the industry cut its labor hours at least 0.15 log points after increasing labor hours in eighteen of the prior twenty years (U.S. Bureau of Labor Statistics 2010b). As expected for an industry that cuts its labor hours without cutting output, the last row of the table suggests an increase in other inputs. The wireless telecommunications industry appears to be engaged in factor substitution: substituting other inputs for labor hours, rather than cutting all inputs in order to reduce output.

Admittedly, the wireless telecommunications industry is just a fraction of the overall economy, but so are the manufacturing and residential construction industries; the latter two industries combined accounted for less than 20 percent of business sector value-added in 2007, and less now. The final column of the table therefore examines the entire business sector, apart from manufacturing and residential construction.[25] Their real value-added fell 0.03 log points, while labor hours fell 0.06. The other input residual *increased* 0.04 log points. In this regard, most of the economy appears to be substituting other factors for labor hours, rather than reducing all factors.

Because efforts to reduce output should be associated with reductions in some of the other inputs, the fact that the other input residual increased on average for the entire economy (Figure 2.4) and for the nonmanufacturing, nonconstruction parts of the business sector (Table 2.2) calls into question the assertion that most industries cut their employment because of a lack of customer demand. A more obvious explanation for a substitution away from labor and toward other inputs is that businesses perceive labor to be more expensive than it was before the recession began. Below I use the consumption and productivity data to begin to quantify labor cost effects like this, and Chapter Three separately quantifies labor cost effects using public policy measures.

Neither Wealth Effects Nor Intertemporal Substitution Effects Explain the "Supply" Shift

Although my finding that the marginal productivity schedule (Figure 2.4) has been stable or shifting up since 2007 rules out reductions in the usage or efficiency of complementary production factors as the primary explanation for the sharp labor decline and prolonged recovery, this still does not tell us why the economy was on one part of that schedule in 2007, and a quite different part in the years thereafter. Economists often interpret movements along the schedule as changes in the supply of labor, or changes in the ability of the labor market to coordinate supply and demand (hereafter, "labor market distortions") and interpret the schedule itself as the demand curve for labor.

An influx of immigrant workers into the economy is an example of a supply change. The influx would, in the short term, push down wages as people compete for jobs, and lower wages would induce employers to hire more. In the process of putting more people to work, output would increase but productivity would fall. This would be a movement along Figure 2.4's marginal productivity schedule in the direction of more labor and less productivity. A reduction in the wealth of working households is another supply change that would increase labor and reduce productivity.

A reduction in worker marginal tax rates—that is, an increase in the share of additional earnings a worker keeps after taxes—can also be interpreted as a supply change, and it would also move the economy down the marginal productivity schedule. But a reduction in employer payroll taxes would, for similar reasons, also increase labor and reduce productivity, so taxes are often referred to as labor market distortions.

Consumption and Leisure Have Moved in Opposite Directions

The wealth effect explanation for movements up the marginal productivity schedule says that people work less because they feel richer. The intertemporal substitution effect says that people work less in 2009 because they view 2009 as a relatively bad time to work and produce, either because the return to saving is low or because they expect future labor productivity to be even higher than it is now. Both the wealth and substitution effect theories imply that consumption is *high* during the recession (Barro and King 1984).

Figure 2.2 easily rejects the wealth and intertemporal substitution effect explanations for low aggregate labor because consumption expenditure has been low in this recession. Judging from the consumption drop, wealth and intertemporal substitution effects by themselves would be moving the economy down the marginal productivity schedule shown in Figure 2.4—in the direction of more labor—so something else must be moving the economy up the schedule even more than the total change that combines the wealth and intertemporal substitution effects with other effects. In other words, if labor and productivity remained constant while consumption dropped, that itself would indicate an important change in the labor market because we expect adverse wealth effects to be associated with more labor and lower labor productivity.

A Metric for Labor Supply Puzzles

Real wages appear to have increased since 2007, which helps to explain why employers would be hiring less and using more of the production factors other than labor hours. But on the employee side of the market, we have a puzzle: low consumer spending leaves the impression that people feel poorer, or that they began to view the years since 2007 as a good time to save, or some of both. Either way, they should be eager to work; yet their eagerness is not showing up as cheaper labor for employers.

Before attempting to solve the puzzle, it helps to first quantify its size: the amount of the leftward labor supply shift (or labor market distortion change) that is needed to explain why people would be working less at the same time their consumer spending is low and labor productivity and wages are high. Might, for example, the aging of the baby boom shift labor supply enough to explain much of the movement along the demand curve shown in Figure 2.4? A "marginal rate of substitution" (MRS) function is a device for such a quantitative exercise.

I assume that the month t MRS is proportional to real consumption per person, and increases with work hours per adult:

$$MRS_t \sim \frac{c_t}{P_t}\left(\frac{n_t}{N_t}\right)^{1/\eta}$$

(2.5)

where c_t is aggregate real consumption of nondurables and services (including public nondefense consumption), P_t is population (adults and children), N_t is the age-adjusted adult population,[26] and n_t is total labor time. η is a constant, assumed for the moment to be one. η is sometimes interpreted as the Frisch elasticity of labor supply with respect to wages, although its interpretation is not important until Chapter Four.

The MRS function can be interpreted as a quantitative model of the relative preferences for consumption and leisure of a typical or representative family in the economy (see Chapter Five). The MRS can also be interpreted as describing the reservation wage of the marginal worker: the marginal worker is willing to work if and only if offered a wage that equals or exceeds the MRS. According to (2.5), this reservation wage increases with the marginal worker's living standard as measured by real consumption per capita: the lower the living standard, the lower the wage the marginal worker will accept. The dependence of the MRS on the amount of work hours n means that people are not willing to work still more hours unless offered an hourly wage that is especially high. In other words, the equation version of (2.5) graphed in the $[n,MRS]$ plane is a kind of labor supply function, with an upward slope whose magnitude is determined by η, and with consumption shifting the function up (a "wealth effect").

Absent labor market distortions and determinants of the marginal rate of substitution omitted from (2.5), labor market equilibrium is described by the equation of the marginal rate of substitution function (2.5) to marginal labor productivity. Given the Cobb-Douglas assumption (2.1), marginal productivity is proportional to labor productivity, so that both average and marginal productivity have the same log changes over time. As explained by Mulligan (2005), changes in the gap between (2.5) and average productivity y_t are therefore measures of the combined effect of changes in labor market distortions and other (omitted) determinants of the marginal rate of substitution. Denoting that gap as $(1-\tau_t)$, its changes can be calculated as:

$$\Delta \ln\left(1-\tau_t\right) \equiv \left[\Delta \ln\left(c_t / P_t\right) + \frac{1}{\eta}\Delta \ln\left(n_t / N_t\right)\right] - \Delta \ln y_t \qquad (2.6)$$

In words, each log point that consumption declines is a log point that distortions must increase in order to offset the wealth effect and explain a given path for labor and productivity.

Equations (2.2) and (2.6) together make up a simple model of the labor market that determines log changes in labor hours n and labor productivity y as a function of log changes in four determining variables: production inputs

A other than labor hours, consumption per capita c/P, the size of the adult population N, and the gap term $(1\text{-}\tau)$. Equation (2.6) by itself quantifies the labor supply puzzle noted above, because it tells us the amount of the gap change that is needed to explain why the consumption change term and labor change term would both be negative at the same time that the productivity term change was positive.

So far, the gap $(1\text{-}\tau_t)$ is just a residual. With only the data presented in this chapter, one cannot determine whether the gap $(1\text{-}\tau_t)$ captures measurement errors, unobserved preference changes, model specification errors, or genuine market distortions.[27] Henceforth, for the purposes of brevity, and anticipating the results of later chapters, I refer to $-\ln (1\text{-}\tau_t)$ as the amount of labor market "distortion."

Appendix 2.2 to this chapter as well as Chapters Four and Five examines sensitivity of the results to alternative assumptions about functional form, elasticity magnitude, and consumption concepts. However, only weak assumptions are needed to conclude that equation (2.6) is correct at least in terms of the qualitative effects of consumption, labor hours, and productivity on the labor market distortion.[28] Given that consumption and labor clearly fell during the recession, and labor productivity clearly rose, we must conclude that the distortion increased; the only questions are the amount of the increase, and its origins.

Labor Market Distortions Since 2007

Figure 2.6 graphs quarterly changes in the labor market distortion, together with its supply or "reservation wage" component (the square bracket term in equation 2.6) and its productivity component y_t. Distortions increased throughout 2008 and 2009. During 2008, much of the increase can be described as falling consumption and labor in the face of fairly constant productivity. In other words, by the end of 2008 living standards declined—consumption per person fell 2 percent—and this by itself reduced the reservation wage schedule by 2 percent. With a lower reservation wage and constant productivity, we expect people to work more, not less. As noted in Chapter Six, the elderly did work more after 2007, and likely for this reason; nonetheless Figure 2.1 shows that the average person was working less by the end of 2008. With people working less, we further suspect that reservation wages were low: an additional 3 percent lower as of the end of 2008. Thus the reservation wage or MRS value for 2008-Q4 shown in Figure 2.6 is −0.052 (see the light red curve). To rationalize these outcomes in the face of productivity that was

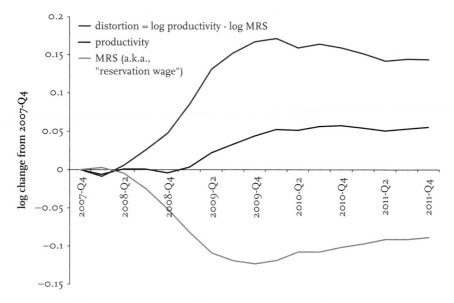

FIGURE 2.6 Supply, Demand, and Distortions since 2007-Q4

essentially constant, the distortion term must have changed about 5 percent in the direction of greater distortion; +0.048 is graphed in Figure 2.6 as the 2008-Q4 value for the distortion (see the red curve).

During 2009, productivity increased and the reservation wage fell further, which implies that labor distortions increased further. The total distortion change from 2007-Q4 to 2009-Q4 was 0.167. To put this in perspective, to explain the labor market events with, say, an across-the-board labor income tax hike, the amount of the hike would be about 15 percentage points.[29] Since 2009, productivity, the reservation wage, and the distortion have been fairly constant.

As shown in Appendix 2.1, the residuals in the 1981–82 recession were quite different: the input residual fell while the labor supply residual was constant. In addition to having much larger reductions in labor and output, the Great Depression of the 1930s was also different: both the input and labor supply residuals fell.

Wage measures are not part of equation (2.6), but to the degree that aggregate wages can be reliably measured they could be used to decompose the overall distortion—the difference between log productivity and log MRS—into a difference between log productivity and the log wage and a difference between the log wage and the log MRS. The former difference is sometimes associated with employer-side distortions, such as employment costs they

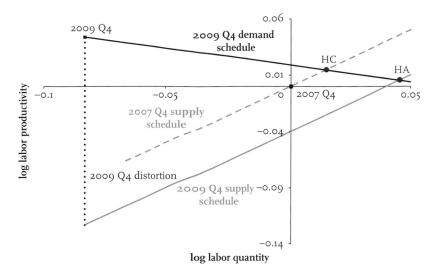

FIGURE 2.7 The 2009 Q4 Distortion, and Two Hypotheticals

incur apart from wages, and the latter difference is associated with employee-side distortions such as income taxes owed by employees on their wage income and government subsidies received by employees who are out of work. However, given that the gap between wage changes and productivity changes is small by comparison with the overall distortion (compare Figures 2.3 and 2.6), I leave that decomposition for the sensitivity analysis in Appendix 2.2 and for now note that most of the distortion since 2007 appears to be employee-side rather than employer-side.

The calculation of the distortion for any particular date can be illustrated in a diagram like Figure 2.4 by adding an MRS or reservation wage schedule (2.5) to the marginal productivity schedules already shown. Figure 2.7 therefore expands the scales of the axes in Figure 2.4 to make room for a reservation wage schedule, and it deletes all of the observed values of labor and productivity except for 2007-Q4 and 2009-Q4. Because of their familiar geometric shapes and conceptual relations with demand and supply, marginal productivity schedules are labeled as "demand" and MRS schedules are labeled as "supply." In a labor market without distortions, the quantity of labor is determined by the intersection of supply and demand.

The 2009-Q4 demand schedule (solid black) is the schedule satisfying formula (2.2) and taking on the other inputs value A that fits the actual labor and productivity for 2009-Q4. The 2007-Q4 supply schedule is the schedule satisfying formula (2.5) for a fixed amount of consumption per person. The

2009-Q4 supply schedule is the same as the 2007-Q4 supply schedule, except that it is shifted vertically in the amount of the log per capita consumption change over those eight quarters, −0.031, and shifted out horizontally by 0.010 to reflect the age-adjusted growth in the adult population over that time. In other words, the reservation wage schedule was about 4 percent lower in 2009-Q4 than eight quarters earlier. As illustrated in Figure 2.7, the actual 2009-Q4 values for labor and productivity do not lie on the 2009-Q4 supply schedule, and the distortion is measured as the vertical distance between the supply schedule and the actual values, which turns out to be 0.167.

As graphical representations of equations (2.2) and (2.6), Figure 2.7's black demand curve and light red supply curve together constitute a simple model of the labor market that determines log changes in labor hours n and labor productivity y as a function of log changes in production inputs A other than labor hours, consumption per capita c/P, the size of the adult population N, and the distortion or labor supply residual τ. As such, the model can be used to simulate log changes for labor and labor productivity under hypothetical changes for some or all of the determining variables A, c/P, N, and τ. If τ had remained unchanged since the beginning of the recession yet consumption, population, and the input residual had followed their actual values, the hypothetical outcome would have been the point labeled HA in the Figure at the intersection of the 2009-Q4 supply and demand schedules. If instead of falling 0.083 log points, labor had *risen* 0.045 log points (as at the hypothetical outcome HA), the outcome would have been exactly on the 2009-Q4 supply schedule and the distortion term would have been zero. In other words, the actual labor supply distortion (whatever it was) not only prevented an increase in labor that would have been consistent with the consumption drop but actually reduced labor.[30] In this sense, the labor supply distortion is responsible for more than 100 percent of the labor decline since 2007. As the remaining chapters of this book seek to explain the origins of growing labor distortions since 2007, Figure 2.6's red series will be a guide as to how much their growth must have been.

Conclusion: Productivity Patterns Begin to Reveal the Recession's Causes

Employment, hours, and consumption per person declined significantly in 2008 and 2009, while real wages and labor productivity rose. Since 2009, none of these variables have returned to their prerecession values. This chapter decomposes the hours and productivity changes into three types of "causes":

1. *Changes in other production inputs* that change labor and output in the same direction
2. (Unmeasured) *labor distortions and labor preferences* that raise productivity, reduce labor, and reduce consumption
3. *Wealth and intertemporal substitution* effects that reduce labor and raise consumption

The macroeconomic concept of the "marginal productivity schedule" relating wages or output per hour worked to the number of hours worked—a concept shared by real business cycle models, New Keynesian models, and even Keynes's *General Theory* (2008/1936)—helps to isolate the first group of causes. Output declined sufficiently less than work hours to make it appear that other production inputs (aside from work hours) tended to *increase* during the recession. When viewed through the lens of *any* model in which aggregate output is a function of labor hours and other inputs with an elasticity of output with respect to hours of about 0.7,[31] the recession and slow recovery cannot primarily be explained by, or even associated with, adverse productivity shocks such as interruptions to the production process created by unusually bad weather, strikes, labor immobility, or business sector attempts to economize on raw materials.

Perhaps the most commonly cited theories of the 2008–09 recession are that the housing collapse, stock market crash, or the banking crisis caused people to spend less, so that the businesses serving those spenders experienced less demand for their products. Rather than cutting prices to induce customers to continue buying the quantities that they did before the recession began, those businesses decided to cut output. These spending-impulse theories may be a good description of the declines in manufacturing, residential construction, and perhaps a couple of other industries, and they can explain why labor productivity increased. But such theories cannot explain the apparent increased use of other production inputs that occurred on average for the whole economy.

Factor substitution motivated by a perceived increased cost of labor can explain why output and work hours fell while the usage of other inputs increased. That increase can come on the employer side, as with an anticipated and often discussed employer tax credit for new hires, which amounts to an implicit tax hike on the payroll that employers have before the tax credit goes into effect.[32] Another example is that health care reform or some other forthcoming employer regulation will create employer liabilities based on the number of employees they had in the past.[33] Yet another possibility is that, thanks to the banking crisis, employers find payroll management more costly. In all these employer-side examples, labor productivity growth is consistent with a drop in labor demand, as evidenced by lower labor compensation per hour, to which marginal workers respond by not working. For this reason, the finding in Figure 2.3 that both labor productivity and labor compensation per hour are greater now than they were before the recession began suggests that perceived employer costs are not the primary reason for the sharp drop in labor usage between 2007 and 2009. On the other hand, the gap between productivity and hourly compensation changes since 2009 is consistent with the hypothesis that employment is recovering slowly, in part because employers perceive employment costs that exceed measured labor compensation.

Employee-side distortions, shifts in labor supply, and a failure of nominal wages to fall enough to clear the labor market are all consistent with rising productivity and real wages during the recession. The last part of this chapter used the theory of labor supply to quantify the combined amount of the distortions or supply shifts. The labor supply theory, also shared by real business cycle and New Keynesian models, says that workers' reservation wages increase with living standards and with the amount of time worked. With consumption and work time so much lower than they were when the recession began, the theory says that people would be more willing to work now than they were then,[34] unless something else were significantly reducing their reward to work, or reducing their willingness to work. Pinpointing such "distortions" is beyond the scope of this chapter, but it does find that the distortions were, at their peak, as large as a 15 percentage point increase in the labor income tax rate (on a base rate of zero). The next chapter begins the task of finding the origins of (increases in) labor market distortions since 2007.

Appendix 2.1: Productivity, Labor, and Residuals in Prior Downturns

This appendix examines the input and labor supply residuals for four previous postwar recessions, and for the Great Depression of the 1930s.[35] The changes during the 2008–09 recession were much less in magnitude than during the Great Depression, but often larger in magnitude than the changes during recessions since then. Of particular interest is that 2008–09 recession is quite different from (1) both the 1981–82 recession and the Great Depression in terms of the direction of the input residual, and (2) the 1981–82 recession in terms of the direction of the labor supply residual.

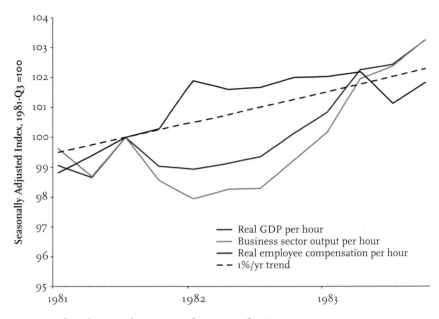

FIGURE 2.8 Labor Productivity, 1981-Q1 to 1983-Q4

Figure 2.8 is the 1980s version of Figure 2.3 for the years 1981–1983, except that real GDP per capita and real employee compensation is divided by a slightly different measure of hours (see below) than used in Figure 2.3. Note that the NBER dates the business cycle peak in 1981-Q3 and the trough in 1982-Q4. Both real GDP per hour and business sector output per hour decline significantly, although the two series disagree about the exact amount of the decline. Both series remained below prerecession levels until the recovery was under way.

Real employee compensation per hour actually rises during the 1981–82 recession and does not fall until the recovery. Both productivity and real wages are likely subject to a countercyclical composition bias (see the section in the body of this chapter entitled "On Average, Real Wages Did Not Fall"), but composition bias probably cannot explain why average hourly earnings increased rather than decreased.[36]

The input residual A_t is measured in the quantity dimension—that is, it is a horizontal distance in Figure 2.7—while the labor supply residual is measured in the price dimension (a vertical distance in the figure). To examine the two residuals in the same units, I transform the other input residual into a "productivity residual" by multiplying it by nonlabor's share 0.3. Figure 2.9 is a scatter diagram of the labor supply residuals and productivity residuals for

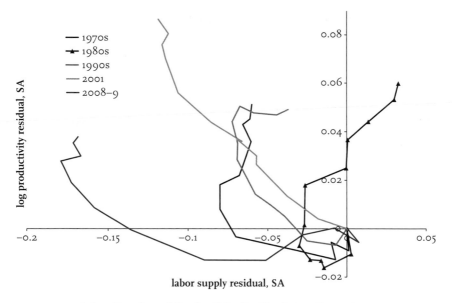

FIGURE 2.9 Labor Supply and Productivity Residuals in 5 Recessions

five recessions that began in 1974, 1981, 1990, 2001, and 2008. The chart's origin indicates the values for the quarter designated as the NBER business cycle peak, and the axes measure each residual as a gap from its value at the NBER business cycle peak.

The 1980s (black with triangles) and 2008–09 (red) recessions show two very different patterns. The 1980s recession was characterized by a reduction in the productivity residual, and little change in the labor supply residual.[37] The recovery from that recession involved a large increase in the productivity residual, but again little change in the labor supply residual by the eighth quarter after the NBER peak (1983-Q3; the business cycle trough was 1982-Q4).[38] The 2008–09 recession began with a reduction in both residuals, but it was the labor supply residual that dropped the most. Later in the recession, the productivity residual increased beyond its prerecession values, while the labor supply residual continued to fall.[39]

The recession beginning in 1990 may be the one most similar to the 2008–09 recession, because the productivity residual increased significantly from peak to trough, while the labor supply residual fell. Growth in the productivity residual stopped during the 1990s recovery, while the labor supply residual returned near to its prerecession value.

The Great Depression of the 1930s was unique in its magnitude, and therefore not shown in Figures 2.8 and 2.9. Table 2.3 offers a comparison of

Table 2.3 **Residuals for the 2008–9 Recession and the Great Depression**

	Residual Changes	
	(Log Points, in the Price Dimension)	
	Productivity	**Labor Supply**
2007 Q4–2009 Q4	+0.019	−0.17
2007 Q4–2011 Q4	+0.041	−0.16
1929–30	−0.053	−0.17
1929–1933	−0.150	−0.46

Sources: Cole and Ohanian (1999), Mulligan (2005).

the early 1930s to the economy since 2007. In this recession, the productivity residual has increased. The productivity residual fell more than 5 percent 1929–1933 (Cole and Ohanian 1999), which is many times more than it did in the 1980s recessions. Both the 2008–09 recession and the Great Depression saw labor distortions of about 0.17 appear within a year or two, but after four years the Great Depression labor distortion (Mulligan 2005) was much larger than it is now. Although it is not clear whether the Great Depression was just an amplified version of the 1970s recession—with both the labor supply residual and the productivity residual falling—it is qualitatively different from the 2008–09 recession, when the productivity and labor supply residuals moved in opposite directions.

Appendix 2.2: Sensitivity Analysis

Many of the conclusions in this chapter derived from the empirical finding that aggregate work hours dropped significantly more than output. Fortunately, aggregate work hours have been measured in various ways, depending on the sampling method, the concept of work time, and the means of eliciting work time. Regarding sampling method, the U.S. government conducts a monthly survey of employers (the "establishment survey") and another monthly survey of households (the "household survey"). The establishment survey asks employers about their employees' paid work time (that is, including paid sick days and paid vacation days) during the reference week. The Bureau of Labor Statistics projects sample measures to the entire economy for that month, and those aggregate hours can be divided by total persons aged sixteen and over (regardless of employment status) to arrive at an estimate of weekly hours worked per adult.

The household survey asks respondents about their work status (and the status of other adults in the household) during the reference week and, if at work during that week, hours worked. These hours worked, counting zeros for persons not at work, can be averaged across respondents to arrive at another measure of hours worked per adult. The two differ somewhat in terms of the population covered (the establishment survey does not include agriculture or self-employed workers).[40]

The BLS combines the establishment and household surveys to form industry- and sector-specific measures of hours worked, which (as noted in the main text) I use for some of my productivity estimates.

But sometimes surveys can be misleading about hours worked, because there is a tendency for people to report round numbers like "forty hours" or "thirty-five hours" even when actual hours worked are not a round number (more than 40 percent of employed persons in the household survey reported that they worked forty hours in the reference week, as opposed to a mere 0.4 percent who reported thirty-nine hours of work). It is logically possible that a number of employed people were working more hours in recent years but continue to report the round number of forty.

Since 2003 the Census Bureau has supplemented its household survey with a time diary study—the "American Time Use Survey" (ATUS)—dedi-

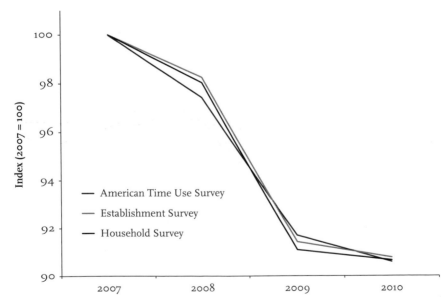

FIGURE 2.10 Work Hours per Person from Three Sources

cated to measuring time use. Participants in that survey are ask to account for all of their waking hours in a specific day along with their various activities that day, including eating, watching TV, working, traveling, caring for children, etc. The diary study therefore has no automatic bias toward finding that masses of people work exactly eight hours every day for exactly five days per week. The BLS averages daily hours worked across respondents, days of the week, and survey months to arrive at an annual average daily hours worked per person aged fifteen and over. Figure 2.10 displays changes in hours worked per person for each of the three measures. They closely agree: the indices for 2009 range from 91.1 to 91.7, while the 2010 indices range from 90.6 to 90.7.

The establishment survey and ATUS measures shown in Figure 2.10 are not available for previous recessions, and the previous recessions were too short to have a large enough sample from the household survey to accurately estimate hours changes from peak to trough. The BLS does form an index of hours of production and nonsupervisory employees for all private industries from the establishment survey, and it has an index of hours of all business sector employees that is part of their productivity calculations (formed

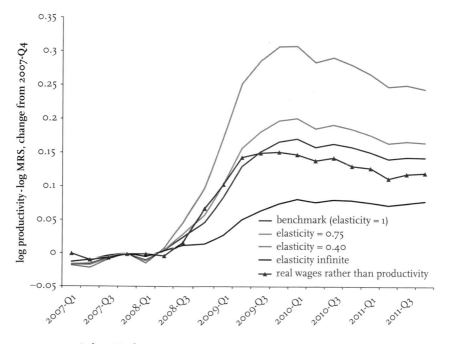

FIGURE 2.11 Labor Market Distortions: Sensitivity Analysis

from both the establishment and the household surveys). These two series disagree as to the amount that work hours dropped from 1980s peak to trough, by almost 2 percentage points. The household and establishment surveys for that time period disagree almost as much as to the peak-to-trough percentage employment change.

Figure 2.11 displays sensitivity analysis for the labor market distortion esti-mates. The red series is the same series shown in Figure 2.6, which assumes a wage elasticity of labor supply of one. Figure 2.11's light red, gray, and black series show the results for alternative assumptions about the wage elasticity, ranging from 0.4 to infinite. In all cases, the labor market distortion is significant. The magnitude of the wage elasticity is important for a number of the results in later chapters; Chapter Four discusses the magnitude in more detail.

Equation (2.6), copied as the top equation below, shows that the distortion is a gap between log productivity and log marginal rate of substitution (MRS) and how the distortion is calculated from the major macroeconomic vari-ables:

$$\Delta \ln\left(1-\tau_t\right) \equiv \left[\Delta \ln\left(c_t / P_t\right) + \frac{1}{\eta}\Delta \ln\left(n_t / N_t\right)\right] - \Delta \ln y_t$$

$$= \left\{\left[\Delta \ln\left(c_t / P_t\right) + \frac{1}{\eta}\Delta \ln\left(n_t / N_t\right)\right] - \Delta \ln w_t\right\} - \left\{\Delta \ln y_t - \Delta \ln w_t\right\}$$

(2.7)

As noted in the main text, the overall labor market distortion change can be decomposed into a gap between log wage changes and log MRS changes (the first curly bracket term in the second line above) and a gap between log pro-ductivity changes and log hourly compensation changes (the second curly bracket term). w denotes hourly employee compensation. Figure 2.11's red-with-triangles series displays changes in the difference between log real hourly labor compensation and log MRS, which is the first curly bracket term above multiplied by -1. The figure shows that the compensation-based version of the distortion (red with triangles) is similar to the overall distortion calculated from labor productivity (red), with the main departure between the two occur-ring in 2010. See also Figure 2.3.

3

The Expanding Social Safety Net

DURING THE RECESSION, a variety of private and public sector practices moved in a direction that would likely distort the labor market, and thereby reduce labor hours and increase output per hour. Among those are recent changes in regulations, such as the federal minimum wage hikes of 2007, 2008, and 2009. In addition, markets and governments have been allocating an increasing amount of resources on the basis of "means": household income and employment status. This chapter documents the surprisingly large changes in means-tested resource allocation since 2007; Chapter Eight analyzes minimum wage changes.

One increasingly prevalent instance of means-tests resulted from the large number of homeowners who owed more on their mortgage than their house was worth, and both private and public sector renegotiations of the mortgage contracts served as a massive implicit tax on their earning during the recession because borrowers can expect their earnings to affect the amount that lenders will forgive (Mulligan 2009a). A new-home-buyer's $8,000 tax credit was made available but phased out as annual family income varied beyond the income limitation. Other parts of the 2009 "stimulus law" increased the generosity of means-tested subsidies such as food stamps, and employment-tested subsidies such as unemployment insurance.

All of these safety net expansions help cushion individuals and businesses from reductions in their incomes. A necessary, but presumably unintended, byproduct of means-tested benefits is that they act as a penalty for raising one's market income: the more someone earns, the more of the "cushion" that has to be given back. The penalty reduces the rewards to activities that raise market incomes, and it thereby causes at least some people to do less toward earning their own market income. The magnitude of these effects depends on the amount and characteristics of safety net expansions (the subject of this chapter) and the sensitivity of work hours to those expansions (the subject of Chapters Four and Five).

Many economists noticed that the allowable duration of unemployment benefit payments was extended during the recession and have attempted to determine the impact of the extensions on employment.[1] However, aside from the duration extensions, much analysis of the labor market since 2007 assumes that marginal tax rates have otherwise been constant.[2] This chapter's measures of marginal tax or "replacement" rates since 2007 suggest that other changes to the safety net increased the overall replacement rate significantly more than duration extensions did, and that the overall replacement rate change is similar in magnitude to the previous chapter's estimates of labor market distortion changes based on productivity, work hours, and consumption behavior.

The quantitative incentive effects of many, if not all, of the safety net events since 2007 are complex and varied, and they might therefore seem beyond the reach of aggregate analysis. The purpose of this chapter is to select the large subset of these events that can be characterized as changing means-tested transfers to individuals either from the government or from lenders, begin to quantify the combined amount of labor market distortion that they might create, and begin to identify the types of workers who might be most affected (see also Chapter Six). One result is a monthly time series for the overall safety net's marginal income tax rate from the point of view of the average marginal worker.

A Framework for Quantifying the Generosity of the Safety Net as a Whole

This chapter examines the social safety net for the purpose of quantifying the role of public policy in labor market changes since 2007. One of the challenges of the exercise is that the benefits received from any one safety net program depend on the participating household's characteristics: its income, assets, employment status, presence of children, knowledge of the program, and other factors. As a result, the degree of safety net generosity varies by demographic groups, some of which are more relevant for aggregate outcomes than others. At the same time, convenient summary measures of program activity, such as program spending, are often a complicated mixture of changes in program rules and changes in the relative size of demographic groups that differ in terms of the program benefits they are awarded. The former have the potential to affect labor market behavior, whereas the latter are merely reflective of it.

The task is complicated by interactions among the programs. For one, an increased generosity of safety net program A might reduce labor hours, and the reduced labor income obligates safety net program B to spend more, even though program B's benefit rules are unchanged. From the point of view of program B, it appears that "the recession" caused it to spend more, but in fact at least part of its spending growth derives from an overall safety net that became increasingly generous because that safety net includes program A.

Second, a single program's quantitative impact on the labor market depends on the generosity of the rest of the safety net, because an important determinant of labor market behavior is the effect of working on a person's disposable income. A person earning, say, $30,000 per year might react differently to program A's $5,000 annual benefit for nonworkers when the rest of the safety net provides nothing, than he or she would when the rest of the safety net provides $25,000 in annual benefits for nonworkers. In the first case, not working would mean giving up $25,000 of disposable income ($30,000 in lost income from working, minus program A's $5,000 benefit), whereas in the second case the $5,000 benefit from program A makes it possible to stop working without losing any disposable income. More generally, the benefit paid by a single program to people with low income has a larger percentage impact on the reward to earning income the more that the rest of the safety net helps people with low income.

The labyrinth of programs available to help people without work can be summarized by measuring the combined value of benefits available to a person who does not work, less taxes paid, and comparing it to the net of tax value of benefits available to the same person if he or she were working.[3] The difference between the two combined values is the causal effect of working on the value of benefits available. The more that working reduces the net of tax value of available benefits, the more the programs have reduced the reward to working.

In doing so, it is important to recognize that people do not always participate in all available programs and that the reward to working is not affected by a program from which no benefits are received (regardless of work status) and to which no taxes are paid. Once it includes an accounting for program participation, the comparison of combined net of tax benefits received when not working to the value received when working quantifies the contribution of the programs to the reward to working. This chapter makes this comparison at several points in time—every month since 2007—because new program rules have taken effect over time that add to or subtract from the benefits received when not working, the net benefits received or taxes paid when working, or both.

My approach begins by forming two time series for each safety net program j: a statutory eligibility index $\{E_{jt}\}$ and a statutory benefit-per-participant index $\{B_{jt}\}$. The indices, and therefore their product, change only at dates t when new program rules ("statutes") go into effect. A time series for overall statutory safety net generosity $\{b_t\}$ is obtained by aggregating the product of the two indices across programs using a set of time-invariant program weights ω_j.

$$b_t \equiv \sum_j \omega_j E_{jt} B_{jt} \qquad (3.1)$$

where t indexes time and j indexes safety net programs.

Any program's weight depends on the population of interest and is estimated as the fraction of the population of interest that typically participates in the program, holding eligibility constant. For example, the unemployment insurance program would receive a positive weight if unemployed people were the population of interest, but zero weight if persons out of the labor force were the population of interest. Regardless of the exact values for the program weights, the overall generosity index (3.1) changes over time only to the extent that one or more of the component programs had a change in eligibility rules, benefit rules, or both.

This chapter focuses on the group of household heads and spouses under age sixty-five, which it divides into those unemployed, out of the labor force, underemployed (defined later), and the remainder (the employed but not underemployed). Thus, each safety net program in principle has four weights—a weight used for unemployed population calculations, a weight used for out of the labor force population calculations, etc.—and my framework delivers three time series for overall safety net generosity relative to the remainder group.[4] At the end of the chapter, I combine the three time series into a single aggregate time series by weighting each component according to the share of its population's contribution to the reduction in aggregate hours between 2007 and 2010.

Children and youths qualify for a number of programs on the basis of their parents' or guardians' income or employment, not their own, which is why this chapter examines safety net expansions from the perspective of (nonelderly) household heads and spouses.[5] Table 3.1 displays some of their characteristics in 2007 and 2009.

Weekly employment fell 2 percent among married women, and about 6 percent for the other three demographic categories. Overall, employment

Table 3.1 Number and Characteristics of Household Heads, Spouses

	Employed			Not Employed		
	2007	2009	Chg	2007	2009	Chg
	Millions			Millions		
Married male	42.6	40.2	–6%	6.3	8.1	28%
Married female	33.6	32.9	–2%	16.4	16.8	3%
Unmarried male	16.0	15.0	–6%	4.1	5.6	36%
Unmarried female	18.5	17.5	–6%	6.7	7.7	15%
Total	110.8	105.6	–5%	33.5	38.2	14%
Among the Employed						
Weekly hours, average	40.5	39.2	–3%			
Weekly earnings, average	846	853	1%			
Weekly earnings, median	692	696	1%			
Weekly earnings, first quartile	438	435	–1%			
Underemployment rate	0	0.030				

Notes: Persons under age sixty-five only. Employment, hours, and earnings refer to the survey reference week. Hours are measured only for persons at work.

Among the employed, the underemployment rate is 1 minus the ratio of average hours to average hours in 2007. Because 2009 employment was 105.6 million, the absolute amount of underemployment was 3.2 million among the employed.

Earnings are measured in 2007 dollars.

fell, and nonemployment increased, about five million between 2007 and 2009. Among those employed, weekly work hours fell about 3 percent. Inflation-adjusted weekly earnings, measured at the mean, median, and first quartile were pretty stable, reflecting the increase in earnings per hour shown in Figure 2.3.

Between 2007 and 2009, the number of household heads and spouses not working increased 14 percent, which is one crude estimate of how much aggregate safety net spending would have increased during that time if benefit rules had remained constant. This measure potentially neglects weekly income losses among the employed that might also create more safety net expenditure. For this reason, I also measure employed persons' contribution to underemployment, according to the amount by which their weekly work hours fall short of average weekly work hours among heads and spouses employed in 2007. Thus total underemployment in 2009 is 3 percent of the number of people employed, plus the number of persons not employed, which is a total of 41 million.[6]

This chapter examines two categories of safety net programs: means-tested (or work-tested) government subsidies and means-tested loan forgiveness. Taxes are omitted for the moment; later this chapter adds taxes to the calculation. Regarding the first category, Table 3.2 displays the various means-tested or work-tested subsidies that appear in the personal income accounts as government social benefits. For each program, the table displays the 2006–2010 average fractions of program expenditures that go to the nonelderly and indicates the result in the "inclusion factor" column of the table.[7] The Medicaid inclusion factor also contains a 50 percent reduction for the possibility that Medicaid benefits are a poor substitute for cash benefits. I then add up each program's product of inclusion factor and 2009 expenditures and show the contribution of each program to the total in the last column of the table. The three largest programs for persons under age sixty-five in 2009 were Medicaid, Unemployment Insurance (UI), and Supplemental Nutrition Assistance

Table 3.2 Means-tested Public Subsidies Found in the Personal Income Accounts, 2009

Program	Inclusion Factor[a]	Percentage of Total[b]
Federal		
Unemployment Insurance	0.97	30%
Supplemental Nutrition Assistance Program	0.93	12%
Supplemental Security Income	0.88	9%
State and Local		
Medicaid	0.40	35%
Family Assistance	0.93	5%
Supplemental Security Income	0.88	1%
General Assistance	0.93	3%
Energy Assistance	0.93	1%
Other[c]	0.93	4%

Notes: [a] Inclusion factor is an estimate of the fraction of program spending on nonelderly persons. For Medicaid, it is multiplied by an estimate of the relative value of in-kind versus cash subsidies (0.5).
[b] Percentage of total is proportional to a program's transfer amount times its inclusion factor; percentages sum to 100 across programs.
[c] "Other" consists of expenditures for food under the supplemental program for women, infants, and children; foster care; adoption assistance; and payments to nonprofit welfare institutions.

(SNAP). These are also the three government programs featured in major federal legislation and with the largest spending changes since 2007; the remaining means-tested government programs are lumped into a single "other" category for the purposes of applying formula (3.1).[8]

The rest of this chapter first derives statutory eligibility and benefit indices for the major government programs. The indices are used to decompose government safety net program spending changes into statutory changes and changes in population characteristics. The chapter then measures the amount of resources redistributed to persons underemployed or not employed through mortgage and consumer debt forgiveness, and how the availability of such resources changed over time. Readers interested only in results for the entire safety net can jump to the "Conclusion: Replacement Rates for Aggregate Analysis" section near the end of this chapter, which combines the government safety net and loan discharge results into a single overall replacement rate series for the marginal worker that is the cornerstone for the aggregate labor market analysis in later chapters of this book.

Legislation Made the Safety Net Available to Millions More

The fraction of households receiving benefits from safety net programs increased dramatically since 2007. Figure 3.1's red series shows the average weekly number of persons aged twenty-five to sixty-four receiving unemployment benefits as a ratio to the average weekly number of persons of the same age range who are unemployed.[9] Figure 3.1's black series displays the average monthly number of households receiving SNAP benefits as a ratio to total households with annual income below 125 percent of the poverty line (as defined by the Census Bureau on the basis of their money income). Many more households have money income below the poverty line than in 2007, and many more household heads and spouses find themselves unemployed, yet the two ratios shown in Figure 3.1 rise because the number of safety net program participants increased even more. For example, the number of families with income below 125 percent of the federal poverty guideline (FPG) increased about 16 percent from 2007 to 2010, yet the number of households receiving SNAP benefits increased 58 percent over the same time frame. As a result, the SNAP recipiency ratio shown in Figure 3.1 increased 37 percent.

Millions of households received safety net benefits in 2010 that would not have been eligible for benefits in 2007 even if their circumstances had been the same in the two years, because the rules for receiving safety net benefits

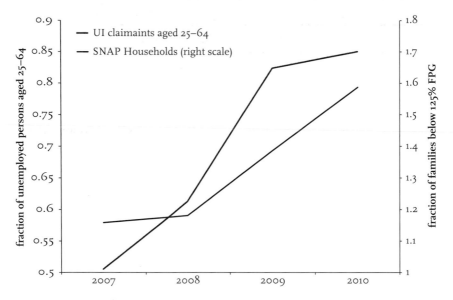

FIGURE 3.1 UI and SNAP Recipiency Rates since 2007

had changed. Table 3.3 displays some of the major government benefit rule changes that are quantified in this chapter. The table is organized in panels: the top panel lists unemployment insurance and associated initiatives, the middle panel list SNAP changes, and the bottom panel lists Medicaid changes. The left column indicates rule changes related to program eligibility, and the right column (discussed further below) indicates rule changes related to the amounts received by eligible beneficiaries. All together, I quantify the nine major eligibility expansions embodied in eight pieces of legislation shown in the left column of Table 3.3. For the most part, those expansions went into effect in 2009 or in the second half of 2008. Most of the expansions are indefinite in that the initial legislation either specified no termination date or, as with the unemployment insurance eligibility period additions, had the original termination date repeatedly extended by subsequent legislation and thereby continue in force as of the time of my writing.

Unemployment Insurance Eligibility: Benefit Duration and Modernized Rules

The unemployment insurance (UI) program is jointly administered and financed by federal and state governments, offering weekly cash benefits to people who have lost their jobs and have as yet been unable to find and start a

Table 3.3 Major Government Benefit Rule Changes Since 2007

Eligibility	Benefit Amounts
Unemployment Insurance and Related	
Automatic extended benefit trigger Add 13 weeks of eligibility July 2008–indefinite	*American Reinvestment & Recovery Act* Exempt $2,400 UI from '09 inc. tax April 2009–December 2009
Supplemental Appropriations Act of 2008 Add 13 weeks of eligibility July 2008–indefinite	*American Reinvestment & Recovery Act* Cover 65% of COBRA expense after layoff April 2009–May 2010
Unemp. Comp. Extension Act of 2008 Add 20 weeks of eligibility December 2008–December 2012	*American Reinvestment & Recovery Act* $25 weekly bonus April 2009–June 2010
American Reinvestment & Recovery Act Reward states for modernizing eligibility April 2009–indefinite	*American Reinvestment & Recovery Act* Eliminate extended benefit experience rating April 2009–indefinite
Worker, Homeownership, & Business Assistance Act of 2009 Add 20 weeks of eligibility December 2009–May 2012	
SNAP	
Farm Bill of 2002 Begin diffusion of broad-based categorical eligibility Median implementation in Oct'08	*Farm Bill of 2008* Increase maximum benefit; exclude more income from benefit formula Oct 2008–indefinite
Farm Bill of 2008 Relax asset and net income tests October 2008–indefinite	*American Reinvestment & Recovery Act* Increase max. benefit; more inc. excluded April 2009–November 2013
American Reinvestment & Recovery Act Grant states relief from work requirement April 2009–October 2010	
Medicaid	
Patient Protection and Affordable Care Act of 2010 Admit able-bodied adults up to 133% FPG January 2014–indefinite	

new job. On average they receive about $300 a week until they start working again, or they stop looking for work, or their benefits are exhausted. Before the recession, an unemployed person in a typical state without high unemployment would often have benefits limited to a maximum of twenty-six weeks (U.S. Department of Labor 2007). The federal law in place before the recession included some local labor market "Extended Benefit" (EB) triggers that, based on the statewide unemployment rate, would automatically lengthen the maximum benefit period. These automatic triggers began to extend the duration of benefits around the nation in the middle of 2008 (U.S. Department of Labor 2011b), as indicated in Table 3.3's first entry. At about the same time, the Supplemental Appropriations Act of 2008 included new "Emergency Unemployment Compensation" (EUC) legislation that extended maximum benefit periods for the entire nation. The Worker, Homeownership, and Business Assistance Act of 2009 further extended the EUC periods, so that unemployment insurance benefits could be paid up to ninety-nine weeks (U.S. Department of Labor 2011e). The maximum unemployment benefit duration was not changed by the February 2009 American Recovery and Reinvestment Act, but the ARRA did expand eligibility by encouraging states to "modernize" (and relax) their eligibility requirements by processing earnings histories through an "alternative base period" (National Employment Law Project 2003a), including persons who quit their job for compelling family reasons, adding twenty-six weeks of eligibility for persons enrolled in training programs, and/or paying benefits for persons who search only for part-time work (U.S. Department of Labor 2009b).

For each safety net program, I create a monthly statutory eligibility index. Each program's index is normalized so that it averages 1 in fiscal year 2010 and changes only when eligibility rules change. The amount of the change is calculated according to a time-invariant measure of the fraction of program participants affected by the eligibility rule change. The index increases when eligibility rules are relaxed and decreases when eligibility rules are tightened. For example, if a program's only eligibility rule change was January 1, 2009, the rule change was permanent, and on average eighty persons would participate in the program under the pre-2009 rules for every hundred participating under the post-2009 rules, then the eligibility index's value would be 0.8 for all months prior to January 2009, and 1.0 for all months thereafter. By construction, the eligibility index does not change when eligibility rules remain fixed, even though population characteristics may be changing (e.g., more people lose their jobs) in a way that changes the fraction of the population that participates in the program.

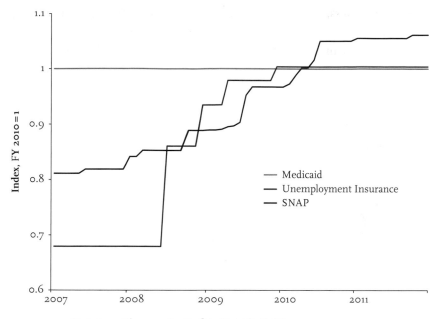

FIGURE 3.2 Statutory Changes in Safety Net Eligibility
nonelderly household heads and spouses

Figure 3.2 displays the eligibility indices for unemployment insurance, SNAP (food stamps), and Medicaid. The eligibility index for unemployment insurance (red series) has changed four times since January 2007, at the four initiation dates indicated in the first column of Table 3.3. The largest index change occurs in July 2008, when the maximum benefit period went from twenty-six to fifty-two weeks, because about half of the people who are unemployed more than twenty-six weeks are still unemployed less than fifty-two weeks. The smallest jump is for the extension of the maximum benefit period, from seventy-two to about ninety-six weeks.[10]

Overall, the eligibility index increases almost 50 percent from 2007 to 2010, which suggests that a majority of the increase in the fraction of unemployed receiving benefits (see Figure 3.1) was the result of the legislation changes shown in Table 3.3. Indeed, the average weekly number of unemployed persons aged twenty-five to sixty-four not receiving unemployment insurance actually fell between 2007 and 2009, even though the number of unemployed people in that age range increased by more than five million.[11]

SNAP Eligibility: State-by-State Elimination of Asset and Work Status Tests

The Department of Agriculture's food stamp program, now known as Supplemental Nutrition Assistance (SNAP), provides funds to low-income households for the purpose of buying food (Social Security Administration 2008), often in conjunction with cash assistance programs. SNAP benefits are potentially available to households earning less than 130 percent of the prior year poverty line, which is adjusted every fiscal year according to the rate of inflation. For example, 130 percent of the prior year poverty line was, on a monthly basis, $1,430 for a household of two in fiscal year 2007, and $1,578 in fiscal year 2010.[12] With an essential exception noted below, a household having sufficiently few assets and satisfying other eligibility criteria has its monthly benefit calculated as the program's maximum benefit for its household size minus 30 percent of its net income, where net income is money income minus deductions for shelter and other items. For this reason, essentially every participating household's benefit is linked to the program's maximum benefit.

An important legislative change during fiscal years 2007–2011 was the adoption by at least twenty-seven states, plus the District of Columbia, of "broad-based categorical eligibility," which means that states confer automatic SNAP eligibility on all households receiving a specified social service informational brochure.[13] Households that participate in SNAP under this rule still have benefits determined by the same formula (of household size and net income) as the other SNAP beneficiaries.[14] A practical result of broad-based categorical eligibility (BBCE) is therefore that households can receive benefits solely on the basis of their net income, and not on the value of their assets.[15] Even SNAP households not participating through BBCE saw the asset test relaxed as the values of individual retirement accounts and education savings accounts were excluded from the test by the 2008 Farm Bill and, between 2006 and 2010, as almost 20 states eliminated their consideration of vehicles (Eslami, Filion, and Strayer 2011, 6).

Between fiscal years 2007 and 2010, the number of SNAP households increased 37 percent more than did the number of households with income at or below 125 percent of the poverty line, and the inflation-adjusted average income of participating households actually increased (Eslami et al. 2011, table A.27). More than 100 percent of the increase in participating households occurred among those qualifying under broad-based categorical eligibility and, with the exception of residents of the three states noted in note 15, therefore households not subject to asset tests.[16]

Prior to the recession, able-bodied adults without dependents who were not working or participating in a work program had their receipt of SNAP benefits limited to three months in a three year period (U.S. Department of Agriculture, 2012a).[17] Entire states could obtain waivers from the work requirement whenever the Department of Labor indicated that the state was eligible for extended unemployment benefits (U.S. Department of Agriculture 2009). The American Recovery and Reinvestment Act waived all states through October 2010. Since then, almost all states have obtained waivers pursuant to the Department of Labor triggers (U.S. Department of Agriculture 2011b). Altogether, the state-wide waivers and ARRA changed eligibility requirements in the direction of making SNAP eligibility more inclusive than it would have been if able-bodied adults without dependents were required to work (or have their benefits limited), as they typically were before the recession began.

Figure 3.2's SNAP eligibility index reflects the combination of the relaxation of work requirements and the dynamics of the BBCE legislation. Aside from a one-time jump of 2.3 percent in October 2008 associated with the relaxation of work requirements, the index shows an increase if and only if BBCE went into effect in at least one state on that date, and the size of the increase is proportional to the fraction of the U.S. population (measured in 2010) living in states with the new legislation. For example, the largest jump is in July 2009, when California and Connecticut began conferring BBCE. The index is normalized to average 1 in fiscal year 2010, and to have a three-year logarithmic change equal to 0.21, based on previous estimates of the effects of asset tests and BBCE on program participation and my 2.3 percent estimate of the participation effect of work requirements.[18]

Temporary Assistance for Needy Families (TANF, sometimes known as "welfare") has been operated in conjunction with SNAP since 1997 and offers, among other things, cash assistance for poor families. Prior to the recession, "federal rules also require[d] states to show that at least half of the [TANF] caseload participates in work-related activities" (Zedlewski 2008). The ARRA changed this in 2009, providing "a 'hold-harmless' clause for states that experienced caseload increases, stating that they could still receive the same caseload reduction credit toward the work participation rate requirement that they had received in 2007 or 2008" (Lower-Basch 2010, 5). In other words, the ARRA gave states more flexibility to allow unemployed people to participate in TANF.[19]

TANF was not a new safety net program, but it was more available to unemployed people after ARRA than it was before. Nevertheless, TANF's enrollment and real spending per capita has increased little since 2007 (Food and Research Action Center 2011). Moreover, the ARRA increased TANF subsidies, by about $1 billion, to working people through subsidized employment programs (Zedlewski 2011). Because TANF's rule changes may be relatively small and have both positive and negative effects on the reward to working, I include TANF together in a single "all other" means-tested subsidies category, whose eligibility and benefit rules are assumed constant over time.

Medicaid: A Historic Expansion Planned for 2014

The state-administered Medicaid program pays health care providers on behalf of low-income individuals and families (Centers for Medicare and Medicaid Services 2011). It is the largest single program shown in Table 3.2, spending about $8,000 per beneficiary per year.[20] Due to the high rates of spending on the elderly and disabled, spending per nonelderly, nondisabled beneficiary is about half the average for the entire program (Henry J. Kaiser Family Foundation 2011a). An average family eligible for Medicaid would obtain more than $10,000 in benefits per year, even without any elderly or disabled members.[21] As explained below, the sheer size of this program is important for understanding the economic effects of expansions of the other safety net programs.

Unlike the UI and SNAP programs, the Medicaid program has not yet significantly expanded its eligibility or average benefit since 2007.[22] Some states have restricted Medicaid benefits in order to control costs. A number of states have expanded eligibility (Smith et al. 2011), but those expansions were small enough that nationwide Medicaid enrollment and inflation-adjusted Medicaid spending actually grew slightly less between 2007 and 2010 than did the number of Americans in poverty.[23] To a first approximation, Medicaid spending and enrollment have expanded since 2007 because of the number of families who have seen their income decline (2011, 15), rather than relaxation of eligibility rules.

The Patient Protection and Affordable Care Act was passed in March 2010. As a result of this legislation, Medicaid enrollment and spending are expected to increase significantly in 2014, when the program is made "available to able-bodied adults with incomes up to 133 percent of the federal poverty level" (Sack 2010). The Medicaid eligibility index shown in Figure 3.2 is therefore 1 prior to 2014, at which time it jumps up an amount reflecting estimates of the number of newly eligible beneficiaries who will participate in the program (see Appendix 3.1). Thus, even though the safety net has already expanded because of recent changes in eligibility rules for the UI and SNAP programs,

Medicaid may be the main way for the safety net to further expand in the near future.

Legislation Increased the Amount of Benefits Received per Program Participant

For each safety net program, I create a monthly statutory real benefit index. Each index is normalized so that its fiscal year 2010 average is equal to the program's average real monthly benefit per participant in fiscal year 2010.[24] A real-benefit index changes only when benefit rules change the amount that a program participant with a given set of characteristics would receive. The results are displayed in Figure 3.3.

The major benefit rule changes are indicated in the right half of Table 3.3. The four provisions shown in the top panel were put in place by the ARRA and serve to increase the amounts received by persons laid off from their jobs. The first provision exempts from 2009 federal income tax the first $2,400 of unemployment benefits received by an unemployed person (U.S. Department of Labor 2011e). Because the provision serves to reduce that person's personal income tax, I estimate it to be worth about $57 per month for each of the nine months April 2009 through December 2009 (details in Appendix 3.1), which is why the red unemployment insurance series in Figure 3.3 jumps down that amount in January 2010.

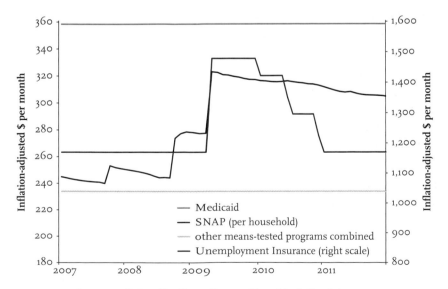

FIGURE 3.3 Statutory Safety Net Benefits per Nonelderly Participant

For laid-off workers who wanted to remain on their former employer's health plan, the ARRA offered to pay 65 percent of the cost. For a $13,027 annual family health insurance premium (Crimmel 2010), that subsidy is worth $706 per month. However, I estimate that the number of people receiving the benefit when it was available was only one-fifth the number of people receiving unemployment benefits, so the effect of the provision on the index is only $143 per month (see Appendices 3.1 and 3.2). The third provision is worth a bit more than $100 per month.

SNAP had two major federal legislative changes in benefits since 2007: the 2008 Farm Bill (effective October 2008) and the 2009 American Recovery and Reinvestment Act (effective April 2009). Both laws increased the per-household benefit amount across the board, far in excess of the rate of inflation, which is why the real SNAP benefit index shown in Figure 3.3 jumps up at the two legislation dates. A smaller nominal benefit increase went into effect in October 2007. The benefit formulas were unchanged in nominal terms in between these three dates, which is why the SNAP real benefit index trends slightly down between jumps.[25]

At all three dates, benefit amounts were changed by increasing the maximum benefit. The maximum benefit increased about 8.5 percent on October 1, 2008, and another 13.6 percent on April 1, 2009 (Eslami et al. 2011, 22). The dollar amount of the maximum benefit change depends on household size and averaged $27 on October 1, 2008, and $47 on April 1, 2009.[26] In addition, the 2008 Farm Bill revised the standard deduction and expanded the child care deduction and would thereby increase benefits by about $2 per household per month, holding fixed the composition of SNAP households. The net effect of legislation and accumulated inflation was to increase the statutory real SNAP benefit index by $73 per month from fiscal year 2007 to fiscal year 2010, or about 30 percent.

Most of the Increase in Government Safety Net Expenditure Is the Direct Result of Program Rule Changes

When eligibility and benefits per participant are combined, the law changes shown in Table 3.3 create very large changes in UI and SNAP generosity. From statutory rule changes alone, UI's eligibility index increased more than 40 percent from the end of 2007 to the end of 2009, and its benefit index increased more than 25 percent, for a combined generosity increase of 84 percent. From statutory changes alone, SNAP's eligibility index increased more

Table 3.4 UI and SNAP Spending Growth Attributable to Benefit Rule Changes

	2007 $ per Capita			Changes from 2007	
	2007	2009	2010	2009	2010
Unemployment Insurance					
Actual spending, all programs[a]	109	411	427	279%	293%
Regular state programs only	109	251	180	131%	66%
Regular state programs, adj. for ARRA eligibility[b]	109	242	172	123%	59%
Regular state programs, adj. for ARRA eligibility and $25 weekly benefit increase	109	227	163	109%	50%
Food Stamps/SNAP					
Actual spending[a]	102	173	205	68%	100%
Under 2007 eligibility rules[c]	102	151	164	48%	60%
Under 2007 eligibility rules, and constant real benefits rules[d]	102	120	127	17%	24%
Addendum: per capita persons in poverty[e]	0.173	0.189	0.201	9%	16%
UI and SNAP combined					
Actual spending[a]	211	584	632	177%	199%
Under 2007 eligibility and benefit rules	211	347	290	64%	37%

Notes: [a] Actual spending amounts from the personal income accounts, and thereby exclude program administrative costs.
[b] Adjusts for changes in the "modernization" component of the statutory UI eligibility index.
[c] Adjusts for changes in the statutory SNAP eligibility index.
[d] Adjusts for changes in the product of the statutory SNAP eligibility index and real benefit index.
[e] Fraction of persons below 125 percent of the poverty level from U.S. Census Bureau's American Community Survey.

than 20 percent from the beginning of 2007 to the beginning of 2010, and its benefit index increased almost 30 percent, for a combined generosity increase of 56 percent.

Table 3.4's top row displays actual unemployment insurance spending (all programs) for calendar years 2007, 2009, and 2010, adjusted for inflation and measured as a ratio to the entire U.S. population.[27] Actual spending increased almost 300 percent (that is, spending almost quadrupled) in two years.

The second row displays actual spending on state UI programs, which would be essentially the only UI payments if benefits were limited to twenty-six weeks, as they were in 2007. The third row adjusts state program spending for an estimate of the effect of ARRA on state program eligibility rules (the same estimate built into Figure 3.2's eligibility index). If we assume for the moment that eligibility rule changes had no effect on the number of people unemployed from zero to twenty-six weeks, then the second and third rows can be interpreted as estimates of what per capita real UI spending would have been if UI eligibility rules had remained what they were in 2007: it would have grown about 60 percent through 2010, rather than 293 percent. By 2010, less than half of actual spending—less than $180 per person out of a total of $427—was on unemployed people who, so far, were unemployed one to twenty-six weeks and therefore could have been eligible for benefits under the 2007 rules.

The fourth row of the table shows hypothetical program spending using the 2007 eligibility rules and subtracting the $25 per week of federal additional compensation paid pursuant to the ARRA. With the caveat noted above, this row suggests that unemployment insurance spending would have increased only 50 percent between 2007 and 2010, rather than 293 percent, if eligibility and benefit rules had remained as they were in 2007.

The second row of the table's SNAP panel estimates the program's hypothetical spending growth with 2007 eligibility rules by adjusting actual spending for the changes in the statutory SNAP eligibility index. This row suggests that the growth in real spending per capita would have been about one-third less if SNAP eligibility rules had remained constant. The next row estimates the program's hypothetical spending growth with 2007 eligibility rules and constant real benefit rules by adjusting actual spending for the changes in the product of the statutory SNAP eligibility index and the statutory SNAP benefit index. It suggests that, if eligibility rules had remained constant and benefit rule parameters increased only with inflation, then real SNAP spending per capita would have grown only 8 percentage points more than the change in the fraction of people living in households with income less than 125 percent of federal poverty guidelines.

Overall, Table 3.4 suggests that most of the growth in spending on UI and SNAP is due to changes in eligibility rules, and increases in payments per eligible person. The programs' combined spending certainly would have grown if benefit rules had remained as they were in 2007, but much less than it actually did. As shown in the table's bottom panel, the two programs combined increased their spending $421 per capita (from $211 to $632), whereas an increase of only $79 per capita would have been enough to keep up with the greater number of people in 2010 who qualify for SNAP and UI benefits under the 2007 eligibility rules. Because about three-quarters of the increase in per capita spending by all government safety net programs shown in Table 3.2 can be accounted for by UI and SNAP spending growth, most of the increase in government safety net expenditure per capita is the direct result of UI and SNAP rule changes.

Safety Net Rule Changes and Assistance for the Unemployed

The levels of the eligibility indices shown in Figure 3.2 cannot be compared across programs because all the program indices are set to 1 in FY 2010, even though the eligible populations vary across programs. For the same reason, the benefit indices shown in Figure 3.3 cannot be compared across programs. However, they can be compared, and summed together, when adjusted for a time-invariant measure of the likelihood of participation in each program. Recall formula (3.1) for overall statutory safety net generosity:

$$b_t \equiv \sum_j \omega_j E_{jt} B_{jt} \tag{3.1}$$

where t indexes time and j indexes safety net programs. E_j is program j's statutory eligibility index and B_j is its statutory per-participant benefit index, measured in inflation-adjusted dollars per month. The program aggregation weight ω_j is the fraction of the population of interest that typically participates in program j, holding eligibility constant.

Program Aggregation Weights

Ultimately I use formula (3.1) to consider both government and private sector safety net programs as they apply to various persons on the margin of working, but for the moment I limit attention to the government safety net programs listed in Table 3.2 as they apply to household heads or spouses who are unemployed. The first column of Table 3.5 indicates the program weights for this purpose.

The first column weight on unemployment insurance could be 1 only if, under the fiscal year 2010 eligibility rules, all unemployed heads and spouses received unemployment benefits some time during their unemployment spell. Historically, many unemployed persons have not collected unemployment benefits because of ineligibility, lack of awareness, or simply unwillingness to

Table 3.5 Government Safety Net Program Weights

		Labor Force Status		
	Unemployed	Out of the Labor Force	Employed with Reduced Hours	Average Marginal Worker
UI sometime during spell	0.63	0	0	0.37
SNAP	0.50	0.42	0.50	0.49
Medicaid	0.47	0.47	0.47	0.47
All other government safety net	0.37	1.00	0.37	0.43
Demographic weights	0.58	0.09	0.33	

Note: Demographic weights are used to define the average marginal worker. Program weights are used to aggregate program-specific statutory generosity measures. Medicaid weight reflects a 50% discount factor for in-kind benefits.

collect benefits (Anderson and Meyer 1997), so a proper first entry in Table 3.5 is likely less than 1. One way to estimate that entry is as the ratio of the number of regular UI recipients aged twenty-five to sixty-four to the number of persons aged twenty-five to sixty-four who are unemployed but not yet for more than twenty-six weeks, times the fraction of unemployed with spells no greater than ninety-six weeks (the 2010 eligibility rule), which is typically 0.63.[28]

At first glance, it would appear that most of the marginal workers would not be able to participate in a program like SNAP that is targeted to the poorest segment of the population. However, I explain further below how, with asset tests eliminated, the SNAP program is often available during times of unemployment even for a person who normally was at the median of the earnings distribution and is receiving unemployment benefits that count as income for SNAP purposes. Moreover, millions of unemployed people actually participated in the program: using data from the Department of Agriculture, Eslami, Filion, and Strayer (2011, table A.25) report that on average almost four million unemployed people were heads of SNAP households during fiscal year 2010. In order to measure the SNAP program weight ω_j for the population of nonelderly heads and spouses who are unemployed, I therefore take the ratio of the average number of nonelderly SNAP household heads and spouses who were unemployed during fiscal year 2010 to the weekly average nationwide total number of nonelderly unemployed household heads and spouses (regardless of SNAP participation), which is 0.50.[29] It appears that, with fiscal year 2010 eligibility rules in place, about half of the unemployed heads and spouses would participate in SNAP.

To measure the participation fraction ω_j for the Medicaid program, I take the ratio of the change in nonelderly Medicaid enrollment (including children) from June 2007 to June 2010 to the 2007–2010 change in the average weekly number of nonelderly heads and spouses who were not employed or underemployed, which is 0.946,[30] and discount the result by 50 percent to reflect the fact that Medicaid benefits are distributed in-kind, rather than in cash or cash equivalents.[31] I assume that eligibility and benefit indices for "all other safety net programs" are constant over time, and that the nonelderly parts of those programs pay equal benefits to all nonelderly heads and spouses who do not receive unemployment insurance in a given week. The average inflation-adjusted monthly benefit is therefore $234, and the program weight for the population of unemployed heads and spouses is the fraction of them not receiving UI under 2010 eligibility rules, 0.37.

Note that all program weights $\{\omega_j\}$ are based on actual program participation, and not the participation that would theoretically be possible if all eligible persons participated. At the same time, changes over time in the weighted sum (3.1) do not reflect *changes* in program participation aside from those associated with changes in program eligibility rules because the program weights do not change over time.[32]

Results, and Multiprogram Participation Examples

The red series in Figure 3.4 shows the results of aggregating, according to formula (3.1), the product of the statutory eligibility and benefit indices across programs using the weights shown in Table 3.5. The red series can be interpreted as the combined monthly benefits received from all government safety net programs by the average unemployed household head or spouse as a function of when the person was unemployed, holding constant the characteristics of the average unemployed person. The average combined monthly benefit was about $850 in 2007 and the first half of 2008. By the beginning of 2009, it had increased about $210 per month entirely as a result of the eligibility and benefit rule changes cited above. The series peaks another $280 higher at the end of 2009. By 2011, the statutory benefit series was down to about $1,200, but still $300 greater than it was in 2007. Simply put, safety net program rules were the most generous to the unemployed in the twelve months or so after the ARRA went into effect, and they remain significantly more generous than they were before the recession began.

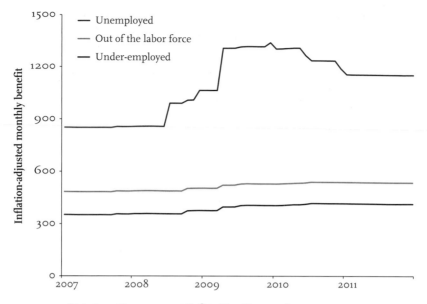

FIGURE 3.4 Statutory Government Safety Net Generosity
for nonelderly household heads and spouses, by labor force status

As demonstrated below, aggregate quantitative estimates of changes in safety net generosity, such as the series shown in Figure 3.4, are both helpful for quantitative analysis of the major macroeconomic variables and critical for many of this book's conclusions. It is therefore helpful to examine a few hypothetical families, and how their safety net benefits would have been different in, say, 2009-Q4 if the eligibility and benefit rules from two years earlier had remained in place.

Consider a family of four, with the primary earner unemployed during 2009-Q4. The primary earner is entitled to a $275 weekly UI benefit, plus the ARRA's federal additional compensation, but only until benefits expire. The household can either purchase health insurance through the former employer (at a cost of $13,027 per year) or participate in Medicaid (if eligible on the basis of assets and income). Its monthly deductions for SNAP purposes are $410 (the FY 2010 average for all SNAP households without earnings) plus 20 percent of spousal earnings.[33] Its marginal federal income tax rate for the purposes of changes in the amount of unemployment benefits is 21 percent.[34]

If the primary earner has so far been unemployed four months, as with hypothetical households A, C, and E shown in Table 3.6, the household would be receiving unemployment benefits under both 2007-Q4 and 2009-Q4 eligibility rules. However, it receives the federal additional compensation ($25 per

Table 3.6 Changes in Safety Net Generosity for Hypothetical Households with Four Members

Household Characteristics	Monthly Amounts, Levels					
	HH A	*HH B*	*HH C*	*HH D*	*HH E*	*HH F*
Months of unemployment so far	4	9	4	9	4	9
Real spousal income	2,500	2,500	0	0	0	0
Passes 2007 SNAP asset test?	1	1	1	1	0	0

2009-Q4 Benefit Generosity Relative to Inflation-Adjusted 2007-Q4 Benefit Rules, When Primary Earner Not Earning

	Monthly Amounts, Policy Impact					
Unemployment insurance	108	1,300	108	1,300	108	1,300
SNAP	0	0	108	108	401	401
Medicaid	0	0	0	0	0	0
COBRA subsidy	706	706	0	0	706	706
Payroll tax savings	0	0	0	0	0	0
Federal income tax savings	33	−217	33	−217	33	−217
All provisions combined	824	1,789	227	1,191	1,225	2,190

Assumptions: Each hypothetical household participates in the above programs whenever eligible. Each has a 21% marginal federal income tax rate. The primary earner's weekly UI benefit (before exhaustion) is $275, plus the ARRA's federal additional compensation. Household does not use secondary earner's health insurance. Household lives in a state that began conferring broad-based categorical eligibility, without an asset test, sometime between 2007-Q4 and 2009-Q4. Health insurance costs $13,027 per year. The Medicaid asset test is the same as the 2007-Q4 SNAP asset test. Monthly deductions for SNAP purposes are $410 plus 20 percent of spousal earnings.

week, which is $108 per month) only under the 2009-Q4 rules, so Table 3.6 shows a policy impact on UI of $108 for those three households. Any household receiving UI receives a tax exemption of $2,400 of UI income—$267 per month when amortized over the nine months of 2009 when the ARRA was in effect. For a household with more than $2,400 of UI income for the calendar year, the total monthly tax savings from the 2009-Q4 policies is $33 (21 percent of $267 minus $108).

If the primary earner has so far been unemployed more than six months, the person qualifies for unemployment benefits only under 2009-Q4 rules, and the entire $1,300 monthly benefit is the policy impact. The household owes tax on this monthly benefit, so 2009-Q4 rules cost such a household $217 more per month in federal income tax; see Table 3.6's hypothetical households B, D, and F.

If the primary earner has a spouse or other household member who earns much more than $2,000 per month (such as the $2,500 per month shown in Table 3.6's first two columns), the hypothetical household will not qualify for SNAP benefits, even under BBCE. In this case, the policy change has no impact on the household's SNAP benefits.

Without any spousal earnings, the household qualifies for $401 SNAP benefits under 2009-Q4 rules.[35] If the household's assets exceeded SNAP limits under 2007 rules, as with hypothetical households E and F, the policy impact is the full $401. If the household would have qualified for SNAP under 2007-Q4 rules, then the policy impact is the $108 difference between $401 and its $293 benefit under inflation-adjusted 2007-Q4 rules; see Table 3.6's hypothetical households C and D.

Hypothetical households C and D have sufficiently little in assets and spousal earnings to qualify for Medicaid. For this reason, I assume that households C and D do not obtain health insurance through the former employer and therefore do not benefit from the ARRA's COBRA subsidy.[36] Only for the purpose of Table 3.6, I assume that households not qualifying for Medicaid (A and B fail to qualify because of spousal income; E and F fail to qualify because of assets) opt to obtain health insurance from the former employer through the COBRA provision. The 65 percent subsidy for COBRA costs is available only under 2009-Q4 rules, so the policy impact on the COBRA subsidy is $706 per month (706 = 0.65*13027/12).

Added together across all six safety net provisions, the policy impact on the disposable income of the household with an unemployed primary earner and fixed characteristics ranges from $227 and $2,190 per month among the six hypothetical households.[37] These amounts are policy impacts, the amounts that 2009-Q4 rules *add* to safety net benefits relative to the benefits that would be paid under inflation-adjusted 2007-Q4 rules. Five of the six hypothetical households experience a policy impact of $824 per month or more. Half of the households experience a policy impact of more than $1,000 per month even without the COBRA provision.

By comparison with the amounts shown in Table 3.6, the $450 increase in Figure 3.4's red series measuring statutory safety net generosity over time is not particularly large. As shown in Appendix 3.2, the statutory safety net generosity increases shown in Figure 3.4 and elsewhere in this chapter are also congruent with changes over time in aggregate benefit payments per non-employed or underemployed household head or spouse. The safety net actually did become significantly more generous, and the payments actually received by unemployed people and other potential beneficiaries reflect this increased generosity.

Unemployment Insurance Experience Rating

By offering people a potential source of income while they are not working, unemployment insurance can reduce employment through a couple of channels. One channel is the decision by workers and employers to separate, especially to separate by layoff. Employers and employees understand that, after a worker quits or is laid off, earnings and production will be lost for the duration of time that the employee is unemployed and the duration of time that the employee's work tasks are not performed. These losses by themselves discourage separation, and they do so to a greater degree the more earnings and production are expected to be lost. Safety net benefits help mitigate such losses and thereby reduce the cost of separation from the point of view of employers and employees. A second channel of unemployment benefits reducing employment is through exit from unemployment: at least some unemployed people might find, accept, or begin a new job more quickly if the unemployment insurance program were not providing an alternative source of income. For either channel, the benefits shown as Figure 3.4's red series are a component of employment decisions.

Layoff taxes are excluded from Figure 3.4's red series, as well as the related unemployment insurance calculations in Figure 3.3 and Table 3.4, but they may also affect employment through the separation channel because they add to the cost of separation. The "experience rated" unemployment insurance systems run by the states resemble layoff taxes, because a layoff that results in an unemployment insurance claim can increase the amount the employer owes in payroll taxes to the state unemployment insurance system. Layoff taxes are presumably much less relevant for unemployment exit (the second channel) than for employment separations (the first channel) because the unemployed often have no contact with their former employer and thereby would have little reason to consider the effect of their continued unemployment on their former employer's tax liabilities. In theory, layoff taxes may increase or decrease employment, although they probably reduce the amount of employment changes over the business cycle.[38] Henceforth, I exclude former employer UI liabilities from most of my calculations of safety net generosity indices. Appendix 3.2 estimates that the excluded liabilities amount to about

$260 per month for the average unemployed household head or spouse, shows that the amount is essentially constant over time, and explores the effect on the chapter's main conclusions of including those liabilities in the safety net calculus.

Means-Tested Loan Forgiveness

Household debt was already increasing during the 1980s and 1990s, but the rate of increase was extraordinary between 2000 and 2007. In 2000, household sector debt was less than 80 percent of annual personal income. By 2006, it had reached 114 percent of the nation's personal income (Dynan and Kohn 2007)—more than $13 trillion. The change was almost entirely due to accumulation of home mortgage debt; nonmortgage debt remained about one-quarter of personal income throughout the period (2007). The mortgage debt had grown more or less in proportion to the growth in residential real estate values (2007); by that year home mortgage debt was almost 90 percent of annual personal income.

Means-Tested Home Mortgage Collection

The combination of housing market events and the profit motive for mortgage lenders turned trillions of dollars of household debt into a kind of safety net, because one of the consequences of unemployment would increasingly be a lender-provided discount on home mortgage expenses. Normally, lenders do not offer discounts on home mortgage expenses because the mortgages are fully secured by a residential property: if a homeowner fails to make the scheduled payments in full and on time, the lender can seize the property and sell it to obtain his principal, interest, and fees.[39] When the lender has this valuable foreclosure option, borrowers overwhelmingly either make their home mortgage payments, or sell their property in an orderly fashion in order to obtain the funds to repay the mortgage lender. As long as a property could be sold for enough to repay its mortgage, even homeowners who had become unemployed could be expected to pay their mortgage in full.[40] The vast majority of mortgages were paid in full and on time, and homes were typically owned by occupants, not by banks.

When residential property values plummeted in 2008 and 2009, a number of residential properties were suddenly under water: worth less than the mortgages that they secured. In those cases, the lender's foreclosure option was no longer valuable: selling the property would likely yield too little funds to cover principal, let alone interest and fees. For the same reason, a homeowner who suddenly owed more than the house was worth might minimize losses by stopping the mortgage payments.

A homeowner always has the option to stop paying her mortgage, even if she can afford the payments. Although state laws are somewhat different, to a good approximation the worst-case scenario for a homeowner who stops paying is that he can no longer own or occupy the house, may suffer a reduction in his credit rating that might raise his future borrowing costs, and may personally suffer a loss in pride for his failure to pay as promised.[41] But if the combined value of the house and these costs were less than the present value of the promised mortgage payments, then the homeowner could do better than paying in full. That's probably an important reason why, as of early 2009, more than five million homes were already either in foreclosure (lenders were seizing the collateral as a consequence of lack of payment) or their owners were delinquent on their mortgage payments.

In order to minimize lending losses, it helps to encourage at least some of the underwater borrowers to make their scheduled mortgage payments, and thereby pay more than their homes are worth. As explained above, insisting on full payment from everyone probably would not minimize losses because lenders would find themselves owning millions of unoccupied homes. Lenders could essentially eliminate foreclosures by reducing all mortgage amounts enough that homeowners were no longer under water, but that would eliminate their chances of collecting from the subset of borrowers who would pay in full despite being under water.

Lenders needed a way to estimate which borrowers would pay in full, and for other borrowers try to work out a mortgage modification that would give them an incentive to pay at least a bit more than their homes were worth. Naturally, a borrower's income is a factor to be considered; borrowers with high income can be expected to repay more than borrowers with low income. Thus, a partial solution to the lenders' collection problem is to insist that high-income borrowers pay more, and allow some low-income borrowers to pay less. Lenders have been doing exactly that.

Chapter Nine examines the microeconomics of mortgage modification in more detail, and the role of public policy in determining mortgage modification formulas, but a couple of examples begin to put mortgage modification in the context of the overall safety net. Table 3.7 shows some of the mortgage modification arithmetic based on the federal guidelines for a hypothetical dual-earner household. When working, both earners earn $727 per week, or $3,148 per month (2010 dollars), which is the median among working heads of households and spouses at work during the average week in 2007. The household has

Table 3.7 Home Mortgage Interest Payment Forgiveness for A Hypothetical Dual-Earner Household

Household Characteristics	UI Eligible	UI Ineligible
Monthly earnings when working	3,148	3,148
Monthly UI when not working	1,574	0
Spousal earnings	3,148	3,148
DTI when working	31%	31%
Modification characteristics if one earner was unemployed		
DTI when not working, unmodified	41%	62%
Monthly modification that hits DTI = 31%	488	976
LTV needed to pass NPV test	1.13	1.29

Assumptions: Insurance and real estate taxes are 20% of overall (unmodified) housing expenses. The annual interest rate is 7%. Unemployment occurs, if at all, for the full year that income is examined for the purposes of modification.

DTI = debt-to-income ratio

LTV = loan-to-value ratio

NPV test = modification must be at least as profitable as foreclosure.

monthly housing expenses, inclusive of mortgage principal and interest payments, that are 31 percent of their income when both earners are working.

If one of the earners were not working and eligible for unemployment insurance (Table 3.7's first column), then unemployment benefits would replace half his or her salary, or $1,574 per month. Otherwise unemployment benefits are zero. Either way, unemployment thereby reduces household income and increases the household's debt-to-income ratio, or DTI.[42] According to federal modification guidelines, home mortgage interest payment should be reduced so that the household's DTI returns to 31 percent. For the household shown in Table 3.7, the required reduction is zero if both earners are working, and either $488 or $976 per month if one of the earners is unemployed, depending on whether the unemployed earner is UI-eligible.[43] In this regard, mortgage modification provides a $488 monthly unemployment benefit, in addition to the $1,574 received from the unemployment insurance system (the table's first column), or a $976 monthly benefit by itself (second column).

The only remaining question is whether the lender could do better by foreclosing rather than agreeing to reduce interest payments by $488 per month, or $976 per month for the UI-ineligible household, for five years.[44] That depends on the value of the collateral: if the home's value is low enough that the loan-to-value ratio is no greater than 1.13 for the UI-eligible household, or 1.29 for the UI-ineligible household (see the last row of the table), then the modification is more profitable than foreclosure.[45]

To put mortgage modification in the context of the overall safety net, I calculate an eligibility index, a benefit index, and a program weight for mortgage modification so that it can be added to the other safety net programs using formula (3.1). The modification eligibility index is not based on statutes, however, but rather on the propensity of homeowners to have negative equity in their home—because a homeowner with positive equity is not eligible for modification if unemployed.[46] Figure 3.5 displays a time series for the modification eligibility index, which is calculated as the ratio of the fraction of owner-occupied homes with negative equity to the average fraction in fiscal year 2010 (0.189). The eligibility index has more than tripled since 2007 as residential property values collapsed and home equity was more often negative than it was before the recession began. By the end of 2009, the average amount of negative home equity was $70,700, and the aggregate amount was $801 billion (First American CoreLogic 2010). Home mortgage modification thereby had the potential to redistribute as many resources as the expansion in unemployment insurance or food stamps.

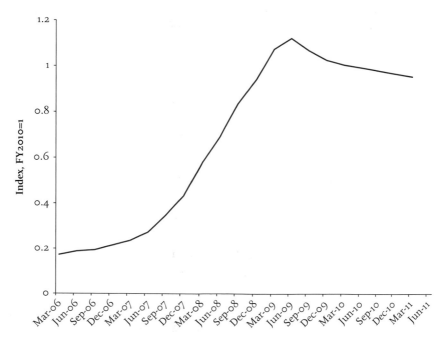

FIGURE 3.5 Eligibility Index for Mortgage Modifications

I estimate that 37 percent of the 2007–2010 change in average hours worked by household heads and spouses is covered by unemployment insurance and the rest is not (often because the person is underemployed, rather than unemployed). With these weights, I set the (time-invariant) modification benefit index to the $797 weighted average of $488 and $976.

Mortgage modification provides no safety net to someone who does not have an underwater home mortgage, which in fiscal year 2010 described about 87 percent of household heads and their spouses because they did not own their home or had nonnegative home equity. Nor is modification a safety net for a household that has access to, and is satisfied with, a nonmeans-tested resolution such as foreclosure without lender recourse. A number of other homeowners are technically eligible for modifications but do not pursue them, perhaps because they are unaware of the possibility, or they prefer to pay their mortgage as promised at origination. Others apply for a modification but have their application lost or delayed by lenders and their servicers. As for the other safety net programs, the proper program weight ω_j reflects the actual number of modifications rather than the number that would hypothetically occur if all eligible homeowners received a modification, so I multiply the fraction of heads and spouses owning an underwater home by the ratio of the actual number of home mortgage modifications under the Obama administration's Making Home Affordable Program through the end of 2011 (1.1 million) and the number that the program originally targeted (3.5 million).[47] As a result, mortgage modification adds (in fiscal year 2010) a $29 monthly benefit per month of nonemployment or underemployment of the head or spouse to the income of the average household experiencing that reduced employment. In fiscal year 2007, the monthly benefit was only $8 because negative home equity was less common.

Means-Tested Collection of Unsecured Consumer Loans

Consumers also borrow with credit cards and other forms of consumer debt that is unsecured in the sense that the loans are not collateralized by a specific asset such as a home or automobile. Aside from paying back in full, consumers potentially have three ways to obtain a discharge of some of their unsecured consumer debt: negotiating a settlement with creditors, filing Chapter 7 bankruptcy, and filing Chapter 13 bankruptcy. In all three cases, more debt is expected to be discharged the less that the debtor earns; in effect, part of the debtor's earnings goes to the lender. Implicit wage taxation is obvious during the three-to-five-year period following Chapter 13 bankruptcy when creditors receive all of the income, beyond amounts set aside for necessary expenses, of debtors who are not scheduled to pay in full (Li and Sarte 2006). Wage taxation is also relevant during the settlement process not only because wage garnishment (that is, having a specific percentage of the debtor's paycheck withheld on behalf of creditors) is one of the debt collection tools but also because the debtor can eschew a settlement and opt for Chapter 13 instead. The lower the debtor's income, the more creditors are threatened by the Chapter 13 possibility. The debtor's income is not considered when discharging debts under Chapter 7 bankruptcy, which is the majority of non-business bankruptcies. However, under current law, Chapter 7 bankruptcy is not permitted for high-income debtors.[48]

To ignore bankruptcy law changes for the moment, means-tested consumer debt discharges are nothing new. Moreover, contrary to the amount of mortgage debt, the amount of unsecured consumer debt was not historically unusual in 2007 (Moore and Palumbo 2010). To a first approximation, unsecured consumer debt discharge is a cushion for a debtor against income declines, but the size of the cushion has been constant over time. This suggests treating unsecured consumer debt discharges like Medicaid expenditures: a positive but time-invariant component of safety net benefits. To estimate the size of this cushion, I average the fiscal year 2007 and 2010 ratios of inflation-adjusted consumer loan discharges by commercial banks to the number of nonelderly heads and spouses not employed or underemployed, which is $100 at a monthly rate.

In fact, a new federal bankruptcy law went into effect in October 2005. To the degree that the new legislation achieved its goal of making it more difficult for high-income debtors to discharge debts under bankruptcy, the generosity of the consumer debt discharge component of the safety net is not time-invariant but rather has increased since the new law went into effect. However, the legislation implemented its goal by means-testing eligibility for Chapter 7, yet the ratio of Chapter 7 bankruptcies to Chapter 13 bankruptcies was not substantially different during the 2008–09 recession than it was in the 2001 recession (Administrative Office of the United States Courts 2011b). To be slightly conservative as to the change in the generosity of the overall safety net, I treat consumer loan discharges as a time-invariant benefit.

Conclusion: Replacement Rates for Aggregate Analysis

The amount of earnings replaced by the aggregate safety net—that is, the increase in benefits from all programs that occurs per dollar that income falls—varies across households, and within households according to how their earnings are reduced (e.g., employment versus hours, or primary earner versus secondary earner). A simple average across households and circumstances is one way to simplify this complex reality, although many of those households and circumstances are irrelevant for determining equilibrium employment and hours. For example, a large fraction of elderly persons are not about to return to work, even if there were a significant change in labor market circumstances. Many other persons obtain a large surplus from working and would not change their work hours in response to safety net rules. For the purposes of understanding equilibrium employment and how it changed since 2007, two particularly important groups are (1) persons working in 2007 but near the margin of not working and (2) those not working in 2007 but near the margin of working. The safety net rules affecting these two groups are the majority, if not all, of the safety net rules that affect equilibrium employment.

Unfortunately, the usual datasets do not indicate exactly who is near the margin of working, let alone the distance from that margin. I therefore take a couple of steps to attempt to isolate marginal workers and the safety net benefits they would receive if not working. First, as noted at the beginning of this chapter, I exclude elderly people and safety net programs targeted toward the elderly, at least for the moment. Second, I measure replacement rates separately for unemployed people, people out of the labor force, and employed people with reduced hours. Third, I consider the possible size of these three groups among the larger group of people who would be working more hours if the labor market had remained as it was in 2007. An appropriately weighted average of replacement rates for unemployed people, people out of the labor force, and employed people with reduced hours is then the aggregate replacement rate series used for aggregate analysis in later chapters. As with its component replacement rate series, the aggregate series changes only when there are changes in the rules for eligibility or benefit amounts of one or more of the safety net programs.

As noted above, the red series in Figure 3.4 measures overall government safety net generosity for unemployed nonelderly heads and spouses by weighting the indices for the UI, SNAP, Medicaid, and "all other" programs. The gray and black series are weighted sums of the same component-program series, but with weights appropriate for the out-of-the-labor-force (OLF) or underemployed group. The UI program weight is zero for both the OLF and underemployed groups (see also Table 3.5). On the approximation that the underemployed have about the same income (inclusive of unemployment benefits) and assets as the unemployed, I set all other program weights equal for the two groups. The SNAP weight for the OLF group is the ratio of fiscal year 2010 nonelderly OLF SNAP household heads to the average monthly number of nonelderly OLF household heads in the nation, which is 0.42.[49] The Medicaid weight for the OLF group affects only the level of the replacement rate, and not its changes prior to 2014, so I assume it is the same as for the other two groups. The "other program" weight for the OLF group is calculated in the same way as for the unemployed group: 1 minus the UI program weight.

The main difference between the OLF and underemployed series and the series for the unemployed is that the latter exclude UI and related programs. As a result, the gray and black series are less than the other two and show no tendency to decline as the ARRA expires. Note that the underemployed series is the average monthly benefit received by the underemployed *per month underemployed*, holding constant the composition of the underemployed. The level of this series is lower than the others because, on average, safety net programs spend less on the underemployed per hour of underemployment: they typically do not qualify for unemployment insurance and sometimes have too much income to qualify for other safety net programs.

Aggregate Replacement Rates

The bottom row of Table 3.5 shows the relative contribution to the 2007–2010 reduction in average hours worked among nonelderly heads and spouses of changes in their propensity to be unemployed, OLF, or underemployed. The contributions in that row sum to one[50] and I use them as weights to average the overall government safety net series in Figure 3.4. The results are shown in light red in Figure 3.6.

Because the light red series is a weighted average of weighted sums, it can itself be interpreted as a weighted sum across programs of the form (3.1), using the single set of "average marginal worker" program weights shown in the last column of Table 3.5.[51] I henceforth refer to the series in Figure 3.6 as measures for the average marginal worker among nonelderly heads and spouses, or simply for nonelderly heads and spouses.

The eligibility indices, benefit indices, and program weights, constructed in the previous section for means-tested mortgage modification and consumer debt discharges, were themselves calculated for nonelderly heads and spouses, so that their product can be added to the light red series in Figure 3.6. The results of their addition are shown in gray and black in Figure 3.6. The mortgage

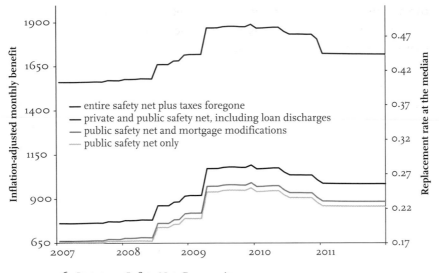

FIGURE 3.6 Statutory Safety Net Generosity for nonelderly heads or spouses

modification addition is the smaller of the two since owning a home with negative equity is still relatively rare, but it is the only addition of the two that varies over time because the prevalence of negative equity changed over time.

The final addition is for taxes on earnings. For brevity, and probably without much loss of accuracy, I consider only changes in payroll taxes and treat personal income taxes as a constant 10 percent.[52] With the exception of the former employer liability noted previously, the payroll taxes do not apply to any of the safety net benefits and do not apply to income that a person fails to earn because of being unemployed, out of the labor force, or underemployed. However, they do apply to a person who is employed, which is the baseline to which I have been comparing all of the other groups, so their amount is appropriately added to any and all of the series in Figures 3.5 and 3.6. Prior to 2011, I calculate the payroll tax amount as 15.3 percent of the median monthly earnings of heads and spouses ($3,148, at 2010 prices), which is $482. The amount is constant through December 2010. Beginning January 2011, it is reduced by $63 owing to the 2 percentage point FICA payroll tax cut that was part of the Tax Relief, Unemployment Insurance Reauthorization, and Job Creation Act of 2010. The result is shown as the red series in Figure 3.6.

The overall net monthly safety net benefit series averaged $1,560 during fiscal year 2007, and was about $300 per month greater during fiscal year

2010 and much of fiscal year 2009. The net benefit averaged $1,745 during fiscal year 2011. Of course, increases in the amount of time that people could receive unemployment benefits contribute to the increase in the overall net monthly safety net benefit series since 2007, but Appendix 3.2 shows that the contribution of benefit durations is well less than half of the overall change. In this regard, we cannot have an accurate assessment of the role of fiscal policy changes in the labor market or in the distribution of resources on the basis of means if we limit our attention to the duration of unemployment benefits.

A key indicator of the employment incentive effects of means-tested sub-sidies is the replacement rate: the fraction of productivity that the average nonemployed person receives in the form of means-tested benefits.[53] Another indicator is the self-reliance rate—the fraction of lost productivity not replaced by means-tested benefits—and is merely 1 minus the replacement rate. The larger is the self-reliance rate, the more that a household has to rely on its own earnings rather than subsidies in order to maintain its living standard. If none of the means-tested subsidies and discharges went to any household whose head (and, if present, spouse) was continuously employed, then Figure 3.6 can be used to measure the replacement rate by dividing the dollar amounts in the figure by the amount of production lost from the median head or spouse missing work for a month. Under the assumption that productivity is lost at the rate of $3,885 per month, the right scale in Figure 3.6 shows the replacement rate.[54] Before the recession began, Figure 3.6's measure of the self-reliance rate was about 60 percent (1 minus the replacement rate of about 40 percent), but by the second half of 2009 it had fallen about 8 percentage points. By any standard, that's a large and sudden change in the aggregate self-reliance rate for middle-income households and thereby a large and sudden change in the incentives to work for a large fraction of the population.

My findings of high replacement rates and low self-reliance rates during the recession are not surprising when benefit expansions since 2007 are put in the context of some of the previous literature on antipoverty programs. Holt and Romich (2007) look at self-reliance rates from tax and subsidy programs in the year 2000 and find them to be about 50 percent, and potentially much smaller if program participation rates had been greater, as they were since 2007. It is well known that a large number of households have seen their market incomes fall below the poverty line since 2007, but Sherman (2011, figure 2) shows that only 0.6 percent of the population saw their living stan-dards fall below the poverty line between 2007 and 2010, thanks to expan-sions in means-tested subsidy programs. For every forty-two people whose market income declines would have put them in poverty, government assistance pulled thirty-six back out. Roughly speaking, Sherman's results suggest that the government absorbed six-sevenths of market income declines, at least for households with income in the neighborhood of the poverty line. That is a low self-reliance rate.

Once we recognize the amount of new safety net legislation that relaxed eligibility requirements, increased benefits, or both, it is no surprise that replacement rates increased significantly. The hypothetical households shown in Table 3.6 illustrate that a larger benefit became available for a variety of household circumstances because of changes in program rules. Just as important, the rule changes are obvious in safety net program spending, which has increased at a faster rate than the population that was once considered eligible (see Table 3.4 for UI and SNAP, and Appendix 3.2 for all safety net programs).

I have not quantified several other areas of expanding means-tested benefits or increasing marginal tax rates such as student loan discharges, forgiveness of income tax debts, child support enforcement, other nutrition programs with eligibility automatically linked to SNAP eligibility, and tax credits targeted to low-income households that presumably reduced self-reliance rates still further during the recession.[55] Moreover, some of the credit market discrimination (on the basis of income) may have served to reduce replacement rates before the recession began; creditors rewarded high income prior to the recession by extending more credit and rewarded low income during the recession by extending more forgiveness. The fact that I omitted the former effect means I underestimated self-reliance rate declines. This chapter does not consider the safety net for businesses, especially financial businesses (Morgenson 2011), but Chapter Ten does touch on this subject and its possible role in starting the recession.

Aggregate Replacement Rates and Aggregate Distortions

The decline in self-reliance rates is, by definition, a decline in the rewards to time and effort that raise market incomes. In theory, at least some people respond by doing less toward earning their own market income. As people work fewer hours, and fewer businesses attempt to expand, output will be lower, and output per hour will be greater. In other words, as safety net rules change to reduce self-reliance rates, economic theory predicts that the gap between productivity and consumers' marginal rate of substitution (MRS) will widen, as will the gap between hourly employee compensation and the MRS.[56] Moreover, the theory says that, holding constant employer-side distortions, the magnitudes of the two changes (self-reliance rates and gap) are identical in percentage or logarithmic terms. For example, if safety net benefit rules changed to reduce the self-reliance rate by 10 percent, then the theory predicts that the ratio of MRS to labor productivity would also fall by 10 percent. With Figure 3.4 measuring changes in the self-reliance rate, and the previous chapter measuring the gap between productivity and MRS (conditional on a particular model of the MRS function), we are now in a position to begin to evaluate the theory.

Figure 3.7 graphs the productivity-based distortion series from Figure 2.6 (black) together with (-1 times) log changes in the self-reliance rate implied by safety net statutes since 2007-Q4 (red). The red series tends to increase over time because safety net benefit rules change in the direction of increasing replacement rates and reducing self-reliance rates. Assuming that I used the correct marginal rate of substitution function in Chapter Two, that employer-side distortions were constant, and that all of the measurements were exactly correct, the theory says the red and black series should be identical. Note that the two series are based on very different data sources—the former comes from data on aggregate consumption and productivity while the latter comes largely from changes in government benefit rules—which means the two series are not automatically equal. Nevertheless, the two series follow each other closely. They both increase about 0.07 or 0.08 during the first five quarters of the recession. The total increase through the end of 2009 was 0.14 for the log self-reliance rate and 0.17 for the productivity-based distortion. By the end of 2010, the gap between the red and black is about 0.04.

Most of the taxes and safety net programs included in the red series create employee-side distortions rather than employer-side distortions, and all of the measured program changes change employee-side distortions. If all of the measurements were correct, and employer-side distortions possibly changed over time, then the theory says that the red series would follow a wage-based measure of the distortion at least as well as it follows the productivity-based measure shown in black. A wage-based measure is shown as a gray series in Figure 3.7 (see also the red with triangles series in Figure 2.11). It follows the self-reliance rate series closely through late 2010. By the end of 2010, the safety net series is closer to the wage-based series than the productivity-based series.

Reasonable alternative measures of either distortions or safety net self-reliance rates could introduce more gaps between the two types of measures than are shown in Figure 3.7.[57] But a couple of lessons derive from even a rough agreement between distortions and safety net self-reliance rates. First,

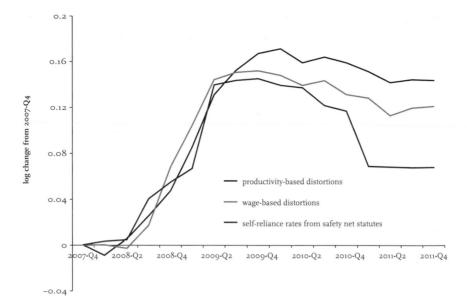

FIGURE 3.7 Labor Market Distortions Measured from Productivity, Wages, and Safety Net Statutes

the safety net expanded, and then stabilized at a more generous level, at about the same times that employment rates dropped, and then stabilized at a lower level. Second, the amount of the safety net expansion was large, and possibly large enough to cause a significant part of the employment drop. Both of these lessons are consistent with the reasonable ideas that the recession motivated at least some of the safety net expansions (see especially Chapter Ten), and that the entire recession cannot be attributed to expansions in the safety net.

Appendix 3.1: Calculation and Aggregation of Statutory Eligibility and Benefit Indices
Statutory Eligibility Indices

The government safety net eligibility indices displayed in the main text represent five federal changes in UI eligibility rules. In each case, the one-time change in the eligibility index reflects the typical size of the population eligible under relaxed eligibility rules relative to the size of the population eligible under the stricter rules.

The UI eligibility index changed three times since January 2007 due to changes in the maximum allowable period of benefit collection. For an eligibility rule change that involves extending the duration of benefits from A weeks to B weeks, the relative population size is measured by the ratio of the fraction (measured for 2007 and 2010, and then averaged) of unemployed nonelderly heads and spouses whose spell has not yet surpassed B weeks to the fraction of unemployed nonelderly heads and spouses whose spell has not yet surpassed A weeks.

The first instance was July 2008, when an additional twenty-six weeks of unemployment benefits became possible with the combined startup of the extended benefits and tier I emergency benefits programs.[58] Sixty-six percent of unemployed nonelderly heads and spouses had a spell lasting so far zero to twenty-six weeks (66 percent is an average of 80 percent for 2007 and 52 percent for 2010) and 83 percent have a spell lasting so far zero to fifty-two weeks, so the statutory UI eligibility index jumps by a factor of 1.3 (= 83/66) in July 2008. In December 2008, the index jumps again by a factor of 1.09 when Tier II emergency benefits (lasting thirteen weeks) begin and seven weeks of eligibility are added to Tier I. The 1.09 amount of the index's jump is determined from the unemployment duration data in the same way as for July 2008. The third jump associated with benefit duration is a factor of 1.03, occurring in December 2009 when Tier III and IV emergency benefits (thirteen and six week durations, respectively) begin, another week is added to Tier II, and Tier II is made available to all states.[59]

The maximum unemployment benefit duration was not changed by the February 2009 ARRA, but the act did extend eligibility by encouraging states to "modernize" (and relax) their monetary eligibility requirements by processing earnings histories through an "alternative base period," including persons who quit their job for compelling family reasons, adding twenty-six weeks of eligibility for persons enrolled in training programs, and/or paying benefits for persons who search only for part-time work. I am not aware of direct estimates of the number of people affected, so I assume that the index jumps by a factor of 1.047 owing to modernized eligibility.[60]

In order to quantify participation effects of the relaxation of SNAP asset tests, it helps to distinguish states conferring BBCE from the rest of the nation, where the federal eligibility rules (that began exempting retirement and education savings accounts from asset tests and expanded deductions thereby relaxing the net income test) would still be relevant, and states were continuing to add vehicle exemptions (Dean, Pawling, and Rosenbaum 2008). Previous research has found that vehicle exemptions are an important determinant of participation, with one vehicle exemption increasing log participation by 0.08 to 0.16 (Ratcliffe, McKernan, and Finegold 2007, 15). Because estimates of the effects of exempting retirement accounts vary so widely,[61] I use the midpoint of the vehicle estimate range, thus assuming that eligibility changes from the 2008 Farm Bill and state-by-state changes in vehicle policies would, in combination, increase log participation by 0.12 in the fourteen states not conferring BBCE by the end of 2010, as compared to the actual increase of 0.40. I assume the log participation increases an additional 0.09 in the thirty-six BBCE states plus D.C., which is the population-weighted log participation change gap between the two types of states (see also Klerman and Danielson 2011). Nationwide, this means that, holding work requirements fixed, eligibility changes would increase log participation 0.18 log points,[62] which is 58 percent of the three-year increase in the log of the ratio of participation to families with incomes below 125 percent of the poverty line. I assume that, holding work requirements fixed, the nationwide dynamics of the eligibility rule changes follow the time pattern of the population-weighted adoption of BBCE by the states (as dated by Trippe and Gillooly 2010 and updated by BBCE Memos from the USDA), although arguably part of the increase in the statutory SNAP eligibility index should occur immediately upon the implementation of the 2008 Farm Bill.

If we hold work requirements fixed, the SNAP eligibility index for month t is therefore measured as a time-invariant linear function of the 2010 population of all states that were conferring BBCE as of month t. The slope and intercept of this function are chosen so that (1) the index's fiscal year 2010 average is 1 and (2) the index's fiscal year 2007 average is $e^{-0.18}$. As a result, the SNAP eligibility index changes in all of the seventeen months between January 2007 and December 2011 in which at least one state (or D.C.) began conferring BBCE and the size of the change is proportional to the 2010 population of the state or states beginning BBCE at that time.

I am aware of only one study quantifying the participation effects of SNAP work requirements. Ziliak, Gundersen, and Figlio (2003) use state-level panel data for the federal fiscal years 1980–1999 to relate per capita food stamp case loads to state economic and political variables and state-specific characteristics of program administration. During this period of time, states sometimes obtained waivers from the work requirements for able-bodied nonelderly adults without dependents, and in many of those cases the waivers applied only to specific geographic areas within the state. They find that a 10 percentage point increase in the share of the state's population waived increased statewide food stamp caseloads by 0.5 percent. A waiver of the entire state might therefore be expected to increase caseloads by 5 percent. However, the 5 percent estimate is an extrapolation outside most of their data, and the authors caution that their estimate of the waiver effect may be exaggerated for failure to fully control for state economic conditions.

Using the SNAP quality control micro data files prepared by Mathematica Policy Research, I found that 1.4 million additional able-bodied nonelderly adults *without* children participated in SNAP in fiscal year 2010 than would have if they had remained 40 percent of able-bodied nonelderly adult SNAP participants *with* children as they were in 2007. Assuming that half of these 1.4 million were the result of relaxed work requirements (the requirements never applied to adults with children), and weighting by pro-rated benefits, I conclude that relaxed work requirements had the effect of increasing total program participation by 2.3 percent,[63] or about half of Ziliak, Gundersen, and Figlio's point estimate. In order to obtain an eligibility index that reflects changes in work requirements, I therefore multiply the work-requirements-fixed SNAP eligibility index cited above by 0.977 before October 2008, which began the first fiscal year following the triggering of extended unemployment benefits that is a condition for statewide work requirement waivers.[64] Under these assumptions, less than 10 percent of the overall change 2007–2010 in the SNAP eligibility index is associated with the work requirement waivers, as opposed to BBCE and other changes in SNAP eligibility rules.

The statutory eligibility indices for consumer debt discharges "all other government safety net" and payroll taxes are set to 1 in all months. The statutory eligibility index for Medicaid is also 1, except after December 2013 when it is 1.274, from estimates that Medicaid enrollment would increase by 27.4 percent as a result of the relaxed eligibility criteria going into effect January 2014 (Holahan and Headen May 2010).

Statutory Benefit Indices

The contributions of federal additional compensation ($25 per week federal addition to UI benefits) and the federal income tax exclusion for unemployment benefits (the value of which is converted to fiscal year 2010 dollars) are explained in the main text. The monthly value of the COBRA subsidy is $706 for someone who receives it (see the main text), but I assume that only about one-fifth of UI beneficiaries received it; the Treasury Department reported that two million unemployed workers took advantage of the subsidy in 2009 (U.S. Department of Treasury 2010a), as compared to about ten million people receiving UI benefits in the average week during that time.[65] A more aggressive estimate would allocate the $25 billion budgeted for the subsidy by the ARRA (Hossain et al. 2009) over the persons receiving UI during the fourteen months that the COBRA subsidy is reflected in my statutory benefit index. However, the COBRA provision's expenditure could overstate the value it added to the safety net, because Medicaid is sometimes available to unemployed persons who do not participate in their former employer's health plan.

To quantify statutory changes in the real benefit amount received by the average SNAP participating household, I begin with the fiscal year 2010 average nonelderly family benefit amount of $316 per month. That nominal benefit amount is assigned to all dates after March 2009. The nominal benefit assigned to October 2008–March 2009 is $45 less, and $28 less than that before October 2008, because $45 ($28) is the combined effect on monthly benefits of the April 2009 (October 2008) changes in the maximum benefit, minimum benefit, and allowable deductions, holding fixed the composition of SNAP households, respectively (see note 26). The same type of subtraction is made for fiscal years 2006 and 2007, which each began with a small nominal maximum benefit increase that was due to a change in the cost of living over the prior year, built into the prior law. The fixed SNAP household composition used for all four calculations is quantified by the average frequencies by household size, and average nonelderly frequencies by propensity to receive the minimum benefit, for fiscal years 2007 and 2010. The statutory SNAP real benefit index is the nominal series converted to fiscal year 2010 prices with the monthly seasonally adjusted chain type price index for personal consumption expenditures.

The statutory Medicaid real benefit index is set at a constant $358 per month ($4,296 per year) as an estimate of what Medicaid spends per nonelderly nondisabled enrollee (Henry J. Kaiser Family Foundation 2011a). The statutory real benefit index for government safety net programs aside from UI, SNAP, and Medicaid is set to monthly fiscal 2010 program benefits times the elderly exclusion factor shown in Table 3.2 divided by the fiscal year 2010 difference between the average monthly amount of nonemployment and underemployment among nonelderly household heads and spouses (the calculation shown in Table 3.1, except for fiscal year 2010) and the average monthly number of persons aged twenty-five to sixty-four receiving UI.[66]

Appendix 3.2: Sensitivity Analysis

This appendix explores the sensitivity of the overall replacement rate series to two types of changes: (1) changes in the methodology from statutory replacement rates to "effective" (that is, program expenditure based) replacement rates, and (2) changes in the weights and other parameters used to construct the statutory series.

Replacement Rates Based on Safety Net Program Spending

The amount of subsidies available to people who are not employed can also be measured as a ratio of government safety net program spending to the size of the eligible population, as in Mulligan (2011b). In principle, the spending approach could be different from the statutory approach implemented in this chapter because of changes in the composition of the eligible population. On the other hand, laws are not always enforced—e.g., a tighter eligibility law could be passed but not reduce program spending because of lack of enforcement—and the spending approach has some advantages in terms of simplicity and transparency.

To form the numerator, I aggregated the product of aggregate benefits and inclusion factors across the means-tested and employment-tested programs shown in Table 3.2, and then I added amounts of home mortgage modifications and consumer debt discharges. All dollar amounts were converted to fiscal year 2010 prices with the monthly seasonally adjusted chain type price index for personal consumption expenditures. To quantify the size of the loan modification safety net and its changes over time, I estimate the amounts that "home retention actions" (as the federal government calls them) actually changed mortgage payments from the original mortgage contract, which specified only payment in full or foreclosure. To estimate those amounts for 2008–2010, I first measure the number of residential properties in each quarter receiving loan modifications, lender permission for short sale, or lender permission for deed-in-lieu of foreclosure.[67] Second, I multiply the number of transactions by a $20,319 average value of each loan modification.[68] For the years 2006 and 2007, for which I do not have data on the number of home retention actions, I assume that 2006 and 2007 had a dollar value of these discharges that was, as a proportion to discharges in 2008, the same as total mortgage loan discharges by commercial banks.[69]

The combination of discharges of other consumer loans and discharges of home mortgages by home retention actions was almost $150 billion in 2010, which exceeds peak spending for the entire unemployment insurance system.

I measure the denominator as the average weekly number of nonelderly household heads and spouses not employed or underemployed relative to

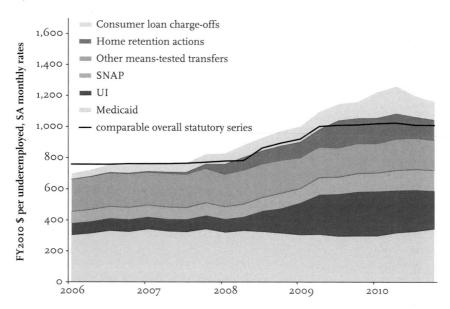

FIGURE 3.8 Transfers and Loan Discharges for the Nonelderly Unemployed and Financially Distressed

2007. This population, which grew 24 percent between fiscal years 2007 and 2010, became less poor in the sense that the number of families at or below 125 percent of the federal poverty guidelines increased only 14 percent over the same time frame.

The quarterly results are stacked program by program in Figure 3.8. Before the recession, housing collapse, and expansion of means-tested programs, the inflation-adjusted combination of the nonelderly portion of safety net benefits was only about $300 billion per year, or almost $800 per month per nonemployed or underemployed household head or spouse. The combination was flowing at an inflation-adjusted annual rate of more than $600 billion per year by the second half of 2009, or about $1,100 per month per nonemployed or underemployed household head or spouse.

The black series in Figure 3.8 is the black statutory safety net series from Figure 3.6, except that the COBRA and federal income tax exclusion provisions have been excluded in order to be consistent with the program expenditure data. The black statutory index series is the only series in Figure 3.8 that uses any information about the safety net eligibility rules or benefit formulas. Nevertheless, its level is similar to that of the combined expenditure per underemployed, although its change is somewhat less.[70] At a program level, the two loan forgiveness programs contribute more to overall spending than they do to the statutory rate, perhaps because the statutory series understates the importance of loan forgiveness.

Replacement Rates That Include Experience-Rated Employer Payroll Taxes

Economists have found that, on average, every $100 paid to a former employee in the form of state unemployment benefits adds about $50 to the employer's payroll tax.[71] For this reason, it is worth considering statutory generosity series that include the former employer's liability as a subtraction. Specifically, I consider the unemployment experience rating system to be another program to be included in sum (3.1). Because alternative base periods are the only eligibility change relevant for this liability—unemployment benefits paid beyond twenty-six weeks are federally funded[72]—the eligibility index for the experience rating program is equal to the alternative base period component of the UI eligibility index times the fraction of unemployed heads and spouses at a typical point in time whose spells are twenty-six weeks or less. The benefit index is equal to the base unemployment benefit, excluding any federal additional compensation, times -1 because the experience rating program is a tax rather than a benefit. The program weight is the program weight for unemployment insurance benefits multiplied by the fraction of unemployed people with spells so far no more than ninety-six weeks whose spells are so far no more than twenty-six weeks (and thereby have their UI count against their employer). The result is simply the red series shown in Figure 3.4 minus $249 ($261) dollars per month prior to (after) the ARRA became effective, respectively. See also Table 3.8, discussed further below.

Replacement Rate Variants

Medicaid, other government means-tested programs, consumer debt discharges, federal income taxes, and payroll taxes all have constant eligibility and real benefit indices prior to January 2011. As a result, they affect log changes in the self-reliance rate only through its level. Doubling the Medicaid eligibility index, doubling its benefit index, or doubling its program weight would subtract about 4 percentage points from the self-reliance rate. Doubling the eligibility index, benefit index, or program weight for "other means-tested government programs" would subtract about 3 percentage points from the self-reliance rate. Doubling federal income taxes (but keeping the marginal rate constant for the purpose of valuing the FIT UI exclusion)

Table 3.8 Self-Reliance Rate Changes: Sensitivity Analysis

	Log Changes from 2007-Q4		
	2008-Q4	2009-Q4	2010-Q4
Benchmark	−0.05	−0.14	−0.12
Replacement rate level			
+ 5 pct points	−0.06	−0.16	−0.13
− 5 pct points	−0.05	−0.13	−0.11
COBRA incidence among the unemployed[a]			
+ 5 pct points	−0.05	−0.15	−0.12
− 5 pct points	−0.05	−0.14	−0.11
Unemployment Insurance layoff tax			
Subtract half of the tax from UI benefits	−0.05	−0.14	−0.11
Subtract all of the tax from UI benefits	−0.05	−0.13	−0.11
Debt forgiveness components			
Set both benefit indices to zero	−0.05	−0.13	−0.10
Double mortgage modification	−0.06	−0.15	−0.12
SNAP			
Log BBCE factor set to 0.3	−0.06	−0.15	−0.12
Log BBCE factor set to 0.1	−0.05	−0.14	−0.11
All rules frozen at FY2007[b]	−0.05	−0.12	−0.09
Labor force weights			
Move 10 pct points from UE to OLF	−0.05	−0.12	−0.10
Move 10 pct points from UE to underemployment	−0.05	−0.12	−0.10
Additional UI taxation			
Ignore PIT exclusion	−0.05	−0.13	−0.12
5% discount to UI extensions and FAC	−0.05	−0.14	−0.11
Unemployment Insurance duration alone[c]			
Actual duration schedule	−0.04	−0.06	−0.06
Duration limited to 52 weeks	−0.04	−0.04	−0.04

Notes: [a] Benchmark incidence is 0.2.
[b] The SNAP eligibility and real benefit indices are held constant at their 2007-Q4 values.
[c] All other eligibility indices and real benefit indices, including those for COBRA and federal additional compensation, are held constant at their 2007-Q4 values.

would subtract about 8 percentage points from the self-reliance rate. Thus, the effect of any of these changes on changes in the log self-reliance rate can be determined from the effect of the level of the self-reliance rate.

Table 3.8 displays log changes in the self-reliance rate under various assumptions about the components of (3.1). The top row displays the results of the benchmark assumptions, which coincide with data points from Figure 3.7's red series. The next two rows show results with alternative levels of the self-reliance rate. The next two rows show the effects of altering the assumed fraction of UI beneficiaries who receive the COBRA subsidy. The UI layoff tax rows show the effects of subtracting all or part of the portion of unemployment benefits funded by former employers through the states' experience-rated tax system (see above). The two rows after that show the effects of altering assumptions about means-tested mortgage modification and consumer debt discharges. The SNAP rows show the effects of altering the assumed three-year log participation effect of BBCE and other SNAP eligibility rules. In all of those variations, the quantitative results are a bit different from the benchmark, but still the log self-reliance rate decreases by at least 0.13 through 2009-Q4 and 0.10 through 2010-Q4.

Freezing SNAP eligibility and real benefits at 2007-Q4 amounts results in a somewhat larger departure from the benchmark: the log self-reliance rate decreases about 0.12 through 2009-Q4 and 0.09 through 2010-Q4. Moving 10 percentage points of the labor force weight (see the last row of Table 3.5) from unemployed to either OLF or underemployed has a similar effect on the results.

The benchmark calculation treats personal income taxes on unemployment benefits as a constant dollar amount, with the exception of the personal income tax exclusion during part of 2009.[73] Table 3.8 shows two the results of two alternative assumptions. One possible assumption is that income taxes collected on UI benefits are negligible, in which case the benefit of the 2009 personal income tax exclusion is also negligible.[74] This possibility is examined in the first row, which might also be combined with an increase in the baseline replacement rate in order to recognize the excessive (under this assumption) taxation of state UI benefits included in the benchmark. A second assumption is that income taxes were collected on the federal additional compensation (FAC) and on Extended (EB) and Emergency (EUC) benefits (in addition to the personal income taxes collected on regular state benefits already included in the benchmark). Because of the progressivity of the personal income tax system, the rate paid on EB and EUC benefits is probably lower than the rate paid on regular state benefits (and maybe zero), because the regular state benefits are more likely paid in a tax year in which the worker also had wage and salary income. For this reason, a 5 percent discount on FAC, EB, and EUC benefits is considered in Table 3.8.

The final two rows of the table show that, despite the attention given them in the literature and in the media, the lengthening of the duration of unemployment explains well less than half of the reduction in self-reliance rates. The "actual duration schedule" results are calculated by holding all eligibility and real benefit indices constant at the 2007-Q4 values, except for the changes in the UI eligibility index in July 2008, December 2008, and December 2009, when UI beneficiaries were given more time to collect benefits. The final row of the table makes the same calculation, except that the UI eligibility index is also held fixed after July 2008, by which time benefits could be collected for fifty-two weeks (such an eligibility index corresponds more closely to the index that might be constructed for prior recessions). The results show that the log self-reliance rate is reduced by about 0.04 over time in the (hypothetical) scenario with unemployment insurance benefits allowed to last fifty-two weeks rather than twenty-six, and it is reduced by another 0.02 when the benefits are allowed to last up to ninety-six weeks (the actual duration schedule for UI). But the other 0.09 reduction in the self-reliance rate seen in the benchmark calculation through 2009-Q4 comes from other changes in safety net program rules.

Program Participation Costs and the Marginal Tax Rate

Eligible people do not always "take up" the safety benefits that are available to them. This appendix sketches a model of take-up and how that affects the proper measurement of self-reliance rate changes. The model considers a group of people who are identical in terms of their earning potential, which I normalize to 1, willingness to work, and the benefit $b < 1$ available to them if not working (no benefit is available if working). People differ in terms of their cost $x \geq 0$ of participating in the program, which is distributed F in the population. The net benefit a person receives when not working is therefore $\max\{b - x, 0\}$, where the zero is always attainable by declining to participate. The model participation rate is therefore the fraction $F(b)$ of the population with participation cost less than or equal to b. Because the self-reliance rate for people with $x > b$ is one (not working will yield them no net program benefits), the average log self-reliance rate in the population is:

$$E[\ln SRR] = \int_0^b \ln(1 - b + x)dF(x) \tag{3.2}$$

The magnitude of the marginal effect of the statutory benefit b on the average log self-reliance rate is:

$$-\frac{\partial E[\ln SRR]}{\partial b} = \int_0^b \frac{dF(x)}{1-b+x}$$

$$= \frac{F(b)}{1-bF(b)} + \frac{1}{2}\frac{v(x\,|\,x\leq b)F(b)}{\left[1-b+E(x\,|\,x\leq b)\right]^3} + \frac{\left[1-F(b)\right]b - E(x\,|\,x\leq b)}{\left[1-b+E(x\,|\,x\leq b)\right]\left[1-bF(b)\right]}F(b)$$

(3.3)

where $E(x|x{\leq}b) \geq 0$ is the average participation cost among participants and $v(x|x{\leq}b) \geq 0$ is the participation cost variance among the participants. The second line of equation (3.3) is a second-order approximation in the neighborhood of $E(x|x{\leq}b)$ and has three terms. The first term is identical to the marginal effect of my approach (3.1), which, lacking data on the magnitude of participation costs, scales statutory benefit changes by a fixed program participation rate (it's part of my program weight ω) and evaluates the self-reliance rate at average benefits received $1 - bF(b)$, gross of participation costs. The second term is positive or zero because it is proportional to the participation cost variance. The third term is related to the gap between $[1-F(b)]b$ and average participation cost among participants, which can be positive or negative. Unless the third term were negative enough to cancel the second term, my approach to measuring the effect of statutory benefits on average log self-reliance rates would tend to understate the magnitude of log self-reliance rate changes over time.

Appendix 3.3: The Self-Reliance Rate Outlook

I found that self-reliance rates fell significantly between 2007 and 2010 because the social safety net became more generous than it was before the recession began, especially its debt discharge, unemployment insurance, and food stamp components. To understand what will happen to the labor market in the years beyond 2010, and in order to fully understand what happened to consumption and investment during the recession, it is important to consider market expectations of self-reliance rates for the years beyond 2010. As I explain in more detail in the following chapter, people consume less, and businesses invest less, the longer they expect self-reliance rates to remain low.

Some of the subsidy expansions contributing to the changes shown in Figure 3.6 had lapsed by the end of 2010 and by themselves result in ongoing self-reliance rates that are greater than they were in 2009 and 2010. In principle, other expansions such as the extension of unemployment benefit duration to as long as ninety-nine weeks will lapse too, but Congress has repeatedly renewed them (U.S. Department of Labor 2011e) and only time will tell how long the renewals will continue.

Negative home equity will not forever remain the pervasive problem that it is now, and for this reason the contribution of mortgage discharges to the safety net will eventually decline. However, it seems that little of the decline will occur in the near future; as of the fourth quarter of 2011 the fraction of home mortgages whose par value exceeded the value of the property securing it was about the same (23 percent) as it was during 2009 (First American CoreLogic 2012), and needs to decline by a factor of five in order to return to prerecession levels.

Other factors suggest that self-reliance rates could remain low indefinitely. The payroll tax cut that began in January 2011 will expire. Medicaid enrollment and spending are expected to increase significantly beginning in 2014. By 2019, Medicaid's enrollment is expected to increase by sixteen to twenty-two million and its spending to increase by 13 to 16 percent (Holahan and Headen 2010). In the future, the government may also be subsidizing private health insurance participation, beyond the Medicaid program as we know it, and means-test those subsidies. According to the methodology of my Figure 3.6, the 2014 Medicaid expansion alone would add more than 1 percentage point to the replacement rate (returning it about to its level of mid-2010) and thereby subtract that amount from the self-reliance rate.

Early in 2009, the Obama administration began talking about a tax credit for employers who expanded their payrolls. Along these lines, the administration proposed in September 2011 "a full holiday on the 6.2 percent payroll tax firms pay for any growth in their payroll up to $50 million above the prior year, whether driven by new hires, increased wages or both" (White House 2011).[75] During the time prior to such a law actually taking effect, both the credit and holiday proposals actually serve as an expected employer tax on payrolls and would have many of the effects of *increasing* the safety net's replacement rate.

To see this, suppose that the tax holiday law had passed in 2011, to be effective for the calendar year 2012. The law said that, in 2012, employers owed 6.2 percent of their 2012 payroll spending P_{2012} minus the amount $(P_{2012}-P_{2011})$ of that spending that was an increase from the prior year. In terms of arithmetic, the 2012 payroll tax liability would be 0.062 times $[P_{2012}-(P_{2012}-P_{2011})]$, which is just 0.062 times P_{2011}. In words, the 2012 tax liability depends on 2011 payroll rather than 2012 payroll because increments to payroll go tax-free. The 2011 tax liability was, of course, 0.062 times P_{2011}, so 2011 payroll is, in effect, taxed twice: once in 2011 and again in 2012. Employers who anticipate such a tax holiday will understand that payroll spending in the year before the tax holiday (2011 in this example) is almost 12.4 percent more expensive[76] than it will be during the holiday because payroll in the year before is effectively taxed twice and payroll during the holiday is not taxed at all. Just as important, anticipation of the holiday makes payroll prior to the holiday more expensive (a tax rate as large as 12 percent) than it would have been if no holiday were anticipated (a tax rate of 6.2 percent).[77]

As of the end of 2011, 12 percent of the nation's population lived in a state that did not confer SNAP BBCE; the SNAP eligibility index has the potential of increasing by a factor of 1.14 even without any additional federal legislation, which would increase the overall replacement rate by another 0.5 percentage points.

The overall safety net generosity series from Figure 3.6 is also displayed in Table 3.9, together with some of its components.

Appendix 3.4: The Making Work Pay, Earned Income, and Child Tax Credits

The 2009 American Recovery and Reinvestment Act created or changed three federal individual income tax credits: the Making Work Pay Tax Credit (hereafter, MWPTC), the Earned Income Tax Credit (EITC), and Additional Child Tax Credit (ACTC). According to Recovery.gov, the ARRA spent (in terms of forgone tax revenue) $104 billion, $5 billion, and $18 billion on these changes.[78]

All three of the changes are credited with reducing poverty (Sherman 2011), which by itself suggests that, if anything, they reduced work incentives for the median household head or spouse who normally is not in poverty. The purpose of this Appendix is to examine the degree to which the credits affected the reward to working, and thereby their potential effect on time seri's measures of statutory marginal labor income tax rates such as those developed in this chapter.

The 2009 American Recovery and Reinvestment Act created a refundable personal income tax credit for calendar years 2009 and 2010 called the "Making Work Pay Tax Credit".

For single (married) filers with wage, salary, and self-employment income for the calendar year less than $75,000 ($150,000), the amount of the MWPTC

Table 3.9 Overall Safety Net Generosity, 2010 $ per Month, Displayed with its UI and SNAP Components

Impact of Working on Net-of-tax Benefits, All Programs, Adjusted for Typical Take-up Rates

Month	UI		SNAP		Overall	Month	UI		SNAP		Overall
	Elig.	Benefit	Elig.	Benefit	Safety Net		Elig.	Benefit	Elig.	Benefit	Safety Net
Jan-06	0.680	1,169	0.805	243	1,556	Jan-09	0.935	1,169	0.890	278	1,718
Feb-06	0.680	1,169	0.805	243	1,556	Feb-09	0.935	1,169	0.890	277	1,718
Mar-06	0.680	1,169	0.805	243	1,556	Mar-09	0.935	1,169	0.891	277	1,718
Apr-06	0.680	1,169	0.805	242	1,556	Apr-09	0.979	1,478	0.895	323	1,870
May-06	0.680	1,169	0.805	241	1,556	May-09	0.979	1,478	0.897	323	1,870
Jun-06	0.680	1,169	0.805	241	1,556	Jun-09	0.979	1,478	0.903	321	1,870
Jul-06	0.680	1,169	0.805	240	1,556	Jul-09	0.979	1,478	0.952	321	1,876
Aug-06	0.680	1,169	0.805	239	1,555	Aug-09	0.979	1,478	0.967	320	1,878
Sep-06	0.680	1,169	0.805	240	1,556	Sep-09	0.979	1,478	0.967	319	1,878
Oct-06	0.680	1,169	0.805	247	1,559	Oct-09	0.979	1,478	0.967	318	1,876
Nov-06	0.680	1,169	0.805	247	1,559	Nov-09	0.979	1,478	0.967	317	1,876
Dec-06	0.680	1,169	0.812	246	1,559	Dec-09	1.004	1,478	0.967	317	1,889
Jan-07	0.680	1,169	0.812	245	1,560	Jan-10	1.004	1,421	0.967	316	1,867
Feb-07	0.680	1,169	0.812	244	1,559	Feb-10	1.004	1,421	0.973	316	1,868
Mar-07	0.680	1,169	0.812	243	1,559	Mar-10	1.004	1,421	0.988	316	1,870
Apr-07	0.680	1,169	0.812	243	1,560	Apr-10	1.004	1,421	1.002	316	1,872

May-07	0.680	1,169	0.812	242	1,560	May-10	1.004	1,421	1.002	316	1,872
Jun-07	0.680	1,169	0.819	241	1,560	Jun-10	1.004	1,350	1.016	316	1,848
Jul-07	0.680	1,169	0.819	241	1,562	Jul-10	1.004	1,295	1.050	316	1,832
Aug-07	0.680	1,169	0.819	241	1,562	Aug-10	1.004	1,295	1.050	315	1,832
Sep-07	0.680	1,169	0.819	240	1,562	Sep-10	1.004	1,295	1.050	315	1,832
Oct-07	0.680	1,169	0.819	253	1,570	Oct-10	1.004	1,295	1.050	314	1,831
Nov-07	0.680	1,169	0.819	252	1,569	Nov-10	1.004	1,295	1.050	314	1,831
Dec-07	0.680	1,169	0.819	251	1,569	Dec-10	1.004	1,223	1.050	313	1,804
Jan-08	0.680	1,169	0.842	250	1,576	Jan-11	1.004	1,169	1.055	312	1,721
Feb-08	0.680	1,169	0.842	250	1,576	Feb-11	1.004	1,169	1.055	311	1,721
Mar-08	0.680	1,169	0.853	249	1,577	Mar-11	1.004	1,169	1.055	309	1,720
Apr-08	0.680	1,169	0.853	248	1,580	Apr-11	1.004	1,169	1.055	308	1,719
May-08	0.680	1,169	0.853	247	1,579	May-11	1.004	1,169	1.055	308	1,719
Jun-08	0.680	1,169	0.853	246	1,579	Jun-11	1.004	1,169	1.055	308	1,719
Jul-08	0.861	1,169	0.853	244	1,660	Jul-11	1.004	1,169	1.055	307	1,719
Aug-08	0.861	1,169	0.853	244	1,660	Aug-11	1.004	1,169	1.055	306	1,718
Sep-08	0.861	1,169	0.853	244	1,660	Sep-11	1.004	1,169	1.055	306	1,718
Oct-08	0.861	1,169	0.889	274	1,681	Oct-11	1.004	1,169	1.061	306	1,719
Nov-08	0.861	1,169	0.889	277	1,682	Nov-11	1.004	1,169	1.061	305	1,719
Dec-08	0.935	1,169	0.889	278	1,714	Dec-11	1.004	1,169	1.061	305	1,719

was the lesser of 6.2 percent of that income and $400 ($800), respectively (U.S. Internal Revenue Service 2010). For incomes beyond those amounts, the MWPTC was phased out at a 2 percent rate until it reached zero.

The MWPTC did not enhance the reward to working for any person whose spouse earned $12,903 or more for the calendar year because the amount of the MWPTC for the household would be at most $800, and it would only be *reduced* or unchanged as the result of more work for this person. For example, if the spouse earned $36,000 for the year and the person in question could earn at most $36,000, then the household's credit would be $800 regardless of whether the person earned zero or the full $36,000. Because the purpose of my safety net generosity index is to measure the difference between safety net benefits received when not working versus benefits received when working, the index for such a person would not be affected by MWPTC because it adds $800 to both components of the difference.

Moreover, if the spouse earned $150,000 for the year, then the MWPTC would actually reduce the reward to working for the person in question because his or her wages and salary would reduce the household's credit at a 2 percent rate. Persons like this are not very common and are certainly not like the median household head or spouse that was examined in this chapter, which is one reason MWPTC had no effect on my calculations of the index.

Whether MWPTC enhances the reward to working for single filers depends on the work decision time interval considered. That is, we might consider the consequences of working or not during a particular week, month, quarter, year, or some other time interval. If we are considering the work decision for any time interval that is less than a year (or even if it is longer than a year but excludes part of calendar year 2009 and part of calendar year 2010), then the effect of MWPTC on the reward to working during that interval is zero, or less, as long as the person earned more than $6,451 for the remainder of the calendar year. Suppose, for example, that a single earner earned $9,000 in the first quarter of 2009 and would earn less than $75,000 for the entire calendar year no matter how much he worked. Then the amount of his MWPTC for 2009 would be $400 regardless of how much or little he worked for the final three quarters of the year.

The only work decisions that were enhanced by MWPTC were those involving earning less than $6,451 ($12,903 for a married person with spouse who has no earnings for the entire year) for the entire calendar year. Even in those few cases, the contribution of MWPTC to the replacement rate is only about a percentage point for the household head or spouse with median earning potential. This is the second reason that MWPTC does not enter my calculations of the safety net generosity indices.

The Earned Income Tax Credit (EITC) is a federal income tax credit of a few thousand dollars per year paid to families with positive but low earned income (that is, wages or salaries) for a calendar year. As such, it encourages people to earn positive income during a year but discourages them from earning more than maximum annual family earnings (roughly $15,000 per year, depending on the number of children present) allowed to receive the maximum credit.

Holding constant family composition, the EITC specifies a schedule relating the credit amount to family earnings for the year. As annual earnings increase from zero to about $9,000,[79] the credit increases. Above that, there is a range of incomes over which the credit is constant. For still higher incomes (above the maximum earnings cited above), the credit is phased out: more earnings means less credit. The maximum amount of the credit depends on family size and composition.

Because the EITC is an annual credit based on family earnings, its effect on work incentives for a given day, week, month, or quarter depends on how much the person would be earning during the remainder of the calendar year and how much other family members earn during the entire calendar year. For example, a person who earned $13,000 during the first nine months of the calendar year would not be rewarded by the EITC for working during the final quarter of the year, and may well be discouraged from working by the EITC, depending on how much other family members were earning.

Even in 2009, the median nonelderly household head or spouse had annual personal earnings of $28,000 (from the March 2010 Current Population Survey Annual Demographic File; this counts nonelderly household heads and spouses with zero annual earnings), and more family earnings. Even among those individuals with at least five weeks of unemployment in 2009, median 2009 personal earnings were $13,000, and thereby above the range in which the EITC encourages more work. Simply put, the EITC discourages a range of work decisions that the median household head or spouse might consider.

The EITC was already in place before the recession began, so more important for the purposes of this chapter is how *changes* in the EITC since 2007 affect work incentives. The 2009 ARRA widened the range of maximum credit incomes for joint-filing married couples (the phase-out range was shifted accordingly, without changing the marginal tax rate in the phase-out range) and increased the credit amount for families with three or more children (Kneebone 2009). The act thereby had essentially no effect on work incentives for unmarried households with fewer than three children. It also had little net effect among married people with fewer than three children: it reduced marginal tax rates in an annual income range with width $3,000 and increased marginal tax rates by the same number of percentage points in another annual income range with the same width.

Among families with three children or more, the $629 increased maximum credit effectively widened the range of incomes over which EITC marginal tax rates are positive (and about 21 percent). About nine hundred thousand such families (Kneebone 2009), or about 0.9 percent of all nonelderly households, were expected to have incomes in that range, which from an aggregate point of view is roughly a 0.2 percentage point increase in the marginal tax rate. Given that the EITC changes tended to increase marginal tax rates, but to a small degree, I omit the EITC from the calculations in the body of this chapter.

Since 2007, there has been no significant change in the Child Tax Credit (CTC), which by itself is a nonrefundable $1,000 tax credit for every child under age seventeen in a single-headed household with annual income less than $75,000 or in a married household with annual income less than $110,000 (each child credit is phased out at a 5 percent rate thereafter). The CTC's companion, the Additional Child Tax Credit (ACTC), is refundable for households with tax liability (inclusive of payroll taxes) less than the CTC, with an amount equal to 15 percent of income in excess of a threshold, limited by the amount of the remaining CTC. For this reason the ACTC by itself induces a -15 percent marginal tax rate on a range of incomes beginning with the threshold and extending as much as $6,667 per child.

The 2009 ARRA changed the 2009 ACTC threshold from $12,550 to $3,000 and thereby moved the negative marginal tax rate income range. In other words, this ARRA provision reduced marginal tax rates for some low incomes and increased them for some less-low incomes. To a first approximation, the two marginal tax rate changes offset for the purposes of aggregate analysis, which is why I do not include the ACTC changes in my marginal tax rate series. Given that the median nonelderly household head or spouse earned more than $12,550 in 2009 as an individual, and even more as a household, a closer calculation would likely find that the ACTC changes increased the marginal tax rate appropriate for aggregate analysis.

4

Supply and Demand

LABOR MARKET CONSEQUENCES
OF SAFETY NET EXPANSIONS

THE NEXT STEP is to trace out the possible consequences of the safety net expansions for the major macroeconomic variables—including GDP, consumption, investment, and labor hours. Chapter Five simultaneously estimates dynamic safety net impacts on all four variables using the neoclassical growth model, which embeds the reservation wage and labor productivity schedules from Chapter Two into a dynamic economic model with capital accumulation. It turns out that an important part of the conclusions drawn from the dynamic model depends only on the reservation wage and labor productivity schedules and can thereby be illustrated in a supply and demand diagram like those shown in Chapter Two. The purpose of this chapter is to introduce the reader to one of the book's major conclusions by presenting the supply and demand illustrations, and using the self-reliance rates calculated in the previous chapter for the median worker.

A basic economic principle in this chapter, and much economic analysis of the labor market, is that the pecuniary reward to working is an important determinant of how much people work. By definition, the pecuniary reward to working is the effect that a person's work has on what he can spend on himself and his family: the difference between what he has to spend if he works and what he has to spend if he does not work. When social programs increase what they pay to someone who does not work, they diminish this difference, and the result is that some people work less.

The (theoretical) effects of the reward to working can also be seen from the perspective of wages. The more that the safety net pays for not working, the less reason people in low-wage jobs have to keep their job and the less reason unemployed people have to accept a low-wage job. In this way, the safety net raises wages, to which employers respond by hiring less.

Economists capture this basic idea in a variety of ways: with search models, principal-agent moral hazard models, growth models, selection models, etc. This chapter uses perhaps the simplest and most widely recognized economic model: the supply and demand model, as applied to the labor market. The social safety net appears in that model as a shifter of the supply or reservation wage curve, with the amount of shift determined by the amount that safety net programs pay people for not working.[1]

None of this necessarily implies that the safety net is a bad thing, because few of us want to live in a society where starvation is the penalty for not working (see also Chapter Ten). But it does imply that safety net expansions reduce the amount of work, at least a little bit, and perhaps a lot. The predicted amount of the labor decline depends critically on the magnitude of the slope of the supply curve. This sensitivity is found in much labor market analysis, and as a result a large econometric literature offers many estimates of the labor supply curve's slope, and many estimates of the effects of safety net programs on employment. This chapter explains how that prior work can be relied upon to help estimate the labor market effects of the safety net expansions since 2007.

I conclude that at least half, and probably more, of the drop in aggregate hours since 2007 would not have occurred, or at worse would have been short-lived, if the safety net had been constant. As shown below, this result is driven by the amount of enhanced safety net generosity documented in Chapter Three plus the economic ideas that, even during a recession, the combination of labor supply and labor demand determines the total amount of labor, and that the allocation of jobs is determined by comparative advantage.

Readers interested in the full mathematical detail and all of the dynamic results may want to skip ahead to Chapter Five; other readers may want to examine this chapter and then skip ahead to Chapter Six. This chapter has essentially the same quantitative results as Chapter Five because both have the same labor market model building blocks.[2] Appendix 4.1 and Chapter Six discuss the fact that log self-reliance rate changes varied across demographic groups, and it lays out the assumptions implicit in my use here and in Chapter Five of a single "marginal worker" time series for the self-reliance rate. The concluding section of this chapter addresses a number of the mischaracterizations of the supply and demand model of labor market changes, especially as regards the economic analysis of recessions.

The Income-Maximization Fallacy

It is sometimes claimed, by noneconomists at least, that the safety net does not prevent anyone from working because everyone strives to have more income rather than less and will gladly take any available job that pays them more than the safety net does. This "income maximization" hypothesis is contradicted by the most basic labor market observations, not to mention decades of labor market research.

Before the recession began, well over one hundred million Americans were not working. To be sure, some of them could find no reward in the labor market and would be stuck without gainful employment no matter how lean the safety net got. But many others were not working by choice. We all know skilled stay-at-home mothers or fathers who could readily find a job but believe that the pay from that job would not justify the personal sacrifices required. They are examples of people who deliberately do not maximize their income. Others are people who turn down an out-of-town promotion in order to avoid relocating their family, and workers who eschew higher-paying but less safe occupations. Earning income requires sacrifices, and people evaluate whether the net income earned is enough to justify the sacrifices.

When the food stamp or unemployment programs pay more, the sacrifices that jobs require do not disappear. The commuting hassle is still there, the possibility for injury on the job is still there, and jobs still take time away from family, hobbies, sleep, etc. But the reward to working declines, because some of the money earned on the job is now available even when not working.

Decades of empirical economic research show that the reward to working, as determined by the safety net and other factors, affects how many people work and how many hours they work. To name a small fraction of the many studies: Hoynes and Schanzenbach (2012) show how potential participants stopped working or reduced their work hours when the food stamp program was introduced. Studies of unemployment insurance (see Appendix 4.2) find that program rules have a statistically significant effect on how many people are employed, and how long unemployment lasts. Yelowitz's research (2000) shows how a number of single mothers found employment exactly when, and where, state-level Medicaid reforms increased their reward from working. Gruber and Wise (1999) and collaborators show how the safety net for the elderly results in less employment among elderly people. Autor and Duggan (2006) and the Congressional Budget Office (2010) explain how the number of disabled people who switch from work to employment-tested disability subsidies depends on the amount of the subsidy relative to the earnings from work. Murphy and Topel (1997) show how poor wage growth among less-skilled men helps explain their declining employment rates during the 1970s and 1980s. Jacob and Ludwig (2012) show that means-tested housing assistance reduces labor force participation and earnings among able-bodied working-age adults.

Because economists have identified many other cases in which means-tested and employment-tested subsidies caused people to work less, it is entirely possible that the same kinds of behavioral responses have occurred since 2007: a larger safety net reduced aggregate employment.[3] Indeed, studies have already found statistically significant post-2007 effects of unemployment insurance rules on employment and unemployment (Farber and Valletta 2011 and Rothstein 2011). I therefore proceed with the old idea that safety net expansions affect labor supply, and then I turn to the critical issue of the magnitude of those effects in the calibration section and in later chapters of this book.

Labor and Output Effects of Safety Net Expansions
The Supply and Demand Framework

Recall from Chapter Two that labor supply and labor demand can be used to calculate hypothetical market outcomes. Chapter Two develops equations (2.2) and (2.6) as a simple model of the labor market that determines log changes in labor hours n and labor productivity y as a function of log changes in production inputs other than labor hours A, consumption per capita c/P, and the age-adjusted size of the adult population N. Those equations are copied here and rearranged to highlight their relationship with Figure 2.7.

$$\Delta \ln y_t = -0.3 \Delta \ln n_t + 0.3 \Delta \ln A_t \tag{4.1}$$

$$\Delta \ln y_t = \frac{1}{\eta} \Delta \ln \left(n_t / N_t \right) + \Delta \ln \left(c_t / P_t \right) - \Delta \ln \left(1 - \tau_t \right) \tag{4.2}$$

The top equation is the labor demand or marginal productivity schedule. The bottom equation is the labor supply or reservation wage schedule.

The demand curve has only one shifter, A, the amount of "other production inputs." If those other inputs were constant over time, then log changes in productivity y would be perfectly proportional to log changes in labor hours n. As shown in Chapter Two, especially Figure 2.4, the measured values of those two changes were not exactly proportional but pretty close, which suggests that A did not change much over time. Moreover, to the extent that A did change over time, it stayed pretty close to its prerecession trend. For these reasons, I do not attempt to model changes in A over time and instead use its actual values whenever using the demand equation (4.1).

The supply curve has three parallel shifters: total population P, the age-adjusted adult population N, and the distortion term τ. As with the input variable A, I do not offer detailed explanations for changes in P and N, because there were no real surprises for those variables. I use their actual changes whenever using the supply equation (4.2). Consumption c is also a shifter of the supply equation. The consumption changes were surprising and need explanation: I offer explanations later in this chapter and especially in Chapter Five. For the moment, I use actual consumption changes when using the supply equation (4.2).

The supply equation also includes a constant slope parameter $\eta > 0$. It says that the supply curve slopes up when displayed in a graph of labor versus productivity. But for now I do not assign a single value to η as I do for the slope of the labor demand curve, because economists do not agree on the exact value for the aggregate labor supply curve slope.

Results with a Supply Elasticity Equal to 1

Mild changes in other production inputs and in the amount and composition of population growth are not mysteries. The real mystery that has so many economists wondering what happened to the labor market is that models such as (4.1) and (4.2) require a large and so far unexplained change in the supply equation's distortion term τ in order to be consistent with the observation that labor hours fell so much. Chapter Two's Figure 2.7 is an illustration of why the labor market changes seem so surprising, at least if safety net expansions are ignored. Figure 2.7 presents two model simulations of hypothetical log changes in labor and productivity from 2007-Q4 through 2009-Q4. Both of them assume that other production inputs and population changed as they actually did, but that labor market distortions were constant. One of them (the hypothetical outcome labeled HC in the diagram) assumed that per capita consumption was also constant, while the other (the hypothetical outcome labeled HA in the diagram) assumes that log consumption changed as it actually did. HA and HC are far from the actual data; the model with constant labor market distortions explains little of what happened in the labor market since 2007.

But Chapter Three shows that labor market distortions were not constant between 2007 and 2009, because the social safety net increasingly replaced earnings lost to non-employment or underemployment. Moreover, economic theory says that an expanding safety net increases log reservation wages by exactly −1 times the log change in the self-reliance rate.[4] Chapter Three finds that the log change in the self-reliance rate was −0.144 between 2007-Q4 and 2009-Q4 (see Figure 3.7), which means that the expanding safety net increased log reservation wages by that amount.

Figure 4.1 is a simulation of the changes in labor and labor productivity between 2007-Q4 and 2009-Q4 that recognizes changes in four of the fundamental determinants of labor market outcomes—(1) labor productivity, (2) wealth effects (as evidenced by consumption changes), (3) population growth and its age composition, and (4) the self-reliance rate—but assumes that all other determinants of labor were constant. The figure's black demand curve, and two light red supply curves (with slope equal to 1), are exactly the same lines as shown in Figure 2.7. Both figures also graph the same actual outcomes for labor and labor productivity as black squares. Figure 4.1's vertical axis has a different scale, though, so it can also show (as a red line) the 2009 supply curve that accounts for the expansion of the safety net between 2007 and 2009. The red supply curve is calculated simply by shifting the solid light red supply curve up by the amount that the log self-reliance rate fell, 0.144. Accounting for the safety net expansion, the model's predicted outcome for 2009-Q4 is shown as the intersection of the red supply curve and the black demand curve.

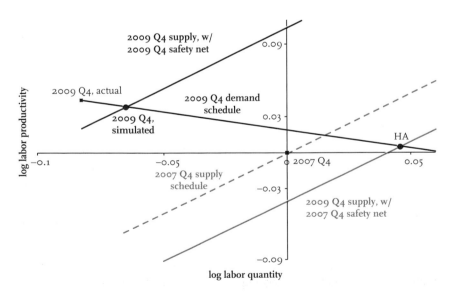

FIGURE 4.1. Actual and Simulated Labor Hours, 2009 Q4

The model's predictions for the log labor change between 2007-Q4 and 2009-Q4 are entirely different when accounting for the expanding safety net. Unlike the hypothetical outcome HA shown in Figure 4.1, which ignores the expanding safety net (that is, assumes that safety net generosity did not change between 2007-Q4 and 2009-Q4) and predicts that log labor would have increased 0.045, the model with the safety net expansion says that log labor would have decreased 0.065, log productivity would have increased 0.039, and (based on the difference of the two) log output would have declined 0.027 over those eight quarters.[5] In fact, log labor declined 0.083, log productivity increased 0.044, and log output declined 0.039.

The model says that log labor per (age-adjusted) adult would decline 0.075, as compared to the actual decline of 0.093. In this way, the simple supply and demand model in Figures 2.7 and 4.1 explains 81 percent of the labor market contraction from 2007-Q4 and 2009-Q4, as long as it incorporates the labor supply effects of the expanding social safety net. The remaining 19 percent of the contraction is "explained" by unmeasured market distortions—that is, still unexplained by the measured factors present in the model.

Recall that labor productivity rose about 4.5 percent over those eight quarters. A person producing $46,600 (annual rate) at the beginning would, if work schedule were constant and pay grew with productivity, would be producing $48,700 by 2009-Q4. Ignoring taxes and the safety net, it would seem that the reward from working had increased $2,100. But Chapter Three finds that the self-reliance rate fell from 0.596 to 0.516 over that time, which means that the effect of this person's work on income including taxes and means-tested subsidies actually fell from $27,800 to $25,100 at annual rates. A fraction of the population will react to a reduction in the reward from working by working less, which is why the model predicts that aggregate labor falls.

Sensitivity Analysis

The exact amount of the log labor change, −0.083, is an important ingredient in these calculations, but I have confidence in that estimate because it is confirmed by three separate data sources (recall Figure 2.10). Three other model ingredients are also important, but less precisely estimated: the labor productivity change, the slope of the supply curve, and the log change in the self-reliance rate.

Chapter Two explains that individual-level wages and labor productivity likely increased between 2007-Q4 and 2009-Q4, but probably less than the 4.4 percent increase measured from the aggregates because of changes in the composition of the labor force. Indeed, my hypothesis that the expanding safety net contributed significantly to the labor decline implies that the composition of the labor force would change (see also Chapter Six), so that aggregate labor productivity would increase more than it does for the average individual. Bureau of Labor Statistics (2011a) estimates that composition bias from 2007 to 2009 served to exaggerate aggregate labor productivity changes by 1.4 percentage points (although less relative to preexisting trends for labor force composition). Thus, instead of using the 4.4 percent measured productivity change, one could use 3.0 percent. With the 3.0 percent assumption, the model explains 93 percent of the decline in labor per capita instead of 81 percent because less 2009-Q4 productivity has been assumed and productivity increases the amount of labor supplied.[6]

A reasonable range for the supply slope parameter η is from 0.4 to 1.1 (more on this below). If I repeat Figure 4.1's simulation changing only η from 1.0 to the low end value of 0.4, the model explains 38 percent of the log per capita labor change. If, in addition, I make the aforementioned 1.4 percentage point adjustment to the measured productivity change, the model explains 43 percent. Thus, the expanding safety net is a large factor depressing aggregate work hours even if one assumes a low sensitivity of labor supply to the financial rewards from working. At the midrange supply slope parameter η estimate of 0.75, and including the composition bias adjustment, the model explains 74 percent of the log per capita labor change.

All of the above assumes that the safety net reduced the log self-reliance rate changed −0.144 from 2007-Q4 to 2009-Q4, as calculated in Chapter Three. Arguably the change was more negative because Chapter Three does not consider all of the changing means-tests in the economy and my estimates of the contributions of debt discharges and food stamp eligibility expansions may have been on the conservative side because they underpredict the change in the amount of revenue involved with those programs. Table 3.8 examines a number of other parameter changes that sometimes add or subtract 0.02 or 0.03 from my −0.144 point estimate. If I repeat Figure 4.1's simulation, changing only the vertical amount of the labor supply shift from 0.144 to 0.174 (0.114), the model explains 106 (56) percent of the log per capita labor change, respectively. If, in addition, I use the midrange supply slope parameter η estimate of 0.75, the model explains 84 (45) percent of the log per capita labor change, respectively.

My preferred estimate is that the expanding safety net explains about three-quarters of the 2007-Q4 to 2009-Q4 decline in log labor per capita. The model ingredients are uncertain enough that the expanding safety net might plausibly explain as little as half, or perhaps almost all, of the decline.

Predictions for Consumption and Investment

The 2009-Q4 supply and demand for labor do not by themselves explain what happens to consumption, because consumption depends not only on present labor income but also on expectations about future labor income. If the safety net were expected to remain permanently expanded, and thereby labor permanently 9 or 10 percent below trend, then in theory consumption would drop by about the same percentage because the nation cannot indefinitely consume a sharply higher fraction of its labor income. If the safety net were expected to quickly return to prerecession generosity, then the consumption impact of the safety net expansion would be minimal.

Only time will tell exactly what happens to the safety net in the future, but Chapter Three gave indications as to some possible scenarios for the safety net. In particular, many of the expansions are expected to last for several more years, while the Medicaid program still has large and potentially permanent expansions ahead. For this reason, the immediate consumption response to the safety net expansion would in theory be somewhere between zero and the fully permanent expansion case of 9 or 10 percent. In fact, consumption fell almost 5 percent below trend, almost exactly in the middle of the two boundary possibilities.

Assuming, as economists usually do in aggregate analysis, that capital enhances the productivity of labor, and labor enhances the productivity of capital, then the efficient reaction to less labor is to have less capital. Investment is the rate of change of the capital stock, so even small reductions in the capital stock may be achieved by large investment reductions for a short period of time. For this reason, investment is expected to decline by a much greater percentage than consumption in the short term, and by the same percentage in the long term. In this view, the investment decline is entirely a reaction to the labor market, and not a cause of the low rates of labor usage.

Another interesting labor market hypothetical holds the safety net constant as it was in 2007-Q4 and assumes that population, production inputs other than labor hours, and other labor market distortions evolved as they actually did.[7] The result depends on what happens to consumption per person, which is one reason the full neoclassical growth model presented in the next chapter is valuable. We can bound the possibilities at one extreme by assuming that consumption was not affected by the safety net (in which case the model says that log labor per capita is essentially constant) and at the other extreme by assuming that the entire decline in consumption per capita was due to the safety net expansion (in which case log labor per capita decreases 0.020). In other words, the eight-quarter decline in labor per capita, if any, would have been minimal without the expanding safety net because the unmeasured part of the labor market distortion is hardly enough to offset the increase in the marginal productivity schedule.

Figure 4.2 shows how simulated values for log labor per adult vary with the assumed value of the wage elasticity of aggregate labor supply, η, when the model's consumption change is linked to the model's predicted output change rather than its actual change as in Figure 4.1. For each value of η in the range discussed above, I calculate a hypothetical log labor change from 2007-Q4 through 2009-Q4 assuming that (1) the changes in population and nonlabor inputs A were the same as actual, (2) the change in the log self-reliance rate was −0.144, (3) the simulated log change in consumption per capita is two-thirds of the simulated change in output per capita, and (4) all other labor distortions or labor supply residuals were constant.[8] Even for the low end supply elasticity of 0.4, the expanding safety net explains about half of the change in log labor hours per adult. The results in Figure 4.2 also suggest that the expanding social safety net may well be the largest single factor reducing labor during the 2008–09 recession.[9]

FIGURE 4.2. Simulated Labor per Person: Sensitivity to the Supply Elasticity log change from 2007-Q4 to 2009-Q4

Calibrating the Wage Elasticity of Aggregate Labor Supply

Figure 4.1 and Figure 4.2 show that the predicted size of the labor decline depends critically on the magnitude of the slope of the supply curve. Given Chapter Three's 0.144 estimate of the log change in the self-reliance rate as a result of the expanding safety net, economic theory tells us that the supply curve shifts up by 0.144. But an upward shift of the supply curve would be a minimal horizontal shift of the supply curve if the curve were wage-inelastic (that is, steep when drawn in Figure 4.1), and it's the horizontal distance that determines the predicted change in log labor.

Economists generally agree that the safety net shifts the aggregate labor supply curve up—that is, raises workers' reservation wages—and that the amount of the shift is quantified by the replacement rate. Beyond that, they disagree about two basic issues: the sensitivity of labor supply to incentives and whether the labor supply curve is even relevant for determining aggregate labor hours during a recession.

Assuming for the moment that labor supply is relevant (more on this in Chapters Seven and Eight), a first step in quantifying aggregate effects of the expanding social safety net is to obtain an estimate, or range of estimates, of the sensitivity of aggregate labor supply (in the quantity dimension) to self-reliance rates. This sensitivity is a critical part of much economic analysis, and as a result a large econometric literature offers many estimates, and many surveys and syntheses of estimates. I rely on that prior work to calibrate my aggregate models of the labor market, rather than putting forward an econometric estimate of my own.

Studies differ in terms of how they measure work and changes in the reward to working, which is one of the reasons the results can appear to vary across studies. This book examines aggregate or average hours worked, including zeros for people not working, which can change over time as families vary their hours per day, days per week, number of members in the labor force, etc. Yet a number of the studies of labor supply look at only one or a few of these margins, and as a result they measure only part of the response to the reward to working.[10] Other studies examine tax changes that affect small groups of people. To the degree that labor market participants need to coordinate their work schedules, the members of these small groups may have little flexibility to change their work hours in response to their idiosyncratic tax incentives. The safety net expansions examined in this book, on the other hand, directly affect tens of millions of people. As noted by Chetty et al. (2011), these are all reasons that the results of individual-level labor supply studies need some adjustment before using them for aggregate analysis such as mine.[11]

I leave it to Chetty et al. (2011) to survey and synthesize the micro-econometric evidence and properly adapt it for aggregate analysis. They conclude that the Frisch elasticity of aggregate hours is particularly pertinent for aggregate business cycle analysis and that "Micro estimates imply a Frisch elasticity of aggregate hours of 0.78" (2011, 3) and "it would be reasonable to calibrate representative agent macro models to match a Frisch elasticity of aggregate hours of 0.75" (recall that my slope parameter η can be interpreted as the Frisch elasticity of aggregate hours).[12]

The Frisch elasticity of aggregate hours is not a universal constant known with many decimal places of accuracy for every application. In his work on business cycles, Hall (2009, 284, 319–20) concludes "the Frisch elasticity [of hours conditional on working] is taken to be 0.7, consistent with the findings of research with household data." The Frisch elasticity of aggregate hours is the sum of the elasticity of the probability of working and the elasticity of hours conditional on working and therefore greater than the latter (Heckman 1993). If Hall's conclusion about micro-econometric estimates of the elasticity conditional on working were correct, then the aggregate hours elasticity could easily be 1 or a bit more.[13] I therefore consider values for η as large as 1.1 and, in order to keep the 0.75 recommendation of Chetty et al. (2011) in the middle of the range, values for η as low as 0.4.[14]

For my purposes I need to know the labor response to safety net expansions over a one-or-two-year time frame, and it would be nice to know the response over an even shorter horizon. The micro-econometric literature is not especially helpful on this issue, which is another reason to consider a range of elasticities rather than settling on a single value.[15]

Chapter Three notes that the safety net expansions were of (at least) three types: increases in the weekly amount of various benefits, extensions of the amount of time that UI benefits can be received, and other eligibility expansions. In my framework for quantifying changes in safety net rules, each type of expansion contributes a specific amount to the total expansion. I then take the total amount of the expansion and use it for aggregate labor market analysis, implicitly assuming that, on a per dollar basis, each type of expansion shifts the supply curve the same amount, or at least that underestimates for some types are offset by overestimates for other types. An alternative approach worth pursuing in further research might have a separate supply analysis for all the types of expansion (and account for their interactions) and draw on the somewhat separate empirical literatures quantifying labor market effects of each type.

I pursue an intermediate approach that draws on the separate empirical literatures but still maintains the assumption that all the types of expansion create the same per dollar supply shift in the wage dimension. This approach has the disadvantage that comparisons across literatures are imperfect, but the advantage that it might detect significant differences between the supply behavior of the subjects of the wage studies surveyed by Chetty et al. (2011) and the supply behavior of safety net program participants (Meyer 2002).[16] Appendix 4.1 gives the details and explains how a number of the safety net program studies are consistent with a wage elasticity of aggregate labor supply in the range 0.4 to 1.1.

Conclusions and Interpretation

This chapter completes a significant part of the book's affirmative case that the 2008–09 recession and lack of labor market recovery has a lot to do with labor supply distortions. I conclude that at least half, and probably more, of the change in aggregate hours between the end of 2007 and the end of 2009 would not have occurred if safety net program rules had been constant. The expanding social safety net may well be the largest single factor reducing labor during the 2008–09 recession.

A few readers may be surprised by my conclusion, for a variety of reasons. Another demonstration of why the safety net expansion is expected to reduce employment by millions starts with Elsby, Hobijn and Sahin's (2010) low-end estimate of the effect of UI eligibility extensions: more than two million are unemployed because the extensions induce them to return to work more slowly. But the UI extensions are only 36 percent of the overall safety net expansion measured in Chapter Three for the time frame 2007-Q4 to 2009-Q4. If the rest of the expanded safety net spending were equally effective at keeping people out of employment, that would be an employment effect of the entire safety net expansion of six million. If the rest of the safety net expansion were half as effective, that would still be an employment effect of four million. The four and six million estimates are just back-of-the-envelope calculations built from Elsby et al.'s (2010) low-end estimate; the more thorough and accurate equilibrium calculations are the subject of the body of this chapter. But they illustrate why it would be misleading to ignore the aggregate effects of a safety net whose expenditure increases as much as documented in Chapter Three.

My supply and demand model also predicts that labor per capita in 2009-Q4 would have been only slightly less than it was in 2007-Q4 if the safety net had been constant, rather than expanding as it actually did. It is more difficult to know what would have happened to labor for the eight quarters in between, given that housing prices were collapsing and financial market functioning was highly abnormal at the end of 2008, because the supply and demand elasticity magnitudes used in my model were not intended for week-to-week or month-to-month analysis. We do know that the safety net expanded significantly in the middle of 2008, again at the end of 2008, and again in the first half of 2009 (see Figure 1.1), but predicting the month-to-month effects of these expansions probably requires estimates of transitional supply effects that are beyond the scope of this book. For this reason, my results may be consistent with the view that, with the safety net constant, labor per capita still would have declined sharply at the end of 2008, but it would have recovered quickly to its prerecession level rather than continuing lower and then recovering only partially during 2010 and 2011.[17]

One possible objection to my overall conclusion is that safety net rules changed many times in recent history yet failed to cause a recession or boom of the magnitude of what happened in 2008 and 2009. I agree that a labor hours change as large as 2008–09 is historically unusual, and that whatever impulse or combination of impulses caused the 2008–09 labor change is unlikely to be a historically common impulse, or common combination of impulses. But safety net changes of the size seen since 2007 are not historically common. Discharges of household debt are an important part of the safety net changes since 2007, and that amount of discharges could not have happened in the decades prior to 2005 because the unsecured amount of household debt was much less (Dynan and Kohn 2007). A long-term study of unemployment insurance take-up is beyond the scope of this book, but the data I have going back to 1986 show that the (twelve-month moving average) percentage of unemployed people receiving UI peaked at 68 percent in 2009, whereas the peaks in the previous two or three recessions were around 50 percent. Anderson and Meyer (1997) find that the percentage of unemployed people receiving UI between 1960 and 1994 was about 50 percent at its maximum.

In addition, the secular increase in earnings inequality, the secular growth of the Medicaid program, and to some extent the secular growth in the Food Stamp program probably meant that the safety net's replacement rate was larger when this recession began than when prior recessions began.[18] This means that each percentage point increase in the replacement rate during the recession had greater percentage effects on the self-reliance rate during this recession than during previous recessions. In other words, economic theory suggests that, holding constant the elasticity of labor supply with respect to the self-reliance rate, today's safety net spending might be more potent at reducing labor supply because it is more potent at reducing the log self-reliance rate.

Another possible objection is that the couple of hundred billion dollars added to the annual spending of safety net programs is small in comparison to the losses people have experienced since 2007, and therefore the losses cannot be explained by the expansion. But I have not put forward an estimate of the effect of safety net expansion on home values, or stock market values. Rather, I find that the safety net expansion is the primary reason aggregate labor fell, rather than increasing in response to those losses. Indeed, part of the safety net expansion came directly from the collapse of home values (recall Chapter Three, and see also Chapter Nine). Moreover, the 2008 financial crisis probably made the 2009 "stimulus" law and other legislation expanding safety net eligibility rules politically feasible. For these reasons, my results are consistent with the idea that drops in home values or stock values caused labor to decline, as long as the safety net is the primary mechanism by which values affected labor.

An important implication of the economic model of labor supply is that the safety net helps determine the total amount of labor, but exactly who works is determined by comparative advantage. As a result, a subsidy for not working can have a relatively large effect on the total amount of labor, especially if the subsidy were targeted toward the people with the least comparative advantage from working. Take the case when the wage elasticity of labor supply is close to zero, so that a person's surplus from working is essentially her wage. According to the wages measured among the CPS Merged Outgoing Rotation Groups, a $415 weekly benefit targeted to 12.5 million marginal full-time working household heads and their spouses (costing a total of $5.2 billion per week, which is about the $270 billion per year extra safety net program spending measured in Chapter Three) would fully replace their earnings and could induce essentially all 12.5 million to take the week off.[19] Even if only a quarter of the safety net expansions were spent on marginal full-time workers, that could be more than four million full-time workers who could have their earnings fully replaced.[20] To the degree that the wage elasticity of labor supply is greater than zero, the employment effects of targeted subsidies are even greater.

Admittedly, the principle of comparative advantage says that the aggregate losses from a subsidy that reduces labor per adult by, say, 6 percent are significantly less than 6 percent of the nation's labor income because, among other things, the subsidy primarily changes behavior for the 6 percent of the workforce with the least comparative advantage. On the other hand, we must recognize that the safety net expansion's deadweight loss (that is, the amount that losers from the safety net expansion, such as taxpayers, lose in excess of what the "winners" gain) also depends on the magnitude of preexisting labor market distortions, such as the preexisting safety net, income taxes, payroll taxes, sales taxes, and distortions created by imperfect competition in product or labor markets (Galí, Gertler and Lopez-Salido 2007). Appendix 4.3 estimates the deadweight loss in fiscal year 2010 to be almost $200 billion, minus any insurance benefits of the expansion.

It is sometimes claimed that a safety-net induced recession would be obvious because lots of people would quit their jobs in order to participate in safety net programs, which did not happen during this recession. This claim is incorrect about the theory of a safety-net-induced recession, and it fails to reference the relevant data from this recession. The first point is best addressed with an explicit model of job flows that is beyond the scope of this book, but for now we should recognize that a large fraction of the safety net benefits added since 2007 were available to people who were laid off from their jobs and unavailable to people who quit their jobs. Thus my approach likely predicts that quit rates (the number of people who quit their job expressed as a fraction of total employment) would fall, layoff rates would increase, and the sum of the two would increase, especially among nonelderly household heads and spouses.[21]

Another objection says that the recession came as a surprise, whereas the expanding safety net was anticipated well before 2008. But markets were generally surprised at the degree to which homeowners would be under water on their mortgages, and the discharges of unsecured household debt are an important part of the safety net. I also doubt that markets anticipated the fear that made the 2009 stimulus law and the 2010 health care law, and the safety net eligibility changes they implemented, politically feasible. In fact, markets might have anticipated tightening safety net eligibility rules as the retiring baby boom put increasing demands on Treasury revenues.

A number of economists assume that the total amount of labor is not affected by labor supply during a recession, and perhaps even that jobs are not allocated by comparative advantage. However, Chapter Six shows that employment and labor income changes were not randomly distributed across the population but rather were disproportionately shared by groups expected to be most responsive to safety net expansions and to minimum wage hikes. Chapter Eight confirms that labor supply does affect the total amount of labor during the 2008–09 recession and during previous recessions.

Appendix 4.1: Comparative Advantage with Heterogeneous Effects of the Safety Net Expansions

To quantify the labor market effects of changes in redistribution since 2007, I use the market level labor supply and labor demand framework that is familiar from labor and macroeconomics. In that model, an across-the-board increase in marginal tax rates shifts up the labor supply curve (think of wages or productivity as being graphed on the vertical dimension and the quantity of labor graphed on the horizontal dimension, as in Figure 4.1). The amount of the shift is, in logarithmic terms, the absolute amount of the log change in the self-reliance rate that results from changes in safety net program rules.

In this view, it does not really matter whether the across-the-board safety net expansion occurs through one program or several programs. What matters is the combined total value of what people can receive when they do not work as compared to what they receive when they do work. Chapter Three calculates that combined total, or as much of it as possible.

The numerical value for the slope of the market level labor supply curve depends on a number of factors, one of which is the degree and incidence of what economists call (tax-adjusted) "comparative advantage." Comparative advantage refers to the fact that people differ in terms of their willingness to work, and in terms of the value of what they produce when working. The degree of an individual's comparative advantage is sometimes summarized as the surplus or difference between the amount she produces when working and the cost to her of working,[22] which includes safety net benefits forgone (Heckman 1974). In this way of thinking, some people have more surplus than others. In theory, persons with positive surplus work, and people with negative surplus do not work. An expansion of the safety net will affect the work behavior only of persons with surplus near zero, and have no effect on the work behavior of people with large positive surplus or people with large negative surplus.

It is easy to name examples of people whose work behavior would not be affected by a safety net expansion. For example, a student who is initially not working because he values (in dollar terms) his time at school far in excess of what the market will pay him for working will not drop out of school and go to work if the safety net expands or contracts. A highly paid CEO of a large corporation will not quit his position if food stamps become more generous. Few, if any, disabled octogenarians would go back to work because the amount of unemployment benefits changed.

The heterogeneity in the surplus of working is relevant for the purposes of this book because the safety net expansions were not "across the board." There is no single log change in the self-reliance rate that applies to all people (see also Chapter Six). Application of the supply and demand framework therefore requires not only a numerical value of the supply curve slope, and a numerical value for the amount of the supply curve shift, but also an understanding of the effect of the safety net on comparative advantage.

The conceptually simpler possibility is that the actual safety net expansions did not significantly affect comparative advantage—that is, they did not take a large group of people who had a large positive surplus from working and change their surplus to negative. In the simpler case, there is no significant effect of the safety net expansion on the slope of the labor supply curve in the neighborhood of the market equilibrium, and the effect of the safety net expansion can still be simply calculated by shifting up the market labor supply curve. The amount of the shift is, in logarithmic terms, the absolute amount of the log change in the self-reliance rate for the marginal worker, which is the amount Chapter Three attempts to calculate.

Comparative advantage did change to some degree. Chapter Six explains that the elderly and teenagers seem to have little if any change in their marginal tax rates, and that work hours among the elderly actually increased since 2007. The approach of this book is to treat the relatively small labor market(s) for teenagers and the elderly as separate from the rest of the labor market, in a way made mathematically precise in Chapter Five. I thereby assume that the rest of the labor market is not significantly affected by changes in the teen and elderly labor markets, and that the safety net expansions did not significantly change comparative advantage in the former market. Chapter Six notes that the latter assumption may be reasonably accurate, given that marginal tax rates increased for many demographic groups, and that even the groups with lesser marginal tax rate changes may still have after-tax rewards from working that fell since 2007. More work should be done on these issues.

Appendix 4.2: Calibrating the Supply Elasticity from Unemployment Duration Studies

As far as I know, economists have so far considered only one potential mechanism by which public policy might reduce labor supply during the 2008–09 recession: the effect of UI extensions—federal and state government policies increasing the amount of time that unemployed people can receive unemployment benefits—on an unemployed person's probability of starting or returning to a job. The purpose of this appendix is to relate the results of such studies to the goal of this chapter of quantifying potential aggregate labor market effects of the safety net expansions since 2007. In doing so, I note that the academic attention given to UI extensions exaggerates the contribution of UI expansions to the overall safety net's expansion. The majority of the changes in the return to working documented in Chapter Three are the combined result of other safety net rule changes: the food stamps program became more generous; UI eligibility was modernized; unemployed people received bonuses, tax breaks, and health insurance subsidies; etc. If one were to focus on low-skilled people, whose work hours fell disproportionately, the importance of UI extensions would be even less relative to these other safety net provisions (see Chapter Six).

Econometric studies of UI extensions attempt to quantify the amount that the labor supply curve shifts in the quantity dimension as a result of UI extensions.[23] My self-reliance rate calculations quantify the amount of the shift in the wage dimension as a result of all safety net expansions, and they can be scaled down to UI extensions by calculating the share of the safety net benefit index change that derives from UI extensions. I thereby have quantified the same labor supply shift in both the quantity dimension (the previous econometric studies) and wage dimensions (my estimates of the self-reliance rate) and can estimate the implied wage elasticity of labor supply.[24]

Extended or emergency unemployment benefits account for 36 percent of the change in the replacement rate from 2007-Q4 through 2009-Q4. Because 36 percent of the total log self-reliance rate change is 0.05, we might say that the benefit extensions contributed 0.05 to the total 0.144 upward shift of the labor supply curve over those eight quarters.[25]

Elsby et al. (2010, 40) offer estimates of the fraction of unemployment that is a result of emergency benefits ranging from 0.12 to 0.31, on the basis of econometric studies of the effect of UI extensions on unemployment duration and assuming that UI extensions have no effect on separations.[26] As a fraction of actual employment in 2009, their range is 0.012 to 0.031.[27] To get a corresponding estimate of the wage elasticity of aggregate labor supply, I scale any estimate from their range to reflect the seventy-week combination of EB and EUC that was in place by the end of 2009 in the average state (and therefore 32 percent longer than the fifty-three-week extension they considered), and then divide by the aforementioned log change in the replacement rate associated with the combination of EB and EUC, yielding a wage elasticity range of 0.3 to 0.8.

However, Elsby et al. (2010) and much of the recent literature on the behavioral effects of UI extensions ignore the effect of UI extensions on layoffs or separations. Because UI extensions are primarily federally funded,[28] they reduce the share of unemployment benefits that must be paid by the beneficiary's former employer and increase the expected amount former employees will receive from UI beyond what is funded by the employer. In other words, federally funded UI extensions can be understood as a bundled pair of policies: an experience-rated extension of the eligibility period that has the unemployment duration effects noted by Elsby et al. (2010), plus a reduction in the amount of experience rating for a given eligibility period. The second part does not have the duration effects of the first part, but it nonetheless would likely increase the amount of unemployment because it reduces the employer tax penalty for layoffs.[29]

To know the full labor supply effect of the UI extension episodes since 2007, beyond their effects on unemployment duration, we therefore need to add the effect of the extensions on the number of job separations.[30] A couple of studies have looked at effects of imperfect experience rating on layoffs, and they have all found large effects.[31] Moreover, the UI extensions since 2007 have roughly tripled the amount of benefits received by the insured unemployed beyond what their former employer funds.[32] Because a wage elasticity range of 0.3 to 0.8, derived in this way, ignores the layoff effects and ignores spousal supply effects (Cullen and Gruber 2000), I find the slightly shifted range of 0.4 to 1.1 to be more appropriate for the purpose of aggregate analysis.

Rothstein (2011) uses data on unemployment spells from May 2004 through January 2011 and finds that "extended UI benefits do reduce the rate at which unemployed workers reenter employment."[33] However, he concludes that the statistically significant effect is nonetheless economically insignificant and that "the vast majority of the 2007–2009 increase in the unemployment rate was due to demand shocks." His conclusions are unjustified, and his data do not support the view that safety net expansions had a minimal effect on labor supply. First and foremost, he ignores every aspect of the safety net expansions since 2007 except the extensions of the amount of time that UI benefits can be received. According to Chapter Three, all UI extensions combined made up only 36 percent of the safety net expansion. Second, Rothstein (2011, 2) assumes that UI can raise unemployment only through its effect on search effort among the unemployed, even though economists have long recognized that UI affects layoffs too (see above). Third, his data grossly underpredict the actual amount of unemployment (see his figure 7) and therefore might underpredict the effect of UI on the amount of unemployment.

The UI literature also offers estimates of the effect of benefit amounts (conditional on eligibility) on the probability of exit from unemployment, which can also be used to quantify the horizontal amount of the aggregate labor supply shift. Reviewing that literature, Chetty (2008) concludes that a 10 percent increase in benefit levels increases the duration of unemployment by 4–8 percent. Chapter Three reports (and see also Figure 1.1) that government safety net generosity to the unemployed increased from about $10,000 per year to about $16,000 per year from the end of 2007 to the end of 2009. One might assume that the effect of benefit amount on unemployment duration is independent of the level of benefits, but this would rule out the likely possibility that average unemployment durations become quite long once the benefit exceeds what a person can earn from working. Instead, I assume that the elasticity of unemployment duration with respect to the self-reliance rate (1 minus the payroll and income tax rate minus the ratio of unemployment benefit amount to potential earnings) is constant and infer a range for the magnitude of that duration elasticity from Chetty's (2008) range of marginal effects. Assuming, as in Chapter Three, annual labor productivity of $46,600 and payroll and income taxes of $9,600, the end of 2007 and end of 2009 self-reliance rates associated with the $10,000 and $16,000 benefit levels are 0.57 and 0.45, respectively. At the initial self-reliance rate of 0.57, Chetty's range implies that the magnitude of the duration elasticity ranges from 1.0 to 2.1. The log self-reliance rate change is −0.24 for unemployed people, so the range for predicted log duration changes is 0.25 to 0.49.[34] By comparison, log actual average unemployment duration for persons aged twenty five to sixty-four increased 0.49 between 2007-Q4 and 2009-Q4. None of this accounts for the effect of unemployment benefit levels on the number of people laid off from their jobs, or for safety net expansions omitted from Figure 1.1, yet it appears possible to explain a large fraction of the increased unemployment duration by applying Chetty's (2008) interpretation of the UI literature to my estimates of the amount of safety net expansion for unemployed people.[35]

Appendix 4.3: Safety Net Distortions Measured in Dollars per Year

This appendix uses the methodology of Galí, Gertler, and Lopez-Salido (2007) to quantify the welfare cost of the labor market distortions created by the safety net expansions, which is essentially a Harberger triangle calculation (see also Hausman 1981) for the labor market that recognizes preexisting distortions. As explained in Chapter Ten, this welfare cost is only part of an overall cost-benefit analysis of the expansions that would also count their insurance benefits. For the purposes of this appendix, I estimate the fraction of the total labor decline from fiscal year 2007 to fiscal year 2010 attributable to the safety net expansion as 64 percent, based on the estimates in the main text corresponding to a labor supply elasticity of 0.75.

To a first-order approximation, the Gali, Gertler, and Lopez-Salido welfare cost is the area of the trapezoid in a supply and demand diagram like Figure 4.1, except that prices and quantities would be expressed in levels per capita rather than logs. The parallel sides of the trapezoid are bounded by the amount of labor per capita with the expansion and the amount of labor per capita without the expansion, which makes the trapezoid's height (a horizontal measurement in a supply and demand diagram with labor quantity measured on the horizontal axis) equal to the magnitude of the impact of the safety net expansions on labor $(n'-n)$, where n denotes actual labor per capita and n' denotes what labor per capita would have been without the expansion (both adjusted for the age of the population). Per capita employment among nonelderly household heads and spouses fell by 0.039 between fiscal years 2007 and 2010, adjusted for age.[36] Underemployment (among the employed) per capita increased 0.018, for a total per capita increase of non-employment and underemployment of 0.057. I take the safety net impact to be 64 percent of that, or 0.037. In aggregate, that is a non-employment and underemployment impact of 5.2 million.

The shorter base's length is equal to the safety net benefit amount b' without the expansion (inclusive of taxes and other preexisting distortions), which I take to be the safety net benefit amount in fiscal year 2007 of $1,560 per month of non-employment or underemployment inclusive of income taxes plus an estimate of 5 percent of the after-income and payroll tax median head-spouse monthly wage for sales and excise taxes ($118 per month) plus $777 per month for the 20 percent product market markups over labor costs assumed by Galí, Gertler, and Lopez-Salido.[37] The shorter base therefore has a length of $2,454 per month of non-employment or underemployment. The longer base's length is the shorter base's length plus the safety net benefit added by expansion, which was a $300 addition in fiscal year 2010. Thus the area of the trapezoid is about $13.6 billion per month, or $163 billion for fiscal year 2010. More should be added for (1) impacts of the expansion on the labor and sales tax amounts (and markups) per employee-month to the degree that they increase with labor productivity and (2) distortions to the labor market for persons who were not household heads or spouses. As shown in Chapter Six, it also appears that the safety net expansions changed the composition of the workforce, which would be yet an additional deadweight cost to the extent the expansions increased heterogeneity in log self-reliance rates.

5

Means-Tested Subsidies and Economic Dynamics Since 2007

THE PURPOSE OF this chapter is to estimate impacts of the expanding social safety net on the major macroeconomic variables—including GDP, consumption, investment, and labor hours—in a dynamic economic model with capital accumulation. The neoclassical growth model has a number of advantages for this purpose: it has the minimum number of components needed to offer predictions for the aforementioned macroeconomic variables; its components are fully consistent with the "partial equilibrium" calculations of productivity, labor distortions, and marginal tax rates presented in previous chapters of this book; the model has predictions for entire time series, and not just the economic measurements at a single point in time (such as 2009-Q4, which is emphasized in the previous chapter); the model can help explore the effects of impulses other than the expanding safety net; and the model has long been used to interpret business cycle events, marginal tax rate impulses, and cross-country consequences of the social safety net.[1]

The model takes time series for marginal labor income tax rates (hereafter, "marginal tax rates") as inputs and delivers time series for the major macroeconomic variables as outputs. The exercise begins with a baseline version of the neoclassical growth model with constant marginal tax rates in which equilibrium labor per capita is constant over time and other macro variables continue to grow at a constant rate. I then replace the constant marginal tax rate series with one of three marginal tax rate scenarios: (1) the labor market distortion series derived in Chapter Two for all distortions, (2) the safety net marginal tax rate series derived in Chapter Three, or (3) the combination of the safety net marginal tax rate series and employer-side distortions. In the all-distortion scenario, the simulated macro time series are, according to the model, the macroeconomic effects of all distortions combined, relative to the constant distortion baseline. In the safety-net-only scenario, the simulated macro time series are the macroeconomic effects of the safety net expansions by themselves (also relative to the constant distortion baseline). The third scenario indicates the macroeconomic effects of the combination of two types of distortion changes: safety net expansions and employer-side distortions.

I do not assume that the labor market would have been constant absent the safety net expansions. In addition to the safety net marginal tax rate series from Chapter Three, I measure an employer-side or "labor demand" distortion according to the gap, if any, between labor productivity and hourly labor compensation. I also define a labor supply "residual" distortion to be the part of the measured gap between labor productivity and the marginal rate of substitution between consumption and work that cannot be explained by safety net expansions or the employer-side distortions. If my model and the safety net marginal tax rates from Chapter Three are taken literally (more on this below), then the employer-side and labor supply residual distortions were not affected by safety net expansions, and therefore would have been present even if the safety net rules had remained constant. Model outcomes simulated from the employer-side and labor supply residual distortions alone can therefore be interpreted as outcomes for the economy in the hypothetical scenario in which safety net rules were constant, rather than expanding as they actually did.

In modeling the recession as a transition to an increasingly distorted labor market, I assume that production and capital markets are always efficient, or have rates of inefficiency that were unchanged during the recession, so that their dynamics are understood solely as reactions to the rising work disincentives stemming from expanding means-tested subsidy programs, and to other labor market distortions.[2] In this sense, my results do not depend on assumptions that the economy is efficient or that all markets are perfectly competitive, but rather on the assumption that *changes* in efficiency or competitiveness over time are limited to changes in the labor market as represented by changing distortions between labor productivity and reservation wages.

With these assumptions, an increase in the marginal tax rate originating, say, with changes in safety net program rules causes consumption, investment, and labor to decline in the short term, albeit in differing proportions. Labor declines in the short term because (by construction) the sole impulse is the rising work disincentive. Consumption declines because of the permanent income effect. Thanks to the legacy of a capital stock accumulated prior to the safety net expansions, the marginal product of capital falls with the workforce, which creates an intertemporal substitution effect on consumption partially offsetting the permanent income effect. Thus, consumption declines less than labor in the short term, regardless of whether the new work disincentives are temporary or permanent. For the same reason that the marginal product of capital falls, the marginal and average products of labor initially rise.

If the marginal tax rate increase is expected to be long-lasting, then the labor reduction will be long-lasting and investment will be low for long enough to eventually reduce the capital stock by the same proportion as labor. Once the work disincentives stabilize at a higher level, the marginal product of capital can rise again and reduce the intertemporal substitution effect that had mitigated the consumption decline. After enough time has passed with the greater marginal tax rate in place, the cumulative reductions in labor, consumption, and capital are all in the same proportion.

The model's paths for consumption and investment given a long-lasting marginal tax rate hike are compared with the monthly and quarterly aggregate time series since December 2007, when this recession began. The model and data agree that investment expenditure would fall 20–30 percent, although the data show investment dropping about three-quarters sooner than predicted by the model. Consumption dynamics in the model are similar to those in the data. Consistent with the model, the percentage consumption decline has so far been much less than the percentage decline in work hours.

I conclude that much of the aggregate changes in the labor market since 2007 can be interpreted as the result of changes in marginal tax rates or some other impulse with many of the characteristics of marginal tax rate changes. Moreover, the marginal tax rate changes coming from safety net expansions were enough by themselves to generate changes in the major macro aggregates that resemble the actual changes in direction, amount, and timing. The neoclassical growth model also offers an unconventional causal interpretation of the sharp drops in consumption, investment, and capital market values during 2008: the drops were, in significant part, a reaction to, and anticipation of, labor market contractions created by the expanding social safety net. In this view, it is incorrect to attribute the labor market contraction to drops in investment and consumer spending.

The analysis in this chapter has a lot in common with an extensive labor wedge literature beginning with Barro and King (1984) and as recent as Shimer (2010a) emphasizing the significance of labor wedges over several previous business cycles.[3] However, this chapter is more like McGrattan (1994), Mulligan (2002), and Ohanian (2010) in that the labor distortion or wedge is associated with specific public policies, in this case means-tested government subsidies.

The Neoclassical Growth Model with Targeted Means-Tested Subsidies

Consider an economy with many identical families, each with many adult family members. Family members will ultimately differ in terms of whether and how much labor they supply to the market, and in their expectation that they will be eligible for a means-tested subsidy in the event that they are not working. To simplify a complex reality in which there are many means-tested subsidy programs each with its own eligibility rules, I partition the family into just two groups: "prime" members, who have a probability $p > 0$ of receiving a means-tested subsidy in the event they are not working (more below about this probability); and "others," who are never eligible for means-tested subsidies. The relative size of the two groups, which I assume to be constant over time, is not relevant for my qualitative results or even many of my aggregate quantitative findings, but elsewhere in this book I measure the prime group as nonelderly household heads and their spouses, because they are more likely than the rest of the population to have a recent history of employment covered by unemployment insurance, be heads of households with children, or have home mortgages and consumer credit that may be partly forgiven by lenders on the basis of "ability to pay."

Time is continuous. Gross output is produced with capital and prime labor and is (exhaustively) used for market consumption goods and gross investment.

$$An_t^\alpha k_t^{1-\alpha} = c_t + \dot{k}_t + \delta k_t \tag{5.1}$$

where n denotes prime labor input (measured in hours per capita). k denotes capital input and c denotes market consumption, each relative to a constant exponential trend that reflects the constant exogenous growth rates for population and technology (Barro and Sala-i-Martin 2003). t is the time subscript and $A > 0$ and $\alpha \in (0,1)$ are constant technology parameters.[4] Dots denote time derivatives, and $\delta > 0$ reflects the rate of capital depreciation as well as population growth and rates of technical progress.

When the date t flow of market consumption is c_t, prime members supply n_t units of labor, and other members supply m_t units of labor (also measured in hours per capita), the representative household's flow of utility u_t is:

$$u_t = \frac{\sigma}{\sigma - 1} c_t^{(\sigma-1)/\sigma} - \gamma_n \frac{\eta}{\eta+1}(n_t - \beta m_t)^{(\eta+1)/\eta} - \gamma_m \frac{\eta}{\eta+1} m_t^{(\eta+1)/\eta} \tag{5.2}$$

where the positive constants σ, η, β, γ_n, and γ_m denote preference parameters. σ is the constant elasticity of substitution of consumption over time, and η is the constant Frisch elasticity of labor supply. In order to rule out unrealistically large intertemporal substitution effects, I make the weak assumption that σ ≤ $1/(1-\alpha)$.[5] For simplicity, and because of my lack of emphasis on the composition of employment, equation (5.2) assumes that the utility function is homothetic in the two labor amounts, and that the two types of labor enter additively in utility.[6] Households discount the utility flows at constant rate ρ > 0, which may also reflect exogenous growth rates of population and technology.

Firms rent the labor of prime family members at rate w_t in the labor market (market consumption c is the numéraire good). Prime members who work at date t supply one unit of labor, receive pretax wage rate w_t, and pay a linear labor income tax. Prime members who do not work at date t receive subsidy b_t with probability $p_t \in [0,1]$ and no subsidy with probability 1 - p_t; their expected replacement rate from the time t subsidy is $p_t b_t / w_t$. Other family members work, if at all, producing household services, as indicated by utility function (5.2). Assuming that households own the capital and rent it to firms at gross rental rate r, a household's dynamic budget constraint is:

$$n_t w_t + \left(\Gamma - n_t\right)\tau_t w_t + r_t k_t = c_t + \dot{k}_t + \delta k_t + L_t \tag{5.3}$$

where L_t denotes the date t taxes owed by any 100 percent working household (hereafter, lump sum taxes), Γ is the prime worker time endowment, and the combined marginal tax rate τ_t is the sum of the time t labor income tax rate and the expected replacement rate $p_t b_t / w_t$. I assume that τ_t is less than one for all t. In practice, much of τ_t's variation over time comes from the safety net replacement rate, but for brevity I hereafter refer to the combined marginal tax rate τ_t as "the marginal tax rate" for time t.

Given values for the scalar taste and technology parameters, a value for the initial capital stock k_0, and a time path for the marginal tax rate, a market equilibrium is a list of time paths on $t \geq 0$ for utility flows, consumption flows, capital, both types of labor, wage rates, capital rental rates, and lump sum taxes such that: the subsidy program's budget constraint $L_t = (\Gamma - n_t)\tau_t w_t$ balances at each date; and—taking the time paths for factor rental rates, marginal tax rates, and lump sum taxes as given—the paths for utility, consumption, labor, and capital (1) maximize profits $A n_t^\alpha k_t^{1-\alpha} - w_t n_t - r_t k_t$ at each date and (2) maximize the present discounted value of utility $\int_0^\infty e^{-\rho t} u_t dt$ subject to (5.2), the household's sequence of dynamic budget constraints (5.3), and a no-Ponzi condition on capital ownership.

Equilibrium factor rental rates equal their marginal products, so the equilibrium time paths for consumption, prime labor, and capital are the solution to a two-dimensional system of differential equations (5.1) and (5.4), plus the algebraic equation (5.5), whose boundary conditions are the initial capital stock and the usual transversality condition:

$$\dot{c}_t = \sigma \left[(1-\alpha)A\left(n_t / k_t\right)^\alpha - \delta - \rho \right] c_t \qquad (5.4)$$

$$n_t^{1/\eta} = \frac{1-\tau_t}{\gamma} \frac{\alpha A}{c_t^{1/\sigma}} \left(k_t / n_t\right)^{1-\alpha} \qquad (5.5)$$

where the constant $\gamma > 0$ is a combination of the preference parameters η, β, γ_n, and γ_m. Differential equation (5.4) is the usual consumption Euler equation equating the intertemporal marginal rate of substitution of consumption to the net marginal product of capital. Algebraic equation (5.5) equates the marginal rate of substitution between consumption and prime labor to the marginal product of prime labor net of marginal tax rates. A marginal tax rate $\tau_t > 0$ is a labor distortion in the sense that it causes the marginal product of labor to differ from the marginal rate of substitution.

Many studies have put a wedge in condition (5.1) by letting the productivity parameter vary over time. Other studies have also put a wedge in the consumption Euler equation (5.4), perhaps with a rate of time preference or price of investment goods that varies over time. But a result of this chapter is that a large fraction of this recession can be understood as a consequence of a time-varying labor wedge alone, and that much of the wedge has to do with subsidies available to the unemployed and financially distressed,[7] so I have omitted productivity and intertemporal wedges as sources of time variation.

Because equation (5.5) includes labor productivity rather than the wage rate, the marginal tax rate τ in that equation captures not only labor income taxes paid by workers and marginal tax rates implicit in government subsidies to individuals but also payroll taxes and other marginal employment costs paid by employers. The primary difference between the former two distortions and the latter is that the former drive a wedge between the wage rate and the consumer marginal rate of substitution, whereas the latter drives a wedge between productivity and the wage rate.

The functional form (5.5) for the marginal rate of substitution function implies that consumption and leisure are normal goods and has been occasionally used in the macroeconomics literature,[8] although for various reasons. My purposes here are simplicity and a maximum of analytic results and to have consumption, capital, and labor all change in the same proportions in the long term.[9]

Dynamics of the Stationary System

If the labor distortion were constant over time, the dynamical system (5.1), (5.4), and (5.5) would be stationary and saddle path stable, with only the saddle path satisfying the transversality condition. The stationary state of the system (c_{ss}, k_{ss}, n_{ss}) has a closed form solution:

$$k_{ss}^{1/\eta+1/\sigma} = \frac{1-\tau}{\gamma} \frac{\alpha}{(\delta+\rho)^{(1/\eta+1)/\alpha-1}(\alpha\delta+\rho)^{1/\sigma}} A^{(1/\eta+1)/\alpha} (1-\alpha)^{(1/\eta+1)/\alpha-1+1/\sigma}$$

$$(1-\alpha)A(n_{ss}/k_{ss})^{\alpha} = \delta+\rho \tag{5.6}$$

$$c_{ss} = \frac{\alpha\delta+\rho}{1-\alpha}k_{ss}$$

The last two equations in (5.6) determine the steady state ratio of market consumption and prime work to the capital stock and do not depend on the value for the marginal tax rate τ. Thus, a permanent increase in the marginal tax rate reduces the long-term capital stock, and it reduces market consumption and work in the same proportion.

When the marginal tax rate is constant, a phase diagram for saddle path stable systems describes the dynamics of the system from any initial capital stock. The $\dot{k} = 0$ schedule in the $[k,c]$ plane is implicitly defined by:

$$c = \left[AN(c,k;1-\tau)^{\alpha} - \delta \right] k$$

$$N(c,k;1-\tau)^{1-\alpha+1/\eta} \equiv \frac{1-\tau}{\gamma} \frac{\alpha A}{c^{1/\sigma}k^{1/\eta}} \tag{5.7}$$

where $N(c,k;1-\tau)$ is the labor-capital ratio that satisfies the labor market condition seen in (5.5) for given values of consumption, capital, and the marginal tax rate. Along $\dot{k} = 0$, market consumption equals net market output, so the schedule slopes up if and only if net market output increases with capital, taking into account the positive effect of capital on labor for a given marginal utility of consumption. The maximum of this schedule therefore occurs at a capital stock that exceeds the "golden rule" capital stock that maximizes net output for a given labor, which itself exceeds the steady state capital stock for which the marginal product of capital equals the rate of time preference ρ. A larger value for the marginal tax rate τ is associated with a $\dot{k} = 0$ schedule that is lower at each value of k.

The $\dot{c} = 0$ schedule is implicitly defined by:

$$N\left(c,k;1-\tau\right)^{\alpha} = \frac{\delta+\rho}{1-\alpha}\frac{1}{A} \tag{5.8}$$

Thus, the schedule slopes down and has elasticity equal to $-\sigma/\eta$. A larger value for the marginal tax rate τ is associated with a $\dot{c} = 0$ schedule that is lower at each value of k.

Figure 5.1 shows $\dot{c} = 0$ and $\dot{k} = 0$ schedules and the implied dynamics of the system. When capital is below (above) its steady state value, there is an initial value for market consumption that is necessarily below (above) its steady state value so that the dynamics of the system asymptotically approach the steady state. Proposition 1 characterizes the stable arm containing such paths.

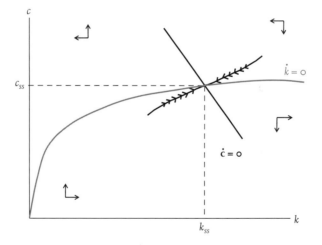

FIGURE 5.1. Capital-Consumption Phase Diagram for the Stationary System
The Figure shows the stationary system's steady state, dynamics, and stable arm.

Proposition 1.   If $\sigma \in (0,(1-\alpha)^{-1})$, the stable arm of the system slopes up in the $[k,c]$ plane and crosses the ray from the origin from above.

Proof   In the $[k,c]$ plane, both the stable and unstable arms solve the ordinary differential equation

$$c'(k) = \sigma \frac{(1-\alpha)AN\big(c(k),k;1-\tau\big)^{\alpha} - \delta - \rho}{AN\big(c(k),k;1-\tau\big)^{\alpha} - \delta - c(k)/k} \frac{c(k)}{k}$$

$$N\big(c(k),k;1-\tau\big)^{1-\alpha+1/\eta} \equiv \frac{1-\tau}{\gamma}\frac{\alpha A}{c^{1/\sigma}k^{1/\eta}}$$

(5.9)

The elasticity of these two arms in the neighborhood of the steady state can be found by using L'Hopital's rule and noting that the resulting quadratic equation is satisfied for both elasticities. One of the quadratic equation's solutions is in the interval (0,1),[10] while the other is in (-∞,1). The unstable arm's elasticity corresponds to the lesser solution, which means that the elasticity of the stable arm at the steady state is in (0,1). The steady state lies on the ray from the origin, which means the stable arm crosses that ray at the steady state from above.

For any capital stock below (above) its steady state value, the stable arm is below (above) the $\dot{k}=0$ schedule, which implies that the denominator of equation (5.9) is positive (negative), respectively. At the steady state, the numerator is zero and the arm slopes up. Because the net marginal product of capital term in the numerator declines in both c and k, it would be positive (negative) even if $c'(k)$ were zero, which means that $c'(k)$ is positive for any capital stock less (greater) than the steady state, respectively.

A number of analytical results can be obtained for this model. Others of the results are better displayed numerically, in which case parameter values are assumed as shown in Table 5.1 below (Appendix 5.1 has more on calibration).

Short-Term Effects of a Permanent and Immediate Increase in the Marginal Tax Rate

Proposition 2 A permanent increase in the marginal tax rate reduces the steady state capital stock, labor hours, and consumption in the same proportions.

Figure 5.2 shows the steady states and stable arms of the stationary system with marginal tax rate τ and the stationary system with higher marginal tax rate $\tau' > \tau$. Because the steady states lie on the same ray from the origin, and both stable arms cross that ray from above, the stable arm corresponding to the lesser marginal tax rate lies above that corresponding to the greater marginal tax rate.[11]

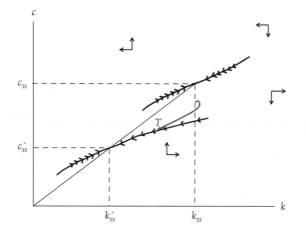

FIGURE 5.2. Stable Arms for High and Low Marginal Tax Rates
The Figure shows the system's dynamics and stable arm. The dynamics shown by the red arrows correspond to the low tax rate that prevailed before date o. When the new tax rate path is first anticipated at date o, consumption falls, but not as far as it will fall in the long term. The new stable arm (shown as a black path) describes dynamics once the tax rate has reached its higher long-term value.

Lemma   If $\sigma \in (0,(1-\alpha)^{-1})$, the elasticity of labor with respect to capital is less than the elasticity of consumption with respect to capital along the stable arm of the stationary system.

Proof   See Appendix I of Mulligan (2010a).

Proposition 3   If $\sigma \in (0,(1-\alpha)^{-1})$, the initial effects of a permanent and immediate increase in the marginal tax rate are to reduce labor and consumption, but consumption declines in a lesser proportion.

Proof   As shown in Proposition 2, the steady state consumption and labor impacts are in the same proportion. Because the initial capital stock exceeds the steady state capital stock, initial consumption must exceed steady state consumption. Initial labor may (or may not, depending on parameter values) exceed steady state labor, but the Lemma guarantees that the percentage gap between initial and steady state is greater for consumption.

A Gradual and Permanent Increase in the Marginal Tax Rate

The sudden and immediate increase in the marginal tax rate is intellectually cumbersome because it combines two types of initial effects: the wealth effect of the news that the present value of output is less than previously thought,

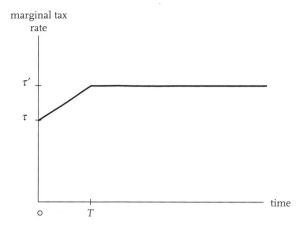

FIGURE 5.3. Time Path for the Gradually Increasing Marginal Tax Rate

and the substitution effect of the initial marginal tax rate increase creating an increase in leisure and a reduction in consumption. More important, the actual marginal tax rates in the economy may accumulate over time, as for example the housing market repeatedly deteriorates, or various means-tested government subsidies are introduced or expanded at staggered dates.

For this reason, I consider a marginal tax rate that evolves over time rather than jumping immediately to its long-term value. At time T, the marginal tax rate reaches its long-term value, which I assume exceeds its initial value. Suppose that the marginal tax rate increases continuously and monotonically with time for T years and then remains forever after T at that higher level, as shown in Figure 5.3. As of time T, the system must be on the stable arm corresponding to the long-term value for the marginal tax rate, which is shown in Figure 5.2 as a black curve. Consumption cannot jump any time after time zero, so time paths for consumption and capital prior to time T satisfy differential equations (5.1) and (5.4), satisfy the labor market condition (5.5) for the marginal tax rate amount assumed at each date, satisfy the given initial capital stock, and terminate at time T at an allocation $[k(T),c(T)]$ that is on the stable arm of the stationary system with the high marginal tax rate. Furthermore, as shown in Figure 5.2's light red curve, the time path in the $[k,c]$ plane approaches the stable arm from above, and with an amount of capital that exceeds its long-term value, because the marginal tax rate is less before time T than at time T.[12]

Not surprisingly, the initial reduction in consumption is less than it would be if the entire marginal tax rate change occurred immediately at time 0, because the wealth and substitution effects on labor supply are both smaller in this case. Labor initially increases a bit, because of the adverse wealth effect and the fact that too little increase in the marginal tax rate is initially present to create a substitution effect. The initial labor increase raises the marginal product of capital and consumption growth (after consumption's initial jump down), which motivates some investment in the short term. As the marginal tax rate increases, labor, investment, and consumption growth fall. The amount and duration of the initial high-labor period turn out to be little for the marginal tax rate series examined here; in general they depend on the size of relative wealth and substitution effects on labor supply, and how quickly the marginal tax rate approaches its long-term value.

Table 5.1. Parameter Values Assumed for the Purposes of Numerical Results

Parameter		Value(s)	Units	Comments
α	Labor's share	0.7	Share	
ρ	Time preference rate, adjusted	0.5%	Per year	Chosen to produce a steady-state investment to adjusted output ratio of 0.27
δ	Capital depreciation rate, adjusted	7.5%	Per year	5.5% pure depreciation, adjusted for 1% population growth and 0.5% technical change, and 0.5 percent expected investment price trend
σ	Intertemporal consumption elasticity	[0.5,2]	Elasticity	Benchmark value of 1.35 (Mulligan, 2004)
η	Labor substitution elasticity	[0.4,1.1]	Elasticity	Benchmark value of 0.75
A	Productivity level	Normalized		Normalized so that the initial-MTR steady state
γ	Leisure preference	Normalized		capital and prime labor are one
Γ	Prime-worker time endowment	1.32		Initial-MTR steady state has 76% prime labor usage
θ	Prime-worker's share of labor income	0.9	Share	A function of the preference parameters

At least part of the safety net expansions, such as unemployment insurance bonuses granted by the 2009 American Recovery and Reinvestment Act, were temporary. Others, such as underwater mortgages in certain parts of the country and the extended duration of time that the unemployed are permitted to receive unemployment benefits, may be present for a number of years after the recession is over. Expansions of food stamps and Medicaid may largely be permanent. Moreover, new taxes to pay for (and, sometimes, means-tests associated with the distribution of) growing public pensions and publicly financed health care may replace some of the temporary marginal tax rate effects of the programs examined in Chapter Three, and be present for a number of years thereafter. For these reasons, the marginal tax rates series measured in Chapter Three and used in this chapter are a bit different from Figure 5.3. Nevertheless, they often induce quantitatively similar dynamics: consumption initially jumps down and then declines monotonically thereafter. A second type of dynamics is also possible, depending on whether, and how much, the peak marginal tax rate exceeds the long-term marginal tax rate (see Appendix 5.1).

Data and Simulation Results

Time Series for the Marginal Tax Rate

The marginal tax rate series needed to simulate the model stretches into the infinite future, although the model's predictions for near-future economic outcomes are relatively insensitive to the values of distant-future marginal tax rates. I construct four such marginal tax rate series. One of them measures actual and expected changes in safety net program rules and is created by augmenting Figure 3.6's red monthly marginal tax rate series (as measured on its right scale), which combines labor income taxes with the income replaced by government and lender safety net programs, going only as far as the end of 2011. After that, I assume that the product of the SNAP eligibility and real SNAP benefits indices (two components of Chapter Three's overall marginal tax rate series) erode with inflation through February 2012 and then remain constant through the end of the fiscal year. I assume that SNAP work requirements are reinstated in fiscal year 2013 and beyond. The UI eligibility index falls slightly in June 2012 and again in September 2012 as benefits are no longer paid beyond seventy-nine and seventy-two weeks, respectively. The net result of all of these expected changes is to reduce the marginal tax rate by 0.4 percentage points between December 2011 and December 2012.

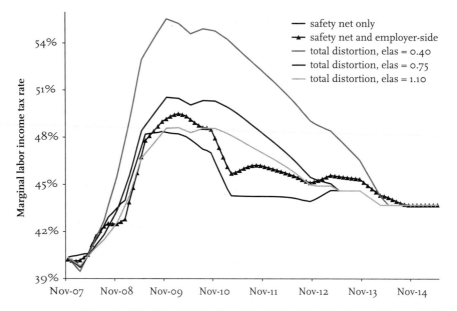

FIGURE 5.4. Marginal Tax Rate Series from the Safety Net, Employer-side, and All Distortions Combined

In January 2013, 0.8 percentage points are added to the marginal tax rate as the payroll tax cuts expire and unemployment benefit duration is reduced from seventy-two weeks to fifty-two, although Congress could extend those provisions yet again.[13] I assume that the marginal tax rate is constant during 2013 and jumps down 0.9 percentage points in January 2014: 2.1 percentage points down from the reduction of unemployment benefit duration from fifty-two weeks to twenty-six, and 1.2 percentage points up because of the scheduled Medicaid eligibility expansion (see also the Appendix to Chapter Three). As noted in Chapter Three, the vast majority of the changes in this marginal tax rate series come from safety net program rule changes rather than changes in labor income tax rates; henceforth I refer to it as the "safety net marginal tax rate series."

Figure 3.6's marginal rate series change on exactly the month that new safety net rules go into effect, which probably exaggerates the precision with which it measures genuine tax rate changes. For example, the series jumps down in June 2010 when the COBRA subsidy expired, even though persons who had already been unemployed as of that date could continue to receive the subsidy for more than one year after June 2010. For this reason, this chapter uses the five-month centered moving average of the statutory safety net marginal tax rate series, which is the black series shown in Figure 5.4.

The second marginal tax rate series quantifies the gap, if any, between labor productivity and hourly labor compensation as measured by the inverse of real unit labor cost. One of the many interpretations of the inverse of real unit labor cost is as an employment cost perceived by employers but not included in current labor compensation. Chapter Two notes that employers may have anticipated a future payroll expansion tax credit, or future health care costs for current employees, both of which act as an implicit payroll tax in the present and drive a wedge between labor productivity and wages.[14] Economists have recently suggested that extraordinary uncertainty has discouraged employers from hiring, which might also reduce measured real unit labor cost (and thereby increase its inverse). A consolidation of goods markets that permitted employers to further mark up prices over marginal cost could affect real unit labor cost. New Keynesian economists have also offered interpretations of real unit labor cost, one of which is the result of an increase in labor supply (such as the increase that might occur when some of the safety net expansions expire) in the face of "sticky" output prices.[15] I refer to changes in the inverse of unit labor cost as changes in "employer-side distortions" and sometimes present it in combination with the safety net marginal tax rate series, that is, the combined change in the gap between labor productivity and reservation wages occurring from both safety net rule changes and changes in the gap between wages and labor productivity. Its combination with the safety net series is shown in black with triangles in Figure 5.4.

Chapter Two calculates a total distortion series through 2011 using only data on actual consumption, labor hours, labor productivity, and population, plus an estimate of the consumption elasticity (assumed to be 1 for the purposes of Chapter Two but assumed to be 1.35 here; more on calibration in Appendix 5.1) and an estimate of the labor supply elasticity η. In theory, the total distortion change from the base period reflects the combined change of all labor market distortions affecting aggregate labor hours, as well as changing model specification errors, and not only the distortions coming from safety net expansions.[16] In order to isolate the other labor market distortions and the specification errors from the safety net distortions and the employer-side distortions, I calculate a residual supply series through early 2011 that has a change that subtracts the log distortion changed implied by the safety net marginal tax rate series and the log inverse unit labor cost change from the overall labor market distortion log change.[17] By construction, the supply residual and total distortion series depend on the assumed labor supply elasticity, but the safety net and employer-side distortions do not.

In order to calculate log inverse real unit labor cost for dates beyond 2011, I fit a quarterly first-order autoregressive model with a linear trend in the data from 1980 to 2007, and use the estimated model (its quarterly autoregressive coefficient is 0.87) to dynamically forecast the dependent variable's deviation from trend from 2012-Q1 through 2014-Q2 and then set it to zero thereafter in order to have all distortions constant in the distant future. In order to calculate a supply residual for dates beyond 2011, I assume that the supply residual returns linearly to its 2007-Q4 value at about the rate it increased before (returning to zero in twenty-four months). Values for the total distortion beyond 2011 are calculated by adding the supply residual and the log inverse unit labor cost back to the log distortion implied by the safety net marginal tax rate series. Total, employer-side (in combination with the safety net series, or not), and residual distortion series are then expressed in terms of marginal tax rates and normalized to 40.4 percent in November 2007 to coincide with the safety net marginal tax rate series at that date.[18] Figure 5.4's monthly gray, red, and light red series display the total distortion series corresponding to labor supply elasticities of 0.4, 0.75, and 1.1, respectively. The marginal tax rate series based on the supply residuals are discussed and shown later in this chapter.

Regardless of the exact value of the assumed labor supply elasticity, the total distortion series follow the marginal tax rates measured from safety net program rules during the first year and a half of the recession, increasing 7 to 13 percentage points from the end of 2007 to May 2009. Between May 2009 and December 2010, the total distortion series for the middle and large elasticity (shown in red and light red in Figure 5.4) increase about the same as the marginal tax rates measured from safety net program rules (shown in black). From this perspective, the safety net program rule changes explain most of the changes in labor market distortions for the first 1.5 to 2 years of the recession (see also Figures 1.1 and 3.7).

In mid-2010, some of the safety net expansions expire and the marginal tax rates measured from safety net program rules begin to decline, yet the total distortion series do not begin to decline until late 2010 and even then decline more slowly. The combination of safety net and employer-side marginal tax rates follow two of the total distortion series more closely during this period. From mid-2010 to the most recent observation (end of 2011), the combined marginal tax rate series falls 2.9 percentage points, as compared to 2.2 percentage points for the total distortion with $\eta = 0.75$ and 1.6 percentage points for the total distortion with $\eta = 1.1$.

Monthly and Quarterly Indicators of Aggregate Economic Quantities

The next step is to compare the actual changes in the major economic variables with the model predictions. The model is especially simple in that output has only two uses: as consumption or investment. The national accounts offer more detail than this, so I aggregate nondefense government consumption, private nondurable consumption, and private service consumption into a single quarterly consumption aggregate, which is shown in per capita terms in Figure 2.2. Real gross domestic private investment, real government nondefense investment, and real private purchases of consumer durables are summed together into a single quarterly real investment aggregate, using the same methodology as for the consumption aggregate. I also consider a second measure of investment that excludes residential investment, because housing capital is likely less complementary with labor than business capital. Labor usage is measured monthly as the sum of aggregate private work hours and aggregate public work hours, shown in per capita terms in Figure 2.1, and then adjusted for changes in the population age distribution as measured in Chapter Two.[19] The average product of labor is measured as the ratio of quarterly real GDP to quarterly aggregate private and public work hours.

Model households provide their own household services, but in practice many household services such as child care, or close substitutes for them such as dining services, are traded in the marketplace. The model's best analogue for date t national accounts expenditure on nondurable consumption goods and services is therefore $c_t + \beta(1-\tau_t)w_t m_t$.

The model is expressed relative to constant exponential trends for population and labor productivity.[20] The labor usage data are therefore expressed in per capita terms for the purpose of comparing to the model. To match the other measured series with their model counterpart, each is expressed in per capita terms and then detrended by 0.5 percent per year, about the ratio of the average annual rate of TFP growth over the four years prior to the recession to labor's share, 0.7.[21]

Effects of Marginal Tax Rates on Labor, Consumption, and Output

Figures 5.5a–5.5d display model predictions for labor usage, real consumption, the average product of labor, and real investment, assuming (1) that marginal tax rates followed one of the total distortion series in Figure 5.4, (2) three alternative values for the labor supply elasticity η, using the other benchmark parameter values shown in Table 5.1, and (3) that the detrended capital stock at the end of 2007 coincides with the steady state capital stock corresponding to those parameters and a marginal tax rate of 40.4 percent.[22] The Figures 5.5a–5.5d express model variables as a ratio to their values in the steady state with a marginal tax rate of 40.4 percent (its value at the end of 2007), and measured variables as a ratio to their value in December 2007 (or, in the case of quarterly data, 2007-Q4). Appendix 5.1 explains how I numerically simulated the (nonlinear) model's equilibrium time paths.

Figure 5.5a compares the model with measured labor data. All three model labor paths closely follow one another and the labor data because each total distortion series was constructed to fit the measured relative log changes of consumption, labor, and labor productivity. For this reason, Figure 5.5a shows only that, regardless of the assumed value for the labor supply elasticity, it is possible to find a marginal tax rate series that allows the model predictions to look a lot like the labor data.

Figure 5.5b is more interesting because it shows the model consumption following actual consumption for the same marginal tax rate series used to simulate Figure 5.5a. In other words, the model's consumption and labor can closely follow the two corresponding data series with a single assumed marginal

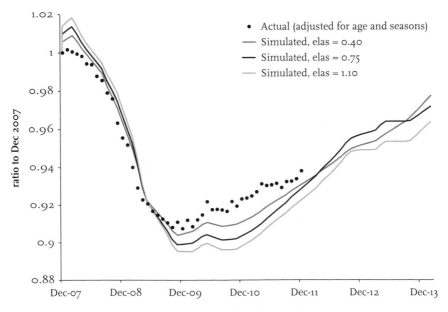

FIGURE 5.5a. Labor per Capita Simulated from the Total Distortion

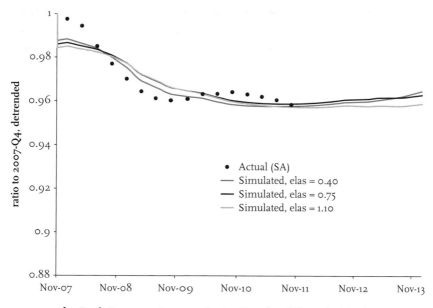

FIGURE 5.5b. Real Consumption per Capita Simulated from the Total Distortion

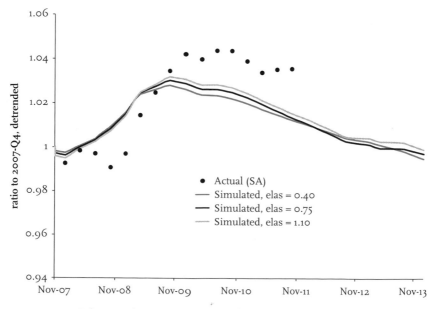

FIGURE 5.5c. Labor Productivity Simulated from the Total Distortion

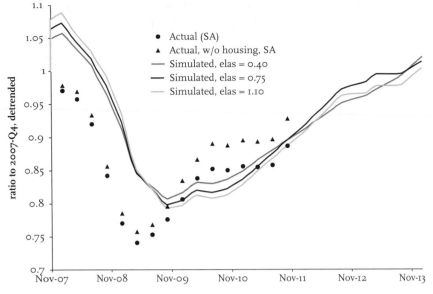

FIGURE 5.5d. Investment per Capita Simulated from the Total Distortion

tax rate series. As explained further below, other economic models cannot simultaneously fit the consumption and labor series.[23] Figures 5.5a and Figure 5.5b show that fitting two series with a single marginal tax rate series does not depend on the assumed value for the labor supply elasticity.

In the model, both the consumption and labor changes are the result of labor market distortions. Nevertheless, model consumption declines before labor does. Thus, the fact that, as of the middle of 2008, consumption had declined more than labor does not by itself imply that reduced consumption caused the labor decline.

Figure 5.5c shows that the model's labor productivity follows a similar pattern to actual productivity, especially from the perspective of alternative models in which labor productivity declines during recessions.[24] Measured productivity peaks about 1 or 1.5 percentage points above model productivity, although Chapter Two notes that measured productivity may be exaggerated about that much because of changes in the composition of the workforce.

Much, But Not All, of the Investment Decline Appears Efficient Given Rising Marginal Labor Income Tax Rates

As shown in Figure 5.5d, model investment declines to about 80 percent of the prerecession value by the end of the recession's second year. Through the middle of the second year, the data also show real investment of about 75 percent of the prerecession value. In this sense, low labor usage explains more than half of the investment decline.[25]

The fact that both labor and investment declined during the recession does not necessarily tell us that the labor decline was the result of a lack of investment. Investment declines in my model because capital and labor are complements in production (in the sense that the marginal product of capital increases with the amount of labor), and the labor market becomes increasingly distorted with time. I interpret the low investment during the recession as the result of labor market distortions, rather than the other way around.

The model and investment data disagree as to the amount of the investment decline during the first year and a half. Part of the disagreement is related to my rather simple modeling of the arrival of information about the future of labor market distortions: I assume that such information arrives completely and fully in December 2007. Model consumption jumps down immediately (see Figure 5.5b), which mitigates the investment drop. In reality, it took about a year for actual consumption to drop as much as it does in the model.

Effects of the Safety Net Expansion

The results above show that marginal tax rates that rose after 2007, and then fell somewhat thereafter, can explain much of what happened to the major economic variables. However, those results by themselves do not indicate what caused marginal tax rates to change over time, or whether the economy experienced other changes that have many of the same characteristics of marginal tax rates. The next step is therefore to simulate the model with the marginal tax rate series from the safety net program rule changes alone—the black series shown in Figure 5.4—or the employer-side distortion alone (the gap between the black-with-triangles and black series), rather than one of the total distortion series from Figure 5.4.

Figure 5.6a's red series displays simulated labor per capita using the safety net marginal tax rate series, a labor supply elasticity of 1.1, and the other benchmark parameter values shown in Table 5.1. Because the underlying marginal tax rate series reflects actual safety net program rule changes and does not account for any other labor market distortion changes, it is labeled as simulated with "safety net MTR, and other distortions constant." Unlike the labor series from Figure 5.5a, the red labor series in Figure 5.6a does not automatically fit the data because it was constructed from safety net program

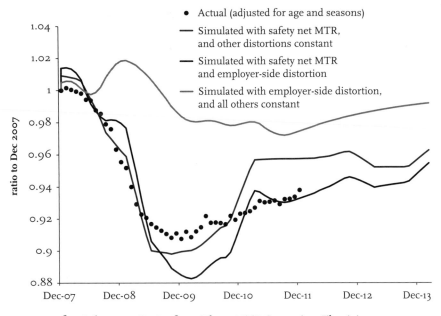

FIGURE 5.6a. Labor per Capita from Three MTR Scenarios, Elasticity = 1.1

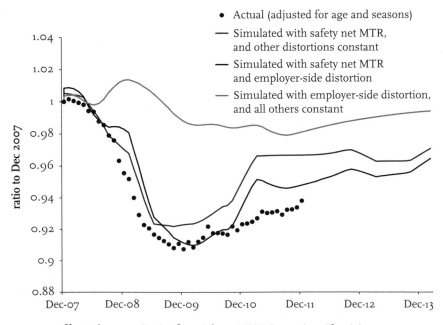

FIGURE 5.6b. Labor per Capita from Three MTR Scenarios, Elasticity = 0.75

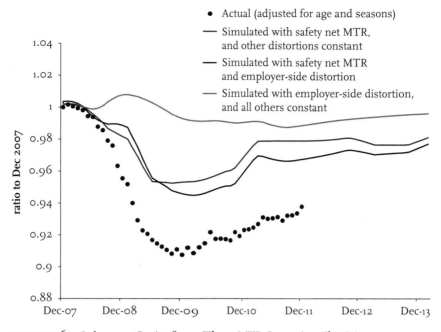

FIGURE 5.6c. Labor per Capita from Three MTR Scenarios, Elasticity = 0.4

benefit rules rather than labor market outcomes. Nevertheless, the model's labor closely follows actual labor through the middle of 2010. In the fourth quarter of 2009, actual labor averaged 0.909 while simulated labor averaged 0.899. From this perspective, the model with η = 1.1 explains 111 percent of the decline in age-adjusted labor per capita between the end of 2007 and 2009-Q4.[26]

The model and the data also agree as to the timing of labor's turn: both say that labor per capita began to increase in early 2010. In the model, labor turns because the safety net expansions begin to expire. The model and data also agree that, prior to the end of 2011, there was no "double dip recession" when labor per capita would peak below prerecession levels and decline significantly from there. The model predicts no double dip recession as long as the safety net does not have a second expansion period.

In a number of previous recessions, work hours per capita were near or past prerecession levels within four years. Nevertheless, the model and data also agree that labor per capita would not be near prerecession levels any time before the end of 2011, a full four years after the recession began. However, with the safety net expansion alone and a labor supply elasticity of 1.1, the model predicts labor to increase more in 2010 than it actually did.

Figures 5.6b and 5.6c display the results with labor supply elasticities of 0.75 and 0.4, respectively. To focus on Figure 5.6c (η = 0.4),[27] many of the results are similar as with η = 1.1: model (with other distortions constant) and data agree that labor declines significantly in 2008 and 2009, labor per capita turns in early 2010, and there is no double dip recession prior to the end of 2011. Not surprisingly, the amounts of the labor changes depend on the assumed value for the labor supply elasticity. The model with η = 0.4 (η = 0.75) explains only 52 percent (85 percent) of the per capita labor decline from the end of 2007 to 2009-Q4, respectively, as compared with 111 percent explained with η = 1.1. On the other hand, the model with η = 0.4 more closely matches the amount of the labor change from the end of 2009 to the end of 2011 than do the models with η = 0.75 and η = 1.1.

I also simulated the model with a combination of safety net marginal tax rates and employer-side distortions and display the results as black curves in Figures 5.6a–5.6c. The model with η = 1.1 actually overpredicts the labor decline from the end of 2007 to the end of 2009, as indicated by the fact that the simulated black series dips below the data series. The model predicts that age-adjusted labor per capita would decline a net 7 percent from the end of 2007 to the end of 2011, which is close to the actual decline over that time frame. Figures 5.6a–5.6c also show that the employer-side distortion does little to reduce labor per capita through mid-2009 (see the gray series in those figures), and its maximum labor impact (found with η = 1.1) occurs in 2011 and is still less than 3 percent. Regardless of the value of the labor supply elasticity, the impact of the safety net expansions through mid-2010 is many times the impact of employer-side distortions. Even in 2011, the cumulative impact of measured safety net expansions is still about double the cumulative impact of employer-side distortions.

Assuming a labor supply elasticity of 0.75 or 1.1, the model with safety net and employer side distortions predicts a consumption path much like the simulated paths shown in Figure 5.5b and an investment path much like the simulated paths shown in Figure 5.5d, and therefore broadly like the actual consumption and investment paths. With an assumed labor supply elasticity of 0.4, labor and therefore consumption fall about half as much in the model as in the data.

Interpreting the Residual Labor Market Distortions

Figure 5.7 displays the labor supply residuals, namely actual log after-tax labor productivity (based on the safety net marginal tax rate series) minus the employer-side distortion and the log of the marginal rate of substitution (based on the functional form (5.2), and a consumption elasticity of 1.35) corresponding to three values for the labor supply elasticity and expressed as a marginal tax rate. For comparison, the figure also displays the safety net marginal tax rate series and the employer-side distortion. All series are normalized so that they are 40.4 percent at the end of 2007. With the labor supply elasticities $\eta = 0.75$ and 1.1, the supply residual is relatively constant for the first 2 to 2.5 years of the recession, and then rises 2 or 3 percentage points through early 2011. They average 42.7 percent and 41.3 percent, respectively, through the end of 2011, as compared to their starting values of 40.4 percent. All three residual distortion measures decline during the second half of 2011 and then decline thereafter by assumption.

The labor supply residuals have some of the same interpretations as the overall labor wedge. Unmeasured labor preference shifts, for example, would in my approach appear as a labor supply residual, which is why the stability of that residual is sometimes said to gauge the stability of the aggregate labor supply curve (Parkin 1988). Model specification errors are another interpretation. Hall (2009) suggests that the labor wedges derived from models like mine for prior recessions are the result of the omission of labor market search from the model. Perhaps the residual distortions since 2007 could be interpreted in the same

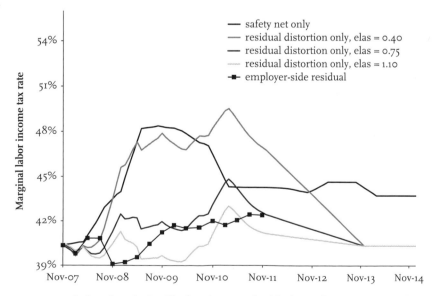

FIGURE 5.7. Labor Supply Residuals Compared with the Safety Net Marginal Tax Rate Series

way, although I wonder why labor market search would be a more important model omission in 2010 and 2011 than it was in 2008 and 2009.

Errors in the measurement of wages and labor productivity would also affect my measures of the labor supply residual. If the U.S. Bureau of Labor Statistics (2011a) is correct that measured wage changes between 2007 and 2009 are subject to a 1.4 percentage point composition bias (i.e., that individual-level wages increased 1.4 percentage points less than aggregate wage measures because different types of people were working after 2007), then adjusting the $\eta = 0.75$ labor supply residual for that composition bias would reduce it to an average of 41.9 percent for 2009, which is closer to its starting value of 40.4 percent. Moreover, the changing workforce composition that creates the composition bias is at least partly the result of safety net expansions, which is one reason that the supply residuals shown in Figure 5.7 might have been different if the safety net had not expanded.

The utility function (5.2) may also be missing dynamic elements such as habit formation and changes in welfare stigma that are potentially important when the safety net changes as dramatically as it has since 2007. More empirical work is needed to measure the response of labor supply to safety net changes at different time horizons.

I have suggested before that labor wedges be interpreted as unmeasured marginal tax rates coming from public policy,[28] and I suspect that part of the supply residuals shown in Figure 5.7 are also unmeasured marginal tax rates. Chapter Three, which produced the safety net marginal tax rate series that is the basis for the residual distortions, notes that, due to limitations of data and scope, it failed to measure changes in means-tested subsidies such as bankruptcy reform. It also failed to measure state and local income tax rates. I suspect that these omissions are of limited economic significance, but so are the magnitudes of the supply residuals, at least if one assumes a labor supply elasticity that is not too much less than 0.75 or too much more than 1.1.

Even for the programs examined in Chapter Three, measurement judgments were required. Perhaps most important for the purposes of interpreting the labor supply residual was my choice of representing the marginal tax rate from the perspective of the median worker, because the dynamics of SNAP expansions (they were largely permanent) were so different from the dynamics of unemployment insurance and related expansions (several of them expired in 2010). It is possible that the overall safety net expansion looks more permanent from the perspective of a worker at the 30th or 40th percentile of the wage distribution than it does from the perspective of the median worker (see also Mulligan 2012).

The "employer-side distortion" is a gap between labor productivity and hourly labor income, and has many economic interpretations. It might reflect anticipation of a payroll expansion tax credit, or future health care costs for current employees. Figure 5.7 shows much of the increase in this distortion during the second half of 2009, which is when the Patient Protection and Affordable Care Act of 2010 was debated in Congress,[29] but I am not aware of any attempt to quantify the amount by which the act or related policies would shift labor demand. Economists have recently suggested that extraordinary uncertainty has discouraged employers from hiring,[30] which might also cause real wages to grow less than productivity. A consolidation of goods markets that permitted employers to further mark up prices over marginal cost could affect real unit labor cost. An employer-side distortion could also be the result of an increase in labor supply (such as the increase that might occur when some of the safety net expansions expire) in the face of "sticky" output prices (see Chapter Seven). The employer-side distortion might not be a distortion at all: it could reflect a technological change, or a shift in the composition of production in the direction of less labor-intensive activities. Under any of these interpretations, the employer-side distortion changes might (or might not) be the result of the safety net expansion or redistribution changes more generally, in which case the employer-side distortion should not be held constant for the purpose of simulating outcomes absent redistribution changes.

No matter how the supply residual and employer-side distortions are interpreted, their changes over time are less—usually much less—than the changes in the safety net marginal tax rate series, at least for labor supply elasticities of 0.75 or more. Even with the low-end labor supply elasticity of 0.4, the safety net marginal tax rate changes through 2010 are at least as large as the labor supply residual.

An Investment Distortion by Itself Does Not Fit Actual Behavior

An alternative view of the recession is that labor usage fell, and safety net expenditures increased, as a consequence of an investment spending collapse stemming from the financial crisis, rather than being caused by an expansion of the safety net or by some other labor market distortion. My model has no investment friction, but its components indicate how the economy might evolve if the supply of funds for new investment were curtailed. Suppose for example that gross investment were frozen at zero on the time interval $[0, T]$. As of time T the economy would be on the stable arm of the stationary system shown in Figure 5.1, with a capital stock less than its steady state value. Prior to time T, labor would be low. Close to time o, labor would be low because of an income effect: potential output remains high and none of it is spent on investment. Closer to time T, capital has fallen because of the lack of investment, consumption would have fallen with capital, and labor would be low because labor productivity had fallen with the capital stock. In summary, the time paths for labor usage and productivity would, for a time, be similar to what they are with the sudden and permanent labor distortion studied above, but the time path for consumption would be very different.

Moreover, unlike this example, actual gross investment has not been anywhere close to zero, and my framework offers a straightforward calculation of the effects of investment distortions (a wedge in the consumption Euler equation 5.4 that had no direct effect on the labor market condition 5.5 or the resource constraint 5.1) that were in exactly the right amounts to replicate actual investment. Given an initial capital stock, a path for investment expenditure, and the taste and technology parameters, an investment-distortion equilibrium is a list of time paths on $t \geq 0$ for utility flows, consumption flows, both types of labor, wage rates, and rental rates, such that the paths for utility, consumption, and labor maximize both profits $An_t^\alpha k_t^{1-\alpha} - w_t n_t - r_t k_t$ at each date and also the present discounted value of utility $\int_0^\infty e^{-\rho t} u_t dt$ subject to (5.2) and to the household's sequence of dynamic budget constraints (5.3).[31]

Figure 5.8a's solid curve is the monthly time path for labor usage from December 2007 to April 2011, which is an investment distortion equilibrium given that the model's investment path over this time is exactly equal to the actual investment path, and given the benchmark parameters.[32] The black circles indicate actual labor usage (the same data shown in Figure 5.5a). For the benchmark wage elasticity of labor supply, the model's labor usage declines in 2008 and 2009, with a minor recovery thereafter, but to a much lesser degree than actual labor usage. In the short term, an investment distortion has essentially no effect on the capital stock and thereby reduces labor solely because of an income effect. As the investment distortion persists, the capital stock is reduced: the income effect is smaller, and eventually in the other direction (increasing labor), while low wages tend to reduce labor. The dashed series shows that model predictions are similar if the elasticities η and σ are set to two times their benchmark values, with the rate of time preference adjusted to maintain the steady state investment-output ratio.

Figure 5.8b shows how the investment distortion model predicts reduced labor for the "wrong" reason—increased consumption. Contrary to the investment distortion model, consumption actually fell during the recession.

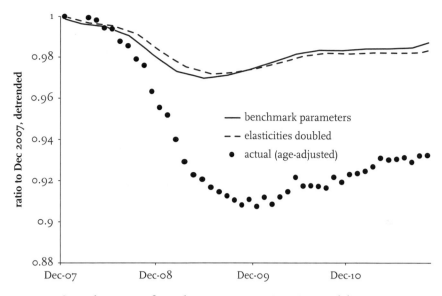

FIGURE 5.8a. Labor Usage from the Investment Distortion Model

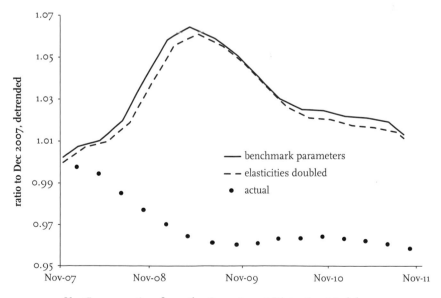

FIGURE 5.8b. Consumption from the Investment Distortion Model

None of these results rule out the possibility that some of the measured investment decline was due to financial frictions. Or still other factors may explain part of the actual investment decline. For example, the option value reasoning of Abel et al. (1996) suggests that, to the extent that additional uncertainty about the efficient amount or composition of capital arose in 2008 and 2009, investment might have fallen even if labor had been constant. Investors may have anticipated an investment tax credit in 2010 and therefore saw investment in 2008 or 2009 as too expensive (Lucas 1976).

Conclusions

Using one of the simplest versions of the neoclassical growth model in which all parameters except the marginal tax rate are constant,[33] this chapter simulates market equilibrium responses to a marginal tax rate that grew steadily during 2008 and 2009 from 40 to about 50 percent. Assuming that the marginal tax rate declined over the next several years (but not all the way to its previous level of 40 percent), and assuming a Frisch wage elasticity of labor supply of 0.75, the model's predictions for labor, consumption, and productivity closely match the data from 2007 through 2011 (the latest data available as of writing).

The model also explains more than half of the actual investment decline as a response to the labor decline. The model's investment series changes are greater than its labor changes in percentage terms, even though the labor declines are not caused by investment changes. The fact that investment is higher in the model than in the data may have a couple of explanations: (1) consumption adjusts immediately in the model, whereas the actual consumption drop of 2008 took several months; and (2) actual productivity did grow during late 2008 and early 2009, but slightly below the trend assumed in the model. Since investment is a small fraction of total spending, these small deviations between model and data consumption and output create larger percentage deviations between model and data investment.

Essentially the same results are obtained with lesser (greater) values for the wage elasticity of labor supply if the marginal tax rate series is assumed to deviate more (less) from 40 percent, respectively.[34] In this sense, much of the aggregate changes in the labor market since 2007 can be interpreted as the result of changes in marginal tax rates or some other impulse with many of the characteristics of marginal tax rate changes.

When the model's marginal tax rate impulse is assumed to follow the marginal tax rate series measured in Chapter Three for safety net programs (and labor income taxes), and the wage elasticity of labor supply is assumed to be 0.75, then model labor dynamics closely resemble the actual aggregate labor dynamics, except that model labor per capita troughs at about 8 percent below December 2007, as compared to almost 10 percent in the data. As noted in Chapter Four, an 8 percent drop as the result of the safety net expansions is roughly in line with a quantitative equilibrium interpretation of micro-econometric studies of the effects of unemployment benefits, once we recognize the array of safety net expansions as captured by Chapter Three's safety net marginal tax rate series. For these reasons, the measured safety net expansions can be interpreted as causing about 80 percent of the decline in labor per capita between the end of 2007 and the end of 2009, with the remainder caused by other impulses that are much less in magnitude, but similar in economic character.

A number of economists thought in 2010 and 2011 that the U.S. economy would enter a second recession as the provisions from the 2009 "stimulus law" expired.[35] The model suggests the opposite: the turning point for labor per capita would occur only when the marginal-tax-rate-increasing provisions of the stimulus law (or some other legislation) began to expire.[36] In fact, the model and the data agree that labor per capita began to increase in early 2010. As long as those expirations were not followed by some other significant safety net expansion, the model says that a double-dip recession would not occur. At least through the end of 2011, the data agree. Despite the contrast with prior recessions, the model and data also agree that labor per capita would not be near prerecession levels any time before the end of 2011—a full four years after the recession began—because marginal tax rates did not return near to prerecession levels by that time.

This chapter also helps characterize the "other impulses" operating during this period. In particular, a gap between productivity and real wages began to appear in the second half of 2009, and it continued to widen through mid-2010. The gap, which has a number of economic interpretations broadly consistent with changes in "labor demand" or "employer-side" distortions, is much less significant than the marginal tax rate changes associated with the safety net expansions, but it still is not negligible. Again assuming a labor supply elasticity of 0.75, the model with the marginal tax rate series combining the safety net marginal tax rates with the employer-side distortions predicts per capita labor dynamics that are similar to actual dynamics (recall Figure 5.6b).

The important model ingredients are the safety net marginal tax rate series from Chapter Three and a value for the wage elasticity η of the supply of aggregate labor hours calibrated from the micro-econometric literature. None of these ingredients is known with several decimal places of accuracy, which is why this chapter displays results with various values for η and various marginal tax rate series. But enough is known about the ingredients to conclude that a large fraction of the labor decline and lack of full recovery since 2007 is the result of safety net expansions. This surprising result raises some of the same objections noted in Chapter Four: that safety net expansions prior to 2007 did not cause recessions, that the added safety net expenditures since 2007 have been small in comparison to the losses people suffered, and that (unlike the recession itself) the safety net expansions were anticipated. The concluding section of Chapter Four explains why these objections point to some important facts, but those facts actually are consistent with the theory featured here and in Chapter Four.

Another objection is that the neoclassical growth model is too simple or too old-fashioned to yield reliable quantitative results, and that it lacks an explicit accounting for job search behavior (Diamond 2010). This objection is incorrect, for several reasons. First, economists need to examine the entire safety net and judge whether its expansions had a significant effect on the labor market. A first examination with a simple model permits attention to be focused on the safety net itself, rather than on economist's assumptions about various auxiliary pieces of the economy. Complexities can be added later. Second, to the extent that search theory has the marginal product of labor and the willingness to work as the primary long-term determinants of employment and the search elements just add dynamics to the process, the first step must be to understand the long-term employment effects of the safety net expansion, and these effects are the primary focus of the neoclassical growth model. Moreover, recent research suggests that the "long term" might not be that long in a search model calibrated to the 2008–09 recession, because actual monthly unemployment rates seem to closely follow the steady state unemployment rate implied by flows into and out of unemployment (Elsby, Hobijn, and Sahin 2010).[37] A related observation is that labor remains depressed more than four years after the recession began. Is it that search takes so long, or that the rewards to a successful search have changed? My approach focuses on the latter.

Third, search theory itself may not yet be ready for quantitative analysis of safety net expansions. Much applied search theory ignores many parts of the social safety net such as food stamps, the modernization of UI eligibility, debt discharges (Herkenhoff and Ohanian 2011 is an exception), and Medicaid. For tractability, many search models shut down one or more of the quantitatively important margins of response to safety net program rules.[38] This book suggests that we can begin to learn about the consequences of safety net expansions even before applied search theory has fully matured.

The model in this chapter rather mechanically links the work hours of "nonprime" members of the population—especially teenagers and the elderly—to the work hours of prime-aged people, and it is therefore probably not well suited for analysis of teen and elderly labor markets. I expect that a proper analysis of those labor markets since 2007 would need to consider their unique marginal tax rate changes, changes in statutory minimum wages, changes in the composition of production, and a possibly different sensitivity of labor supply to wages.

Appendix 5.1: Calibration, Simulation, and Additional Sensitivity Analysis

Aside from the marginal tax rate time path (the topic of Chapter Three), the model has seven parameters to be calibrated (two of which are irrelevant for most of the calculations): labor's share α, the adjusted depreciation rate δ, the adjusted time preference rate ρ, the wage elasticity of labor supply η, the consumption elasticity σ, prime labor's share of prerecession after-tax labor income $1-\left[2+\left(\gamma_m/\gamma_n\right)^\eta/\beta^{n+1}\right]^{-1}$, and the amount Γ of the prime labor time endowment.[39] Labor's share is taken as 0.7, in order to coincide with measured values of the share of employee compensation in nonproprietors' private national income.[40]

The adjusted depreciation rate is taken as a pure depreciation rate minus population growth minus (TFP growth)/α: the rate of gross investment expenditure on a balanced growth path. TFP growth (specifically, real private sector GDP growth adjusted for hours of labor usage and real nonresidential private fixed assets) varied considerably prior to the recession: it averaged 0 percent/year in 2005–2007, 0.3 percent/year 2004–2007, and 1.0 percent/year 2003–2007 (which was also close to its 1.2 percent/year average over longer periods).[41] I use the value of 0.35 percent per year to reflect the likely possibility that, by 2008, TFP growth was expected to be positive, but less than it was in the 1990s and early 2000s. That value implies that per capita consumption grows at 0.5 percent per year in the long term. I also consider alternate TFP growth values corresponding to long-term per capita growth rates of 0 percent/year and 1.0 percent/year.

Model population growth is taken as 1.0 percent per year. The annual pure depreciation rate is taken as 5.5 percent plus 0.5 percent, where the 5.5 percent is the ratio of private fixed asset depreciation per dollar of real private fixed assets in the national accounts. The model's investment is produced with the same technology as consumption goods, so it is best interpreted as investment expenditure deflated with the consumption deflator, and as such it is expected to "depreciate" an additional amount according to the expected rate of decline of the real price of investment goods, which I take to be 0.5 percent per year. The benchmark adjusted depreciation rate is therefore 7.5 percent/year, with alternative values of 7.0 percent/year and 8.0 percent/year depending on the alternative assumed value for expected TFP growth.

Prime labor's share of prerecession after-tax labor income, which matters only for inferring total consumption expenditure $[c + (1-\tau)w\beta m]$ from market consumption expenditure c, is assumed to be 0.9. The amount Γ of the prime time endowment matters only for simulating the equilibrium size of the subsidy budget and is taken to be 1.32, because 76 percent (= 1/1.32) of persons aged twenty-five to sixty-four were employed during any given week in the years before the recession.

The "consumption elasticity" is more precisely the elasticity of consumption growth with respect to the marginal product of capital. Some of the macroeconomics and consumption literature has assumed that this elasticity is necessarily the same as the elasticity of consumption growth with respect to the real return on safe short-term loans, which in some models is closely related to the marginal product of capital. However, the asset pricing literature has shown that the marginal product of capital and the risk-free interest rate often change quite differently, so I stick with the more literal interpretation. Mulligan (2004) finds an elasticity of consumption growth with respect to the (after-tax) marginal product of capital to be about 1.35. This chapter also reports sensitivity analysis using an alternative value of $\sigma = 0.68$.[42]

The model's steady state ratio of consumption to output is, adjusted to include the output of the nonprime workers,

$$\frac{\dfrac{\alpha\delta+\rho}{\delta+\rho}+(1-\tau)\alpha\dfrac{\theta}{1-\theta}}{1+(1-\tau)\alpha\dfrac{\theta}{1-\theta}}$$

where θ is the share of after-tax labor income going to prime labor. I choose the adjusted rate of time preference ρ to be 0.5 percent/year so that the consumption output ratio is 73 percent as in the data in the second half of 2007.

My benchmark values are 0.75 for the labor supply elasticity, 1.35 for the intertemporal elasticity of substitution of consumption, and 0.5 percent per year for long-term per capita growth. With these values, a two-year increase of

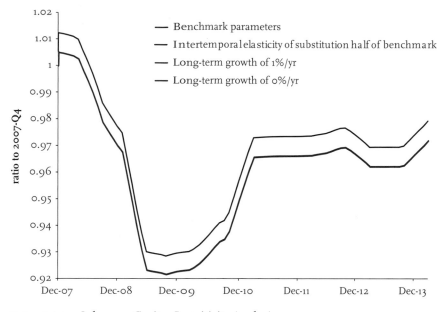

FIGURE 5.9a. Labor per Capita: Sensitivity Analysis

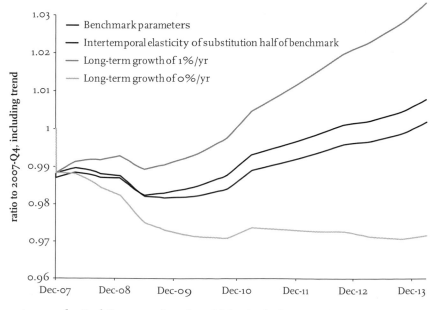

FIGURE 5.9b. Real Consumption: Sensitivity Analysis

the marginal tax rate by about 8 percentage points explains much of the labor decline over the first two years of the recession (see Figure 5.6b). The red series in Figures 5.9a and 5.9b are simulated for the baseline parameters (all series assume the safety-net-only marginal tax rate scenario), and the black series is for an intertemporal elasticity of consumption σ assumed to be half of its baseline value. Both have quite similar changes over time, but the low σ version has a greater initial jump in labor hours because (Figure 5.9a), with σ low, forgone leisure is a better way than forgone consumption to save for temporarily high distortions. The low σ version has consumption follow its trend (which depends on TFP growth, not σ) more closely, as shown in Figure 5.9b.

Labor results are quite insensitive to the assumed long-term growth rate, as shown in Figure 5.9a. I simulate the model once with long per capita growth of 1.0 percent per year and the other benchmark parameters, and a second time with zero long-term growth. The resulting two labor series were so close to the benchmark labor series that I color all three in red in Figure 5.9a.

Consumption results are more sensitive to assumptions about TFP growth, as shown in Figure 5.9b, because TFP growth determines the long-term trend. As compared to Figure 5.5b, which displays multiple simulations with the same long-term trend on a single detrended scale, the series in Figure 5.9b have three long-term trends (0 percent per year, 0.5 percent per year, and 1.0 percent per year) and are therefore displayed with their trends.

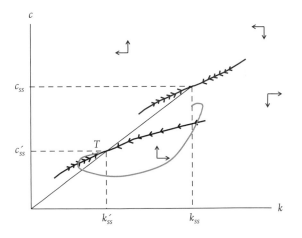

FIGURE 5.10. Dynamics when the MTR Increase is Largely Temporary
The Figure shows the system's dynamics and stable arm. The dynamics shown by the red arrows correspond to the low tax rate that prevailed before date 0. When the new tax rate path is first anticipated at date 0, consumption falls, but not as far as it will fall in the long term. The new stable arm (shown as a black path) describes dynamics once the tax rate has reached its higher long-term value.

Two kinds of model dynamics are possible depending on how much the peak marginal tax rate exceeds its long-term value. If the peak is not too much above the long-term value (i.e., the marginal tax rate's time path is sufficiently close to monotonic), then the dynamics are like Figure 5.2's light red curve except that the path in the $[k,c]$ plane approaches the stable arm of the stationary system with the long-term marginal tax rate from below. As for the path shown in Figure 5.2, this one has consumption and capital falling as time T approaches, and there is never a time during which capital is rising from a value below its initial one.

If the marginal tax rate's peak is high enough relative to its long-term value, capital will drop below its long-term value for some time subinterval of $[0,T]$. In this case, consumption and capital reach their lows before time T and are rising thereafter.[43] Figure 5.10 shows a time path for this case in the $[k,c]$ plane.

Time paths were simulated in three steps. First, the stable arm for the stationary system having the initial (long-term) marginal tax rate was calculated by numerically solving the ordinary differential equation in k (5.9) evaluated at the initial (long-term) marginal tax rate, respectively, using the steady state as the boundary condition. Second, I guessed a time T point on the stable arm for the stationary system having the long-term marginal tax rate and numerically solved the dynamical system (5.1) and (5.4), which is nonstationary because the marginal tax rate varies with time, backwards T time units.[44] I then checked whether the simulated capital stock k corresponded to the initial steady state capital stock, and if not I repeated the procedure after taking as my guess another point on the stable arm for the stationary system having the long-term marginal tax rate. Third, dynamics in the time dimension after time T were simulated by numerically integrating the capital accumulation equation (5.1), imposing that consumption be on the stable arm for the stationary system having the long-term marginal tax rate.

6

Cross-Sectional Patterns of Employment and Hours Changes

ON AVERAGE, THE replacement rates offered by safety net programs increased significantly since 2007. But the various expansions of means-tested programs are more relevant for some people than for others. In theory, employment and hours worked should fall more for groups of people for which safety net program expansions resulted in larger reductions in their log self-reliance rates,[1] because the employed among them (and their employers, jointly) have less to gain in percentage terms from continuing their employment relationship and the nonemployed among them have less to gain in percentage terms from starting a new job. Groups of people, if any, with no self-reliance rate changes should, on average, have increased their employment or hours worked, because wages and labor productivity have increased, and perceived wealth decreased, since 2007.

Simply put, the expanding safety net not only distorts the total amount of labor but also distorts the composition of the workforce. The purpose of this chapter is to test this theory versus the alternative hypotheses that (1) the recession uniformly reduced employment and hours for all demographic groups, or (2) the recession reduced employment and hours for all, although in amounts related to the group's average human capital.

The chapter begins by examining the degree to which log self-reliance rate changes vary by demographic group and region. Self-reliance rate changes tended to be less for persons who were capable of earning a lot. Self-reliance rate changes were also less for members of dual-earner households, or members of households without children, because they were less likely to qualify for a number of safety net programs even if they were not working. Self-reliance rate changes were also less, if not zero, for elderly people.

The second half of the chapter examines the relationship across groups between employment or work hours changes and proxies for log changes in the self-reliance rate, as well as proxies for labor demand changes. One finding is that hours per capita tended to fall more for less educated groups. A more surprising finding is that work hours fell significantly less for married people, even when controlling for race, schooling, age, region and other variables related to demographics and industry. The marital status gap is especially large among women. The education pattern of work hours changes varies by marital status, as predicted by my theory that log self-reliance rate changes created many of the cross-sectional patterns of work hours changes during the recession.

Cross-Sectional Patterns of Self-Reliance Rate Changes
Patterns by Income and Marital Status

Chapter Three's statutory replacement rate series is measured for a nonelderly household head or spouse who, if not underemployed or without a job, would earn $692 per week, which is what the median nonelderly working household head or spouse earned in 2007. Some people do, or can, earn more than $692 per week (hereafter, "high skilled"), and others necessarily earn less even when they work full-time (hereafter, "low skilled"). The replacement rate changes are different for high- and low-skilled workers, and they also vary by household composition.

Recall that the replacement rate is the amount of benefits received as a consequence of not working, expressed as a ratio to the amount produced when working. Holding constant worker characteristics, the replacement rate changes over time because of changes in the amount of benefits received as a consequence of not working. One example is the addition of $25 per week of unemployment benefits by the American Reinvestment and Recovery Act's Federal Additional Compensation provision: the provision added to benefits received by program participants and thereby caused the replacement rate to be greater after the ARRA than before it for anyone who would be eligible for benefits when they were not working. However, the magnitude of the effect of Federal Additional Compensation on the replacement rate differs for high- and low-skill workers: it is inversely proportional to the amount produced when working because the replacement rate change is the ratio of the benefit change ($25 per week) to the amount produced when working. Results are similar for any other benefit change that is a fixed dollar amount, or close to it, such as the federal income tax exclusion for UI benefits, and COBRA subsidies.

Another reason that replacement rate changes differ for high- and low-skill workers is that the amount of some of the benefit changes with income.[2] For example, the weekly amount of unemployment benefits tends to be proportional to earnings on the previous job, up to a cap.[3] Among workers whose prior earnings put them below the cap, additional weeks of unemployment compensation would add to benefits received roughly in proportion to the amount they produce when working, thereby adding roughly the same amount to the replacement rate. Among workers whose prior earnings put them at the cap, additional weeks of unemployment compensation add a fixed dollar amount (namely, the dollar amount of the cap) to benefits and, like federal additional compensation, add to the replacement rate an amount that is inversely proportional to the amount produced when working.

Chapter Three assumes that safety net benefits were zero unless a person was not employed or underemployed. The assumption is accurate for someone capable of earning about $700 per week, or more, because $700 per week is roughly twice the federal poverty guideline, above which households usually cannot pass the income tests required for program eligibility. Even someone working forty hours per week at the minimum wage—earning only $290 per week—would not be in poverty (by the federal definition) if his spouse was earning more than $100 per week on her own. But a sole earner earning only $290 per week would have household income below the federal poverty guideline and thereby could be eligible for, say, Medicaid regardless of employment status, and therefore Medicaid benefits would not contribute to the replacement rate as they do for higher-skilled workers.

A full-time minimum wage worker who was a sole earner would also be eligible for SNAP (food stamps), although the amount of the benefit would be greater if weekly earnings were below $290.[4] A proper calculation of the contribution of SNAP to the numerator of the replacement rate for such a worker is therefore the difference between SNAP benefits received when not working and SNAP benefits received when working. This difference is about 30 percent of the $290 that could be earned.[5] The difference was essentially unchanged when SNAP benefit levels were increased, although its contribution to the numerator of the replacement rate is proportional to the statutory SNAP eligibility index.

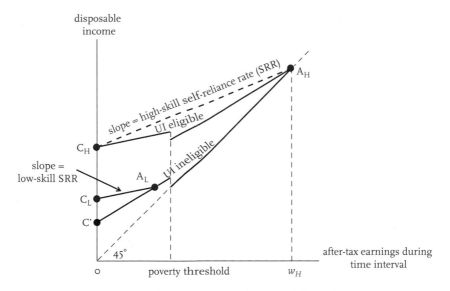

FIGURE 6.1 Measuring Self-Reliance Rates for Two Skill Levels

The result for sole earners can be derived from Figure 6.1's budget set diagram, showing the relationship between a head or spouse's after-tax earnings from employment (horizontal axis) and the earner's disposable income available after receiving safety net benefits (vertical axis), for a specific time interval, such as a quarter, six months, or calendar year. The dashed 45 degree line indicates the possibilities available for a member of a household ineligible for any safety net benefits; his or her disposable income during the time interval is exactly equal to after-tax earnings. The point A_H indicates the outcome for a high-skill person who works full-time throughout the time interval. The point is on the 45 degree line because that person's unemployment benefits would be zero (working throughout) and income would be too much to qualify for means-tested benefits such as SNAP or Medicaid.

If we assume for the moment that the high-skill person is UI eligible throughout the time interval, the point C_H indicates the outcome if the person were unemployed throughout the time interval. The point C_H is above the 45 degree line—disposable income exceeds after-tax earnings—because the household possibly receives benefits from SNAP, Medicaid, and other means-tested programs. The point's exact height depends on the amount of benefits available from each program, the household's probability of participating in them, and a discount (if any) for the value of in-kind benefits such as Medicaid. Ignoring taxes and fringe benefits for the moment, the self-reliance rate measured in Chapter Three is the slope of the straight dashed red line connecting A_H and C_H, where, for the purposes of that chapter, the two points were evaluated for the median employed household head or spouse (without regard for whether they were dual earners or sole earners). Those two points alone show how the self-reliance rate tends to be greater for higher-skill persons: holding fixed the point C_H, the point A_H is further from the origin the greater is the person's ability to earn income, and the red dashed line's slope is greater.

The solid red segments between A_H and C_H indicate the possibilities or "budget set" for a UI-eligible high-skill person who works only part of the time interval. If the person were employed enough that income for the time interval exceeded the poverty line, the segment to the right applies because the household receives UI but is not eligible for SNAP or Medicaid.[6] If earnings for the interval were below the poverty threshold, the household would be eligible for UI as well as means-tested subsidies, and the slope of the budget set would be less because earning in that range reduces both UI benefits and SNAP benefits.[7] The various slopes of the budget set show how there is no single definition of "marginal tax rate"; the definition used in Chapter Three and in this chapter is the slope of the red dashed line capturing the average slope along the entire budget set.[8]

If the high-skill person were not eligible for UI, then the budget set would be the two black line segments. Without UI, the budget set coincides with the 45 degree line above the poverty threshold, and it exceeds the 45 degree line below it according to the amounts received from SNAP, Medicaid, and other means-tested programs. The point C′ indicates disposable income for a UI-ineligible high-skill person who has no earnings during the time interval. The self-reliance rate for this person could be calculated as the slope of the straight line (not shown in Figure 6.1) connecting the points C′ and A_H. Comparing that high-skill self-reliance rate with the self-reliance rate shown in Figure 6.1 shows how an UI-eligibility expansion reduces the self-reliance rate: it shifts the zero earnings point from C′ to C_H for persons who become eligible.

The point A_L in Figure 6.1 indicates the outcome for a low-skill person who works full-time throughout the time interval. Unlike the point A_H, the point A_L is above the 45 degree line because the low-skill person qualifies for SNAP, Medicaid, and other means-tested programs regardless of how much she works. The point C_L indicates the outcome for a UI-eligible low-skill person who has no earnings during the time interval. It is above the point C′ because it includes both UI benefits and other means-tested benefits. The self-reliance rate for a low-skill UI-eligible person is therefore the slope of the line segment connecting the points A_L and C_L.

An increase in the maximum SNAP benefit, or an expansion of SNAP eligibility, shifts the points C', C_L, A_L, and C_H, up in Figure 6.1 by the amount of the (eligibility-adjusted) benefit increase, but it has no effect on the point A_H. For this reason, the SNAP maximum benefit amount and SNAP eligibility expansions reduce the high-skill self-reliance rate but have no effect on the low-skill self-reliance rate. This is important in explaining why changes in the self-reliance rate since 2007 could be somewhat less for the low-skilled than for some of the persons who are capable of earning beyond the poverty threshold.

Assuming that essentially all household heads and spouses would earn at least $290 per week if they worked full-time, the self-reliance rate $SRRS$ in 2007-Q4 and 2009-Q4 for a single-earner household can be calculated as a function of potential weekly earnings y (that is, the weekly income that would be earned if working full-time) using formula (6.1):[9]

$$
\begin{aligned}
SRRS_t(y) \equiv 1 - \frac{T}{1.234} - \frac{\omega_{UI}E_{UI,t}\left[12B_{UI,t}/52 - 270 + \min\{yr, 400\}\right]}{1.234y} - \frac{\omega_{debt}E_{debt,t}B_{debt}}{1.234^*727}\frac{12}{52} \\
- \left[1 - I\left(y \leq FPG/52\right)\right]\frac{12}{52}\frac{\omega_{SNAP}E_{SNAP,t}M_{SNAP,t} + \omega_{Medicaid}B_{Medicaid} + \omega_{other}B_{other}}{1.234y} \\
- I\left(y \leq FPG/52\right)\left\{\frac{\left[\omega_{SNAP}E_{SNAP,t} + \omega_{other}B_{other}/M_{SNAP,2007}\right](y - y_{SNAP})}{1.234y}0.3\right\}
\end{aligned}
\tag{6.1}
$$

where t indexes time (2007-Q4 and 2009-Q4) and y is no less than $290. All dollar amounts in equation (6.1) are in fiscal year 2010 dollars in order to be comparable with Chapter Three's results. T is the combined rate of payroll and income taxation, assumed to be 25.3 percent prior to January 2011. It is divided by the economywide ratio of employee compensation to wages paid, 1.234, because the self-reliance rate is defined to be a ratio to marginal labor productivity, not to weekly earnings. For the same reason, weekly earnings y is scaled by the same factor in the denominator of equation (6.1)'s remaining ratio terms.

As in Chapter Three, ω_j denotes the program weight for program j, $E_{j,t}$ is the program's time t eligibility index, and $B_{j,t}$ is its time t monthly benefit index.[10] Their product indicates the amount received from the program, as a consequence of not working, by an average marginal worker with median earnings. The factor 12/52 converts monthly amounts to weekly amounts.

The second ratio term in equation (6.1) calculates unemployment insurance and related benefits (COBRA subsidies, etc.) for a UI eligible person with prior weekly income of y. r is the ratio of the weekly unemployment benefit to prior weekly earnings, assumed to be 40 percent for persons below the UI cap. The UI cap is assumed to be $400 per week, and $270 is the weekly UI benefit (not including related programs) for an eligible unemployed person with prior earnings equal to the median. The third ratio term in equation (6.1) is the contribution of mortgage modification and consumer debt discharges to the self-reliance rate, assumed to be independent of potential weekly income y.

The second line of equation (6.1) applies only to potential incomes above the federal poverty guideline (FPG); $I(\cdot)$ is a 0–1 indicator for whether y is less than FPG on a weekly basis. Such a person does not qualify for Medicaid, SNAP, or other means-tested programs when working full-time. The SNAP benefit received by a participating sole-earner household with no earnings is the statutory maximum SNAP benefit $M_{SNAP,t}$, rather than the SNAP benefit index $B_{SNAP,t}$ used in Chapter Three.[11]

The final line of equation (6.1) applies only to potential incomes below the FPG. As shown in Figure 6.1, the self-reliance rate for persons who cannot earn above the FPG must be adjusted for the fact that they receive some of the means-tested benefits even when they are working full-time. For them, the SNAP penalty for working is the subtraction of its net income (y_{SNAP} is the average deduction taken by SNAP households in fiscal year 2010) from SNAP benefits at approximately a 30 percent rate, as reflected in the SNAP term in the last line of equation (6.1). Medicaid program participation is assumed to be independent of income for any employed single earner with income below the FPG, which is why the final line of equation (6.1) has no Medicaid term. The "other means-tested programs" are assumed to be phased out continuously with income at the same rate that SNAP is.

Figure 6.2 shows the results of the application of formula (6.1) for 2007-Q4 and 2009-Q4 (left axis, on a log scale), and their log difference (right axis). The figure's horizontal axis measures the "potential" amount that would be earned per week if working full-time. In either quarter, the self-reliance rate generally increases with potential earnings, except when potential earnings fall below the poverty line so that means-tested subsidies are available even when working full-time. The rate of increase of the self-reliance rate with potential earnings changes abruptly at $1,000 per week, because

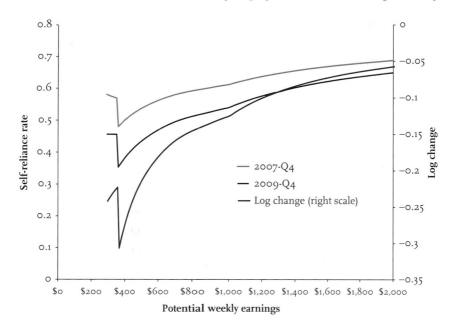

FIGURE 6.2 Self-Reliance Rates, and Changes, as a Function of Earnings Potential (sole earners)

that's about where unemployment insurance benefits hit the cap. An important result for the purpose of examining cross-sectional patterns of self-reliance rates is that log self-reliance rate changes are greatest for someone capable of earning an income that is near but above the FPG—even greater than the changes for the (relatively few) sole earners not capable of earning above FPG.[12]

The prerecession replacement rate level was the greatest, and self-reliance rate the least, for households that would earn between the FPG and about 200 percent of FPG (Holt and Romich 2007), the latter of which is close to the 2007 median earnings of a full-time employed nonelderly head or spouse. In this case, the effect on the log self-reliance rate of an increase in safety net benefits that was proportional to earnings potential (extending UI benefit durations are an example) would be particularly large. The log self-reliance rate effect of a fixed dollar addition to safety net benefits (as with food stamps) would also be large for this group, especially for households nearer to the FPG than to 200 percent FPG.

For a person with a spouse whose income exceeds FPG by itself, the replacement rate is simpler because the household necessarily earns over the poverty line regardless of whether this person works, holding the spouse's income constant. The self-reliance rate SRRD for a member of such a dual-earner household just depends on taxes, unemployment insurance benefits, and debt forgiveness:

$$SRRD_t(y) \equiv 1 - \frac{T}{1.234} - \frac{\omega_{UI}E_{UI,t}\min\{yr,400\}}{1.234y} - \frac{\omega_{debt}E_{debt,t}B_{debt}}{1.234^*727}\frac{12}{52} \quad (6.2)$$

To put it differently, the sole-earner self-reliance rate SRRS is SSRD minus terms that account for the effect of access to income-tested programs on the reward for working.

Figure 6.3 compares the self-reliance rate change schedules for the aforementioned single- and dual-earner households.[13] With the exception of the relatively few sole-earner household heads who are not capable of earning above FPG, the two schedules have essentially the same shape, except that the sole earner schedule is below the dual earner schedule and has a steeper slope. Thus, if hours worked by sole earners and dual earners were equally sensitive to their log self-reliance rate, then hours worked should fall more between 2007-Q4 and 2009-Q4 for sole earners and the amount of the drop should be more sensitive to potential earnings for the sole earners because their self-reliance rate change varies more with potential earnings.[14]

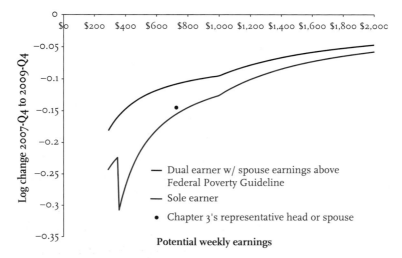

FIGURE 6.3 Self-Reliance Rate Changes for Single and Dual-Earner Households

Safety Net Rules Affected Even High-Skill Workers

As shown in Figure 6.3, the self-reliance rate fell between 2007-Q4 and 2009-Q4 even for persons with high earnings potential. At $2,000 per week—a "six figure" salary on an annual basis—the log self-reliance rate fell 0.05 for a dual earner with spousal earnings above the federal poverty guideline, and 0.06 for a sole earner. A detailed analysis of the labor market for high-skilled people would refine these self-reliance rate measures to account for factors especially important for that group, such as the asset tests for Medicaid and other means-tested programs, but the result remains that program rule changes somewhat reduced the gains that high-skill people obtain from working.

Readers of this book are typically high-skilled people, and they might conclude from their personal experience that means-tested government subsidies, and perhaps even means-tested mortgage forgiveness and loan discharges, are irrelevant for the work decisions of high-skill people. As a rough approximation, I agree with such a conclusion, for the same reason that a value of −0.05 shown in Figure 6.3 can be roughly approximated as zero. But a more accurate analysis must recognize that means-tested government subsidies are a real part of the lives of a small minority of high-skilled people.

Take, for example, household heads aged twenty-five to sixty-four with a professional school degree beyond college, such as a medical degree, law degree, or master of business administration degree. According to the U.S. Census Bureau's Annual Demographic Survey, 5 percent of these people had someone in their household participating in the Medicaid program sometime during 2007. Almost 1 percent received SNAP benefits sometime during the year, while UI receipt was quite rare. In 2010, 6 percent received Medicaid, more than 1 percent received SNAP, and 3 percent received UI. These percentages are small, but not zero, which means that the high-skill employment effects of the safety net expansions since 2007 should be, in theory, small but not zero.

Patterns by Age and Region

UI and related expansions are less relevant for elderly persons, for a couple of reasons. One of them is that pension income often counts against UI benefits, so that UI benefits for pensioners are small or zero.[15] Medicare is a federal health insurance program for the elderly, available regardless of whether they work or not. The elderly can also receive cash Social Security benefits when they are working. Because the replacement rate depends on the difference between safety net benefits received when not working and safety net benefits received when working, Medicare and Social Security contribute essentially zero to the elderly replacement rate and thereby nothing to its changes since 2007. Moreover, the benefits received from Social Security and Medicare, not to mention lifetime wealth accumulations, render many of the elderly ineligible for means-tested programs, and therefore not directly affected by the recent expansions in such programs.

Mortgage discharges are more likely in states that experienced larger cycles in residential property values. Mortgages tend to be a greater fraction of income for younger homeowners than for older ones, because younger homeowners have less income and have had less time to accumulate home equity. Entering the recession with lower amounts of home equity, higher ratios of mortgage payments to income, and fewer financial assets for lenders to seize probably made young homeowners more likely to be eligible for mortgage forgiveness, and elderly homeowners less likely. Young adults probably stood to gain more from consumer debt discharges too, because of greater ratios of consumer loan debt to income, and lower amounts of financial assets. Considering age and region simultaneously, and holding income and marital status constant (see above), the young people in large housing cycle states should experience the largest replacement rate changes, whereas replacement rate changes for the elderly are small, or zero, in all states. The replacement rate changes for young people in small housing cycle states should be in between changes for the elderly and changes for young people in large housing cycle states.

Youths—people under twenty-five, especially those who are not head of household or spouse—are a third group to consider. Their replacement rate changes are likely much different from, and maybe less than, those I have shown for household heads and spouses. For one, their employment and earnings histories are many times too limited to qualify for unemployment insurance even under the modernized eligibility criteria. The incomes of people who are not household head or spouse may technically count toward the household income tests of some of the means-tested programs, although it seems likely that such provisions might be loosely enforced because of the additional information-gathering costs and the likely small amounts involved.

A full analysis of the labor market for youths and teenagers is beyond the scope of this book. I suspect that, because of their low skill levels, teenagers usually could not replace adults whose work hours were eliminated or reduced during the recession, so that the net result of events in the adult labor market since 2007 would be to reduce the demand for teenage labor, even if minimum wages remained constant.[16] In addition, the federal minimum wage was hiked three times, and this differentially affects teenagers.[17] Persons under twenty-five who were not heads of household or spouses do not contribute much to aggregate work hours and did not contribute much to the change in aggregate work hours. But youths are an important part of aggregate unemployment statistics, and for this reason a fuller analysis of their labor market could contribute to our understanding of the aggregate business cycle.

Work Hours Changes by Demographic Group and Region

Female Work Hours Fell More Among the Unmarried

According to the U.S. Census Bureau's 2005–2007 monthly CPS Merged Outgoing Rotation Groups micro samples (hereafter, CPS-MORG), the average weekly work hours of unmarried female household heads aged twenty-five to sixty-four fell from 27.4 in 2005–2007 to 25.2 in 2010. Among married female household heads and spouses, the change over the same time frame was from 23.2 to 22.7. Measuring the change in weekly hours, I find that the marital status gap among female household heads and spouses is 1.6. If the change is measured in percentage points, the gap is 6.3, which is almost as large as the entire peak-to-trough decline in hours per capita among household heads and spouses (recall Table 3.1).

Marital status is correlated with other demographic variables that could be related to hours changes during recessions. In order to control for such variables, I first took the CPS-MORG samples of female household heads and spouses and regressed weekly work hours on indicator variables for marital status, white, state of residence, month of year, the interaction of an age quartic with educational attainment, and the interaction of educational attainment and presence of children under eighteen. I used the coefficients from this regression to assign lagged demographic group hours to each of the female household heads and spouses sampled in 2010. I then regressed weekly work hours in the 2010 sample minus lagged demographic group hours on the same vector of demographic variables. The marital status coefficient of 1.4 from this regression can be interpreted as the marital status gap in the 2005–2007 to 2010 weekly work hours change, controlling for the demographic variables.

Marital status is also correlated with industry of employment, but in the wrong direction to explain the marital status gap in the hours change. Controlling for the demographic variables noted above, married women were more likely to be employed in construction during 2005–2007. I also measured the 2005–2007 to 2010 log change in every three-digit industry's work hours per female household head or spouse. The cross-industry average of this industry log hours change is more negative (by the amount 0.002) when each industry is weighted by the number of married women it employed than it is when each industry is weighted by the number of unmarried women it employed.

Employment and hours tended to fall more among less-skilled people (that is, people with less human capital or ability to earn) during prior recessions, and that qualitative pattern continued during this recession. However, the correlation between marital status and labor market skill cannot explain much of the marital status gap among women. Unmarried women probably have more cumulative work experience because their weekly work hours per capita before the recession exceeded that for married women by 18 percent.[18] Unmarried women have less schooling on average, but if we hold constant the demographic variables cited above, the marital status gap in weekly earnings among women working full-time during at least one of the weeks of 2005–2007 was about $5, or less than 1 percent. In other words, industry and skill by themselves suggest that work hours would fall more among married women, at least when the other demographic variables are held constant.

Work hours increased more among married women than unmarried women during the years prior to the recession. For example, average weekly work hours changed 0.0 from 2002–2004 to 2005–2007 among unmarried female household heads, whereas they increased 0.4 among married female heads or spouses. If a prior trend is expected to continue through the recession, then it might explain a small part of the marital status gap among women in the hours change since 2005–2007.

Prior business cycles have exhibited an "added worker effect": married women who joined the labor force because their husbands lost their jobs.[19] An added worker effect might help explain why average work hours fell less among married people, and fell less among women. However, the added worker effect is too small to explain much of the marital status gap noted above. For one, at least three-quarters of married women were already working and therefore could not have begun work when their husband became unemployed. Second, estimates of the added worker effect in 2009 are about two wives for every hundred husbands who become unemployed (Mattingly and Smith 2010).

In summary, female work hours fell significantly more during the recession among unmarried women than they did among married women. This result does not appear to be a consequence of other demographic variables, skill, or industry factors that are correlated with marital status. Moreover, these patterns are expected given that log self-reliance rates fell more for unmarried women.

Marital Status Interacted with Skill, Through the Lens of Self-Reliance Rates

For the purposes of this book, marital status is of interest primarily because it is correlated with changes in the log self-reliance rate. Because log self-reliance rate changes were greater for low-skill people, especially among sole earners with the potential to earn somewhat more than FPG (only a small fraction of sole earners are not capable of earning more than FPG), work hours should have declined more for low-skill people, especially among sole earners. In the relatively few instances in which a sole earner's earning potential is less than FPG, and those earners are otherwise eligible for means-tested programs (e.g., they have children living in their household), then the log self-reliance rate change is less and work hours should decline less. In order to examine the empirical relationship between changes in work hours and log self-reliance rates, I used the monthly CPS-MORG to measure work hours by demographic group and state since January 2007 and to construct proxies for skill.

One of the building blocks of my analysis is prerecession log earnings among nonelderly household heads and spouses by demographic group, which I measure as the fitted value from a regression of log weekly earnings on indicator variables for white; state of residence; month of year; the interaction of an age quartic with educational attainment and sex; the interaction of educational attainment, sex, and presence of children under eighteen; and all interacted with married (spouse present). The log earnings regression sample is household heads and spouses aged twenty-five to sixty-four at work full-time and included in at least one of the January 2005 through December 2007 waves of the CPS-MORG. I interpret these fitted values as proxies for average potential earnings: what the average person in each demographic group would earn in 2005 to 2007 if he or she worked full-time.[20]

Hours changes for demographic groups are measured as average hours in 2010 minus average prerecession hours in 2005–2007, including zero hours for all persons not at work during the CPS reference week.[21] The average prerecession hours are measured as the fitted values from a regression of hours at work during the survey reference week on the same independent variables cited above, using a sample of all household heads and spouses aged twenty-five to sixty-four and included in at least one of the January 2005 through December 2007 waves of the CPS-MORG. Per capita employment and unemployment changes are calculated in the same way from labor force status indicator variables. All of my calculations are weighted with the CPS-MORG "final weight."

Log self-reliance rate changes between 2007 and 2010 were different for sole earners who, aside from the income test, were otherwise eligible for means-tested programs than they were for dual earners who would not be eligible for means-tested programs even if they were not working. The CPS-MORG does not include measures of characteristics precise enough to form a sample of either of these groups, but it does permit the formation of samples that would be good proxies for them. In particular, I took the sample of nonelderly women who do not have a spouse present in their household but do have at least one child under eighteen there (hereafter, "single mothers"), and the sample of nonelderly married (with spouse present) women with no children under eighteen in the household. Single mothers are much more likely than the latter sample to be eligible for SNAP, Medicaid, and other means-tested government programs when not working because (1) they do not have a spouse present whose income by itself would likely put household income above FPG and (2) the latter group has no children (children are the target of a number of means-tested programs). Thus, I expect the relationship between log self-reliance rate changes and earnings potential, and therefore the relationship between hours changes and earnings potential, to resemble Figure 6.3's red series for the single mothers and to resemble the figure's black series for the married women without children. Among other things, the hours changes should be more negative for the single mothers, and the hours changes for the two groups of women should be closer at high incomes, and at incomes below FPG, than they are in the middle income range.[22]

Figure 6.4 shows the results, with the two groups of nonelderly women broken into subgroups by their years of schooling.[23] The red data points are for single mothers, and the black data points for married women without children. Each data point is labeled with the number of years of schooling of the sample members represented by it. As expected, the hours changes measured on the vertical axis are generally more negative for single mothers, even when we control for the amount these women typically earned when they worked full-time in 2005–2007 (measured on the horizontal axis using the methodology cited above).[24] Not surprisingly, women with more schooling tend to earn more, which is why the higher schooling data points are to the right in Figure 6.4. Perhaps more surprising, and consistent with the theory, is that

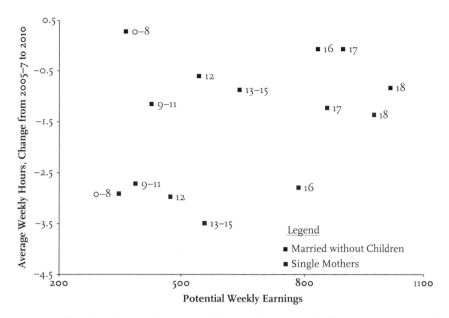

FIGURE 6.4 Female Work Hours Changes by Household Composition and Education

the relationship across schooling groups between hours changes and potential earnings is stronger among the single mothers, especially among those with potential earnings above FPG (schooling groups thirteen to fifteen and higher). More surprising still, and again consistent with the theory, is that the hours changes among single mothers with a high school diploma or less, who tend to earn below FPG,[25] were the same as or greater than hours changes for single mothers with thirteen to sixteen years of schooling. The nonmonotone earnings relationship shown for log self-reliance rate changes in Figure 6.3 (red series) resembles the pattern traced out in Figure 6.4 for the single mothers hours change data.

Proxies for earnings potential such as age or schooling are often found to be correlated with work hours changes during recessions, with the most-skilled groups having less cyclical work hours than less-skilled groups. That general pattern is found in the 2008–09 recession too and is sometimes interpreted as evidence that the demand for low-skilled labor varies more over the business cycle, or that low-skilled groups are more elastic to economic conditions than most workers are. Figure 6.4 shows a pattern like that for single mothers (red squares), because hours changes among single mothers are less negative for those with seventeen or eighteen years of schooling.

However, the education-hours change relationship is not particularly strong among married women without children (black squares). One interpretation of Figure 6.4 is that the elasticity of hours changes with respect to changes in the safety net vary more with potential earnings among single mothers than among married women without children because the former group has more access to safety net benefits.

It is difficult to find additional sizeable samples of household heads or spouses expected to earn below the poverty line and be eligible for means-tested subsidies, and therefore difficult to further test for the non-monotone relationship shown in Figure 6.3's red series.[26] However, more data are available for testing the other prediction that work hours fell more among low-skill people, especially among unmarried medium-to-low-skill people whose household income would fall below the poverty line if they stopped working. Table 6.1 is based on a sample of all household heads and spouses ages twenty-five to sixty-one found in the January 2005 to December 2007 or January 2010 to December 2010 waves of the CPS-MORG. Each column of the table is a regression, with dependent variable equal to average hours worked during the reference week (or, in the last two columns, labor force status multiplied by 100), including zeros for anyone not at work that week, minus the average weekly hours worked (or labor force status) in 2005–2007. The overall sample average weekly hours worked was 30.8 in 2005–2007 and 28.8 in 2010, which is a drop of 6.4 percent. The unit of observation in the regression is a demographic group, as explained further below.

In addition to the indicator variable for marital status, the independent variable of primary interest is the log dual-earner self-reliance rate change from 2007-Q4 to 2009-Q4. The first step in constructing the variable is to calculate the log change over those eight quarters for household heads and spouses working full-time, using formula (6.2) evaluated at y equal to their actual weekly earnings.[27] As I did with log earnings itself, I calculate demographic group averages by regressing the log self-reliance rate change on indicator variables for white, state of residence, month of year, the interaction of an age quartic with educational attainment and sex, and the interaction of educational attainment, sex, and presence of children under 18—all interacted with married (spouse present)—and then projecting fitted values for all sampled household heads and spouses, even those not working full-time. As a result each demographic group is assigned the average log change in the self-reliance rate for its members, which varies in the sample only because earnings vary across demographic groups.

None of the demographic groups, even the married ones, are entirely dual or secondary earners in the sense of equation (6.2) because some of the spouses may not be capable of earning, or willing to earn, over FPG. Nevertheless, the incidence of sole earners should be more common among unmarried groups than among married, and as a result log self-reliance rate changes should vary more with potential earnings among unmarried persons with potential income above FPG than among married persons (see Figure 6.3). For this reason, two additional independent variables are the log change in the dual-earner self-reliance rate interacted with unmarried and potential weekly earnings less than \$400, and unmarried and potential weekly earnings greater than or equal to \$400.[28] Table 6.1's regression model is (6.3):

$$X_i(\theta_{n,2010}-\theta_{n,2007})= \beta_1(X_i\theta_{r,2007})+\beta_2(X_i\theta_{r,2007})(\text{no spouse}_i)(X_i\theta_{y,2007}\geq 400)$$
$$+\beta_3(X_i\theta_{r,2007})(\text{no spouse}_i)(X_i\theta_{y,2007}<400)+\beta_4(\text{no spouse}_i) \quad (6.3)$$
$$+\beta_5(X_i\theta_{y,2007}<400)+\beta_6(\text{no spouse}_i)(X_i\theta_{y,2007}<400)+Z_i\lambda+\varepsilon$$

where i indexes demographic groups: the cross-product of educational attainment, sex, spouse present, children present, age (in years), state of residence, race, and month of interview. X_i is the vector of i's demographic characteristics noted above (including state fixed effects), and Z_i is a vector made up of a constant, four powers of age minus 40, an indicator of the types of industries in which the demographic groups were employed in 2005–2007, and three indicators of prerecession economic conditions in i's state of residence (see below). $\theta_{n,2007}$ is a vector of coefficients from the regression of a scalar labor market outcome (weekly hours at work, employment, or unemployment) on the vector X using the pooled 2005–2007 monthly cross-sections. $X_i\theta_{n,2007}$ is essentially the 2005–2007 average labor market outcome for demographic group i, except that the outcomes are smoothed across age groups by the regression used to estimate $\theta_{n,2007}$ in order to avoid too many averages calculated exclusively from small cells (i.e., the vector $X_i\theta_{n,2007}$ includes an age quartic interacted with schooling, sex, and spouse present, rather than age indicator variables interacted with all other variables). $X_i\theta_{n,2010}$ is essentially the 2010 average labor market outcome, which makes the dependent variable in model (6.3) the change in the labor market outcome between 2005–2007 and 2010. $\theta_{r,2007}$ $(\theta_{y,2007})$ is a vector of regression coefficients from the regression of the log self-reliance rate change (log earnings level) on the vector X using the

Table 6.1 Aggregate Hours and L.F. Status Changes by Demographic Group
Household heads and spouses, ages 25–61 in the monthly CPS-MORG

Independent Variables	Changes from 2005–2007 to 2010					
	Weekly Hours at Work				Empl. per 100	Unempl. per 100
Constant	−1.9	−0.5	−1.0	−0.8	−0.5	0.7
	(0.4)	(0.9)	(1.1)	(1.1)	(2.5)	(0.7)
No spouse present	−1.2	−1.2	0.6	1.4	5.0	−1.4
	(0.4)	(0.4)	(1.1)	(1.1)	(2.4)	(1.2)
ln self-reliance rate chg, 2007-Q4 to 2009-Q4		11.8	7.5	9.1	25.4	−19.6
		(7.6)	(8.9)	(9.1)	(22.0)	(6.3)
* No spouse			15.2			
			(9.0)			
* No spouse * (potential earn. ≥ 400)				21.6	62.5	−21.3
				(9.2)	(20.4)	(9.9)
* No spouse * (potential earn. < 400)				−11.7	−104.6	−55.1
				(65.3)	(171.7)	(85.5)
Potential weekly earnings < $400				0.3	0.8	−1.0
				(0.5)	(1.2)	(0.5)
* No spouse present				−4.3	−22.6	−5.7
				(10.3)	(26.5)	(13.2)
Average ln hours change for industries, deviation from sample avg	19.7	16.4	16.1	16.1	16.1	9.6
	(6.4)	(7.2)	(7.1)	(7.2)	(13.7)	(6.2)
2005–2007 construction share of demographic group employment, deviation from sample avg	−3.5	−4.8	−5.0	−4.7	−4.7	4.4
	(3.6)	(3.8)	(3.8)	(3.8)	(7.6)	(3.2)

Table 6.1 (continued)

Independent Variables	Changes from 2005–2007 to 2010					
	Weekly Hours at Work				Empl. per 100	Unempl. per 100
2007 construction share of state payroll employment, deviation from sample avg	−17.2 (3.5)	−15.4 (3.5)	−15.3 (3.5)	−15.3 (3.5)	−27.1 (7.9)	8.7 (4.6)
ln state housing price index change, 1999–2001 to 2004–2006, dev from sample avg	−1.1 (0.6)	−1.2 (0.6)	−1.2 (0.6)	−1.2 (0.6)	−2.8 (1.6)	4.4 (0.7)
2007 manufacturing share of state payroll employment, deviation from sample avg	3.0 (2.7)	2.2 (2.6)	2.1 (2.6)	2.2 (2.6)	−1.9 (6.7)	8.1 (2.8)
Fixed effects	None					
Sample	All					

Notes: Bootstrapped standard errors in parentheses, clustered by state, sex, and year, and accounting for first stage estimation. Regressions have 78,983 demographic groups made up of 171,941 2010 individual observations and also include a quartic in (age-40). 2005–2007 (2010) hours worked, employed and unemployed are the fitted value from a regression of hours worked in the reference week (or employed times 100, or unemployed times 100) on indicator variables for age, education, state, white, month of year, and sex interacted with spouse and children present, all interacted with marital status, in a sample of all 2005–2007 (2010) household heads and spouses aged 25–61, respectively. The log self-reliance rate (SRR) change is the fitted value from a regression of the log dual-earner SRR change associated with a respondent's weekly earnings on the same independent variables, estimated in the subsample of those employed full-time and projected to the full sample. Omitted categories (fixed effects only) are Ohio and 16 years of schooling. Regression Adj-R-squared ranges from 0.050 to 0.054.

2005–2007 full-time working members of the CPS-MORG cross-sections, respectively. In other words, the regression model (6.3) looks at changes in a labor market outcome as a function of changes in the log self-reliance rate interacted with no spouse and potential earnings below the poverty line, and of the Z variables.

The regression coefficients reported in Table 6.1 are β_1, β_2, β_3, β_4, β_5, β_6, and the vector λ. β_1 is expected to be positive because the amount of the log self-reliance rate change indicates the amount that labor supply was distorted. β_2 is expected to be positive because the sole earner log self-reliance rate change is steeper than the dual earner log change among persons capable of earning above FPG.

In order to relate Table 6.1 to Figure 6.4 and the marital status results cited above, Table 6.1's first column imposes the restrictions $\beta_1 = \beta_2 = \beta_3 = \beta_5 = \beta_6 = 0$; like the marital status (among women) specifications noted earlier in this chapter, the first column has marital status as an independent variable in the hours change regression and does not use the self-reliance rate log change $(X\theta_{\tau,2007})$ or log potential earnings $(X\theta_{y,2007})$ variables noted above. The coefficient on no spouse present is –1.2 (s.e. = 0.4): hours changes among unmarried household heads and spouses are economically and statistically significantly less than hours changes among those who are married.[29]

The amount of the hours change gap by marital status is no surprise given the fact that log self-reliance rate changes are related to marital status. Among nonelderly female household heads and spouses, the dual-earner log self-reliance rate fell an average 0.180 from 2007-Q4 to 2009-Q4 as a consequence of safety net rule changes, holding characteristics fixed as noted above (see also formula 6.2). The sole-earner log self-reliance rate—calculated using formula (6.1) instead of (6.2)—fell an average of 0.122 among female heads of households and spouses over the same time period for the same set of characteristics. Thus, if we had a group of women who were entirely dual earners, and another group who were entirely sole earners, then the gap in their hours changes, holding constant other supply and demand determinants of hours changes, would be approximately the wage elasticity of group labor supply times the average level of hours times the 0.058 group difference in log self-reliance rate changes. Among nonelderly female household heads and spouses, average weekly work hours in 2005–2007 were about 25.4. Thus, for a group wage elasticity of 1.1, the group difference in the hours change would be 1.6 hours per week, holding constant other supply and demand determinants of hours changes.[30] The group difference in hours changes would be less to the extent that one or both of the groups included a mix of dual and sole earners. In fact, the female-only version of Table 6.1's first column has a coefficient of –1.8, which means that the measured marital status gap in hours changes is quantitatively consistent with the hypothesis that the gap was caused by the gap in log self-reliance rate changes resulting from the safety net expansions occurring on top of a prerecession safety net.

Table 6.1's second column introduces the log dual earner self-reliance rate change variable, which is a function, independent of marital status, of the weekly incomes of members of the demographic group who were at work full-time during one of the CPS surveys during 2005–2007 (as a special case of the model 6.3, the second column imposes the restrictions $\beta_1 = \beta_2 = \beta_3$, $\beta_5 = \beta_6 = 0$). As expected, its coefficient is positive and economically significant. Holding constant marital status, I find that demographic groups with greater reductions in their log self-reliance rate had greater hours reductions.

As shown in Figure 6.3 log self-reliance rate changes vary more with potential earnings among unmarried persons with potential income above FPG than among married persons to the extent that sole earners are significantly more common among unmarried household heads. Table 6.1's third column therefore allows the coefficient on the log dual earner self-reliance rate change to be different for unmarried people (as a special case of the model 6.3, the third column imposes the restrictions $\beta_2 = \beta_3$, $\beta_5 = \beta_6 = 0$). As expected, the coefficient on the term interacting the log dual earner self-reliance rate change with no spouse present is positive.

The table's fourth column displays estimates of the unrestricted model (6.3). As expected, the partial correlation between per capita work hours changes and changes in the log self-reliance rate is positive, especially among unmarried household heads with potential income above the poverty line. The coefficient of 9.1 (s.e. = 9.1) on the self-reliance rate variable indicates that more earnings potential among married people is associated with less hours decline from 2005–2007 to 2010 (recall from Figure 6.3 that the log dual earner self-reliance rate change is a monotone function of potential earnings). The coefficient of 21.6 (s.e. = 9.2) on the unmarried and above FPG interaction term indicates that the relationship between potential earnings and hours changes is more than three times as steep among people without a spouse and potential earnings above $400 as it is among married people. The third interaction term shows that there is no statistically significant relationship between log potential earnings and hours changes among unmarried persons with potential weekly earnings below $400. One interpretation of the results in the fourth column is that, as expected from my quantitative analysis of log self-reliance rate changes, safety net expansions had a particularly large negative impact on work hours among unmarried persons with earnings potential that was low but still above FPG.

Expansions in the federal safety net do not stop industry and regional shifts in labor supply and demand, which is why the regressions also include industry and state-level indicators of economic activity.[31] To construct the first industry indicator, I decomposed the hours worked per capita among the samples of household heads and spouses aged twenty-five to sixty-one in each of 2005–2007 and 2010 into a sum of per capita hours worked by three-digit industry. For each industry, I then calculated the log difference between its contribution to the 2010 sum and its contribution to the 2005–2007 sum. Each 2005–2007 sample member at work was assigned his or her industry's log change, and an industry log change was projected to the entire sample in the same way that potential earnings is calculated. For example, the average industry log changes projected to the 2010 sample average –0.111 for men and –0.045 for women because men tended to be at work in 2005–2007 in industries that would subsequently reduce hours more than the industries in which women were typically working. The second industry indicator is the fraction of employed (in 2005–2007) members of the demographic group who were working in construction, estimated by regressing an indicator variable for employment in the construction industry on the vector of demographic characteristics X, using the sample of respondents employed during one of the monthly surveys 2005–2007, and projecting a construction employment rate for the entire sample.

The coefficients on the industry change variable are positive in the hours and employment regressions shown in Table 6.1, which suggests that hours worked per capita fell for demographic groups employed in shrinking industries. The coefficients on the 2005–2007 construction employment variable are negative in the hours and employment regressions shown in Table 6.1, which suggests that hours worked per capita fell more for demographic groups that had been disproportionately employed in construction.

Industry of employment in 2005–2007 explains a lot of the gender gap in hours changes through 2010: the industry change variable is 0.066 less for men, and the group construction employment share is 0.112 greater. Their coefficients in the fourth column of Table 6.1 are 16.1 and −4.7, which together predict a gender hours change gap of about 1.6 as compared to the actual gap of 1.6.[32] As suggested by the economically and statistically significant coefficients on no spouse present and its interaction with the log self-reliance rate change, industry changes do not explain much of the marital status gap in work hours changes.

Of particular interest is the housing cycle, which varied across states. A collapse of a housing price "bubble" is said to reduce aggregate labor demand (Mian and Sufi 2011) and can also reduce labor supply through the channels discussed in Chapters Three and Nine. Table 6.1's regressions include two state-level housing cycle indicators: the share of 2007 state pay-roll employees who were employed in the construction industry and the log difference in the average Office of Federal Housing Enterprise Oversight (OFHEO) housing price index for 2004–2006 and for 1999–2001 (both devi-ated from their sample averages). The negative coefficients on those variables indicate that the housing cycle variables are associated with work hours reduc-tions after 2007, as expected. The final variable is another indicator of the composition of labor demand: the share of 2007 statewide payroll employees who were employed in a manufacturing industry (deviated from its sample average). The point estimate of the state manufacturing coefficient is not eco-nomically or statistically different from zero, holding constant the aforemen-tioned national industry change variable.

The constant terms in each of the work hours regressions have an important interpretation: the average work hours change predicted when the other independent variables are zero. Given my normalization of the first col-umn's independent variables, that occurs for married persons forty years old with unchanged self-reliance rate, in average growth industries, with average hours per capita in 2005–2007, and living in states with the 2007 manufac-turing and construction shares equal to their sample averages and housing price index change equal to its sample average. In this sense, the constant term in the table's second through sixth columns indicate what might have happened to work hours to the parts of the married population that were not exposed to safety net rule changes. Adding the constant to the unmarried level coefficient yields the model's prediction for what might have happened to work hours to the parts of the unmarried population that were not exposed to safety net rule changes and had earnings potential above $400 per week. Interestingly, the constant terms are close to zero (see also the additional spec-ifications shown in Appendix 6.1), which means that the model predicts work hours to be relatively constant from 2007 to 2010 for groups that had a constant self-reliance rate.[33] The final two columns show results for employment (during the reference week) per one hundred persons and unemployment per one hundred persons. Among unmarried people with potential weekly earnings above $400, employment rises more (falls less) and unemployment rises less (falls more) when the log self-reliance rate falls less, as compared to the patterns found among married people.

To the extent that workers compete with each other in the cross-section, supply shifts should generate different wage rate patterns over time than they do in the cross-section. For example, if there were a single national market for labor, a reduction in the supply of one group would not change the group's wage rate relative to other groups. At the same time, imperfect wage measures might show that group's wage to be falling relative to the wages of the rest of the work force because of changes in that group's effort and attachment to the workforce.[34]

I consider two ways to relate measured wage changes to the results shown in Table 6.1. The first replaces the hours change dependent variable with a log wage change dependent variable. Each demographic group's wage change is calculated as a difference between the fitted values from the 2010 and 2005–2007 regressions of log hourly earnings among full-time workers on the same vector of demographics used above. For example, the coefficient on no spouse present in the first column of Table 6.1 is statistically and economically insignificant when the log hourly wage change is the dependent variable. Among female demographic groups, the coefficient on no spouse present is also statistically insignificant in the log wage change regression. Even if we ignore the caveats mentioned above, the point estimate of –0.018 means that the marital status gap among women in measured log wage changes is only one fourth of the marital status gap in log hours changes, which suggests either that there was a significant marital status gap in labor supply changes (my hypothesis) or that the wage elasticity of labor supply among women is about 4.

A second approach with the wage data would be to replace the hours change dependent variable in Table 6.1 with the supply component of the hours change, calculated as the raw hours change minus the measured log wage change scaled by an assumed supply slope. For various assumed supply slopes, the coefficient estimates from this approach are similar to the coefficient estimates shown in Table 6.1, largely because the wage change gaps among demographic groups are minimal.[35]

Regional Shocks

Prior work found that employment and spending fell more after 2007 in regions with larger housing booms prior to 2007 (Mian and Sufi 2011; Mian, Rao, and Sufi 2011). Table 6.1 reports a similar pattern across states, holding constant age, marital status, and proxies for skill or changes in the self-reliance rate.

Chapter Three shows that self-reliance rates increased over time nationwide as the result of more than a dozen changes in benefit rules, any one of which contributed only a small part to the overall change. As a result, I expect it to be difficult for empirical approaches like Table 6.1's to detect work hours effects of one provision by itself.[36] However, Winkler's panel data analysis (2011) for the years 1980–1997 finds that unemployment rises among homeowners relative to renters after an adverse local labor market shock, which might suggest that home ownership may have also affected the labor supply of home owners during the most recent recession.

Interstate migration flows are a small share of the overall population, but in principle they might be informative about the causes of state-specific labor market changes. For example, if the residents of a state were to reduce their labor supply, and workers in the same state were substitutes for each other in aggregate production, then people would migrate into the state in order to take the place of some of the residents who reduced their labor supply.[37] Interestingly, Mian and Sufi (2011) find positive net in-migration between 2006 and 2009 into counties with relatively large housing booms prior to 2006.

The U.S. Internal Revenue Service (2011) measures year-to-year (typically April to April) interstate in-migration, out-migration, and no migration (remain in state) by matching personal tax returns filed under the same social security number in adjacent years and examining each return's filing address. For each state and each pair of adjacent years, I calculate the log of the sum of no migration returns and inflow returns and subtracted the log of the sum of no migration returns and outflow returns. I then accumulate these log differences from 2007 to 2010 for each state and interpret each state's result as its cumulative log net in-migration rate between 2007 and 2010. The results vary from −0.025 for Michigan to 0.048 for the District of Columbia.[38] I regress each state's log migration rate on the independent variables shown in Table 6.1, and the point estimate on the coefficient on the log change in the self-reliance rate is negative (that is, inflows for states with large reductions in the log self-reliance rate and outflows for states with small reductions). However, its statistical significance depends on whether the 2007 construction share and industry change variables are included (the construction variable has a large positive coefficient in the log migration regressions).

Elderly Labor Supply

Work hours changes were quite different for elderly people than they were for everyone else: average work hours for elderly people were actually greater in 2010 than they were before the recession began, even in states that were depressed more than the national average. One way to see this is to divide the nation into "sandy" states—Arizona, California, Florida, Nevada, and Hawaii—and all others. The sandy states as a group are of interest because they had some of the largest housing cycles: the five were among the top nine states in the nation in terms of housing price increases from 1999–2000 to 2004–2006. As shown in the left panel of Figure 6.5, those states had quite a large reduction in work hours among nonelderly household heads and

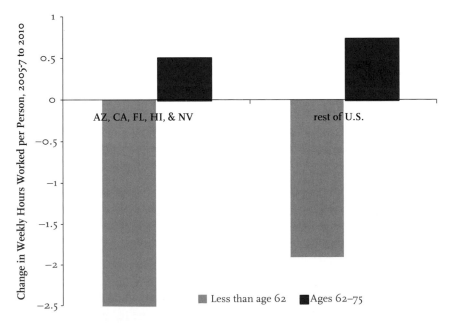

FIGURE 6.5 Work Hours Changes by Age and Region
Household Heads and Spouses

Table 6.2 Elderly Work Hours Changes by Demographic Group

Household heads and spouses in the monthly CPS-MORG

Independent variables Ages:	Average Weekly Work Hours Changes from 2005–2007 to 2010					
	65–75	25–61	65–75	25–61	65–75	25–61
Constant	0.1	−2.1	0.2	−1.9	0.0	−1.7
	(0.2)	(0.1)	(0.2)	(0.1)	(0.3)	(0.3)
(years of schooling	1.1	2.5	1.1	2.5	1.1	2.5
−12)/10	(0.4)	(0.3)	(0.4)	(0.3)	(0.4)	(0.3)
No spouse present	−0.1	−1.2	−0.1	−1.2	−0.1	−1.2
	(0.3)	(0.2)	(0.3)	(0.2)	(0.3)	(0.2)
Lives in AZ, CA, FL, HI, or NV			−0.1	−0.7		
			(0.2)	(0.3)		
2007 construction share of state payroll employment, deviation from sample avg					−14.0	−21.4
					(8.8)	(4.7)
ln state housing price index change, 1999–2001 to 2004–2006					0.4	−1.0
					(0.7)	(0.5)
2007 manufacturing share of state payroll employment, deviation from sample avg					−6.1	−1.1
					(3.6)	(2.6)
2010 observations	30,546	171,941	30,546	171,941	30,546	171,941

Notes: Robust standard errors in parentheses, clustered by state. In the sample of 2005–2007, 2010 CPS-MORG household heads and spouses, weekly work hours (including zeros) are regressed on an indicator for 2010, years of schooling interacted with 2010, an indicator for no spouse present interacted with 2010, the state-specific indicators shown above interacted with 2010, and indicator variables for month of interview, sex, age, state of residence, and age. The coefficients shown in the table are those on the 2010 interaction terms and therefore interpreted as average weekly hours changes from 2005–2007 to 2010. Regression R-squareds are about 0.06 for the elderly and 0.12 for the nonelderly.

spouses, 2.5 hours per week (more than 8 percent). But average work hours among the elderly in those same states actually increased. The right panel shows the rest of the nation, where average nonelderly work hours declined (somewhat less than they did in the sandy states) and average elderly work hours increased.

Table 6.2 is a regression analysis of work hours changes for the elderly (ages sixty-five to seventy-five) and nonelderly (less than age sixty-two).[39] Each column is a regression, and the columns differ according to the independent variables and the sample (elderly vs. nonelderly). In the sample of 2005–2007, 2010 CPS-MORG household heads and spouses, weekly work hours (including zeros) are regressed on an indicator for 2010, years of schooling interacted with 2010, an indicator for no spouse present interacted with 2010, (in some of the columns) state-specific economic indicators shown above interacted with 2010, and indicator variables for month of interview, sex, age, state of residence, and age.[40] The coefficients shown in the table are those on the 2010 interaction terms, and therefore interpreted as average weekly hours changes from 2005–2007 to 2010. The first column's coefficient of 1.1 (s.e. = 0.4) shows that average weekly work hours among the elderly increase more for those with more schooling, although to a lesser degree than for nonelderly people (second column). Marital status is unrelated to hours changes for the elderly, whereas the coefficients of −1.2 in the nonelderly columns of the table indicate that hours changes for the nonelderly are more negative among those who are not married or otherwise do not have a spouse present in the household (see also Figure 6.4 and Table 6.1).

The constant terms in the table indicate weekly hours changes for the benchmark demographic group, the group for which the other variables shown in the table are zero. The benchmark group in the first two columns is persons with twelve years of schooling and spouse present, and their hours changes are 0.1 for the elderly and −2.1 for the nonelderly. All of the other columns also confirm that hours changes are of a different sign for the elderly, holding constant other demographic characteristics.

The middle two columns add an indicator variable for living in the "sandy states" of Arizona, California, Florida, Hawaii, and Nevada and in this regard it is a regression version of Figure 6.5 that holds constant other demographic characteristics. Holding demographics constant, we see that elderly hours changes are not much different in the sandy states from the rest of the nation. But the coefficient of −0.7 in the table's fourth column shows that nonelderly work hours did fall somewhat more in the sandy states than elsewhere. The final two regressions shown in the table include state-level indicators of prerecession housing market and manufacturing activity. The last column shows that the housing indicators are correlated with hours changes among the nonelderly, consistent with Table 6.1's results. The same indicators are not statistically significantly correlated with elderly hours changes, although the coefficient on the construction variable is economically significant and almost as large as the corresponding coefficient in the nonelderly regression.

Figure 6.6 shows that average weekly work time among the elderly tended to trend up between 2000 and 2007. The figure is constructed by pooling all household heads and spouses aged sixty-five to seventy-five found in at least one of the 132 months of CPS-MORG files from the years 2000–2010, and regressing average weekly work hours (including zeros) on indicator variables for age and sex, and indicator variables for the seven schooling levels used in Figure 6.4 interacted with year. The coefficients on the schooling year-interactions are graphed in the figure for the benchmark group of sixty-seven-year-old men.[41] With the exception of the high

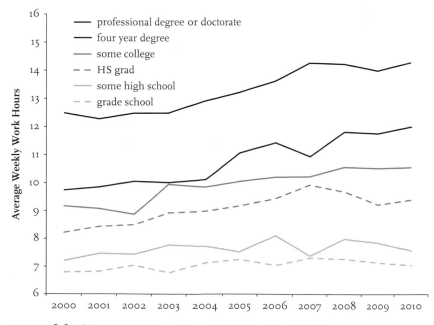

FIGURE 6.6 Elderly Work Hours Trends by Educational Attainment

school graduate group, the hours series after 2007 stay pretty close to the previous trend.

Economists attributed the prerecession trend to labor supply factors such as changing family composition, reduced marginal tax rates, improved health, and anticipation of longer life spans, some of which might be expected to continue beyond 2007.[42] Thus, one interpretation of Figure 6.5 is that the recession years were largely a continuation of prior elderly labor supply trends. Yet a continuation for the elderly is quite remarkable, because other age groups did not see their prior labor market trends continue: nonelderly people saw their work hours drop sharply below that trend. This book explains why elderly work hours would continue to follow prior trends, even while average work hours among the nonelderly fell: the marginal tax rates for the nonelderly increased sharply, while marginal tax rates for the elderly hardly changed.

Program Participation Changes by Demographic Group

In theory, log self-reliance rate changes and hours changes since 2007 vary cross-sectionally for a couple of reasons. The changes are less negative for high-skill people because their earnings potential is high compared to the dollar value of the changes in the generosity of safety net programs. This skill gradient result has nothing to do with the propensity to participate in a safety net program when not employed. Indeed, I assumed in this chapter that program participation among non-employed people is independent of skill, holding family composition constant.[43]

The log self-reliance rate changes and hours changes are, in theory, less negative for married people and people without children in the household because they are less likely to qualify for means-tested benefits when not employed. Their change from 2007 to 2010 in means-tested program participation should be less than the changes for unmarried people and people with children even if all groups had the same employment and hours changes, plus the fact hours fell less for the former group. The relationship between program participation changes and family composition should be weaker (but not zero) for unemployment insurance because UI eligibility is determined by individual characteristics, rather than family characteristics.

Table 6.3 confirms these predictions with data on program participation. Annual program participation is measured retrospectively in the Annual Demographic Survey conducted every March by the Census Bureau. It asks whether the respondent received any unemployment benefits during the prior calendar year, whether anyone in the respondent's family received food stamps during the prior calendar year, and whether anyone in the household is covered by Medicaid.[44] The dependent variables for the regression shown in the table are indicators for receiving program benefits sometime during a calendar year, times 100. The models' demographic variables and state level economic indicators are defined in the same way as in Table 6.1. Independent variables also include a fourth-order polynomial in (age-40), and all independent variables are interacted with an indicator variable for 2010. The coefficients shown in the table correspond to the interaction terms and are thereby interpreted as program participation changes from 2005–2007 to 2010, in percentage points.

The first two columns consider unemployment benefit receipt separately for men (first column) and women (second column). Benefit receipt increases more among the unmarried: 1.0 percentage points more for unmarried men and 2.5 percentage points more for unmarried women. Not surprisingly, UI receipt changes have little relationship to the presence of children, because having children in the household is not a condition for receiving UI. Educational attainment is negatively correlated with UI receipt changes among both men and women. The two state-level housing variables and manufacturing variable are associated with increases in UI recipiency, although the construction variable's coefficient is statistically and economically insignificant for women.

The next three columns consider participation in SNAP, Medicaid, and any one of the three programs (the "Any" column). SNAP, Medicaid, and Any participation increases more among unmarried people. They also increase more in households that have at least one child under eighteen years old. Participation in these programs increased less among more educated households.

The lowest-skill single mothers do not have the most negative log self-reliance rate changes and hours changes because, in theory, they were likely to qualify for means-tested programs regardless of their work hours, even before the recession began. Figure 6.7 confirms this prediction with the program participation data for 2005–2007. Among all single mothers (black series), participation in SNAP or Medicaid sometime during the calendar year falls

Table 6.3 UI, SNAP, and Medicaid Participation Changes by Demographic Group

Household heads and spouses in the CPS Annual Demographic Files

Independent variables	Program Participation Changes from 2005–2007 to 2010, Percentage Points								
	UI	UI	SNAP	Med.	Any	SNAP	Med.	Any	UI
Constant	3.3	1.5	4.0	3.6	6.9	1.2	2.1	3.5	1.4
	(0.8)	(0.5)	(0.7)	(1.0)	(1.0)	(0.7)	(1.8)	(1.8)	(0.6)
No spouse present	1.1	2.4	2.1	0.4	1.9	2.4	−0.6	0.7	−0.2
	(0.4)	(0.4)	(0.4)	(0.5)	(0.5)	(0.9)	(0.9)	(0.8)	(0.4)
Child present	0.2	0.3	2.9	4.1	2.6	−3.1	2.7	2.9	1.8
	(0.5)	(0.3)	(0.4)	(0.6)	(0.5)	(2.3)	(4.0)	(4.2)	(2.0)
Educational attainment	−0.4	−0.1	−1.0	−0.6	−0.8	−0.3	0.2	0.2	0.0
	(0.1)	(0.0)	(0.1)	(0.1)	(0.1)	(0.1)	(0.2)	(0.2)	(0.0)
2007 construction share of state payroll employment, deviation from sample avg	32.4	4.1	−5.4	−2.8	8.5	0.1	67.7	40.4	−9.9
	(14.6)	(8.4)	(13.0)	(27.7)	(29.4)	(22.3)	(47.6)	(50.8)	(10.2)
ln state housing price index change, 1999–2001 to 2004–2006	3.9	2.0	0.1	0.5	2.6	2.1	−3.6	−3.6	0.2
	(1.0)	(0.7)	(1.3)	(1.5)	(1.5)	(1.3)	(3.1)	(3.1)	(1.0)

2007 manufacturing share of state payroll employment, deviation from sample avg	28.6	3.9	4.4	−6.3	7.9	11.2	−30.6	−27.1	−3.8
	(5.2)	(3.5)	(7.6)	(11.6)	(12.3)	(9.7)	(25.4)	(25.9)	(5.1)
Sex	Male	Female				Both			
Ages	Ages 25–61						Ages 65–75		
2010 observations	40,233	45,082		85,305			11,358		
Adjusted R-squared (levels)	0.02	0.01	0.09	0.12	0.12	0.05	0.06	0.07	0.00

Notes: Robust standard errors in parentheses, clustered by state. Dependent variables are indicators for receiving program benefits sometime during a calendar year ("Any" refers to receipt of UI, SNAP, or Medicaid), times 100. UI receipt is for the respondent, SNAP and Medicaid are for the family or household. Only years 2005–2007 and 2010 are included in the sample. Independent variables are the variables shown above, plus a fourth-order polynomial in (age-40), interacted with an indicator variable for 2010. The coefficients shown in the table are on the interaction terms, and thereby interpreted as program participation changes from 2005–2007 to 2010, in percentage points. The educational attainment variable is the CPS code minus the code assigned to high school diploma.

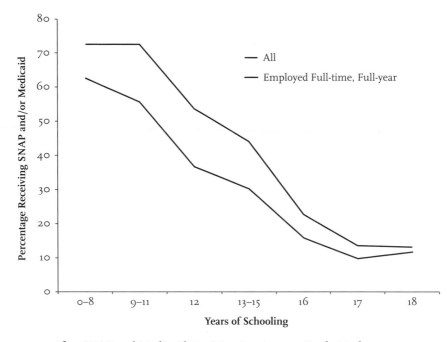

FIGURE 6.7 SNAP and Medicaid Participation Among Single Mothers
Ages 25–61, 2005–7 average

sharply with education, beginning at about 73 percent for single mothers with
zero to eight or nine to eleven years of schooling, and falling to about 14 percent
for single mothers with education beyond college (sixteen years). Even among
single mothers working full-time and at least fifty weeks during the calendar
year, participation exceeds 50 percent for those whose formal education
stopped before graduating high school (indicated in the Figure as twelve years
of schooling).

The right half of Table 6.3 shows cross-sectional patterns of program
participation changes among the elderly. In contrast to the changes for the
nonelderly, changes in elderly program participation rates, if any, were
small and unrelated to family composition or educational attainment.

Conclusion: The Cross-Sectional Patterns of Employment and Hours Changes Are as Expected from a Large Safety Net Expansion

Employment and hours changes during the recession varied by state, by
schooling group, by age group, by sex, and by marital status. Although the

gender gap in hours and employment changes is well explained by changes in the industry composition of employment, many of the other differences among these groups are better explained by differences in the changes in their log self-reliance rates resulting from changes in safety net program eligibility and benefit rules. Average work hours (including zeros for those not at work) typically fell more for low-skill groups than for medium- and high-skill groups, as expected from a safety net expansion and a variety of other factors that might have reduced aggregate hours. Perhaps more surprising are the facts that work hours continued to increase among the elderly and, holding earnings potential constant, hours fell significantly more for unmarried (nonelderly) people than for married people, especially among women. Moreover, the relationship between hours changes and skill is not always monotonic, and varies according to family composition.

If, before the recession began, economists had been asked to predict the consequences of a safety net expansion of the size and character actually experienced since 2007, they might well have predicted that aggregate work hours would fall 8 or 10 percent, that employment and hours reductions would be greater in groups in which the safety net expansions did more to erode their work incentives, and that groups, if any, with no change in work incentives would actually work more. As shown in this chapter, and Chapters Four and Five, all of these things have actually happened since 2007.

Much more work can be done on the cross-sectional patterns of employment and hours changes, and on relating them to supply and demand factors. The cross-sectional empirical results by themselves do not prove that the decline in aggregate labor hours was largely caused by the erosion of work incentives associated with safety net expansions. For example, a (hypothetical) decline in wages and productivity could also produce a similar cross-sectional pattern of hours changes because the prerecession welfare system by itself would cause sole earners, especially those with potential earnings above but near the federal poverty line, to be more sensitive to those changes than the rest of the population. However, at the same time this explanation says that labor supply is a function of safety net benefits, it also implies that expansions in those benefits would affect labor supply, which is the assumption of this book.

Another logical possibility is that work incentives no longer (or never did) have a significant effect on aggregate labor hours, and that the safety net expansions just happened to coincide with a collection of other economic shocks—the real causes of the labor decline—with effects that closely resemble what economists believe would be the effects of safety net expansions. The reader may already judge that logical possibility to lack credibility, but Chapters Seven and Eight offer additional empirical tests of the claim that work incentives no longer matter.

Appendix 6.1: Summary Statistics and Additional Results

As in Table 6.1, Table 6.4's regressions are of the form (6.3). In the first two columns, the male and female demographic groups are put in separate regres-

Table 6.4 Aggregate Hours and L.F. Status Changes by Demographic Group
Household heads and spouses, ages 25–61 in the monthly CPS-MORG

Independent Variables	Changes from 2005–2007 to 2010			
	Weekly Hours at Work			
Constant	2.1	1.4	−0.3	−1.1
	(2.0)	(1.8)	(1.3)	(3.0)
No spouse present	0.5	0.1	1.4	1.2
	(1.5)	(1.4)	(1.2)	(1.1)
ln self-reliance rate chg, 2007-Q4 to	41.7	20.2	10.2	3.1
2009-Q4	(19.6)	(15.7)	(8.0)	(29.5)
* No spouse				
* No spouse * (potential	7.0	16.1	21.9	20.4
earn. ≥ 400)	(13.1)	(11.5)	(9.5)	(9.0)
* No spouse * (potential	−47.5	−31.2	−4.8	7.6
earn. >400)	(220.8)	(67.9)	(65.3)	(66.1)
Potential weekly earnings < $400	0.1	0.3	0.2	−0.1
	(1.2)	(0.6)	(0.5)	(0.7)
* No spouse present	−6.3	−6.2	−3.2	−1.1
	(33.9)	(10.6)	(10.3)	(10.4)
Average ln hours change for industries,	18.2	9.6	11.7	16.3
deviation from sample avg	(9.9)	(12.6)	(4.6)	(9.1)

2005–2007 construction share of demographic group employment, deviation from sample avg	1.5 (4.6)	4.4 (11.6)	−7.0 (2.4)	−4.6 (4.3)
2007 construction share of state payroll employment, deviation from sample avg	−15.0 (5.8)	−19.9 (6.2)		−15.5 (4.0)
ln state housing price index change, 1999–2001 to 2004–2006, dev from sample avg	−1.4 (0.9)	−1.3 (0.8)		−1.2 (0.6)
2007 manufacturing share of state payroll employment, dev. from sample avg	3.6 (4.0)	1.3 (4.3)		2.4 (2.7)
Fixed effects		None	States	Schooling
Sample	Men	Women		All
2010 observations	71,229	79,457	150,686	150,686

Notes: Bootstrapped standard errors in parentheses, clustered by state, sex, and year, and accounting for first stage estimation. See also notes to Table 6.1.

sion samples. According to the point estimates, the interaction between the log self-reliance rate change and spouse present is stronger for women, as would be the case if women were more likely to be the "secondary" earner in a dual earner household.

As an alternative to the regression model (6.3) that includes marital status interactions, separate regressions could be run for persons with spouse present and for persons who are not married (or otherwise without spouse present). The estimated coefficient on the dual earner self-reliance rate variable is statistically and economically significant in both regressions (not shown in any of the tables in this book) but about twice as large among persons who are not married.

Much of the sample variation in the log self-reliance rate change comes from differences among schooling groups, as opposed to states. The third column of Table 6.4 shows how similar coefficients are estimated when state fixed effects are added to the hours change regression from the fourth column of Table 6.1, except perhaps for the coefficient on the industry change variables. Table 6.4's final column shows the results when education indicator variables are added to the hours change regression.

Table 6.5 presents summary statistics for the samples from the CPS-MORG and CPS Annual Demographic Files used to produce Tables 6.1–6.4 and Figures 6.4–6.7.

Table 6.5 Summary Statistics, Household Heads and Spouses Ages 25–61

	CPS-MORG		CPS Annual Demographic Files	
	2005–2007	2010	2005–2007	2010
Median ln self-reliance rt chg (dual earn.)		−0.118	NA	
Median real weekly earnings if at work	753	760	NA	
Mean real weekly earnings if at work	914	920	NA	
Mean real potential earnings		774	NA	
Mean weekly hours if at work	40.8	39.8	NA	
Mean age	43.4	43.8	43.2	43.7
Mean 2007 state construction share	0.085	0.085	0.085	0.085
Mean ln state housing price change	0.397	0.396	0.397	0.396
Mean 2007 manufacturing share	0.102	0.101	0.102	0.101
Percentages				
At work	75.6	72.4	NA	
Employed	78.7	75.1	NA	
Unemployed	2.6	5.9	NA	
White	81.8	81.2	82.1	81.5
Male	48.2	48.1	47.4	47.5
Married with spouse present	70.5	69.2	71.3	69.2
Children under 18 present	46.5	45.0	45.9	43.8
Years of schooling completed (imputed)				
2.5	0.9	0.8	0.8	0.8
5.5	1.6	1.3	1.4	1.4
7.5	1.6	1.5	1.5	1.2
9	1.9	1.8	1.5	1.4
10	2.6	2.1	1.8	1.5
11	3.2	2.9	2.1	2.0
12	31.1	30.8	29.9	28.8
13	6.8	6.9	5.0	6.1

14	13.3	13.6	17.7	17.4
15	3.3	3.0	5.1	4.8
16	17.6	18.7	21.6	22.3
17	2.4	2.2	0.0	0.0
18	13.7	14.3	11.5	12.3
AK, CA, FL, HI, or NV	20.6	20.6	20.6	20.5
UI received by person during year	NA		3.1	6.8
SNAP received by family during year	NA		5.2	9.4
Medicaid received by HH during year	NA		15.0	18.8
UI, SNAP, and/or Medicaid received	NA		18.3	25.5
Observations (unweighted)	536,476	171,941	265,086	85,305

Notes: CPS-MORG (ADF) weighted using the final weight (March Supplement weight), respectively. ADF years refer to the calendar year prior to the interview. "NA" statistics are not available or not in this chapter. Inflation adjustments (to 2010) use the annual PCE deflator. The CPS-MORG industry change (group construction sh.) variable has mean −0.077 (0.071) and std dev 0.046 (.079), respectively.

7

Keynesian and Other Models of Safety Net Stimulus

DURING THE RECESSION of 2008–09, the federal government took a number of steps to help citizens and the economy, including expansion of the food stamp and unemployment insurance programs, helping financially distressed homeowners refinance their mortgages, and offering tax credits to poor and middle-class persons buying homes. In addition to helping the people who receive the funds, these and other programs are sometimes said to stimulate national employment because the programs redistribute resources to persons with a "high propensity to spend," even though the same programs also implicitly raise marginal income tax rates.

High marginal income tax rates by themselves "normally" reduce economic activity, rather than increase it, although there is plenty of room to debate the magnitude of incentive effects. For the same reason, social safety net programs are not expected to increase employment in the long term. But a number of economists believe that recessions are those rare instances when labor markets are "slack": labor supply does not matter and might even affect the aggregates in the opposite direction as usual (Eggertsson 2010b).[1] In their view, it is possible that government spending programs such as unemployment insurance could stimulate economic activity during a recession, even while they eroded labor supply incentives, and even while those programs had very different effects in nonrecession years.

Although my approach agrees that beneficiaries can be helped by safety net expansions, it does not support the national employment stimulus claims. The models presented in Chapters Four and Five assume that aggregate work hours are still determined by aggregate labor supply and demand, even during a recession, and that safety net expansions do not significantly increase labor demand. The purpose of this chapter is to carefully examine the economically substantive differences between the stimulus approaches and mine, and to indicate how to judge and quantify those differences with the help of empirical analysis. The next chapter presents results of three tests of the slack market assumption, which, surprisingly, has not yet been the subject of much empirical testing.

I begin with a discussion of the possible demand effects of transfers that are prevalent in public discussion but largely absent from academic analyses of fiscal policy, "Keynesian" or otherwise. I then give a simple exposition of the "slack market" and "sticky price" or New Keynesian approaches to recession labor markets. The fundamental differences between those two approaches and mine are a matter of testable assumptions, so the chapter concludes with a simple econometric framework that embeds all three approaches. The relevant parts of that econometric model are estimated in the next chapter.

The Safety Net and Consumer Spending

As politicians have debated expansions and contractions in the safety net, news reports on the subject (Orzag 2012), as well as reports by the Congressional Budget Office and other government agencies, claim that safety net programs boost aggregate spending, and by that channel increase employment. It might appear that Chapters Four and Five neglect an important demand effect of safety net expansions.

To consider this critique, we need to be clear what is meant by "spending." If spending includes purchases of investment items, accumulation of liquid assets, and gifts, as well as purchases of consumer items, people are constrained to spend their income and any spending change must involve an income change. Transferring resources from one group to another increases the receiving group's income and spending and reduces the paying group's income and spending. What the spending channel theory really means is that (1) safety net programs change the composition of the nation's final spending, and (2) the composition changes in a direction that raises the demand for labor. Note that their proposition is really a pair of spending hypotheses, neither of which can be refuted or confirmed on the basis of economic logic alone and both of which need to be confirmed with empirical testing. Even if both hypotheses were confirmed, there is still the question of the size of the net result on labor demand relative to the effects on labor supply.

The composition of the nation's spending might change if the government takes resources from one group and gives it to another group (the safety net beneficiaries, which for brevity I call the "poor"), and the two groups are different in terms of how they use their resources. For the moment, let's assume that the government achieves this redistribution through subsidies to the poor and taxes on everyone else. Thanks to the redistribution, the poor have more to spend and everyone else has less. The economy will need more workers to make the things that the poor buy and fewer workers to make the things that everyone else buys. If, relative to everyone else, the poor spend a larger fraction of their income on final goods and services that are labor-intensive in their production,[2] then, holding constant the amount that everyone works, the national demand for labor will increase as the result of the redistribution. The final goods and services that everyone else buys are produced less, but by assumption those final goods and services do not use much labor, and the labor-intensive final goods and services that the poor buy are produced more.

The obvious, and critical, empirical question is whether the poor really do spend a larger fraction of their income on labor-intensive items, but I am not aware of any empirical answers to this question. The answer is far from obvious: for example, some of the most labor-intensive industries are hotels, coal mining, and restaurants, whereas farm commodities and cell phone services are some of the least labor-intensive. If the safety net redistributes resources from people who spend a relatively large fraction of their resources on restaurants and hotels toward people who spend a large fraction on groceries and cell phone services, the redistribution may well reduce national labor demand rather than increase it.

At first glance, this result would seem to depend on the assumption that the government redistributes by levying taxes on everyone else. The result would be the same if the government redistributed by cutting subsidies to everyone else, because everyone else would still have to spend less. The result would even be the same if the government borrowed from everyone else, because everyone else would have to cut their spending (on consumer items, investment items, or both) in order to have the funds to lend to the government.[3]

Studies find that, holding constant labor income, the recipients of unemployment insurance and other transfer payments from the government tend to use those resources to consume, rather than invest or purchase liquid assets.[4] As press articles often say, government transfers such as unemployment compensation "put money in the hands of consumers." The fact that unemployed people tend to consume their benefits when they receive them is an important indicator of the insurance benefits of the UI program, because it tells us that the benefits are especially important for maintaining their living standards (Gruber 1997). But this fact is irrelevant for understanding aggregate labor demand, unless it happens to be that the consumption items purchased by the unemployed are more labor-intensive in their production than are other goods and services in the economy.[5]

New Keynesian models of the business cycle offer a coherent theory about possible effects of safety net redistribution on the composition of demand for final goods and services that has little to do with the distinction between consumption and investment. That theory emphasizes a third spending category: the accumulation of liquid assets. It is usually assumed that liquidity services are not produced with labor (in fact, it assumed that they are not produced at all but rather are in fixed supply). Thus, more demand for consumption and investment goods rather than liquid assets might mean more demand for labor, especially when prices are sticky (more on sticky prices below). But that still does not tell us whether the safety net changes the demand for labor, unless the safety net is somehow connected with the demand for liquid assets, which economists have not done yet. It is possible that the poor use their safety net benefits to purchase consumer items that are of less-than-average labor intensity, and the rest of the country reduces spending on labor-intensive items, so that the net result of redistribution is to reduce aggregate labor demand.

So far I have held constant the amount that everyone works and earns, so that more safety net income for the poor means more total income for them, which permits them to spend more. But the safety net causes some of its beneficiaries to work less. Unless the safety net replaces all of the income lost from reduced work time—it typically does not—then the people who reduce their labor in response to the safety net expansion will spend less as a result of the safety net, and the amount less could be many times more than the amount that the safety net expanded. Now the "hands of consumers" theory is turned on its head: at the same time that the poor spend most of whatever income they have on consumer items, the safety net's redistribution reduces their total spending because it reduces their total income.

For these reasons it is unclear whether safety net expansions shift the composition of final demand in the direction of goods that are more, or less, labor-intensive in their production. Even if we could be sure that the shift was in the direction of more labor-intensive goods, the magnitude of the effect of a safety net expansion on national labor demand would likely be trivial. To see this, take an extreme case in which the poor purchased goods and services that were 100 percent labor-intensive, as compared to the rest of the country, which purchased goods and services that were 65 percent labor-intensive. Without a safety net expansion, total annual spending by the poor would be $2 trillion and total spending by the rest of the country would be $10 trillion, so that the national average labor intensity would be 70.8 percent. Now redistribute $0.25 trillion (about the size of the safety net expansions since 2007) to the poor, and the national average labor intensity increases to 71.6 percent.

Thus, in an extreme case, the safety net expansions since 2007 increased labor intensity by 1 percent (1.01 = 0.716/0.708), which is a trivial increase in labor demand compared with the safety-net-induced reductions in labor supply documented in previous chapters. The small size and ambiguous direction of the safety net's effect on aggregate labor demand are the two reasons my models of the effects of safety net expansions assume zero labor demand effects, and perhaps also why they are often omitted from New Keynesian models of fiscal policy.

Transfers and Government Purchases Are Not the Same

The government safety net program expansions considered in this book are transfer program expansions. Transfers are government payments to individuals who have discretion as to how to spend it and do not have to produce anything in order to receive the payments. Transfers, which include unemployment and social security benefits, are distinct from government purchases of goods and services—"government purchases" for short—such as military spending or highway construction. The businesses or persons receiving payments from the government for its purchases must produce something—such as building a tank or paving a highway—in order to receive the payment.[6]

Economists have cited a variety of reasons that government purchases might increase employment, although they debate the size of the effect. But the debate is hardly relevant for the conclusion of this book—that aggregate work hours would have been significantly greater if the safety net had not expanded—because the safety net program expansions were not increases in government purchases. For the same reason, it does not follow that the

American Reinvestment and Recovery Act of 2009, which is responsible for much of the safety net expansion, necessarily reduced aggregate work hours because the ARRA also included increases in government purchases. For the ARRA in its entirety to increase work hours, the work hours increasing effect (if any) of its purchases would have to be enough to offset the work hours reducing effect of its safety net expansions.[7]

Labor Market Slack and the Marginal Effects of Supply

Another critique of the models used in Chapters Four and Five is that they supposedly predict that unemployment does not exist, and that the labor market is always 100 percent efficient. The critique is wrong in several ways. First of all, time-invariant unemployment frictions and many other labor market distortions are fully consistent with the comparative static exercises in Chapters Four and Five just by reinterpreting some of the time-invariant model parameters such as γ_n in equation (5.2) as inclusive of time-invariant frictions. Under this interpretation, the model can even be used for welfare analysis, as long as the welfare analysis accounts for the inefficiencies associated with the baseline distortions (see Appendix 4.3). Time-varying labor market frictions can also be included in the parameter τ, although admittedly that begs the question of what changed the labor market over time unless the parameter τ is connected with empirical measures of frictions, as I attempted in Chapter Three.

Second, my models clearly predict that employment per person falls.[8] By definition, that means increases in either unemployment per person or out-of-the-labor-force per person, or both. Moreover, given that subsidy rates changed much more for unemployed people than for people out of the labor force (recall Figure 3.4), it is no surprise that the unemployment increase was significantly greater than the increase in the fraction of people out of the labor force.

Third, only minor additions to the model are needed to consider changes in the composition of spending (e.g., consumption versus investment goods) that result from changes in the overall level of spending and would create significant losses for types of workers who saw relative changes in their industry's demand. Suppose, for example, that people respond to the safety net expansion by keeping one automobile for their household, rather than two.[9] A number of people who make automobiles would then find themselves without a job and enduring a painful adjustment to employment in another industry. These former auto workers are not necessarily unemployed because they have access to an enhanced safety net, but rather because the people who used to purchase automobiles have access to an enhanced safety net.

The substantive assumption of my models that differentiates them from recent applications of both New Keynesian and older Keynesian models is that labor supply shifts have had the same aggregate marginal effects since 2007 as they did before. This is not to say that labor supply and demand are the same now as they were before the recession began; both my model and Keynesian models agree that they are not. The question is whether, say, a safety net expansion that would have depressed aggregate work hours by 10 percent if implemented before 2007 still depresses work hours by the roughly the same percentage if implemented since then. Keynesian models offer two theories why safety net expansions might have had different effects since 2007 than they did before: a "slack" labor market theory and a "sticky price" theory.

The "slack market" perspective on the labor market says that real wage rates have a floor—perhaps due to minimum wage laws, unions, or nominal rigidities—that is typically at or below the market clearing wage during non-recession periods, but above it during a recession. Moreover, employment is assumed to be determined only by demand during a recession, but by the combination of supply and demand during nonrecession periods (Galí 2011).[10] For example, an increase in the safety net's replacement rate during a recession would reduce labor supply, but that would reduce only the excess labor rather than actual employment. On the other hand, a labor demand shift during a recession would affect labor usage one for one without being even partially crowded out by factor rental rate adjustments.

The "slack market" view is oversimplified because wage rates are not the only mechanism to help clear the labor market. Suppose, for illustration, that recessions are times when labor unions are able to set a floor on wages with the objective of maximizing labor's surplus. The result could be unemployment in the sense that workers would have an individual incentive, but no opportunity, to work more at the wage floor, but nevertheless the wage floor might adjust according to supply and demand conditions. In fact, if the wage elasticity of labor demand were constant, the union wage markup would be a constant proportion of the marginal worker's reservation wage and the sensitivity of employment to supply and demand parameters would be the same as it would be in a competitive labor market, even while the total amount of employment was less than the competitive level.[11] An expansion of the safety net would cause the labor union to increase its wage floor, because the option of not working is less painful for its members than it would be without the expansion, and through this mechanism the safety net would reduce employment.

The contrast between the "slack market" view and nonwage labor allocation models also appears in studies of statutory minimum wages. For example, employers might react to a binding floor on a job's cash pay by changing the nonpecuniary aspects of the job, in which case equilibrium employment would be depressed by the floor but still be sensitive to workers' willingness to work.[12] The point of these examples is not that recessions are caused by labor unions and statutory minimum wages, but rather that the existence of unemployment does not by itself imply that employment is insensitive to labor supply at the margin.

Another exposition of the slack market theory says that safety net expansions do not prevent people from finding jobs during a recession because there are no jobs to be found. This exposition is literally untrue because millions of jobs were found every month during the recession (de Wolf and Klemmer 2010), but I take it to mean that good jobs are difficult to find during recessions. But a lack of good jobs might mean that the safety net is even more potent at keeping people from working during recessions because safety net benefits look more generous when compared to the pay from a bad job than when compared to the pay from a good job. Only empirical research can resolve the question of whether the labor market distortions that cause employment to be too low necessarily also create a "slack" market in the sense that marginal tax rates and other determinants of labor supply do not affect aggregate employment at the margin. The purpose of Chapter Eight is to present relevant empirical evidence and encourage additional research on this critical but so far neglected empirical question.

Sticky Prices, the Wage Elasticity of Labor Demand, and the Zero Lower Bound

New Keynesian theories offer a second reason safety net expansions might not affect work hours during a recession: because labor demand is especially wage inelastic during recessions. In this view, safety net expansions reduce labor supply regardless of whether there is a recession or not, but in a recession reduced labor supply serves only to raise real wages rather than reduce the

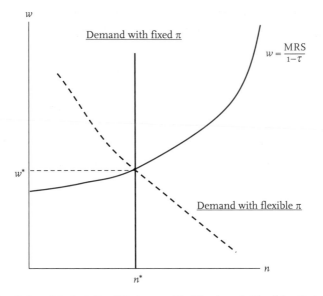

FIGURE 7.1. Labor Market Equilibrium with Fixed and Flexible Output Prices
When the output price is fixed, employers demand the number of employees
needed to produce the output demanded, shown as the vertical curve in the Figure.
When the output price is flexible, employer demand for labor is elastic according
to the marginal product of labor schedule, because he passes on some wage costs
to his customers (who have elastic demand curves). The Figure displays a single
labor "supply" curve that is common to both models.

quantity of labor.[13] This view is consistent with the labor supply analysis shown
in, say, Figure 4.1, but not with my assumption that the labor demand curve
has the same slope now that it did before the recession began. Rather, New
Keynesians view the labor market as shown by the two solid curves in Figure
7.1. Labor usage n is graphed on the horizontal axis, and the real (pretax) wage
rate on the vertical axis. Contrary to the dashed labor demand curve used in
this book, the New Keynesian analysis says that the labor demand curve is
vertical (over a range), as with the solid black curve.

   To understand why labor demand might be wage-inelastic, notice that
prices are one of the ways in which employers might signal to their customers
that the labor market has changed employment costs, and thereby create an
elastic labor demand curve. For example, an increase in the minimum wage
rate makes labor more expensive, in response to which the employers of
minimum wage labor might raise their prices. Customers react to a price
increase by purchasing less and, with fewer customers to serve the employers
can cut back on their labor. This "pass-through" process, as industrial

organization economists call it, links the amount of labor hired to the wage rate through a wage elastic labor demand curve like the one used throughout this book.

New Keynesians rule out the "pass-through" mechanism, at least during recessions, because prices are said to be "sticky": employers cannot change them in order to signal to their customers that the cost of labor has changed. The government can add to employer costs by raising marginal tax rates, imposing minimum wage rules, expanding the safety net, etc., and as long as the prices of final goods and services are fixed they have no effect on labor usage. Labor market conditions in the sticky price model affect wage rates paid by employers and received by employees, without affecting the amount of labor.

The reader may perceive that the sticky price theory seems too powerful, because it says that wages never affect the quantity of labor, regardless of whether there is a recession, because the final prices never reveal updated information about labor costs. But New Keynesian theory has two enhancements, at least for economies that are not in a recession or liquidity trap. One enhancement is that prices are not truly sticky but adjust over a period of years.[14] In that view, a minimum wage hike or safety net expansion does not cause an immediate or sudden price increase and thereby might not cause a sudden or immediate change in aggregate work hours, but as prices eventually adjust, higher labor costs reduce customer demand and reduce the usage of labor. In this regard, New Keynesian models can agree that the safety net expansions of 2008 and 2009 would eventually depress labor below what it was in 2007, but they might suggest that the effects are not seen until 2010 or beyond.

New Keynesian models sometimes include a second enhancement in their modeling of monetary policy. In this view, the stock of money might "normally" respond to changes in minimum wages, safety net expansions, and other labor market events in the direction of stabilizing prices, in large part because of deliberate actions by the monetary authority. Thus, when the safety net expands, the Federal Reserve recognizes that employers will begin to slowly raise their prices to pass on the greater labor costs, and it normally responds by reducing the supply of money in order to discourage employers from doing so. The reduced stock of money reduces consumer demand, and it does so more quickly than employer price adjustments would. Thus the normal situation could well be that safety net expansions quickly translate into less employment.

Simply put, the New Keynesian perspective says that the Federal Reserve's reaction to economic events is the primary mechanism by which labor supply shifts have an impact on employment in the short term. Although flattering to the Federal Reserve, this perspective is difficult for many labor economists to believe. However, rather than relying on labor economists' intuition, this book takes the New Keynesian perspective seriously and asks whether any of the labor market evidence confirms it.

It is true that monetary policy has historically responded to oil shocks (Bernanke, Gertler, and Watson 1997), the seasonal cycle (Sharp 1988), and other changes in economic fundamentals. "Taylor rules" for targeting the federal funds rate prescribe such responses and are said to characterize actual postwar monetary policy in the United States (Clarida, Galí, and Gertler 2000). At first glance, someone adopting the New Keynesian perspective might have expected the same to have occurred with the recent safety net expansions: the Federal Reserve would pursue a more contractionary (or less expansionary) monetary policy than it would have without the safety net expansions as it saw wages and final goods prices rise (or fail to fall as much), and as a result the safety net expansions would have more or less the same impact on employment as they normally do. And maybe this expectation is correct, in which case New Keynesian models would confirm my conclusion that safety net expansions since 2007 significantly reduced employment.

Christiano, Eichenbaum, and Rebelo (2009) and others suggest instead that the usual kinds of monetary adjustments could not occur during this recession because of the "zero interest lower bound." It is also true that money markets behaved quite differently during the 2008–09 recession than they had in the past. For example, the federal funds rate throughout 2009 was close to zero and, contrary to prior years, well above what the Taylor rule prescribed (Rudebusch 2009). For years, the amount of reserves of depository institutions held with the Federal Reserve system corresponded closely to the amount of required reserves, but in late 2008 excess reserves increased by a factor of 400 in a matter of four months (at the same time the fed funds rate fell to zero; see http://research.stlouisfed.org/). During those same four months, consumer prices fell 4 percent (that is, deflation at a 12 percent annual rate; see www.bls.gov).

Thus, it is plausible that neither monetary policy nor other money market events even approximately eliminated deflationary pressures during the 2008–09 recession, and plausible that they would not offset any change in those pressures that might have been created by fiscal policy, or changes in tastes and technology, during the recession. Perhaps this monetary state of affairs is the result of a zero lower bound on the fed funds rate,[15] but in any case it is possible that the simple sticky price comparative statics would better describe the short-term effects of shocks to labor market distortions and spending during the recession than it would during the previous years. It also suggests that evidence on the effects of changes in supply and demand during the recession would be especially valuable for determining whether labor supply continued to have some of the same marginal effects it did before 2007.

An Econometric Model That Nests My Approach with the Slack Market and Sticky Price Hypotheses

These economic hypotheses can be represented formally, and related to the empirical studies presented in Chapter Eight. The model features two groups of potential workers: one group *N* experiencing a labor supply change and another group *L* whose willingness to work is constant. In one application of this model to the market for low-skilled workers over the seasons, I consider the *N* group to be people of schooling age –their willingness to work varies over the academic seasons—and the *L* group to be other low-skilled people who are not enrolled in school any time during the year. In a second application to the market for commercial building, the *L* group consists of long-time commercial building workers and the *N* group consists of home building workers who might consider entering the market for commercial building if there were changes in the market for home building.

Suppose for the moment that wages adjust to clear the labor market, with labor demand and labor supply of the forms (7.1)–(7.4):

$$\ln L_t = \alpha^D(a_t) + \gamma^D(X_t) - \beta_L^D(X_t)\ln w_{Lt} + \left[\beta_L^D(X_t) - \eta^D(X_t)\right]\ln w_{Nt} + \varepsilon_{Lt}^D \qquad (7.1)$$

$$\ln N_t = \alpha^D(a_t) + \gamma^D(X_t) - \beta_N^D(X_t)\ln w_{Nt} + \left[\beta_N^D(X_t) - \eta^D(X_t)\right]\ln w_{Lt} + \varepsilon_{Nt}^D \qquad (7.2)$$

$$\ln L_t = \alpha_L^S(a_t) + \gamma_L^S(X_t) + \beta_L^S(X_t)\ln w_{Lt} + \varepsilon_{Lt}^S \qquad (7.3)$$

$$\ln N_t = \alpha_N^S(a_t) + \gamma_N^S(X_t) + \beta_N^S(X_t)\ln w_{Nt} + \varepsilon_{Nt}^S \qquad (7.4)$$

where L_t and N_t are work hours per person (hereafter, "labor usage") of the two groups and w_{Lt} and w_{Nt} are their real wage rates in month t, respectively.[16] The first two equations (7.1) and (7.2) are the labor demand curves, and the second two equations (7.3) and (7.4) are the supply curves. X_t indicates the state of the business cycle (normalized to have its largest values during business cycle troughs) at month t and a_t the state of the seasonal cycle (e.g., a dummy variable indicating the academic year) or other variable that shifts labor supply and demand separately from the business cycle. I assume that the two types of labor enter the production function homothetically (the wage elasticity of overall labor demand is $-\eta^D$), and that seasonal and business cycles shift overall labor demand but not relative labor demand. I assume that the two types of labor are substitutes (results reported in Mulligan 2011a suggest that the elasticity of substitution between teenagers and persons aged twenty to twenty-four is about 5), so we have the parameter restrictions $\beta_N^D, \beta_N^D - \eta^D, \beta_L^D, \beta_L^D - \eta^D, \beta_N^S, \beta_L^S \geq 0$. Seasonal impulses, business cycles, and month-specific shocks shift both labor supply and labor demand.

According to the "slack market" theory, recession labor supply exceeds labor demand at the going wage. In this view, employers collectively face a more elastic supply of labor during a recession because employees are supplied not only from out of the labor force but also from a large pool of involuntary unemployed. According to the "sticky price" model, aggregate labor demand is completely inelastic during a recession because employers are unable to adjust the price of their output and must produce whatever consumers demand at the fixed prices. The model (7.1)–(7.4) embodies these theories by allowing labor supply and demand elasticities to vary over the business cycle. The hypotheses that labor demand is less (labor supply is more) wage-elastic during a recession are represented as $\beta_i^{D'}(X)<0, \eta^{D'}(X)<0$ $(\beta_i^{S'}(X)>0, i=L,N)$, respectively.

The reduced form for the labor market quantities is:

$$\begin{pmatrix} \ln L_t \\ \ln N_t \end{pmatrix} = \Theta(X_t)v_t^S + \left[I - \Theta(X_t) \right]v_t^D = v_t^D + \Theta(X_t)\left[v_t^S - v_t^D \right] \qquad (7.5)$$

where the 2x1 vectors v_t^S (v_t^D) (each vector has one entry for the L group, and another entry for the N group) are the sum of the α, γ, and ε supply (demand) shifters, respectively. Θ is the incidence matrix; it depends on the relative supply and demand elasticities and shows the degree to which the amount of labor usage is affected by supply or demand at the margin.[17] When the incidence matrix is close to zero (the identity matrix), labor usage is primarily determined by demand (supply) at the margin, respectively. In the special case that both groups have the same supply elasticity, and shocks are common to the two groups—in effect, there is only one group—then the labor usage effects of supply and demand are summarized by the familiar incidence index

$\eta^D(X)/[\eta^D(X)+\beta^S(X)]$, which depends only on the ratio of the overall supply elasticity $\beta^S(X)$ to the (magnitude of the) overall demand elasticity $\eta^D(X)$.[18] For this reason, the slack market and sticky price models have similar implications for the reduced form (7.5)—namely that the incidence matrix is closer to zero during recessions—which are different from my assumption that the incidence matrix does not vary significantly over the business cycle.

If supply were to increase just for the N group and demand were held constant, then the labor usage effects would be represented by the righthand column of the incidence matrix. The bottom entry θ_{NN} in that column is between zero and 1, and the top entry θ_{LN} is in the interval $[-1,0]$: an increase in N supply (weakly) increases the usage of N labor and reduces the usage of L labor. An increase in N demand (weakly) increases the usage of both types of labor. The different effects of N supply and N demand on the usage of L labor help measure the relative size of supply and demand shifts in applications when both are shifting at the same time.

For the purposes of long-term analysis, economists generally agree that labor demand is fairly elastic, but they ultimately disagree about the magnitude of the long-term incidence parameters because estimates of the wage elasticities of group labor supply vary from close to zero to greater than 1. The hypothesis of interest in this chapter and the next is not necessarily whether the incidence matrix Θ is close to the identity matrix but whether it varies with the business cycle.

The model (7.5) and the corresponding wage rate reduced form are used in the next chapter to help identify episodes since 2007 when labor supply and labor demand have shifted by different amounts. Those episodes are used to test the hypothesis that the incidence matrix varies over the business cycle in the direction predicted by the slack market and sticky price theories.

Conclusion: Whether Labor Supply Matters More, or Less, During a Recession Is an Empirical Question

Even if marginal tax rates were held constant, redistribution—taking resources from one group and giving it to another—changes the composition of aggregate spending toward the spending patterns of the receiving group but might affect the total amount of spending in either direction. Empirical research has not yet linked the redistribution patterns of unemployment insurance, food stamps, etc., to the kinds of composition changes that would be needed to increase aggregate spending. Moreover, even if the direction were unambiguous, the magnitude of the aggregate spending effect is small, which is why my models approximate the redistribution effect on aggregate spending as zero and focus on the marginal tax rate effects.

The more interesting question is whether the employment effects of a given-sized marginal tax rate change vary over the business cycle or are different now that the yields on short-term Treasury Bills are so close to zero. My models assume that the employment effects are essentially the same now as they were before 2007, whereas the "slack market" and "sticky price" approaches suggest that they might be different. Economic theory alone cannot resolve this debate, but empirical observations can. This chapter therefore develops a simple econometric framework that embeds all three approaches. The relevant parts of that econometric model are estimated in the next chapter.

Appendix 7.1: The Safety Net, Sticky Prices, and Monetary Policy

This appendix offers a mathematical model of a static "sticky price" economy that demonstrates the proposition from the main text: that neither a safety net expansion nor a labor supply shift reduces labor in the sticky price model unless they induce the monetary authority to reduce the money stock. It has all of the elements of the model considered in Chapter Two, and then some. From Chapter Two, c denotes consumption and n denotes labor. Consumption goods are produced with labor according to the technology (7.6):

$$c = A^{0.3} n^{0.7} \tag{7.6}$$

The economy has another good called "money" that is in fixed supply (i.e., it is not produced with labor). Consumer preferences for consumption goods, money, and working are represented by the single utility function (7.7):

$$\ln c + \ln M - \gamma \frac{\eta}{1+\eta} n^{(\eta+1)/\eta} \tag{7.7}$$

where M is the amount of money that consumers have. Given this utility function, and the facts that (1) π is the price of consumption goods in terms of money[19] and (2) consumers cannot hold more money than the fixed supply that is available in the economy, the real amount of consumer goods purchased is (7.8):

$$c = \frac{M}{\pi} \qquad (7.8)$$

Consumers receive a wage w for each unit of time that they work, and a subsidy τw for each unit of time that they do not work. w is denominated in units of the consumption good. The subsidies are financed with lump sum tax revenue. The labor supply condition equates the marginal rate of substitution between consumption and labor to the real wage net of subsidies $(1 - \tau)w$:

$$\gamma \, c n^{1/\eta} = (1 - \tau)w \qquad (7.9)$$

If the three equations (7.6), (7.8), and (7.9) were combined with a labor demand equation setting the price level π proportional to marginal cost to determine the four economic variables c, n, w, π, then the comparative statics of labor, consumption, and output in this model with respect to the subsidy rate τ and the labor supply parameter γ are exactly the same as I consider in Chapter Two:[20] a greater subsidy rate τ, or a greater disutility of labor γ, means less labor. At the same time, holding fixed the supply of money M, this "flexible price" version of the model says that either a greater subsidy rate or a greater disutility of labor increases the price level π.

Price flexibility is why the labor demand curve would slope down if drawn in Figure 7.1 (see the dashed curve). A more generous safety net, or a greater disutility of work, results in a higher wage rate. Employers pass on their higher labor costs to customers, who purchase less. With customers purchasing less, less labor is needed.

In it starkest form, the New Keynesian model has a fixed price level π. For given values (M,π,τ,γ,η), the three sticky price equilibrium variables—consumption c, labor n, and the wage rate w –are the solution to the three simultaneous equations (7.6), (7.8), and (7.9). We see immediately from the consumption demand expression (7.8) that the subsidy rate τ and the preference parameter γ have no effect on consumer spending holding M fixed, because consumers spending is fixed by the ratio M/π. With no effect on consumer spending, equation (7.6) tells us there is no effect on labor. The only way a safety net expansion or an increase in the disutility of labor can reduce the amount of labor in the sticky price model is that the monetary authority reduces M in response. This monetary response may have been typical historically, in which cases safety net expansions and preference changes reduced labor, but Christiano, Eichenbaum, and Rebelo (2009) and others suggest that monetary responses like this did not or could not happen since 2007.

In terms of Figure 7.1, the sticky price labor demand curve is vertical, at least since 2007. A more generous safety net, or a greater disutility of work, results in a higher wage rate, but employers cannot pass on their higher labor costs to customers. With the price level fixed, the amount of consumer purchases, and therefore the amount of work needed to be done, is unaffected.

Recession-Era Effects of Factor Supply and Demand

EVIDENCE FROM THE SEASONAL CYCLE,
THE CONSTRUCTION MARKET, AND
MINIMUM WAGE HIKES

AS THE FEDERAL government wrote and passed the American Recovery and Reinvestment Act of 2009, which legislated about $800 billion worth of spending and revenue changes—including significant safety net program expansions—purported to "stimulate" the economy, economists revisited the question of whether government purchases might increase private spending, rather than reduce it. With the notable exception of Barro (2010), who explained that the act's tax reductions did not reduce marginal tax rates and that lengthened unemployment eligibility periods raised them, none of the recent analysis considered how the act and other recent fiscal expansions affected marginal tax rates.

When reporting research results that suggest fiscal expansions contract the private sector—as Alesina and Ardagna (2009), Barro and Redlick (2009), Mountford and Uhlig (2009), and Ramey (2011b) did—one might justify as a conservative assumption the neglect of the implicit marginal tax rates created by safety net expansions, because considering marginal tax rates would only strengthen the conclusion. Since those studies examined historical fiscal expansions, it might be argued as well that marginal tax rates were considered to the extent that the historical fiscal expansions also changed marginal tax rates.

However, another group of studies, including Christiano, Eichenbaum, and Rebelo (2009), Eggertsson (2009), Eggertsson and Krugman (2011), and Woodford (2011), report that fiscal expansions do not contract the private sector and furthermore claim that historical output responses to government spending impulses ought to be atypical of those that have occurred since 2007, because recently output is far below potential, and monetary policy is fundamentally different than it was in the past. Because they, and a number of studies attempting to explain what has happened to the economy since 2007, assume that factor supply has little or no marginal effect on employment and output, marginal tax rates are hardly relevant in their view.

Is it possible that factor supply does not matter during recessions in general, or this recession in particular? Does our economy suffer from a "paradox of toil," whereby expansions in factor supply actually reduce aggregate output (Eggertsson 2010a)? The answers to these questions do not have to remain a matter of assumption or economic intuition. The purpose of this chapter is to examine obvious factor supply and demand shifts occurring during this recession, using the framework developed in the previous chapter, to test the propositions that the incidence of supply and demand shifts are quite different than they were in the past, and in the direction assumed by Keynesian analysis. Although the claim that labor supply matters less during recessions is not new, it has not been the subject of much empirical testing.[1] Jurajda and Tannery (2003) find that unemployment insurance affects individual behavior to about the same degree in depressed localities as in less depressed ones. Schmieder, Wachter, and Bender (2012) find that nonemployment spells tend to last longer among otherwise similar people who have unemployment insurance that lasts longer, but that the magnitude of this effect is essentially constant over the business cycle. However, individual-level findings like these are still consistent with, say, the hypothesis that firm-level, industrial-level, or aggregate labor demand is wage-inelastic during a recession because individuals who remain unemployed during a recession as the result of unemployment insurance might merely be replaced by other workers. In other words, the question posed in this chapter is whether a given labor supply shift has a different employment impact during recessions, not whether a given safety net expansion shifts labor supply differently during recessions.

The chapter begins by examining the seasonal cycle, which features an obvious demand change—Christmas—and an obvious supply change: the availability of young people for work during the summer.[2] I then look at the market for commercial building, which saw an increase in factor supply as a result of the collapse of residential building. I conclude with estimates of employment effects of the 2007–2009 federal minimum wage hikes.

The seasonal cycle has advantages for the purpose of measuring the impact of supply and demand shocks. As Jeffrey Miron (1996, 17) explains, "The seasonal fluctuations are so large and regular that the timing of the peak or trough for any year is rarely affected by the phase of the business cycle in which that year happens to fall."[3] Barsky and Miron (1989, table 2) found that GNP falls 8 percent more than normal from Q4 to Q1. In a $14 trillion/year ($3.5 trillion/quarter) economy, that's a sudden reduction of $280 billion. Moreover, the summer and Christmas impulses react little to the business cycle, and thus provide the opportunity to measure differing effects, between recessions and nonrecessions, of a similar impulse. The seasonal cycles have occurred many times: there have been thirteen summers and fourteen Christmases during U.S. recessions since 1948. Even during the present recession—arguably different from many of the previous ones—Christmas and summer each occurred twice.

The summer seasonal impulse is greatest among young people, because they are the ones who attend school. Seasonal fluctuations might therefore be described as informative only about low-skill labor markets, although low-skill labor markets are important enough in their own right to show up in aggregate employment fluctuations. As noted above, the seasonal impulses are large enough to be visible in the national aggregates, and cannot be described as merely a redistribution of a fixed number of jobs among different types of workers.

My examination of the commercial building industry has the advantage that it measures output, which is an important variable in labor market analysis and captures the supply of all factors of production, not just labor. The expansion of the commercial building industry does not by itself indicate much about aggregate employment, although if Keynesian models are correct that wages and prices are sticky and that no other market mechanism serves the same allocative purposes, then it is mysterious as to why commercial building would expand as a result of home building's contraction.

The federal minimum wage hikes do not offer a test of sticky wage Keynesian models, because the point of those models is that wages do not adjust to clear the labor market. But the hikes do offer a test of the sticky price Keynesian model that says wages and labor supply have no effect on a firm's employment or output, at least in the short term, because they do not pass on labor market costs to their customers. The federal minimum wage hikes are interesting in their own right because they help explain why employment fell among teenagers, whose labor market is hardly examined elsewhere in this book.

All of the chapter's tables and charts are selected from Mulligan (2011a) and Mulligan (2011c). Readers interested in additional related results or data processing information should consult those papers.

Christmas and Academic Seasons as Demand and Supply Shifts

Equation (7.5), repeated below, shows that in order to detect the incidence matrix's business cycle—that is, the sign of $\Theta'(X)$—it helps to have a season or seasons in which supply and demand are known to shift by different amounts because the incidence matrix multiplies the gap $(v_t^S - v_t^D)$. Christmas and summer are two such seasons.

$$\binom{\ln L_t}{\ln N_t} = \Theta(X_t)v_t^S + \left[I - \Theta(X_t)\right]v_t^D = v_t^D + \Theta(X_t)\left[v_t^S - v_t^D\right] \qquad (7.5)$$

The Christmas and summer seasonal fluctuations are fundamentally different, in that the former can be interpreted as primarily a labor demand increase and the latter as primarily (although not solely; more on this below) a labor supply increase. Figure 8.1 displays three labor market indicators—weekly hours worked, hourly pay for full-time jobs, and unemployment—for each of two seasons, from the CPS-MORG public use files from January 2000 through December 2009.[4] For the moment I focus on persons younger than thirty-five, because their job turnover rates are expected to be greater and thereby more visibly display the effects of short-term fluctuations such as Christmas or summer. The figure shows seasonal "spikes": the level of the indicator during Christmas (the months of November and December) or the summer (the months of June–August), relative to the indicator during the four months "nearby" the season. Wages and unemployment are measured in logs, and hours spikes are expressed as a proportion to a group's average hours for the entire season and adjacent months. The spikes shown in Figure 8.1 are averages for the years 2000–2009.

The figure's top panel displays weekly hours spikes, where weekly hours are measured as zero for any survey respondent who was on vacation or otherwise not at work during the survey reference week. Each group's spike is positive on Christmas. During the summer, the spikes are positive only for the two younger age groups.[5] All three Christmas wage spikes (middle panel) are positive, while all three summer wage spikes are negative.[6]

Retail sales, which currently average about $360 billion per month, are usually more than 25 percent higher in December.[7] As a result, the retail sector is expected to have especially high labor demand during the Christmas season. One may also expect labor supply to be different, especially during Thanksgiving and during the last two weeks of December, but the Census Bureau data shown in Figure 8.1 do not measure activity during the week of

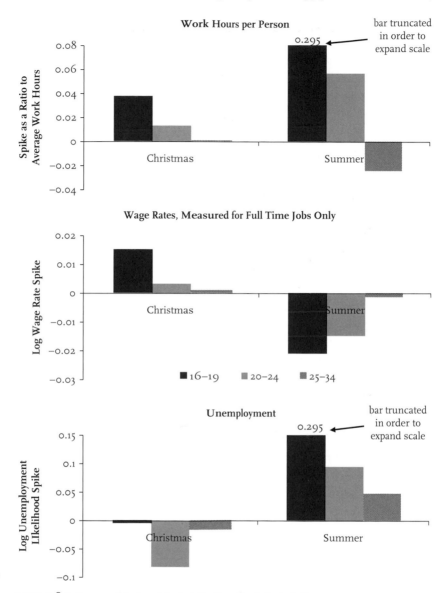

FIGURE 8.1 Seasonal Labor Market Spikes for Selected Groups

Thanksgiving, Christmas, or New Year's Day.[8] According to the common demand shift interpretation, it is no surprise that all groups have work hours and wages that are higher than normal during the Christmas season.

The summer labor supply shift among school aged people is potentially massive. Table 8.1 displays October employment in selected industries, averaged for the years 2000–2009. About twenty million people aged sixteen to thirty-four are enrolled in school during the academic year (especially those aged sixteen to twenty-four), and nineteen million of them are not working full-time. Considered as an "industry," school enrollment is many times larger than, say, the U.S. military or the entire construction industry. Summer vacation makes millions of young people available for work. By itself, this is a supply shift that is specific to school-aged people (the N group in equation 7.5's notation): it should increase hours for school-aged people, reduce hours for people beyond school age (the L group in equation 7.5's notation), and reduce both groups' wages.

Agriculture, construction, and other industries are expected to be more active when the weather is warmer, and school vacation has an impact on family activities. For these and other reasons, the composition of labor demand, if not its level, is expected to be different during the summer. Even so, it is less than obvious that, absent pressures from the supply side, summer labor demand would be *several million* greater and thereby shift as much as labor supply does (see also Miron, 1996, p. 9). More important, the data shown in Figure 8.1 do not suggest any massive summer labor demand shift: persons aged twenty-five to thirty-four actually work fewer hours during the summer, and (unlike Christmas) the summer wage spike is negative for all three age groups.

All three Christmas unemployment spikes (bottom panel) are negative and all three summer unemployment spikes are positive. Taken literally, the model (7.1)–(7.4) is silent about unemployment, but the unemployment data shown in Figure 8.1's bottom panel appear to confirm the hypotheses that

Table 8.1 School Enrollment is a Huge Occupation

2000–2009 average

Selected Activities in October	*Millions of Persons Aged 16–34*
Enrolled in school	20.3
Enrolled in school, not otherwise employed full-time	18.7
Restaurant or other food service worker	4.8
Construction worker	4.0
U.S. military	1.2

Note: U.S. military estimate refers to all military personnel with sixteen or fewer years of service, regardless of age.

Sources: CPS-MORG 2000–2009. U.S. military from FY 2003–FY 2009 issues of U.S. Department of Defense, "Selected Military Compensation Tables Report."

labor demand increases more than supply during Christmas and labor supply increases more than demand during the summer.

Christmas Demand in Recessions and Booms

The business cycles of the Christmas and academic seasons are examined with the same basic annual time series regression specification. The dependent variable is a seasonal outcome measure, and the independent variables are a cubic in calendar time (normalized to zero in 1980) and a measure of the state of the business cycle in November and December (or, for summer analysis, June through August). The time cubic captures demographics and other slow-moving determinants of the seasonal cycle during nonrecession years. The coefficient on the business cycle indicates how much the seasonal is different during recessions than during nonrecession years, if at all.

The Christmas seasonal for a labor market outcome, such as log aggregate employment, is measured as the average of seasonally unadjusted November and December values minus the average of seasonally unadjusted values for the nearby months of September, October, January, and February. I measure the business cycle with a 0–1 indicator for whether November or December (or, in the case of academic seasons, one of the months June, July, or August) was in part of a business cycle peak-trough interval defined by the NBER recession dating committee.[9]

Figure 8.1 uses the CPS-MORG from 2000 to 2009 to examine the typical Christmas and summer seasonal fluctuations. But the purpose of this chapter is to determine the amount, if any, by which seasonal fluctuations are *different* during recession years from what they typically are. For this purpose it helps to have more accurate data for many recessions, which for employment and unemployment have been aggregated by month and age category by the Bureau of Labor Statistics (BLS) dating back to January 1948 for all of the monthly CPS respondents (hereafter, "the household survey"), and not just the outgoing rotation groups. In addition, I use the BLS seasonally unadjusted monthly employment aggregates of the establishment survey, and seasonally unadjusted measures of retail sales (from January 1967) published by the Census Bureau.

Under the assumption that the Christmas season shifts labor demand more than it shifts labor supply, the slack market and sticky price theories predict that a given-sized labor demand increase will increase employment more during a recession. As a result, the labor demand increase will reduce unemployment more during a recession.

I ran three annual time series regressions of the Christmas seasonal on a recession indicator, a third-order time polynomial (with 1980 normalized to zero), and a constant. The three regressions differed in terms of the dependent variable: the employment seasonal measured from the establishment survey, the employment seasonal measured from the household survey, and the unemployment seasonal. The top row of Table 8.2 displays the constant term estimates: the average Christmas seasonal for log employment and log unemployment (from the perspective of the benchmark year in the calendar time cubic, 1980). Not surprisingly, each of them has an economically and statistically significant seasonal. The table's first column shows how, in the average nonrecession year, log aggregate November and December employment is 0.0129 above what it is in the nearby months. Christmas unemployment is below trend. All of the constant terms are broadly consistent with the Christmas hours and unemployment seasonality shown in Figure 8.1.

Table 8.2 Christmas Seasonal Changes in Labor Force Status

Each column of the Table reports a regression result, with the dependent variable varying by column. The dependent variables are 100 times the deviation of November & December log per capita (establishment employment, a household employment, or unemployment) from the average of Sept., Oct., Jan. and Feb. The recession indicator is an indicator variable for NBER recession dates

| | Outcome Measure | | |
Statistic	Emp., Est.	Emp., HH	Unemp.
Nonrecession seasonal,	1.29	0.81	−6.85
100ths of log points	(0.04)	(0.05)	(0.71)
Recession coefficient,	−0.07	0.06	−1.77
100ths of log points	(0.06)	(0.08)	(1.09)
Recession seasonal/nonrecession	0.95	1.07	1.26
seasonal	(0.05)	(0.10)	(0.21)
Recession seasonal/nonrecession	1.00	1.14	1.33
seasonal, relative to retail sales	(0.06)	(0.12)	(0.24)

Notes: OLS standard errors in parentheses.
Independent variables are a recession indicator, a third-order time polynomial (0 = 1980), and a constant.
Log per capita retail sales' recession seasonal is 0.945 times its nonrecession seasonal. These ratios are used to construct the bottom panel from the third panel.

The table's second row displays the various regressions' coefficients on the business cycle term: the estimated gap between the recession seasonal and the nonrecession seasonal. The table's third row displays the size of a recession seasonal relative to a nonrecession seasonal, which is calculated as 1 plus the ratio of the corresponding business cycle coefficient displayed in the second row to the corresponding constant term from the top row. If it were true that labor demand mattered significantly more during recessions, then we would expect coefficients in the second row to differ from zero—in an economically and statistically significant amount—in the positive direction for employment and in the negative direction for unemployment. For the same reason, we expect the coefficients in the third row to be economically and statistically greater than one.

Assuming for the moment that the Christmas seasonal impulse does not vary over the business cycle, one of the three point estimates for employment's seasonal recession–nonrecession gap has the "wrong" sign: the Christmas employment seasonal is smaller during recessions. Unemployment is low during the Christmas season, but results reported in the second row of the table cannot reject the hypothesis that the Christmas unemployment drop is about the same in recession and nonrecession years.

The business cycle for employment and wage seasonality depends both on the business cycle of the incidence matrix and on the business cycle for the underlying seasonal impulse to tastes or technology. Because the business cycle of the incidence matrix is the object of interest here, and employment and wage seasonal changes are readily measured, a seasonal fluctuation that is ideal for measuring the cyclicality of the incidence parameter would derive from a seasonal impulse to tastes or technology whose magnitude is independent of the business cycle, or at least would have a business cycle of a known magnitude. Some of the impulses driving the Christmas seasonal changes, such as seasonal weather patterns, may be independent of the business cycle. But others, such as end-of-year retirements or the preference for Christmas retail purchases, are probably different during a recession.

In order to be conservative relative to the hypothesis that the incidence matrix has no business cycle, I measure the seasonality of the incidence parameter as the seasonality of aggregate log labor activities (employment, etc.) per unit seasonality of retail sales, with retail sales normalized by a seasonally adjusted measure of national labor income.[10] The bottom row of Table 8.2 displays the results. For example, if the Christmas seasonal for log aggregate household employment is 7 percent greater during recessions (see the table's third row) but Christmas seasonal for normalized retail sales is 6 percent less, then 1.14 (= 1.07/0.94) is entered in the corresponding cell of the table's bottom row. None of the entries are statistically different from 1.

Although Christmas is not primarily a supply shock, supply can matter less during recessions only if demand matters more. Formally, the basic equilibrium theory above permits us to infer the business cycle of the supply incidence matrix Θ from estimates of the demand incidence matrix $(I - \Theta)$ made possible from the Christmas season. In particular, Table 8.2 suggests that employment's demand incidence matrix $(I - \Theta)$ seems to have little or no business cycle (Table 8.2, first and second columns), which means that the supply incidence matrix $\Theta = I - (I - \Theta)$ has little or no seasonal.

Figures 8.2 and 8.3 display the time series used in Table 8.2 together with fitted values from the table's employment regressions. Figure 8.2 shows how only four of the twelve NBER recession year payroll employment observations lie above the nonrecession regression function. As shown in Figure 8.3, CPS employment (otherwise known as employment from the "household survey") has a Christmas seasonal that is slightly larger in the average recession year. If we give special attention to the last three years in the time series—the 2007, 2008, and 2009 Christmas seasons, when short-term Treasury Bill rates were low (2007), or essentially zero (2008 and 2009)—we see that those observations lie near the regression line, and usually below it. These data give no

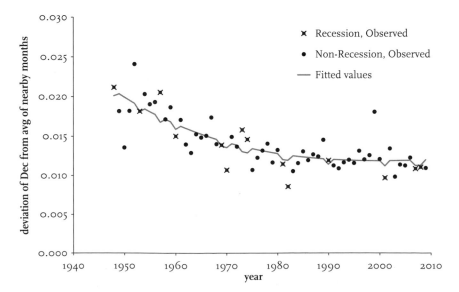

FIGURE 8.2 Christmas Log Payroll Employment Seasonals, All Ages

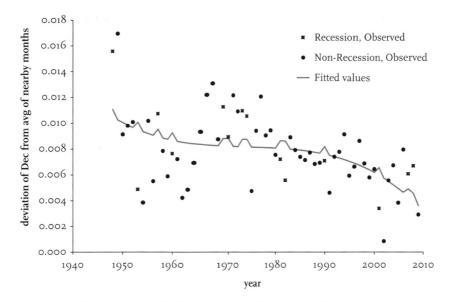

FIGURE **8.3** Christmas Log CPS Employment Seasonals, All Ages

reason to conclude that labor demand shocks matter significantly more since 2007 than they did in the typical nonrecession year.

The Summer Seasonal Change for Employment and Unemployment

Although employment is high in both the summer and in December, the evidence presented in Figure 8.1 and Table 8.1 suggests that the impulses creating high employment in the two seasons are fundamentally different. Among other things, the summer patterns for wages and unemployment are the opposite of the December patterns, which suggests that supply is the more important impulse in the summer and demand is the more important impulse in December. Mulligan (2011a) uses further results on wages and hours, and finds that labor demand is high during the summer, but that its increase is less than half of the increase in labor supply. Thus it is no surprise that summer wages are low and summer unemployment is high. As a result, according to the slack market and sticky price theories, the summer employment surge during recessions should be less than half of what it normally is.

The summer seasonal change for a labor market outcome, such as log aggregate employment, is measured as the June through August average of seasonally unadjusted values minus a seasonally unadjusted average for the nearby months of April, May, September, and October. Table 8.3's first two rows display constant terms from the summer seasonal regressions: that is, the average summer seasonal for employment and unemployment by age group for the nonrecession years (from the perspective of the benchmark year in the calendar time polynomial, 1980). For the younger age groups, the gap between academic year and summer is positive and economically significant for *both* employment and unemployment, which is to be expected given that so many of the younger people become available for work when the academic year ends. For the nonrecession years, summer log employment per capita for teenagers from sixteen to nineteen exceeds the average for nearby months by 0.247 and summer log unemployment per capita exceeds the values for the nearby months by an average of 0.279.

The top row of the table also suggests that the size of the summer seasonal impulse may exceed the impulses associated with the largest postwar business

Table 8.3 Summer Seasonals For Employment and Unemployment, by Age Group
Each column reports results from an employment regression and an unemployment regression. The dependent variable is 100 times the summer deviation of log per capita employment (unemployment) from the average of April, May, Sept., and Oct.

Statistic	Outcome	Age Group			
		16–19	20–24	25–34	16+
Nonrecession seasonal, 100ths of log points	Emp.	24.7 (0.4)	5.1 (0.2)	−1.2 (0.1)	1.6 (0.1)
	Unemp.	27.9 (1.2)	9.6 (0.8)	3.1 (0.9)	9.8 (0.7)
Recession coefficient, 100ths of log points	Emp.	−1.70 (0.70)	0.05 (0.26)	0.03 (0.11)	0.00 (0.11)
	Unemp.	−2.30 (1.84)	−0.82 (1.31)	−0.84 (1.47)	−1.96 (1.18)
Recession seasonal/ nonrecession seasonal	Emp.	0.93 (0.03)	1.01 (0.05)	0.97 (0.09)	1.00 (0.07)
	Unemp.	0.92 (0.07)	0.91 (0.13)	0.73 (0.47)	0.80 (0.12)

Notes: OLS standard errors in parentheses.
Independent variables are a NBER recession dummy, a third-order time polynomial (time 0 = 1980), and a constant.

cycles. Log employment per capita for persons aged sixteen to nineteen fell "only" 0.156 from 1979 to 1983, and "only" 0.295 from 2007 to 2010, whereas it falls 0.247 at the end of a typical summer.

Even without regard to recessions, the summer seasonal varies over time. For example, minimum wages, activities at school, and other factors can change the propensity of teens to work during the school year, and therefore the fraction of teens whose labor supply would shift when summer begins. These factors are considered in my analysis by its inclusion of a smooth function of calendar time among the independent variables.

Table 8.3's middle rows display the estimated coefficients on the NBER recession indicator variable, that is, the gaps between a summer seasonal change during recession years and the corresponding seasonal change for nonrecession years. The gaps for employment are typically in the direction predicted by the various theories—that is, employment would expand less during recession summers—but are not economically significant. For example, the average recession seasonal for log employment per sixteen-to-nineteen-year-old is only 0.017 smaller than the average of 0.247 for nonrecession years, or about 93 percent of the nonrecession seasonal change (see the fifth row of the table). Recall that the slack labor market and sticky price theories predict that the recession employment seasonal would be less than half of what it normally is. The gaps for unemployment are not always in the direction predicted by the theory, and are statistically indistinguishable from zero.

Figure 8.4 displays the annual time series for the summer log employment seasonal change for the sixteen-to-nineteen age group together with fitted values from the regression used for the employment row of Table 8.3's first column. The figure indicates recession year observations with squares and nonrecession year observations with circles. The fitted values follow a smooth curve for the nonrecession years, and small spikes down in the recession years.[11] The employment data also display small down spikes in many (but not all) of the recession years, which is why the recession coefficient of –1.70 is statistically significant.

However, –1.70 is small enough that slack labor market and sticky price theories fail to come at all close to fitting even one of the recession observations better than the hypothesis that the recession and nonrecession seasonal changes are the same. Every single recession economy absorbed large numbers of new teen arrivals into the labor market without a statistically abnormal rise in unemployment; all of the recession employment seasonal observations are much closer to the nonrecession observations than to zero.

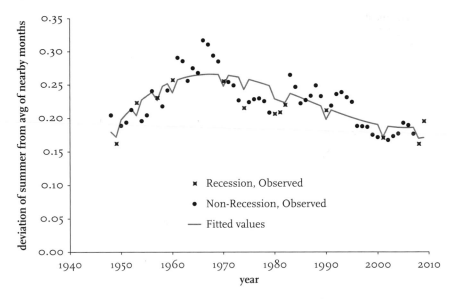

FIGURE 8.4 Summer Log Employment Seasonals, Ages 16–19

Housing Investment Crowds Out Nonresidential Construction

In the sticky price model, a demand increase in one sector increases output in that sector (say, the public sector), without reducing output in other sectors because the competition for factors of production is not passed into output prices that would otherwise cause production to be reallocated to the demanded sector. For the same reason, a reduction in demand in one sector would not cause the other sectors to produce more, unless the former's demand reduction was indicative of a demand shift to the latter sector.[12]

The private residential and nonresidential building sectors are an interesting case study, because the demand for housing surged 2000–2005, and collapsed thereafter. Figure 8.5 displays quarterly real residential and real nonresidential structures investment since 2000 Q1. Nonresidential investment remained low throughout the housing boom. Both residential and nonresidential investment turned at almost exactly the same time, in opposite directions. Nonresidential investment increased throughout 2006, 2007, and 2008, while residential investment was collapsing.

The large reduction in the workforce that became apparent by 2009, not to mention tight credit, likely reduced the desired stock of nonresidential buildings, and this by itself would cut nonresidential investment activity, so it

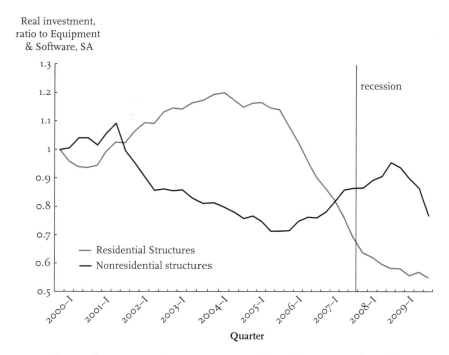

FIGURE 8.5 Real Investment in Structures: Residential vs. Nonresidential

helps to separate the effect of an increased supply of resources for nonresidential investment from reduced demand. I attempt to do so by examining the two investment series in a regression framework that includes measures of the business cycle.

I use quarterly data on male employment rates and per capita real structures investment from 1996-Q1 through 2010-Q3.[13] Each column of Table 8.4 reports estimates of a time series regression with real per capita nonresidential structures investment as the dependent variable. The independent variables include a linear time trend, real per capita residential structures investment, and the log of the male employment rate. In some of the specifications, lags of the independent variables are included in which case the table displays the sum of the coefficients estimated on all lags (including lag zero).[14] Both investment variables are measured in 2005 dollars, so a coefficient of −1 on the residential investment variable would be found if the only fluctuations in building activity were the substitution of building activity in one sector for the same amount of building activity in the other sector. The log employment rate series was rescaled by multiplying by the 1996-Q1–2007-Q4 average of the dependent variable; its coefficient can therefore be interpreted as an elasticity.

Table 8.4 Crowding Out of Real Inv. in Non-Res. Structures

Each column of the Table reports results from a real per capita non-residential structures investment regression.

	(1)	(2)	(3)	(4)	(5)
End sample:	2007-Q4	2007-Q4	2007-Q4	2010-Q3	2010-Q3
Estimation method:	*Levels*	*First Diff.*	*Levels*	*Levels*	*Levels*
No. of current and lagged terms:	4	4	1	1	1
Sum of coeff's on real per capita housing investment terms	−0.32 (0.09)	−0.30 (0.13)	−0.29 (0.09)	−0.29 (0.09)	−0.24 (0.07)
Sum of coeff's on log male emp. rate terms, converted to elasticity	8.05 (1.14)	8.05 (2.00)	2.23 (1.13)	2.22 (1.14)	4.80 (0.78)
Recession measured as:	N/A	N/A	N/A	2008–Q1– 2010–Q3	NBER dates
Recession indicator				−5.10 (2.95)	0.92 (2.05)
Recession indicator * (real per capita housing investment)				0.06 (0.30)	0.11 (0.17)
Recession indicator * (rescaled log male employment rate)				2.98 (1.79)	−0.57 (1.26)
Time trend (constant in first diff.)	0.003 (0.001)	0.003 (0.002)	0.001 (0.001)	0.001 (0.001)	0.001 (0.001)
Constant	−13.6 (2.0)	N/A	−3.4 (2.0)	−3.4 (2.0)	−7.8 (1.4)
Observations	48	48	48	59	59
Adjusted R-squared	0.88	0.26	0.73	0.74	0.78
S.e.	0.010	0.010	0.012	0.012	0.012

Notes: (a) Quarterly observations beginning 1996-Q1.
(b) Regressions are estimated with the Prais-Winsten correction for first-order serial correlation (STATA command "prais").
(c) Standard errors in parentheses.
(d) Independent variables are current and lagged (up to three lags) real housing per capita housing inv. and log male emp. rate (rescaled by the dependent variable's mean) and, when applicable, a recession indicator interacted with those terms.
(e) Both structures investment variables are measured in 2005 dollars per capita.

Columns (1) and (2) differ only in terms of the estimation method—levels versus first differences—and both report an economically and statistically significant negative relationship between structures investment in the two sectors. The point estimates suggest that one hundred units more housing investment is associated with thirty to thirty-two units less nonresidential structures investment, which is consistent with a significant amount of crowding out of one sector's building by building in the other sector. Column (3) omits any lags of the independent variables, but reports a similar negative relationship between the two sectors' structures investment.

Columns (1)–(3) use only data from before 2008, and it has been argued that crowding out would not occur during the recession, even though it occurred in years before. As one way to examine this possibility, I estimated two least squares versions of each of Table 8.4's columns (1) and (2), again using only the data prior to 2008, and then used those estimates to predict nonresidential building through 2010-Q3. One version has the same independent variables as used in columns (1) and (2) of the table. The other version omits the housing investment variable, so that the difference between the two predictions can be interpreted as the expected effect of the housing crash on nonresidential structures investment since 2007. The predictions for nonresidential structures investment were made by using the estimated coefficients (and, for the level specifications, adjusting the constant term so that the models exactly fit 2007-Q4 nonresidential structures investment[15]) and the actual data through 2010-Q3 for housing investment and the male employment rate.

The predictions are shown in Figure 8.6, together with the actual investment series, with the vertical line to the left of 2008-Q1 indicating the end-of-sample quarters that were excluded from the regressions used to make the predictions. When the housing investment variable is ignored, nonresidential building is predicted to drop all quarters (the gray series in Figure 8.6).[16] In fact, nonresidential building peaked in 2008-Q2 and remained pretty flat through the end of the year. The models including the housing investment variable (black series in Figures 8.6) correctly predict this pattern, as well as the actual sharp drop to begin 2009. Overall, the models without housing investment consistently underpredict nonresidential building whereas the predictions based on the housing investment variable are closer, having predictions on both sides of the actual series. Figure 8.6 is inconsistent with the claim that crowding out disappeared during the recent recession.

Table 8.4's columns (4) and (5) further explore the possibility that crowding out differs in recessions from other times by interacting the independent

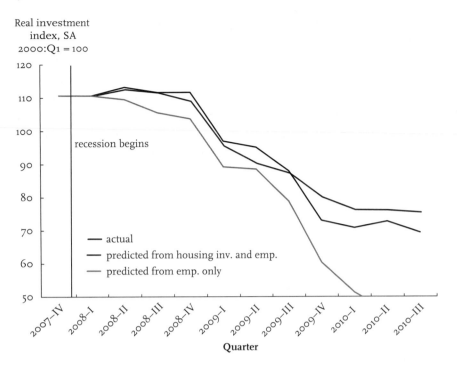

FIGURE 8.6 Real Investment in Non-Residential Structures: Crowding Out (out-of-sample predictions from level specifications)

variables with a recession indicator. One of the recession indicators is a dummy for the quarters since 2007, and the other is an indicator for the quarters coded as recession by the National Bureau of Economic Research. If crowding out were zero during a recession, then the coefficient on the housing investment interaction would be positive and equal in magnitude to the negative coefficient on the uninteracted housing investment term. Instead, the estimated coefficient on that interaction term is economically and statistically insignificant. Thus, Table 8.4 is inconsistent with the claim that recessions have significantly less crowding out.

The Employment Effects of Recent Minimum Wage Hikes Were No Less Than Before

In July 2007, the federal minimum hourly wage was increased for the first time in ten years, to $5.85 from $5.15. It was increased again a year later to $6.55, and increased yet again on July 24, 2009, to $7.25 (U.S. Department of Labor, 2009). Consumer prices were generally rising prior to the summer of 2008, but fell 2.1 percent from July 2008 to July 2009.[17] Thus, the real minimum wage hike was large in July 2009, and began from a higher base than the previous two hikes did.

The effects of the federal minimum wage hikes, especially the last one, are informative for three reasons. First, to the extent that the federal minimum wage hikes had any significant negative impact on employment since 2007, they reject the sticky price hypothesis that the demand for labor has recently been wage-inelastic in the short term. Second, to the extent that the federal minimum wage hikes had an impact on employment since 2007 that was no less than the impact of similar hikes before 2007, they reject the sticky price hypothesis that the demand for labor has recently been less wage-elastic. Third, estimates of the employment impacts of the federal minimum wage hikes might help explain why employment fell among less-skilled people and youths, as well as among the household heads and spouses who have been the subject of much of my analysis.

The minimum wage has been hiked by the federal government and by state governments many times in the past, and hundreds of studies have attempted to quantify the results. David Neumark and William Wascher recently surveyed this literature (Neumark and Wascher 2008) and executed a number of the studies themselves. They report that a majority of the studies find that the elasticity of young people's employment rates with respect to the minimum wage prevailing in their state fall in the range −0.1 to −0.4. The studies given the most weight by Neumark and Wascher control for Federal Reserve policies (through their use of "time effects" or "year effects"), and therefore already seem inconsistent with the New Keynesian sticky price hypothesis that labor demand is affected by wages in the short term only via Federal Reserve policy reactions.

Because all of the studies surveyed used data prior to 2008, none of them can guarantee that minimum wage hikes in 2008 or 2009 would necessarily reduce employment. The study by Even and Macpherson (2010) is informative in this regard, because (1) they use data from January 2005 through April 2010, with most of the relevant minimum wage changes occurring since the middle of 2007; and (2) they employ a methodology that was used prior to 2007 (Burkhauser, Couch, and Wittenburg 2000). Even and Macpherson (2010) find a statistically significant negative effect of minimum wages on teen employment, and their elasticity point estimates are actually a bit further from zero than Burkhauser, Couch, and Wittenberg's.[18] Thus, the Even and Macpherson study gives no reason to believe that labor demand has been wage-inelastic, or less wage-elastic, since 2007.

Neumark and Wascher (2008, 83) explain that the elasticity of teen employment with respect to the prevailing minimum wage is less in magnitude than the elasticity of teen employment with respect to teen wages, because most teens already earn in excess of the minimum wage. For this reason, one might want to adjust the elasticities from the Even and Macpherson (2010) and Burkhauser, Couch, and Wittenberg (2000) studies for the propensity to earn minimum wage before comparing them. Assuming that earning minimum wage was less common for the recent minimum wage hikes than it was historically—that was part of the justification for the 2007–2009 hikes in the first place (Bernstein and Shapiro 2006)—then the adjustment would only strengthen my conclusion that labor demand is no less wage-elastic since 2007 than it was historically.

Proponents of high minimum wages claim that the negative employment impact of minimum wages is small compared to its ability to raise the incomes of low-skilled people who are able to keep their jobs (New York Times Editorial Board 2011). My primary purpose here is not to determine whether high minimum wages are a good idea, but merely to determine whether the wage elasticities of supply and demand are about the same as they were before 2007, so that I might use the historical estimates of those elasticities to understand the labor market consequences of the safety net expansions since 2007. The historical minimum wage changes so far give no indication that those elasticities suddenly became different during this recession.

The Federal Minimum Wage Hikes Likely Reduced National Employment by Hundreds of Thousands, Especially Among the Young and Unskilled

Using the estimates surveyed in Neumark and Wascher (2008) and information about the amount and character of the July 2009 federal minimum wage hike, Neumark (2009) estimated that the July 2009 hike would reduce national employment among teens and young adults by three hundred thousand. Given that about half of all persons earning at or below the minimum wage in 2008 were under twenty-five and the other half over that age (U.S. Bureau of Labor Statistics 2009a), Neumark's teen and youth estimate suggests that the nationwide employment effect (all ages) of the July 2009 minimum wage hike might be a reduction of about six hundred thousand, although this estimate includes employment increases among older persons earning above minimum wage only to the extent that they occur at the same rate among young people. Moreover, only a small fraction of the studies surveyed by Neumark and Wascher (2008) looked at persons over age twenty-five, so little is known about the employment impact among minimum wage workers that age.[19]

My 2011 paper (Mulligan 2011c) estimated a monthly time series model of national part-time and full-time employment per capita for each of twelve demographic groups distinguished according to race, gender, and age, relative to prime-aged white males, whose employment rates were assumed to be unaffected by the July 2009 minimum wage hike. I used the model to estimate the amount and composition of employment losses due to the hike for the average month between August 2009 and December 2010, and found that lower-skill groups had the greater employment losses. The net nationwide employment loss estimate was 829,000, which includes employment gains among more skilled people.

The inflation-adjusted minimum wage increased 32 percent from December 2006 to December 2009, two-thirds of which was the result of the 2007 and 2008 hikes, yet neither Neumark's estimate nor mine includes any effect of the two earlier hikes. Because the minimum wage hikes were cumulative—each increased the minimum wage from the level set by the previous hike—the 2007 and 2008 hikes probably had lesser nationwide employment effects per dollar than the 2009 hike did. For example, only 2.2 percent of persons earning hourly wages were at or below minimum wage in 2006 (U.S. Bureau of Labor Statistics 2007), as compared to 3.0 percent in 2008 (U.S. Bureau of Labor Statistics 2009a) and 4.9 percent in 2009 (U.S. Bureau of Labor Statistics 2010a). If, as a back-of-the-envelope calculation, we assume that the national employment effect per dollar of the 2007 and 2008 hikes combined was half of the 2009 hike's effect, and that the 2009 hike was half the number of dollars, then the nationwide employment impact of all three hikes combined might be twice the impact of the 2009 hike by itself, or about 1.20 million building from Neumark (2009) and 1.66 million building from Mulligan (2011c).

Among persons aged sixteen and over who were neither elderly nor household head or spouse, employment per capita fell from 58.0 percnt in 2007 to 52.3 percent in 2009. If instead their employment rate had continued to be 58.0 percent, about three million more of them would have been working. Thus, the minimum wage hikes since July 2007 might explain about roughly one-third to one-half of the employment decline among persons aged sixteen and over who were neither elderly nor household head or spouse. Much more work can be done to estimate the nationwide minimum wage impacts, and to fully explain why employment fell among young people since 2007.

Conclusion: Labor Supply Still Matters, About as Much as It Did in the Past

The academic year concluded twice during this recession, and both times more than a million teens entered the labor market. Well over a million of them found employment, and as a result total employment for the economy was significantly higher in July than it was in April. This pattern reversed itself the two times that the academic year resumed during this recession.

The commercial building market expanded more, or contracted less, because resources became available from the collapsing home building market (see also Council of Economic Advisers February 2010, 124). The minimum wage hikes of 2007, 2008, and 2009 appear to have significantly reduced employment, especially among less-skilled people.

Despite the presence of perhaps the deepest recession of our lifetimes, and nominal interest rates on government securities that were essentially zero, these episodes show that labor demand is wage-elastic, and that employment continues to be sensitive to the willingness to work. To a first approximation, the wage elasticity of labor demand and the sensitivity of employment to the willingness to work is about the same since 2007 as it was before. For this reason, the historical data continue to be our best source of information on the possible present-day effects of safety net expansions and other changes in the willingness to work on national employment and wages.

This chapter finds that labor supply continues to affect aggregate labor usage at the margin. In other words, *if* there were a reduction in labor supply since 2007, aggregate work hours would be lower as a result. This is not the same as saying that labor supply caused the recession, because in principle labor supply could continue to matter at the margin but have increased since 2007: the situation shown in Figure 2.7. For this reason, Chapter Three is dedicated to measuring the size of the marginal tax rate change that resulted from the safety net expansions since 2007, and Chapter Three examines the magnitude of the slope of the labor supply curve.

Because a few of the seasonal point estimates mildly suggest a slightly smaller effect of the willingness to work during recessions than in other years (other estimates point in the opposite direction), it would not be implausible to assume that short-term labor demand was 5 or 10 percent less wage-elastic during recessions. But quantitative work on the labor market that assumes a zero wage elasticity of short-term labor demand during an era of changing marginal tax rates, as recent New Keynesian models have done,[20] is bound to be inaccurate unless the intent is to significantly underestimate labor supply effects.

9

Incentives and Compliance Under the Federal Mortgage Modification Guidelines

BY SOME MEASURES, U.S. average housing prices fell by a third between 2006 and 2009, and fell further since then. Housing prices fell more than 50 percent in Las Vegas and Phoenix, and nearly as much in Detroit, Miami, and much of California.[1] As a result, more than fourteen million home mortgages nationwide were "under water" in early 2009: the amount owed exceeded the market value of the collateral.[2] About one-third of home mortgages in Arizona, California, Florida, and Michigan, and more than one-half of home mortgages in Nevada, were under water.

The sudden drop in housing prices is an important reason, as of early 2009, that more than five million homes were already in foreclosure (lenders were seizing the collateral as a consequence of lack of payment) or their owners were delinquent on their mortgage payments. When foreclosures are motivated by low home values rather than the quality of the match between a homeowner and a home, a foreclosure is inefficient because it requires the homeowner to live elsewhere. The anticipation of foreclosure of an underwater mortgage probably also creates moral hazard in maintaining the house, because prior to foreclosure the occupant has no stake in the home's value. Nonpayment of mortgage obligations is also said to harm the health of the financial system, and thereby the entire economy. It may be no accident that underwater mortgages were prevalent in the Great Depression (Bernanke 1983), and became so prevalent immediately before this deep recession got started.

So far, mortgage modification initiatives have been the main way the federal government has sought to reduce foreclosures, especially when those foreclosures are motivated by negative home equity (Congressional Oversight Panel 2009, 4). In 2008, the Federal Deposit Insurance Corporation (FDIC), the Federal National Mortgage Association (Fannie), and the Federal Home Loan Mortgage Corporation (Freddie) all announced debt forgiveness or "loan modification" formulas. The Obama Treasury Department continued this work with its Home Affordable Modification Program (HAMP) as part of its Making Home Affordable Initiative,[3] which replaced the Fannie and Freddie programs. HAMP alone targeted three to four million mortgages.

As compared to the several millions of mortgages under water, delinquent, and in the foreclosure process, fewer than two million had actually been modified or otherwise had their payments adjusted through the third quarter of 2009.[4] Moreover, observers lament that most of those modifications adjust interest payments without reducing principal, and thereby may only delay foreclosures rather than genuinely preventing them.[5] It also seems that borrowers are uncertain about the modification process: the degree to which their payments will be reduced, whether lenders will deem them eligible, and when they can expect a modified mortgage to be in place.

This chapter shows how all of these outcomes, and more, may be a direct result of stark incentives created by the FDIC and HAMP programs (hereafter jointly referenced as FH) and their practice of targeting the ratio of housing expenses to borrower income.[6] The FH programs offer modifications on the basis of borrower income reported to the United States Internal Revenue Service. The first section of the chapter shows how the programs resemble government safety net programs, except that the marginal income tax rates from mortgage modification far exceed 100 percent in some instances.

Taken literally, the FH programs create such poor incentives that one is left wondering whether lenders would ever comply with them, that is, willingly make modifications to borrowers deemed eligible by FH, and in the amounts required to hit the FH income share target. The next two sections explain how lenders have an incentive to randomly foreclose on borrowers deemed modification-eligible by FH, because the resulting uncertainty faced by borrowers would discourage them from fully responding to the program's massive marginal income tax rates. The concluding section relates the microeconomics of mortgage modification to the safety net replacement calculations presented in Chapter 3 and used throughout the book to help explain why labor market activity is so much less now than it was in 2007.

Kahn and Yavas (1994) is an early paper modeling foreclosures as the "outside option" in a mortgage renegotiation. This aspect of renegotiation was studied further by Livshits, MacGee, and Tertilt (2007) and White and Zhu (2008), but still considering borrower income as an exogenous characteristic—and therefore not studying the tradeoff between foreclosures and moral hazard in the labor market. Han and Li (2007) consider the combined wealth and substitution effects of mortgage modification on labor supply, but do not attempt to separate them or calculate a labor market deadweight cost of modifications. Grochulski (2008) models personal bankruptcy negotiations as a mechanism design problem akin to Mirrlees (1971). None of these consider the FH programs affecting millions of borrowers during this recession. Mulligan (2009a) considers a stylized version of the economic environment studied here—the paper assumes less borrower heterogeneity, and less detail about mortgage contracts—for the purpose of characterizing the mortgage modification rules that would maximize collections and thereby be the rules preferred by lenders. Assuming that lenders fully and promptly comply with federal modification guidelines, Herkenhoff and Ohanian (2011) embed the FH programs in a model of search for employment and housing locations in order to quantify some of the labor market effects of mortgage modifications.

The Budget Set of a Borrower Facing the FDIC-HAMP Modification Guidelines
Underwater Arithmetic

Consider a mortgage loan with contractual payments in the constant amount h remaining from year zero until year $M > 5$. Assuming payments are expected to be made as contracted, their combined present value as of year t is $hR_{M,t}$, where $R_{M,t}$ is the present value of \$1 paid in each of the years $t, t+1, \ldots M$, from the perspective of year t (except when needed, hereafter I suppress the second element of the time subscript: R_M refers to the time 1 present value of \$1 paid in years 1 through M).

Let H_t be the market value of the loan's collateral in year t. If we ignore for the moment any foreclosure costs borne by the borrower or lender and any difference between the rates at which borrower and lender discount cash flows, a foreclosure at date 1 creates a transfer from lender to borrower with present value $hR_M - H_1$, as compared to the alternative of full contractual payments made for the life of the loan. Hereafter, I use $b = hR_M - H_1$ to denote the "underwater" or unsecured amount of the mortgage as of year 1. Because a borrower can always avoid foreclosure by making the contractual payments, foreclosures during year 1 are expected to be much more common when loans are "under water" $b > 0$ (that is, "home equity is negative"), because foreclosure on an underwater loan can create this windfall for the borrower.[7]

This chapter examines some of the economic incentives created by a "loan modification" occurring in year 1, perhaps to be followed by additional modifications in later years. In other words, time is normalized so that year 0 (or "base year") is the year prior to modification, year 1 is the year of modification, and years 2, 3,... M are the years thereafter. A year 1 loan modification—a change of the contractual loan payments—reduces the borrower's gain from year 1 foreclosure only if the modified payments have a lesser year 1 present value than the contractual payments. The year 1 modification reduces the borrower's gain (if any) from foreclosure in year $t > 1$ only if the payment changes reduce the year t present value of payments to be made in years t through M. Thus, of primary interest in the economic analysis of modification is the timing of payment reductions, and the factors that determine the amount to be reduced.

FDIC-HAMP Guidelines

According to the FH guidelines, year 1 modifications should achieve three objectives:

(1) *Income share target*: a combined housing expense (principal, interest, taxes, and insurance) during each of the years 1–5 that is no greater than μ times borrower income in year 0, y_0.[8]
(2) *NPV test*: the postmodification loan has value at least as great as the value of the collateral to the lender[9]
(3) *Borrower option*: borrowers are free to stay with their obligations under the original mortgage contract (including its foreclosure provisions), and free to request modifications in the future

μ = 31 percent is the typical income share target.[10] In principle, FDIC and HAMP have the same NPV test, although only FDIC has publicized the formula for its NPV test (Congressional Oversight Panel, 2009, p. 85).

The most common modification reduces "interest" in the sense that it reduces payments during years 1–5 and leaves payments after year 5 unchanged.[11] A second possibility is that principal is written down in the sense that payments in all years 1 – M are reduced by the same proportion, thereby reducing foreclosure incentives in all years.[12] Let δ denote the proportion by which principal is written down, and Δ be the absolute amount by which payments during years 1–5 are reduced beyond their reduction (if any) due to reduced principal.

Formally, a date 1 modification reduces the present value of mortgage payments by $\delta h R_M + \Delta R_5$. The guidelines require:

$$(1 - \delta)h - \Delta + T \leq \mu y_0 \tag{9.1}$$

$$\delta h R_M + \Delta R_5 \leq h R_M - H_1 \equiv b \tag{9.2}$$

where h is the contractual mortgage payment (principal and interest), not including the amount T of taxes and insurance. Inequality (9.1) is the income share target, in which year 1–5 housing expenses have been modified from $h + T$ to $(1\text{-}\delta)h + T\text{-}\Delta$. Inequality (9.2) is the NPV test.[13] Hereafter, I suppress the time subscript on base year income y_0.

As part of the NPV test, lenders can consider the probability that borrowers will default on, or request further modification of, the modified loan. To the degree that they consider these possibilities, the parameters R_5 and R_M in the NPV test above should be interpreted to include those effects.[14]

Marginal Tax Rates Under Full Compliance

The policy of no modification passes the NPV test, and sometimes meets the income share target. Specifically, some borrowers have income sufficiently large, or contractual mortgage payments sufficiently small, that income share target is met with no modification because the ratio of housing expenses to income is already less than the program target ratio μ. On the other hand, if income is low enough there may be no modification that meets the income share target and the NPV test. For example, zero interest payments for five years are necessary to meet the income share target for a borrower with zero income, but that amount of interest reduction may exceed the amount of negative equity and thereby fail the NPV test.

As a result, the guidelines result in modifications only when incomes fall in a specific range. Appendix 9.1 derives a formula for that range, and shows how it is especially narrow when principal rather than interest is modified, which is an important reason interest modifications have been so much more common (Mulligan 2010b).[15] Yet, without principal modifications, the negative equity remains, which is thought to be an important cause of foreclosures (Geanakopolos and Koniak 2009). For simplicity, and as a good approximation to actual modifications during the past few years, henceforth I assume that principal is not modified. Also for simplicity, I assume that the eligible income range has zero income as its lower bound.[16]

For any given amount b of negative equity, the present value $x(y)$ of the modified payments satisfying the NPV test and income share target is, in the eligible income ranges noted above, a linear function of base year income y:

$$x(y) = b - \left(\frac{h+T}{\mu} - y\right)\mu R_s \qquad (9.3)$$

Proposition 9.1 examines the slope of this function:

Proposition 9.1   The marginal dollar of income earned by a modification-eligible borrower reduces the value of modifications required to meet the income target, and at a rate that likely exceeds 1.

The marginal income tax rate is the derivative of the modification amount $x(y)$ with respect to y, discounted back from the modification year 1 to the income year 0:

$$MTR = \frac{1}{1+r_0}\mu R_s \qquad (9.4)$$

where r_0 is the one period rate of interest for discounting cash flows from year 1 to year 0. Recall that R_s is the present value of a dollar paid in five consecutive years: at a 6 percent annual interest rate and $\mu = 31$ percent, the marginal tax rate $\mu R_s/(1 + r_0)$ is 131 percent.[17] The marginal tax rate is larger still under the FDIC income share target of $\mu = 38$ percent.[18] A modification that is expected to be the mortgage's final modification has such a large marginal tax rate because a marginal dollar earned in the base year raises mortgage payment obligations by μ cents in *each* of the following five years, if not beyond.

The income share target is based on the borrower's gross income prior to the modification, and borrower's federal personal income tax return is an important document for verifying this income.[19] The payments specified by a modified loan are set in dollars (of much the same form as specified in the original mortgage contract), and is not adjusted for the borrower's income in years after the modification occurs. Future modifications to the loan may occur, but (assuming the program exists in the future) are at the borrower's discretion. Thus, a borrower whose income grows after the modification will not have payments adjusted upward as a result of that growth; the marginal tax rate imposed by a year 1 modification on incomes earned in years 2 and following is zero.

The similarity between mortgage modification and government safety net programs is seen in the geometry of the budget set of a borrower who expects to receive a mortgage modification according to the federal guidelines, conditional on having an income in the eligible range. In each year, that borrower has income that can be spent on mortgage payments and expenditures on items other than mortgage payments. Let *a* denote the year 0 present value of the income stream from years 1 and forward, plus the value of any assets (other than the collateral) the borrower may have. If the mortgage is paid in full, the present value of resources *c* available for expenditures other than future mortgage payments (hereafter, "consumption") is:

$$c = a - \frac{b}{1+r_0} + y \tag{9.5}$$

If instead income falls in the eligible range and the borrower receives a modification according to the federal guidelines, then the present value budget constraint is (9.6):

$$c = a - \frac{b}{1 \mid r_0} + (1 - MTR)y + MTR\frac{h+T}{\mu} \tag{9.6}$$

Figure 9.1 displays this budget set in the [*y*,*c*] plane. Consider first the allocation *X* in which the borrower has no income (in year zero) and consumes the amount $a - b/(1 + r_0)$ while making full mortgage payments. The allocation *Y* indicates the amount of income that equals (full housing expenses)/μ (that is, full housing expenses are equal to $\mu = 31$ percent of income under the HAMP rule). Thus, no allocation to the right of *Y* is eligible for modification under the FH guidelines (recall that, for simplicity, zero is assumed to be the minimum eligible income).

To the left of allocation *Y* in Figure 9.1, the present value of mortgage payments falls $\mu R_s/(1 + r_0)$ or about \$1.31 for each dollar that income is reduced. Because consumption is income minus mortgage payments, consumption therefore *increases* by $\mu R_s/(1 + r_0) - 1$ (about \$0.31) for each dollar that income *falls*. The income share target therefore creates a budget constraint with the wrong slope—it is no longer necessary to increase income in order to increase spending—for incomes near and below the income corresponding to allocation *Y*. At the allocation W_0 (hereafter, the "minimum collection point"),

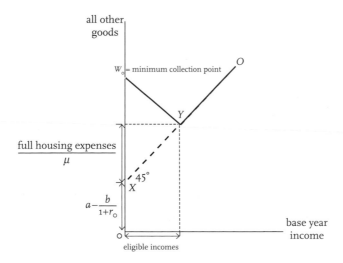

FIGURE 9.1 Budget Set Induced by FDIC-HAMP Means-Tests
The horizontal axis measures borrower income during the base year, from highest to lowest. a denotes the present value of future income available for all other goods and paying the unsecured amount of the mortgage (discounted to the base year), $b/(1+r_o)$.

income is zero and therefore the modification amount is the maximum. To keep the diagram uncluttered, I assume that the NPV test exactly binds at the minimum collection point W_o so that collections are zero there.[20]

It is informative to compare the mortgage modification budget set shown in red in Figure 9.1 with the food stamp and Medicaid budget set shown in blue in Figure 6.1. Both of the budget sets coincide with the 45 degree line for higher incomes, which means that the beneficiary or borrower has only his own income to spend—no help from government or lender. One difference between the two is that the income cutoff for food stamps and Medicaid is the same for all households with the same composition, whereas the income cutoff for mortgage modification depends on housing expenses, which tend to be greater for households that had more income when the mortgage was originated. For this reason, marginal tax or replacement rates from food stamps and Medicaid tend to fall with potential income (recall the rising self-reliance rates shown in Figure 6.2) whereas they are the constant $\mu R_s/(1 + r_o)$ for mortgage modification. The potential-income-independent marginal tax rates from mortgage modification, together with the increased prevalence of negative home equity, are one reason that replacement rates increased since 2007 even for people with high incomes.

Another common feature of the two budget sets is that they are above the 45 degree line for low incomes. Households with low income therefore can spend their own income, plus help they receive from the government (Figure 6.1) and from lenders (Figure 9.1). But the slopes are an important difference between the two: the black slope in Figure 6.1 is positive because the marginal tax rate is less than 100 percent, whereas the red slope in Figure 9.1 is negative (to the left of Y) because the marginal tax rate is greater than 100 percent.

Borrower Reactions Under Full Information and Full Compliance: Spend More and Work Less

Many, although not all, modified mortgages are required to follow either the FDIC or the HAMP guidelines. The purchasers of mortgages owned by failed banks are required to modify mortgages according to the FDIC guidelines (Congressional Oversight Panel 2009, 84). Citi agreed to use the FDIC formula as a condition to its November 2008 bailout (Aversa 2008). Servicers of Fannie Mae or Freddie Mac mortgages are obligated to participate in HAMP for these mortgages. Participants in TARP programs initiated after February 2, 2009, are required to take part in mortgage modification programs consistent with Treasury standards. Years have passed since the initiation of these programs, and yet millions of homes remain under water with homeowners who are delinquent on their payments (Zandi 2011).

In order to help explain why modifications have proceeded slowly, and to understand why borrowers find them frustrating and confusing, I begin by considering the hypothetical situation in which borrowers were fully aware of program rules, and found their applications for modification to be processed promptly and fully consistent with the federal guidelines. I then show that the hypothetical situation is unfavorable to lenders, who would gain relative to that situation by promoting borrower confusion and uncertainty about the disposition of their modification application. To do this, I add two ingredients to the model: foreclosure costs and labor supply.

Costs of Foreclosure

Regardless of whether she is eligible for modification, a homeowner always has the option to stop paying her mortgage. Although state laws differ somewhat, to a good approximation a homeowner who stops paying no longer owns or occupies the house, may suffer a reduction in credit rating that might raise the costs of future borrowing, and runs the small risk of lenders attempting to seize some of her other financial assets (if she has any). I let m denote the combined foreclosure costs of these events (m is for "moving").[21] Foreclosure costs vary among borrowers: I let $G(m; \gamma)$ denote the cumulative distribution of those costs, which may depend on a vector of borrower characteristics γ. A foreclosure would be efficient for a borrower with a negative foreclosure cost, but for simplicity I assume that all borrowers have nonnegative foreclosure costs.[22]

I assume that a borrower must bear the foreclosure cost m unless either he pays the full amount b, or is offered (and accepts) modified payments with present value x, of the unsecured part of his mortgage. As explained above with equations (9.5) and (9.6), the FH programs specify the value $x(y)$ of modified payments as a specific piecewise linear function of income y and negative equity b:

$$x(y)=\begin{cases} b-\left(1+r_0\right)\left(\dfrac{h+T}{\mu}-y\right)MTR & \text{if } y \in \left[0, \dfrac{h+T}{\mu}\right] \\ b & \text{otherwise} \end{cases}$$

(9.7)

$$MTR \equiv \frac{\mu R_S}{1+r_0}$$

where MTR is the constant rate at which the modified payment increases with income, in the range of eligible incomes. The borrower chooses the modified payment or foreclosure, whichever has the lesser cost.[23]

Behavioral Responses

In order to model possible behavioral responses in the hypothetical situation in which mortgages are promptly modified according to the federal guidelines, I assume that borrowers understand those guidelines.[24] If borrowers are free to choose any point on their budget set in the [y,c] plane, and the FH marginal tax rate is at least 100 percent, then the FH budget set might was well be nothing more than the single minimum collection point W_o added to the budget set absent modification, because the other points in the FH budget set—the points between W_o and Y in Figure 9.1—are strictly dominated by the minimum collection point.

To prove this more formally with the type of analysis used in Chapters Two, Four, and Five, I assume that borrowers view the supply of income as a bad, and the available of resources c for expenditure as a good, according to the utility function $u(c,y;\gamma)$. γ is a vector of borrower characteristics that determine, among other things, the marginal rate of substitution between c and y.[25] The marginal rate of substitution is a strictly positive continuous of function of γ. The cross-borrower distribution of the characteristics γ and the foreclosure cost m is continuously differentiable on the set Γ, and has strictly positive density everywhere on the interior of Γ, and zero density outside the set Γ. I assume that the set Γ is broad enough that the support of the distribution of efficient incomes is wider than the eligible income range.[26]

Note that these assumptions are consistent with the idea that borrowers are unwilling to deviate from an "optimal" or "habitual" income, if their unwillingness can be represented in terms of the curvature of indifference curves without denying that the marginal rate of substitution between c and y is positive. These assumptions are weaker than typically assumed in the optimal taxation literature[27] and consistent with a positive, but arbitrarily small, elasticity of income supply with respect to incentives. Thus, outcomes under FH consist of borrowers located at the minimum collection point W_o plus borrowers who make the same choice they would without FH (that is, somewhere near the point O in Figure 9.1).

Lender Incentives to Expand Modification Capacity

Three or four million borrowers are thought to be eligible for HAMP's modification, yet observers appear to be frustrated that only about four hundred thousand modifications occurred under the HAMP program during its first six months[28] and have suspected that its cumulative modifications would never significantly surpass one million (Congressional Oversight Panel 2011, 73). Moreover, borrowers could not be sure whether they would ultimately be offered a modification (Congressional Oversight Panel 2009, 48, 71–72). Fewer modifications occurred than foreclosure proceedings initiated (HOPE NOW 2011, 14). This situation has been blamed on limited lender capacity to process modifications and the complexity of mortgage ownership (Geanakopolos and Koniak 2008; Congressional Oversight Panel 2009, 34, 72), although I show below how the result may be enhanced collections, given the federal guidelines. For some of the same reasons that a fully-enforced FH would have undesirable outcomes, it gives lenders little incentive to comply with the guidelines.

If lenders really do have a limited modification capacity, that capacity would have to be rationed among eligible borrowers. Here I assume that each eligible borrower in year 1 receives a modification with probability p, and has the modification request rejected with probability $1 - p$. In the case of rejection, the original mortgage contract is followed, including its foreclosure provisions, which means that the borrower is either foreclosed or paying in full according to $\min\{m,b\}$. When each borrower makes a year 0 income supply decision, the person knows the modification schedule $x(y)$ for those who will be modified, and knows the magnitude of p, but does not yet know the random outcome (whether it will be modified or rejected).

In order to understand the consequences of the capacity constraint, it helps to compare outcomes with $p = 1$ ("full compliance" with the guidelines) to outcomes with $p = 0$ in the case that the FH marginal income tax rate is at least 100 percent. As shown above, $p = 1$ results in only two types of collections: full collection b from borrowers who would rather pay in full than be foreclosed or pass the FH means test, and zero collections from those modified and those foreclosed.[29] In other words, collections are no greater with $p = 1$ than if lenders made no modifications ($p = 0$), and would be strictly less as long as at least one borrower with $m > b$ would be eligible for an FH modification. Thus, some $p < 1$ maximizes collections.

The borrower payoff to earning zero is increasing in p because a borrower earning zero is paying $x = 0$ with probability p and $\min\{m,b\} > 0$ with probability $1 - p$. Thus, the higher is p, the greater the number of borrowers receiving modification $x = 0$, which proves:

Proposition 9.2   If $MTR \geq 100\%$, then full compliance ($p = 1$) minimizes collections.

Foreclosures are increasing in the rejection rate $1 - p$ by two mechanisms: (1) some of the rejected borrowers opt for foreclosure because they have $m < b$, and (2) the payoff to earning an income in the eligible range is increasing in p, and earning an income in that range is the only possibility of preventing foreclosure for a borrower with $m < b$. Despite its adverse effect on total foreclosures, Proposition 9.2 shows that the capacity constraint increases collections.

A borrower who would be modified under full compliance is strictly worse off with the capacity constraint, but the loss rises with foreclosure costs because foreclosure is one possible result of a rejected application for modification. As a result of the capacity constraint, a high-foreclosure-cost borrower is less willing than an otherwise similar borrower with low foreclosure costs to alter income so as to put it in the FH-eligible range. In other words, at the expense of additional foreclosures, the capacity constraint helps lenders separate those borrowers who are willing to pay in full from those who are not. Lenders that care only about collections have no incentive to expand their modification capacity, so the fact that so many eligible mortgages have not yet been modified may not merely be the result of administrative snafus.[30]

My proof of Proposition 9.2 relies on the FH marginal tax rate's being large enough to attract, under full compliance with the guidelines, a number of borrowers to the minimum collection point, but that MTR might still be less than 100 percent. In fact, even the means-tested modification rule that maximizes collections under full compliance may collect less than would a means-tested modification rule that is to be randomly applied.[31] To see this, note that even the collection-maximizing rule has a range of incomes in which the modifications are generous enough that little is collected in that range as compared to collections from those with greater incomes. If these collections are small enough, lenders would collect more by randomly rejecting modifications from borrowers earning in that range—thereby losing collections from those who are ultimately foreclosed as a result of the rejection—in order to discourage other borrowers from reducing their incomes to qualify for the most generous modification.

For a given means-tested modification rule, incomes under modification capacity constraints are less distorted than they would be if compliance were 100 percent, because the marginal tax rate is $p*MTR$ rather than MTR. Thus, even though a capacity constraint increases foreclosures under FH, it decreases the program's income distortion and may ultimately increase efficiency.[32] Conversely, even if it were observed that the FH programs actually induced only a few borrowers to adjust their income in order to be eligible for a modification, it is still possible that many borrowers would have adjusted if they had anticipated full compliance with the modification rules.

The small number of modifications occurring during 2008 under the FDIC program prompted the Obama administration to allocate about $75 billion, or about $20,000 per mortgage, for subsidies to mortgages modified under the HAMP program. Depending on how these subsidies are incorporated in the NPV test, and the administrative costs involved, a lender may or may not profit from a borrower who locates at the minimum collection point, which helps determine whether the lender can profit from randomly foreclosing on eligible borrowers.[33] But the existence of the subsidy does not change the fact that the FH target income share and NPV test create terrible incentives for borrowers to supply income and for lenders to expand their capacity to modify mortgages.

Conclusions

With the intentions of preventing foreclosures and strengthening the financial system, the FDIC and the U.S. Treasury created guidelines for modifying mortgages, and required that the guidelines be followed for a large class of mortgages. The guidelines include an income share target (for housing expenditures), an NPV test, and voluntary participation by borrowers. This chapter shows how the facts that actual modifications do little to reduce principal, that they are still outnumbered by foreclosures, and that they add to borrower uncertainty may result from incentives created by those very guidelines.

In many instances the programs create implicit marginal income tax rates in excess of 100 percent, and sometimes as high as 400 percent. One might expect a lot of income to be destroyed (or at least detoured off personal income tax returns, where lenders might see it; cf. Feldstein 1999) in an economy where millions of people faced such massive marginal income tax rates. Reasonable people can debate the degree to which the supply of income responds to marginal tax rates, but under the weak assumption that borrowers cannot be expected to perennially locate at points of their budget sets that are strictly dominated by tens of thousands of dollars, lenders that want to enhance collections will take steps to foreclose on borrowers who are deemed modification-eligible by the federal programs. These steps will dull (but not eliminate) the otherwise stark incentives for borrowers to reduce their incomes in order to be eligible for a generous modification, and thereby result in an income distribution impact of the programs that is less than it would be if the guidelines were followed literally.

The purpose of this book is to explain why labor market activity fell so much since 2007, and in pursuing that purpose it examines the work incentives created by various components of the safety net, including mortgage modifications. Proposals for improving mortgage modification formulas, or any other part of the safety net, are therefore beyond the scope of this book. Nevertheless, the basic economic principles used to examine labor market activity suggest that a relatively straightforward direction for safety net improvement is to scale back, if not fully eliminate, the use of marginal tax rates that are near or exceed 100 percent.

By definition, the NPV test excludes all mortgage borrowers with positive home equity, which is why Chapter Three's eligibility index and program weight for mortgage modifications were based on the fraction of household heads and spouses with negative home equity. According to the NPV test, the number of households eligible for mortgage modification increased automatically as housing prices fell and more homeowners found themselves with negative equity. In fiscal year 2010, the product of Chapter Three's mortgage modification eligibility index and program weight was 0.038, indicating that 3.8 percent of nonelderly household heads and spouses would receive a modification sometime after 2007.[34]

Chapter Three formed its mortgage modification benefit index according to the average monthly amount that actual modifications reduce mortgage interest payments. As a result, it concluded that mortgage modification contributed 0.5 percentage points to the total 8.0 percentage point increase in replacement rates between 2007-Q4 and 2009-Q4. Another approach to calculating that contribution would be to multiply a marginal tax rate from this chapter by the eligibility index and by the probability that a nonelderly household head or spouse would receive a modification. For an underwater mortgage that would be modified every year, the marginal tax rate derived above is 29 percent. When multiplied by the modification probability of 0.038, it is 1.1 percent. Multiplied again by the eligibility index for 2007-Q4 and 2009-Q4, respectively, the results are 0.5 and 1.1 percent. Thus, by this alternative method the effect of mortgage modification on the change on the replacement rate over those eight quarters is 0.6 percentage points.[35] Because 0.6 percentage points exceeds the 0.5 percentage points derived in Chapter Three, and because some of the negative equity mortgages targeted but not served by HAMP may have been served by other programs, Chapter Three may have underestimated the contribution of negative home equity to the overall increase in the marginal tax rate from safety net programs since 2007.

Mortgage modification has in common with the rest of the safety net that the amount received by the household falls with its income. But mortgage modification is not all that safe, and the stakes can be large: modification applicants face a gamble as to whether their mortgage will be modified, and the better outcomes involve tens of thousands of dollars in reduced payments.

Appendix 9.1: Principal Modifications and the Eligible Income Range

Some borrowers have income sufficiently large, or contractual mortgage payments sufficiently small, that the guidelines can be met with no modification. For the others, the guideline amount modified is:

$$\frac{R_5 R_M}{\rho R_5 + (1-\rho) R_M}(h + T - \mu y) \le \delta h R_M + \Delta R_5 \le b$$

$$\rho \equiv \frac{\delta h R_M}{\delta h R_M + \Delta R_5} \tag{9.8}$$

As noted, modifications can vary in the degree to which principal rather than interest is modified; the parameter $\rho \in [0,1]$ denotes the amount of the principal reduction, expressed as a share of the total modification amount.[36] The inequalities in (9.8) put upper and lower bounds on the amount modified: the upper bound comes from the income share target (9.1) and the lower bound from the NPV test (9.2).

If year 0 borrower income y is too low, the above interval may not exist, in which case no modification amount can both meet the income target and satisfy the NPV test. Define the modification-eligible income interval to be the range of income y in which income is high enough that the income share target can be met without failing the NPV test (9.2), but low enough that some modification is required in order to meet the income share target (9.1):

$$y \in \left[\max\left\{ 0, \frac{h+T}{\mu} - \left(\frac{\rho}{R_M} + \frac{1-\rho}{R_5} \right) \frac{b}{\mu} \right\}, \frac{h+T}{\mu} \right] \tag{9.9}$$

I refer to the lower income bound as the "minimum income threshold" (*mit*) that, contrary to the simplifying assumption made in the main text, may exceed zero.

For any given amount b of negative equity, the present value $x(y)$ of the modified payments satisfying the NPV test and income share target is a piecewise linear function of base year income y:

$$x(y) = \left\{ b - \left(\frac{h+T}{\mu} - y \right) \underbrace{\frac{\mu R_5 R_M}{\rho R_5 + (1-\rho) R_M}}_{b} \quad \text{if } y \in \left[\text{mit}, \frac{h+T}{\mu} \right] \right.$$

$$\text{otherwise}$$

$$\text{mit} \equiv \max\left\{ 0, \frac{h+T}{\mu} - \left(\frac{\rho}{R_M} + \frac{1-\rho}{R_5} \right) \frac{b}{\mu} \right\} \tag{9.10}$$

where (9.10) assigns no modification to incomes outside the eligible range. The marginal income tax rate is the derivative of the modification lower bound with respect to y, discounted back from the modification year 1 to the income year 0:

$$MTR = \frac{1}{1+r_0} \frac{\mu R_5 R_M}{\rho R_5 + (1-\rho) R_M} \in \left[\frac{\mu}{1+r_0} R_5, \frac{\mu}{1+r_0} R_M \right] \tag{9.11}$$

where r_o is the one period rate of interest for discounting cash flows from year 1 to year 0. Recall that R_5 is the present value of a dollar paid in five consecutive years: at a 6 percent annual interest rate and $\mu = 31$ percent, $\mu R_5/(1 + r_o) = 131$ percent. For a loan terminating in year 25, the marginal tax rate under principal reductions would be $\mu R_M/(1 + r_o) = 396$ percent.

Appendix 9.2: Marginal Tax Rates with Various Horizons and Discount Rates

The marginal income tax rate for incomes in the modification-eligible range depends on the modification horizon (the number of years in which payments will be reduced below the amount specified in the original mortgage contract) and on the rates for discounting future cash flows. For the loan's final modification, the modification horizon is at least five years, and it may be as long as the loan's remaining term. A five-year modification horizon applies when payment reductions are achieved exclusively by reducing interest, and the interest reduction is small enough that it can fully revert to the originally contracted amount in year 6. Typically, "small enough" means that the rate of interest does not have to jump more than one point from year 5 to year 6 (U.S. Department of Treasury, 2009b).

Interest reductions that are somewhat larger will have an impact on payments in year 6 too, reductions that are larger still will affect payments through year 7, etc. (Here I assume that the final payment of the loan occurs in year $M > 8$, so that there are payments beyond year 5 to feel an impact.) For example, if the originally contracted interest rate were 6 percent/year and an interest rate of 2 percent/year were required to meet the income share target, then the interest rate would be 3 percent/year in year 6, 4 percent/year in year 7, 5 percent/year in year 8, and then back to the originally contracted 6 percent/year in year 9. For this reason, the budget constraint shown in Figure 9.1 would more accurately be drawn as convex between allocations Y and W_o. Closest to allocation Y, the slope is $1 - \mu R_5/(1 + r_o)$, but moving toward allocation W_o, the slope is $1 - \mu R_6/(1 + r_o)$, then $1 - \mu R_7/(1 + r_o)$, and then $1 - \mu R_8/(1 + r_o)$. HAMP has an interest rate floor of 2 percent/year, so (if the NPV test still passes) further payment reductions would be achieved by principal reductions, thereby making the slope $1 - \mu R_M/(1 + r_o)$ nearest the minimum collection point W_o. Thus, the budget constraint between Y and W_o can be piecewise linear with as many as five segments and all but one of those segments of equal width in the income dimension.

Note that, under the weak assumption that allocation Y lies below the minimum collection point, a convex budget constraint is observationally

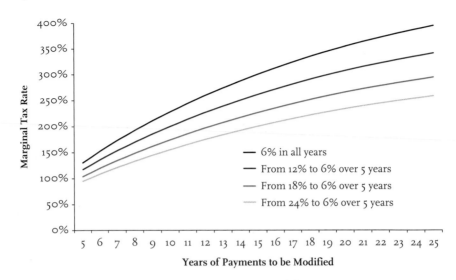

FIGURE 9.2. Marginal Income Tax Rate versus Modification Horizon, Various Initial Interest Rates (share target = 31%)

equivalent to the linear segment YW_o drawn in Figure 9.1—even if some of the segments between Y and W_o slope up, because in both cases all points between Y and W_o are strictly dominated by the zero collection point. Assuming that the mortgage is enough under water that all five segments appear, the average marginal tax rate between Y and W_o is greater than $0.5\mu(R_6 + R_7)/(1 + r_o)$, which is 163 percent if cash flows are discounted at 6 percent/year.

Some borrowers will earn more in year 0 than they otherwise would in order to reach the minimum collection point, and others would earn less. Those earning less would be reducing cash flows in year 0 in order to increase them in years 1–5 and perhaps beyond, which is one reason a borrower might have a higher (one-year) rate for discounting cash flows backward from year 1 than from years further in the future. Year 0 is likely a recession year—perhaps characterized by tight credit for some borrowers, which is another reason some borrowers might have high one-year cash-flow discount rates in the early years of the modification, as compared to later years. This appendix therefore considers one-year cash-flow discount rates that are initially (discounting year 1 to year 0) high and then decline linearly reaching 6 percent by year 5 (a multiyear discount factor is the product of each of the corresponding one-year discount factors). Figure 9.2 shows marginal income tax rates $\mu R_M/(1 + r_o)$ as a function of modification horizon M in four cases that differ according to the initial one-year cash-flow discount rate. In essentially every case, $\mu R_M/(1 + r_o)$ exceeds 100 percent.

Uncertainty, Redistribution, and the Labor Market

AMERICA IS CLEARLY unhappy with the sharp drop in labor market activity in 2008 and 2009, and the prolonged failure of the labor market to return to prerecession levels. If this book is correct to attribute much of the labor decline to public policies expanding the safety net and hiking minimum wages, then it is tempting to condemn the policy changes. At the same time, those who appreciate the value of a generous safety net may be reluctant to concede that the safety net reduces employment, because that concession might appear to diminish the safety net's value.

Neither conclusion can necessarily be supported, at least without further evidence on the origins of the safety net and its recent changes. A significant part of the safety net expansions was likely a reaction to events that originated outside the labor market: perhaps the 2008 stock market crash and financial panic, or the housing crash, or long-term trends that had been increasing labor market inequality. I hope the connections between the labor market and the safety net documented in this book motivate further study of the origins of the safety net's expansions. The purpose of this chapter is to begin sketching a theory of how the financial panic and other events may have motivated an expansion of the safety net, despite its depressing effect on the labor market, and to clarify that a full cost-benefit analysis of the recession must account for the safety benefits of those expansions. The chapter achieves this goal by reviewing the principal-agent theory of the "equity-efficiency tradeoff," and connecting elements of that model with recent economic events.

A Model of the Equity-Efficiency Tradeoff

In the principal-agent model of the labor market, workers devote time and effort n to production. This includes time spent at work, time spent searching for new work, and effort devoted to enhancing and maintaining the productivity of those uses of time. The value produced by that effort is $y = n + v + \varepsilon$, where v and ε are the result of mean zero idiosyncratic random factors beyond the worker's control. For simplicity, the random factors act additively on the worker's effort, rather than multiplicatively as in Mirrlees (1971). My additive model is just a small adaptation of a special case of Holmstrom and Milgrom (1987) that has been applied to executive salaries by Rosen (1982), Garen (1994), and others.

Some of the random factors, embodied in v, are widely observable. The others, embodied in ε, are not observed, except by the worker himself who can infer their combined value by subtracting his effort and v from the value produced. I normalize ε so that it is uncorrelated with v, and assume that the worker is risk-averse (more on this below). As a result, the worker optimally pools the result v of observed idiosyncratic random factors in a full-information insurance market: when v is observed he pays it to the insurance group, or receives $-v$ from the group in case its value is negative. In theory the insurance group is infinitely large and free from administrative costs so that total insurance premiums (from the group members with positive vs) exactly finance total insurance awards (paid to group members with negative vs). In practice, the insurance group may be co-workers, family members, church members, etc.

Even with insurance against the observed random factors, the remaining value produced $n + \varepsilon$ is still random. The purpose of this chapter is to examine possible ways of insuring the ε risk, and deriving the effects of the amount and composition of uncertainty on the efficient amount of that insurance.

Suppose that a worker additionally enters into an imperfect information social insurance arrangement in which she pays a fixed fraction of her earnings $n + \varepsilon$ (net of payments with respect to full-information v insurance) and receives an insurance benefit that is a linear function of net income. Her disposable income c is therefore a linear function of earnings, the intercept of which I denote as b and the slope I denote as μ:

$$c = (n + \varepsilon)\mu + b \tag{10.1}$$

The self-reliance rate for the worker with median potential earnings is μ.

The social insurance system has a budget constraint that relates benefits it pays to people having zero income to payments it receives from people having positive income:

$$b = \frac{1 - \mu}{1 + \phi} \bar{n} \tag{10.2}$$

where $\bar{n}$ is the average effort by members of the insurance system. $\phi \geq 0$ is an administrative or stigma cost reflecting the possibility that social insurance benefits might be worth less than they cost.

Workers have a smooth von Neumann-Morgenstern (1944) utility function u defined over their value of consumption net of the costs of effort, with strictly positive first derivative and strictly negative second derivative in the relevant range. Their expected utility function is therefore:

$$\int u \left(\mu n + \mu \varepsilon + \frac{1-\mu}{1+\phi} \bar{n} - \gamma \frac{\eta}{\eta+1} n^{(\eta+1)/\eta} \right) dG(\varepsilon)$$ (10.3)

where G is the distribution of random factors ε (continuous, with all finite moments), and the constant $\eta > 0$ is the wage elasticity of labor supply. The constant $\gamma > 0$ is a preference parameter, so that the marginal rate of substitution between labor n and disposable income c is a special case of the form (5.2) with no wealth effects on labor. As a result, any worker facing this social insurance program will desire labor in the amount $n = (\mu/\gamma)^\eta$. The desired labor increases with μ because μ is the reward the worker receives for exerting effort; the remaining fraction $(1-\mu)$ of results of effort goes to the social insurance system.

I assume that actual labor coincides with desired labor, which means that the social insurance system has no influence on the worker's labor decision aside from the parameters μ and b of the safety net benefit formula. As a result, average labor $\bar{n}$ is also equal to $(\mu/\gamma)^\eta$, which is generally different from the socially efficient labor $n^* = (1/\gamma)^\eta$ that equates the marginal rate of substitution to the social product of effort.

Because workers choose their effort before knowing the final outcome ε, the only source of randomness in (10.3) is the $\mu\varepsilon$ term. A smaller value for μ therefore means a lesser amount of risk faced by the worker, and more equal disposable income for workers who end up with different values of ε, but it also means less effort and thereby less aggregate income. This is known as the "equity-efficiency tradeoff," or less often as a "safety-efficiency tradeoff."

The equity-efficiency tradeoff can be analyzed quantitatively by considering a measure of equity or safety S that is negatively related to the standard deviation of disposable income $S = (1 + s_c)^{-1} = (1 + \mu s_\varepsilon)^{-1}$, where s_ε is the standard deviation of the random factor ε. By eliminating μ from the safety equation and the average labor equation $\bar{n} = \mu^\eta n^*$, we have a single equation for the tradeoff:

$$S = \frac{1}{1 + s_\varepsilon \left(\dfrac{\bar{n}}{n^*} \right)^{1/\eta}}$$ (10.4)

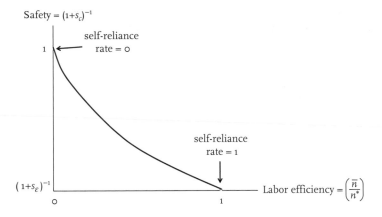

FIGURE 10.1 The Equity-Efficiency Frontier

More safety S achieved with more social insurance (1-μ) means less labor efficiency $\bar{n}/n^*$, and vice versa.[1] Figure 10.1 displays the tradeoff in a simple diagram, with safety measured on the vertical axis and efficiency on the horizontal axis. Points to the northwest on the frontier shown in Figure 10.1 correspond to more social insurance—that is, low values for μ—and points to the southeast correspond to less social insurance. The red line is the equity-efficiency frontier, because combinations of equity and labor efficiency beyond it are not possible since equalizing outcomes reduces incentives to supply labor.

Possible Changes in the Equity-Efficiency Tradeoff, and the Optimal Degree of Social Insurance

Both safety and labor efficiency are desirable, and overall efficiency strikes a balance between the two. The optimal amount of social insurance can be described as the value of μ—a point on the equity-efficiency tradeoff shown in Figure 10.1—that maximizes worker expected utility.

$$\int u\left(\mu \varepsilon + \frac{1+\phi\mu}{1+\phi}(\mu/\gamma)^{\eta} - \gamma\frac{\eta}{\eta+1}(\mu/\gamma)^{\eta+1} \right) dG(\varepsilon) \qquad (10.5)$$

It is straightforward to prove that the optimal amount of social insurance depends on the amount of risk the worker faces, as embodied in the distribution function G.

Proposition 1   The optimal amount of social insurance (1-μ) increases with the standard deviation s_ε of the random factor ε, holding constant higher-order moments of the distribution G.

Proof   Because u is smooth, I prove the proposition by using its Taylor expansion (in the neighborhood of $\varepsilon = 0$) in the worker expected utility expression:

$$u\left(\frac{1+\phi\mu}{1+\phi}(\mu/\gamma)^{\eta} - \gamma\frac{\eta}{\eta+1}(\mu/\gamma)^{\eta+1}\right) + \int \sum_{k=2}^{\infty}\frac{u^{(k)}}{k!}(\mu\varepsilon)^k\, dG(\varepsilon)$$

$$= u\left(\frac{1+\phi\mu}{1+\phi}(\mu/\gamma)^{\eta} - \gamma\frac{\eta}{\eta+1}(\mu/\gamma)^{\eta+1}\right) + \sum_{k=2}^{\infty}\frac{u^{(k)}}{k!}\mu^k G_k$$

where $u^{(k)}$ denotes the kth derivative of u evaluated at $\varepsilon = 0$ and G_k denotes the kth moment of G. The first derivative of expected utility with respect to μ has one term involving the second moment of G, and it is linear with a negative coefficient because u is concave. Thus the optimal μ falls, and the optimal $(1-\mu)$ increases, with the second moment.

There are a couple of reasons to think that standard deviation s_ε of the random factor ε was greater after 2008 than it was before. One is that capital market events made it more difficult for market participants to distinguish bad outcomes that should be blamed on low effort from bad outcomes that were just unlucky. In this view, there was not necessarily any change in the total amount of variation of labor productivity y around labor time and effort supplied, just that more factors since 2007 go into the unobserved category ε than the observed category v. Workers replace part of the full-information insurance lost by adding to their imperfect-information insurance, despite the latter's cost in terms of labor inefficiency. Figure 10.2 illustrates the change that might have occurred between 2007 and 2009. As workers began to face more risk—the equity-efficiency frontier shifted down from red to gray—the safety net could have remained as it was in 2007, in which case labor market efficiency might have remained constant too. But then workers would have substantially less safety, as with the hollow circle in Figure 10.2. In that unfortunate situation, workers may prefer to recover some of the lost safety by reducing labor efficiency, as with the solid circle on the gray 2009 equity-efficiency frontier.[2]

A related argument is that the variance of ε increased without any reduction in the variance of v. Still, workers desire to have more imperfect-information insurance, despite its cost in terms of labor inefficiency. Either way, less labor is the result of the safety net expansion in the sense that the safety net could have been kept constant, in which case labor would have remained constant. But the safety net expansions were themselves a response to another shock—increased uncertainty—and keeping the safety net constant might not have been the best response to that additional uncertainty. The recession, which is

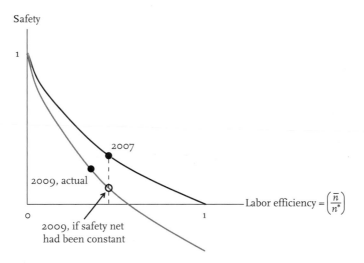

FIGURE 10.2 Changes in the Equity-Efficiency Frontier

by definition a drop in aggregate labor market activity, may have been preventable by keeping the safety net constant, but the cost of preventing it would have been too high in terms of the risks that workers would have borne without government help. In this sense, one might say the ultimate cause of the recession was the change in the equity-efficiency tradeoff mediated through an expanded safety net.

Economists have noted that uncertainty has increased a lot since 2007, and they have offered measures of the amount of added uncertainty (Bloom et al. 2011).[3] One commonly cited measure is the Chicago Board Options Exchange's Volatility Index, sometimes called the fear index or VIX, which is based on market forecasts of the volatility of an index of stock prices. The monthly version of the series is plotted in Figure 10.3, and has percentage units of thirty-day annualized rates of return (Chicago Board Options Exchange 2009). The index increased by a factor of two from the first half of 2007 to the second half, and then by at least another factor of two by the end of 2008. The index returned to its late-2007 level in early 2010 and again in late 2010.[4]

Even if the amount and composition of uncertainty remained constant, the degree of risk aversion could vary over time, which could simultaneously change asset prices (Campbell and Cochrane 1999) and the demand for social insurance (represented in my model as the degree of concavity of the utility function u). For example, the economic expansion prior to 2007 might have been a time of low risk aversion in which people were especially willing to

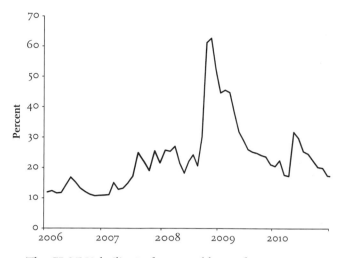

FIGURE 10.3 The CBOE Volatility Index, monthly 2006–2010

purchase risky assets and especially eager to forgo social insurance in order to have a more efficient labor market.

Monetary economists also say that the demand for liquidity increased following 2007 (Diamond and Rajan 2011), and surging prices of U.S. government securities are consistent with their interpretation (Lucas 2008). Safety net payments may share some liquidity and risk characteristics with government securities—indeed, food stamp program beneficiaries receive their benefits on a debit card (Eslami, Filion, and Strayer 2011)—which could be modeled as an increase in the preference for, or a decrease in the preference against, safety net payments. In my model, a reduction in the welfare stigma cost ϕ is another way that the optimal amount of social insurance could increase, and labor efficiency decrease.

Another argument is that the safety net was not generous enough before 2008. If so, then expanding the safety net was, by definition, a good idea even at the cost of reducing labor market activity, and even while the inherent amount and composition of uncertainty in the economy might have been constant. That is, the equity-efficiency tradeoff might be no different now than it was in 2007, but our society had chosen a point too far to the southeast in Figure 10.1. In this view, perhaps we have to thank the Democratic Congresses of the mid-2000s, and finally a Democratic president in 2009, which were finally able to significantly increase the amount of resources available for the poor and vulnerable, and move the economy to a point further to the northwest in Figure 10.1.

But an equally coherent view is that the safety net was already too generous before 2008, so that the recent expansions only made a bad situation worse, although even in this view costs of the labor market distortions that are the subject of this book were partially offset by the safety benefits of the safety net expansions. This book shows that the expanding safety net did a lot to reduce labor market activity, but to a first approximation it has little to say about whether expanding the safety net was worth its labor market cost because it brings little evidence to bear on the questions of whether the safety net was generous enough before 2008, or whether uncertainty, risk aversion, and other shocks were large enough to justify a significant safety net expansion.[5] Nor does the book have much to say about whether safety net expansions should have occurred in the public sector, or the private sector, or some combination thereof.

The Cost-Benefit Analysis of Safety Net Expansions: Necessary Ingredients

The evidence presented in this book can assist future research on calculating the optimal size of the safety net, and how that size should have changed over the past couple of years. For one, the evidence found here and in prior labor market studies helps dispel the notion, embodied in many Keynesian models, that the safety net is a free lunch, that it can help the poor and vulnerable without preventing many people from working.

The Congressional Budget Office, the White House, the Department of Labor, the Department of Commerce, and many other government agencies provide data and policy calculations that made this book, not to mention a huge amount of domestic economic analysis, possible. However, I am not aware that any of these agencies calculate a time series for replacement rates from the safety net as a whole, as I did in Chapter Three, even though replacement rates go a long way toward quantifying the labor market conse- quences of major public policies. To make matters worse, the Congressional Budget Office (2009, 10) and the White House Council of Economic Advisers (2010a) have, at least since early 2009, dismissed, if not ignored, the notion that enhancing payments to people who do not work—as with Federal Additional Compensation, COBRA subsidies, Broad-Based Categorical Eligibility, modernizing UI eligibility, mortgage modification, and a host of other policies—would actually cause a few million people to do what the government paid them to do: not work. When President Obama's advisers released their report forecasting the possible effects of the American Recovery and Reinvestment Act (Romer and Berstein 2009), they failed to mention that the large fraction of the act's funds going toward transfers to individuals might have a negative "multiplier" (that is, a negative effect on employment and output) as opposed to the large positive multipliers attributed to the act as a whole. The Congressional Budget Office and others even refer to marginal-tax-rate-increasing provisions as "automatic stabilizers" (Congressional Budget Office 2012).

The lack of accounting for labor market distortions suggests that the drop in labor market activity as a consequence of redistribution was largely unanticipated by government officials. Although not impossible, it would be impressive, or at least lucky, that the political process would move the safety net in the proper direction and in the proper amount at the same time that the costs of labor market distortions were not acknowledged.

Second, this book has presented and interpreted evidence that is relevant for determining whether the safety net expanded too much for too long. For example, at least some of the measures of uncertainty spiked in 2008 and 2009, and returned to prerecession levels in 2010, yet the safety net remains significantly more generous than it was in 2007, and is scheduled to get more generous. One hundred percent marginal tax rates—when the safety net gets so generous that a number of program beneficiaries receive zero reward for enhancing their incomes—are difficult to justify as a reasonable balance between equity and efficiency, yet even in 2005 some demographic groups were subject to such rates (Romich, Simmelink, and Holt 2007), and the recent safety net expansions documented here added to the number of people facing those rates.[6]

Chapters Three and Nine explain how multiple parties—both governments and lenders—have claims on the income that appears on a person's tax return. Multiple tax collectors can lead to excessive marginal tax rates, as each individual collector might not value the effect of his or her extraction on the revenues received by the other collectors (Olson 2000).

A number of the safety net expansions may be a source of uncertainty via the political process because, among other things, they must be repeatedly renewed by Congress, and taxpayers are still unsure of exactly who will pay for them (Baker, Bloom, and Davis 2011). In addition, Chapter Nine suggests that marginal tax rates in federal government mortgage modification programs were so high that the programs themselves created uncertainty for homeowners, rather than alleviating it. In particular, mortgage modification looks like a gamble from the borrowers' point of view; they do not know whether lenders will process an application for modification, or what factors will govern its disposition, and how modifications affect credit ratings. And one suspects that lenders prefer to keep borrowers guessing about these things, as it helps reduce the losses they experience on their mortgage lending. Minimum wage hikes may also create risk for low-skill workers, and therefore may not find justification in this chapter's equity-efficiency analysis.

Conclusions

Safety net programs face a well-known equity-efficiency tradeoff: providing more resources for the poor can raise their living standards, but it also gives them less incentive to raise their own living standards. Most societies somehow balance the tradeoff by permitting outcomes to vary across people—less-than-perfect equity—and having self-reliance rates less than 1.

The recent housing crash, financial crisis, or even political events may have altered the nature of this tradeoff or altered society's willingness to tolerate labor market inefficiency in order to have more equity. Either way, it should be no surprise that the safety net expanded and labor market activity fell. And, despite the obvious effect of the safety net expansions on the labor market, we cannot necessarily conclude that the costs of those expansions exceed their benefits.

Chapters Three and Nine suggest that settling unsecured debts can increase marginal tax rates directly, because every debt collector is in effect an additional tax collector who keeps part of the borrower's income as it increases. As unsecured debts grew as the housing and financial markets crashed in 2008, marginal tax rates increased. This chapter suggests that there may be a second connection between the financial crisis and marginal tax rates: that the fear, risk aversion, and uncertainty associated with the financial events also cause people to reassess the prerecession tradeoff between equity and labor market efficiency.

11

Conclusions

THE EXPANDING SOCIAL safety net explains a large fraction of the reduction in labor hours, and a large fraction of the increase in labor productivity, since 2007. The federal minimum wage hikes, and the attainment of retirement age by baby boomers, also tended to reduce labor hours, but less than the expanding safety net did. Much of the remaining hours drop might be explained by unmeasured and relatively small labor market distortions, or supply shifts, with many of the same economic characteristics of marginal tax rates.

The time paths for consumption (that is, inflation-adjusted consumer spending) and investment implied by Chapter Five's dynamic model, augmented to include an expanding and partly permanent social safety net, closely follow actual time series for consumption and investment, although the model somewhat overpredicts investment early in the recession. In this view, consumption fell because the safety net expanded, and much of the business investment decline was a response to low labor hours.

A critical, and hardly controversial, empirical observation supporting my conclusions is that labor productivity did not decrease significantly in 2008 and 2009—more likely it increased—and still remains above its prerecession values. Even while slashing payrolls, most of the private sector increased its use of production inputs other than labor hours. These findings help distinguish the 2008–09 recession from some of the previous downturns.

Employment and hours typically fell more for low-skill groups than for medium- and high-skill groups. Holding earnings potential constant, we see that hours fell more for unmarried people than for married people, especially among women. Moreover, the relationship between hours changes and skill is not always monotonic, and varies according to family composition. Work hours increased among the elderly. All of this is consistent with the view that the expanding social safety net was a major factor reducing labor market activity.

Aggregate marginal labor income tax rates, inclusive of the rates implicit in safety net benefit rules, increased from 40 percent before the recession began to 48 percent at the end of 2009. The fact that marginal tax rates increased about 8 percentage points helps explain why the peak-to-trough aggregate hours change was significantly greater than it was in other postwar recessions, yet significantly less than in the Great Depression of the 1930s.

My measures suggest that the safety net expanded a lot in 2008 and 2009, and did not expand significantly between then and the end of 2011. This pattern helps explain why the trough for per capita work hours was at the end of 2009, and why, as of the end of 2011, there had been no "double dip recession" in which labor per capita would peak below 2007 levels and decline significantly for a second time. Moreover, the fact that half or more of the safety net expansions and related labor market distortions remain in place helps explain why the labor market is not even close to a full recovery four years after the recession began.

Figure 11.1 displays my estimates of what would have happened in the U.S. labor market if safety net eligibility and benefit rules, and the federal minimum wage, had remained as they were in 2007. The figure's vertical scale is an index, with 100 representing the actual amount of labor per capita in 2007. For the purpose of preparing Figure 11.1, I assume that the safety net marginal tax rate would have remained constant and that, with no changes in the safety net marginal tax rate or any other redistributive public policy, pretax wages would have grown with labor productivity. Hypothetical labor quantities are simulated from Chapter Four's supply and demand model for three alternative values of the wage elasticity of labor supply (0.4, 0.75, and 1.1). I then add a relatively small estimate of the impact of the minimum wage hikes and display the results as lines in Figure 11.1.[1] The actual amounts of labor are displayed as circles.

The lines in the figure show that the exact results of the hypothetical depend on the assumed wage elasticity of labor supply (a quantification of the degree to which incentives affect time worked), for which economists do not agree on a specific value. Nevertheless, if the proper elasticity is anywhere in the range considered in this book, labor hours per capita would have declined without redistribution, but still significantly less than—probably less than half of –the actual decline. Redistribution is probably the largest single factor reducing labor hours per capita since 2007.

Assuming the middle supply elasticity of 0.75, the index of labor hours per capita would have been about 99 in 2008, and about 97 from 2009 to 2011 without increased redistribution. In other words, even without increased

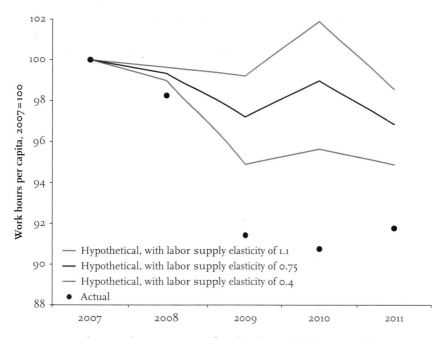

FIGURE 11.1 Labor Market Outcomes if Redistribution had Remained Constant

redistribution, labor hours per capita would have fallen 1–3 percent after 2007. At first, labor hours would have fallen somewhat because of the temporary decline in other production inputs (recall Figure 2.5), which perhaps was the result of the financial crisis, tight credit conditions, or shifts away from the construction industry. Later, the effects of population aging would have been a factor noticeably reducing labor, perhaps about 1 percent. Perhaps also by 2011 a labor market distortion appears that I have not attributed to redistribution through minimum wage hikes or safety net expansions, and this distortion is enough to reduce labor by another 1 or 2 percentage points. But these hypothetical reductions in labor per capita are small on the scale of previous recessions, and not even so large on the scale of a few years' worth of population growth.

More work is needed, however, to estimate the month-to-month evolution of the labor market absent changes in the amount of redistribution. My models are missing dynamic elements such as habit formation, the diffusion of program information, and job search, which are potentially important in the short term when the safety net changes as dramatically as it has since 2007. Moreover, not enough is known about the magnitude of historical responses of labor supply to safety net rule changes at different time horizons.

For these reasons, my results may not indicate whether increases in the amount of redistribution caused labor to drop sharply at the end of 2008, or just prevented the economy from recovering quickly and fully from an inevitable sharp drop.[2]

Additional work is also needed on measuring the work incentives created by the safety net as a whole, especially as they interact with imperfect program knowledge and other obstacles that prevent universal program take-up, and how they affect the likelihood and incidence of layoffs. The distribution of wages is quite different now from what it was thirty-five years ago, and this may affect how safety net programs expand and how the labor market responds to those expansions. It would be nice to measure marginal tax rates for the safety net as a whole over prior business cycles, and for other countries. More estimates of minimum wage effects among adults are needed.

Incentives Matter

Identifying private and public sector practices that would be expected to increase labor market distortions is not difficult, and does not even require the benefit of hindsight. Before the recession began economists understood that the federal minimum wage hikes would reduce employment, especially among less-skilled people.[3] Economists knew that the government's social safety net affects labor supply.[4] Before the end of 2008, if not earlier, it became clear that one of the legacies of the housing cycle would be a large redistribution of resources, on the part of mortgage lenders, on the basis of means (Mulligan 2008). One of the contributions of this book is to quantify the sum total of these and other labor market distortions associated with the expanding safety net.

The sum total is surprisingly large: aggregate marginal labor income tax rates increased 8 or 9 percentage points, on top of the marginal tax rates that were already present in 2007. Figure 11.2 helps illustrate the multitude of safety net rule changes. It displays the contributions of eight types of safety net program rule changes to the average $311 monthly benefits received in 2009-Q4 by the marginal nonworker *in addition* to the benefits that would have been received under 2007-Q4 program rules, following the methodology of Chapter Three. The largest single category consists of the increase from twenty-six weeks to ninety-six weeks of the amount of time an unemployed person is allowed to receive unemployment benefits, but Figure 11.2 shows that this "increase UI duration" category is still well less than half of the combined total of all safety net program changes.[5] The second and third

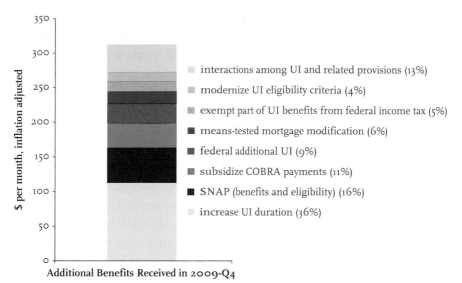

FIGURE 11.2 Decomposition of 2007-Q4 to 2009-Q4 real safety net generosity changes, person characteristics held constant

categories consist of the food stamp program expansions (still available as of the end of 2011, now known as "SNAP") and the COBRA health insurance subsidy (now expired), respectively. By fiscal year 2010, SNAP had become such a significant program for the unemployed that about as many unemployed nonelderly household heads and spouses were receiving SNAP benefits for their household as were receiving regular unemployment insurance benefits.

Focusing on just one of any of the safety net expansion categories is misleading as to the magnitude of the overall increase in marginal tax rates and therefore potentially misleading as to the sources of the major changes in the labor market since 2007. It is even possible that attention to one program in isolation of the wider safety net would motivate backward public policy responses. To see this, imagine that unemployment insurance (UI) rules became more generous, and this added to the number of households that were unemployed and with less income than they have when working. A number of the added unemployed people apply for food stamps, which from the food stamp program's point of view makes it look like "the economy is getting worse," so food stamp officials recommend enhancing food stamp benefits, which further increases the marginal tax rate. But in this example, the added food stamp applications come from higher marginal tax rates created by UI, and the right food stamp policy response may be to reduce benefits in order to stabilize the overall marginal tax rate. My point here is not that the actual safety net expansions were excessive—Chapter Ten explains why a proper welfare evaluation of the social safety net requires critical ingredients that are beyond the scope of this book—but rather that the economics of the safety net can differ when the safety net is viewed as a whole rather than program by program. The distinction is more than academic: recent events involved expansions of the safety net in many dimensions, and all of it occurred on top of a labyrinth of other safety net programs.

Economists recognize that the social safety net creates labor market distortions in the sense of creating a gap between the marginal product of labor and the marginal cost of supplying labor. They also largely agree that, in the aggregate, capital and labor are complements, so that sharp investment declines would be a *consequence* of labor market distortions, if the distortions were large enough to significantly reduce labor hours. The real debates are about (1) the amount by which an 8 or 9 percentage point increase in marginal tax rates (delivered through an expanding safety net) would reduce labor hours and (2) whether insurance and redistributive benefits of an expanding social safety net outweigh the costs of its labor market distortions.

Regarding the aggregate quantitative effects of marginal tax rates, I do not attempt to estimate those effects with the data since 2007 because marginal tax rates were reacting to the economy at the same time the economy was reacting to marginal tax rates. Rather, Figure 11.1 and the rest of the book consider a range of quantitative effects covering many reasonable interpretations of the historical evidence on labor supply and incentives. Throughout the range, the observed safety net expansions are expected to substantially depress labor hours. In this view, any quantitative attempt to describe the labor market since 2007 would be incomplete without including marginal tax rate effects of the expanding social safety net, and not just extending the duration of unemployment insurance payments.

To the extent that wages and other employment costs increased since 2007 without a commensurate increase in total factor productivity, it is no puzzle that employers do not want to return to the number of employees they had before the recession began. Wages and employment costs have been greater since 2007 in part because of the federal minimum wage hikes, but more significantly because the safety net expansions have given employees, and prospective employees, less reason to accept reductions in their compensation.

I am sometimes told that historical changes in personal income tax laws (supposedly) had little effect on the economy, and they prove that the marginal tax rate hikes created by the recent safety net expansions would also have little effect. The results of some of those historical changes are part of what determined the aforementioned range of quantitative effects considered in this book, but we also must recognize that the economic concept of marginal tax rate usually has little to do with what politicians call a "tax increase" or "tax decrease." For example, the New Home Buyers Tax Credit cited in Chapter One was called a tax cut by politicians, but it actually served to increase marginal tax rates in the economic sense of reducing the reward to working because qualified buyers who earned more received less of the credit.

Even when the political and economic tax concepts are correlated, the magnitudes of changes in average marginal tax rates relevant for labor market analysis can be small, in part because personal income taxes are not as closely targeted to marginal workers as safety net benefits are. For example, the National Bureau of Economic Research (2010) calculates that average federal marginal personal income tax rates increased by 1.5 percentage points from 1992 to 1994, largely because of the 1993 law raising federal tax rates. On the same scale, the marginal tax rate change from 2007-Q4 to 2009-Q4 measured in Chapter Three for the average marginal worker was about 10 percentage points.[6] Even if a 1.5 percentage point change had a small effect, it is no guarantee that a 10 percentage point change would have a small effect too.

My results are inconsistent with the Keynesian notion that marginal tax rates and other determinants of labor supply suddenly stopped mattering in 2007 or 2008, when the recession got going and the economy was said to be "caught in a liquidity trap." I find that seasonal fluctuations in labor supply affected aggregate employment after 2007 at about the same rate they did before 2007. I find that seasonal fluctuations in demand still run into supply constraints at about the same rate they did before 2007. I find that nonresidential construction was stimulated because of the supply of workers and materials made available by the housing collapse. I find that the demographic groups with lesser relative reductions in the financial reward to working had their employment increase, or at least fall less than it fell for other groups. Perhaps future research will offer alternative explanations for these findings, and offer proof that marginal tax rates really have not mattered recently. Even then, we would be left with the remarkable coincidence that labor hours, consumption, and investment all fell in amounts that are consistent with the labor supply effects of an expanding social safety net, if only those effects were similar to what they were before 2007.

Perhaps there is a "middle" ground between my conclusions and the Keynesian assumption that marginal tax rates have not affected employment and hours since 2007: that marginal tax rates still matter, just less than they normally do. But even in this case, it is essential to recognize that marginal tax rates changed over time, to measure the amount of that change, and to use that measure to determine how much of the decline in labor hours since 2007 might have been attributed to factors other than marginal tax rates. Chapter Three provides marginal tax rate series for such an analysis. Chapters Four and Five show that marginal tax rate changes might still account for, say, half of the drop in labor hours even if labor hours were significantly less sensitive to marginal tax rates than they were before 2007.

Was the Financial Collapse a Cause, or an Effect?

Compared with other books and articles about the recession, this book devotes little attention to the capital market gyrations that preceded most of the labor market decline. In part, this emphasis reflects the hypothesis of Chapter Five that an increasing labor market distortion makes capital less valuable. In this view, the market value of capital *reacts to* labor market distortions, and declines before labor supply distortions actually appear—namely, when news of labor distortions becomes known in the market place.

However, this book's narrative of the recession also includes labor market reactions to capital market events. One of the events prior to 2007 was the extraordinary accumulation of household debt. Home values peaked in 2006, and their subsequent decline both affected homeowners' incentives to earn income (through means-tested discharges) and drove a number of financial firms to bankruptcy or near bankruptcy. The 2008 financial crisis probably made it politically possible, if not politically inevitable, to expand other parts of the social safety net. If nothing else, people were more scared than usual, and understandably may have preferred more insurance than usual. Third, production inputs other than labor did fall, briefly, during the first year or so of the recession. Productivity affects labor in my model, and the temporary productivity drop may have had something to do with credit market conditions.

Still, these mechanisms linking capital markets to labor markets are fundamentally different from the investment narrative found in much of the economic literature. In this view, the housing collapse disabled bank lending, disabled bank lending prevented businesses from investing, and low investment meant fewer jobs. Other variations on the investment narrative attribute low investment to uncertainty or liquidity demand associated with financial market gyrations, but they have in common the idea that jobs are scarce largely because businesses do not invest. My theory is about collection of old loans, not underwriting of new ones, and I view low business investment as mostly a reaction to the labor decline rather than a cause of it.

Labor Supply and Demand Help Explain an Unhappy Situation

Most recessions are a time when consumption and labor move in the same direction over a short time frame (Barro and King 1984), and the basic pattern repeated itself in this recession. Those changes cannot happen in the textbook model of the aggregate labor market, unless labor productivity falls, leisure preferences change, or marginal tax rates rise. Most economists are reluctant to consider preference changes, and do not believe that productivity falls enough (or at all), or that marginal tax rates rise enough (or at all), to be blamed for many of the recessions of the past. With such an interpretation of the historical evidence, they feel compelled to either abandon or completely overhaul the textbook model in favor of models in which marginal tax rates hardly matter, and did so as this recession unfolded.[7] Although not always acknowledged, marginal tax rates were changing significantly during this recession, and the textbook labor market model does a pretty good job of explaining the major macroeconomic changes since 2007 as reactions to the marginal tax rate changes.

Happiness data are not part of my statistical analysis, but my interpretation of recession events is fully consistent with the common observation that people are less happy with their economic situation since the recession began. First of all, housing prices collapsed. Sometimes housing price changes are considered to merely be redistributive—affecting the lifetime wealth of people who own houses in the opposite direction from how they affect the lifetime wealth of people who expect to consume more housing than they currently own. Even in this view, the former group wishes housing prices were now what they were before the recession began. Moreover, the collection of unsecured mortgage debts costs the debtors more than the lenders ultimately collect. It is also possible that the housing price collapse reflects a reduction in the economy's production set (Mulligan 2010c), which is itself bad news.

Second, the safety net is not free: it is funded by taxpayers, lenders, owners of government debt, beneficiaries of government programs other than the safety net, or some combination thereof. To the extent that the safety net expanded beyond the efficient amount, its benefit to the beneficiaries is less than the cost to those who pay. People are even worse off to the extent that political uncertainty remains as to who will ultimately pay for the safety net expansions, and uncertainty as to who will be eligible for loan discharges and other safety net programs. To the extent that the safety net expansion was an efficient reaction to uncertainty or other bad economic news, people are worse off from the bad economic news, and the expanding safety net at best helped cushion the blow.[8]

As millions of people opt to earn less, they also opt to spend less, as their budget constraint requires. They cut most sharply their purchases of consumer durables. Businesses anticipate having fewer employees and invest less (see Chapter Five). These behavioral changes are a third type of bad news—for employers in general, for people who produce consumer durables and investment goods, and for people who live in places such as Michigan whose economies are especially intensive in the production of such goods. This is a third reason my analysis predicts that a large number of people would be worse off after 2007 than they were before, and may be without work and yet have no direct contact with safety net programs.

The expansion of the safety net does not put a halt to the bad life events—divorce, illness, changes in the composition of market demand, etc.—that a fraction of the population normally experiences, often through no fault of their own. Moreover, the unfortunate people who experience such events may, owing to their income and demographics, be disproportionately represented among the fraction of the population who find reducing employment and market income, and increasing reliance on safety net programs, to be the best response to a bad situation.[9] However true it may be, they may find no consolation in the possibility that the life event they experienced in 2009 would have been even worse if they had experienced it before the recession began—when the safety net was less generous. But this does not change the fact that aggregate employment would be significantly greater in 2009 if the safety net had not been expanded.

Even if we ignore external events that might have caused the safety net to expand, my model says that the deadweight loss of the safety net expansion was about $200 billion for every year that the safety net is as generous as it was in 2010, plus the deadweight costs of the tax hikes that may someday be necessary to pay for it, minus any redistributive or insurance benefits. By itself, $200 billion per year is enough to make people noticeably worse off, and in my model people rationally respond to the expanding safety net and other labor market distortions by cutting their consumption by 4 percent.

The 2009 American Reinvestment and Recovery Act is probably the single piece of legislation with the most provisions expanding the safety net. To name a few: it increased unemployment and food stamp benefits; it expanded eligibility for both programs with its "alternative base period" calculation of the unemployment benefit and by granting states relief from the food stamp program's work requirements; it federally funded extended unemployment benefits, so that employers would not have to pay for the extended benefits received by their former employees. The act's "recovery" and "stimulus" monikers are ironic because, like other legislation that expanded the safety net, the transfer provisions of the act helped keep labor hours low after the act went into effect.

But arguably public policies should not be judged solely on the basis of their employment impacts. An expanding safety net can help equalize living standards across households and, judging from Sherman's findings (2011), federal safety net expansions did exactly that. If the prerecession safety net was too small, then the recent safety net expansions might be a welcome improvement that is well worth the price of its labor market distortions. In addition, much of the population may be more willing now than they were before the recession to tolerate labor market distortions in order to expand the safety net's cushion, which could help maintain their living standards if and when they experience bad life events. On the other hand, the prevalence of 100 percent marginal tax rates and multiple tax collectors may indicate that the safety net could have been expanded in alternative ways that were less depressing to the labor market. There is room to debate the net welfare effect of safety net expansions, but the fact remains that income redistribution has a price: reduced labor, consumption, capital, and market output.

Notes

1. All of the data used in this chapter are seasonally adjusted at the source, unless already measured annually.
2. Appendix 2.2 explains how various sources agree on the amount of the aggregate hours drop.
3. See also Elsby, Hobijn, and Sahin (2010).
4. The book focuses on labor usage—the total hours in the nation that people are working—as opposed to the "labor force," which includes persons who are not working but are looking for work. In most cases, as in Figure 2.1, my hours measures derive from hours tabulations by the Census Bureau or Bureau of Labor Statistics, which are tabulations of hours that employed persons are paid (and thereby include hours of paid vacation, sick days, etc.). In a few cases, noted below, it is important to distinguish paid work hours from hours actually worked, in which case I create my own hours-actually-worked series from the microdata from the Census Bureau's household survey. In a few cases, also noted below, employment is the only available labor usage measure.
5. See Abraham and Haltiwanger (1995) for a review of that literature.
6. See also Mulligan (2009b). "Consumption" refers to inflation-adjusted consumer spending, plus the service value of owner-occupied housing (see below for more details). "Intertemporal substitution" refers to changes in activity in the present that offset, or are expected to be offset by, future behavioral changes in the opposite direction: farmers are said to "make hay while the sun shines" knowing that it is profitable to delay rest until night or until the winter, when there is less farm work to be done.
7. Real consumption is spending on consumption items and services, adjusted for inflation (that is, price changes) for those items and services, and therefore it changes only if people change the number or quality of the items and services they purchase.

8. Chapter Five includes consumer durables purchases as part of private investment. Although I treat public consumption the same as private consumption in terms of their direct contributions to living standards, later I examine private-public differences in terms of how consumption items and services are distributed.

9. Specifically, the "sustainable trend" increases at 0.5 percent per year, according to my estimate (discussed in Chapter Five) of the rate of per capita total factor productivity growth. With some exceptions noted below, employee compensation per hour is thought to indicate marginal labor productivity to the extent that workers are paid their marginal product.

10. The combined series closely follows private sector services because (1) private nondurables and services follow a similar pattern and (2) public nondefense consumption expenditure is small compared to private expenditures on nondurables and services (the latter is the single largest expenditure category).

11. Unadjusted for inflation, hourly compensation had increased almost 7 percent by the end of 2009. Also note that self-employment income is not included in the numerator of hourly compensation, but self-employment hours are included in the denominator. I have not attempted a quarterly adjustment for changes in employees' share of total hours worked, but note that CPS-MORG micro data suggest that the share fell 0.4 percent from 2007 to 2009.

12. Real GDP per hour is a more comprehensive measure of productivity than business sector productivity because the former includes all sectors in its numerator and all workers in its denominator. As a comprehensive measure, GDP per hour is more readily integrated with models of aggregate labor supply in which total hours worked is a key variable. However, productivity by itself is often measured for the narrower business sector because output in the remaining sectors (government, nonprofit institutions, and households) may be measured less reliably. Because the two measures experienced many of the same changes since 2007, henceforth I use the more comprehensive GDP per hour and note a few places where results would be slightly different if based on business sector output per hour.

13. More generally, when factor markets are competitive, the magnitude of the elasticity of productivity with respect to labor input is equal to the share of output paid to nonlabor production factors. I assume the share to be 0.3 and assume that it is independent of the amount of labor and the amount of other inputs. As noted below, this chapter's qualitative results are not sensitive to either of these assumptions. Measures of the nonlabor share depend somewhat on assumptions about the factor composition of indirect taxes and proprietors' income (Mulligan and Threinen 2010); later chapters note how quantitative results would be only slightly different if the share were assumed to be one-third rather than 0.3.

14. The concepts of labor productivity and the "input residual" are different from "total factor" or "multifactor" productivity, which attempt to measure the change

in output that cannot be explained by changes in labor and capital inputs. In practice, the multifactor productivity measures prepared by the Bureau of Labor Statistics do not account for changes in capacity utilization, which is sometimes the primary reason the input residual changes over time.

15. As shown in Figure 2.3, business sector output per hour fell slightly during 2008.

16. My statistics are weighted by the Current Population Survey "Final Weight.". Unlike the labor compensation used for aggregate analysis, earnings measured from the Current Population Survey exclude the value of fringe benefits. Persons with zero weekly earnings are excluded from the average hourly earnings calculations shown in Table 2.1.

17. If 140 million workers were earning an average of $20.20 per hour in 2007 and another 6 million workers were earning an average of $5.50 per hour, the overall average hourly earnings would be $19.60. In other words, the overall average understates the average for the 140 million by 3 percent.

18. The U.S. Bureau of Labor Statistics (2007) and U.S. Bureau of Labor Statistics (2008) calculations for 2006 and 2007 suggest that fewer than two million people earned at or below the federal minimum wage.

19. As part of its work on multifactor productivity, the Bureau of Labor Statistics (2011a) considers changes in age, education, and gender and finds that those sources of composition bias changed measured productivity 1.4 percent from 2007 to 2009, or about 0.8 percent relative to the prior trend. In their study of composition bias for business cycles between 1967 and 1987, Solon, Barsky, and Parker (1994) found that aggregate wage measures fell 0.6 percent for every percentage point increase in the national unemployment rate. The direction of this result by itself shows that something different happened during the 2008–09 recession, but if we take their composition-bias-corrected estimate of 1.0 percent (this is a 2007 weighted average of their separate male and female estimates) and thereby infer composition bias of 0.4 percent for every percentage point that the national unemployment rate increases, then the 4.7 point national unemployment rate change that occurred between 2007 and 2009 resulted in a 1.8 percent increase in average wages due to changes in composition. For the reasons I cited in the text (see also Bils 1985, 684; and Keane, Moffitt, and Runkle 1988), I believe the Solon et al. (1994) composition bias estimates may be exaggerated for my purposes, but still they imply that selection-bias-corrected real wages increased from 2007 to 2009.

20. Young workers and recent graduates are examples of marginal workers, although some of them may also have experienced a relative reduction in the demand for their labor (e.g., the food service industry declined disproportionately during the recession). Nevertheless, real wage changes 2007–2010 for young people do not appear to be substantially negative. For example, I took the full-time employed members of the CPS-MORG micro data aged sixteen to

twenty-four and having positive earnings, and calculated their hourly wage as the ratio of earnings to hours worked during the reference week. I averaged the wages by age (in years) and year of the interview, and then calculated log changes from 2007 to 2010. The resulting change varies by age, but the inflation-adjusted average log change was -0.04 among the twenty-to-twenty-four age groups and 0.09 among the sixteen-to-nineteen age groups (the age sixteen group change is an outlier; without them the change was 0.00). Note that the log real federal minimum wage increased 0.11 over that time period.

21. Regardless of whether other inputs are held fixed, the New Keynesian model with flexible nominal wages predicts that nominal and real wages fall as a result of a lack of demand, which contradicts the empirical findings for the 2008–09 recession.

22. As I explain in Chapter Five, even a recession that was the result of reduced labor supply would create an immediate reduction in the demand for durable goods.

23. For the purposes of applying equation (2.2) to the manufacturing industries (as opposed to the entire economy), I used the labor share of 55 percent rather than 70 percent because manufacturing employee compensation was 55 percent of value-added in 2007 (U.S. Bureau of Economic Analysis 2011; http://www.bea.gov/iTable/index_industry.cfm, last accessed May 30, 2012). Using a labor share of 70 percent would result in a 0.13 reduction in the other inputs residual for manufacturing.

24. Capacity utilization is an example of a factor of production, other than labor hours, that can be adjusted in the short term.

25. Each quarter's log change in real value-added (for business minus manufacturing minus residential construction) is calculated so that, together with the log changes for manufacturing and residential construction, it averages to the log change for the entire business sector, using each component industry's nominal value-added as weights.

26. The age-adjusted adult population is the number of people aged sixteen and over, weighted by the average hours worked by people that age in 2006 and 2007, and normalized so that the adjusted population coincides with the actual population in 2007-Q4, all estimated from the CPS-MORG microdata files. Between 2007-Q4 and 2009-Q4, the log age-adjusted adult population increases 0.007 less than the log unadjusted adult population. As of the time of writing, I have CPS-MORG through the end of 2010, so I assume that the log age adjustment follows its 2004–2010 trend of -0.00023 per month through the end of 2011.

27. For this reason, the gap $(1-\tau_l)$ is sometimes called "the labor wedge" or the "labor supply residual."

28. The marginal rate of substitution function (2.5), which corresponds to the utility function $u(c,n,P,N) = P\ln(c/P) - \gamma\frac{\eta}{\eta+1}N\left(\frac{n}{N}\right)^{(\eta+1)/\eta}$, can be interpreted as a

first-order approximation to the marginal rate of substitution function associated with any utility function $u(c,n,P,N)$ with those four arguments, and having the properties that (1) consumption and leisure are normal goods, (2) the indifference sets are convex, (3) the MRS function depends only on consumption per capita and labor per adult, and (4) consumption per capita and the MRS can have the same trend without any trend for labor per adult.

29. More precisely, from a base tax rate of zero, the hike would have to be 15 percentage points because $0.15 = 1 - e^{-0.167}$; recall that the distortion in Figure 2.6 is measured as $-\ln(1-\tau)$.

30. If 2009-Q4 population and real consumption per capita were the same as in 2007-Q4, if the productivity residual followed its actual values, and if the labor supply distortion did not change over time, then the supply schedule would be unchanged and log labor would increase 0.015 log points, as shown in the figure as the hypothetical outcome HC. Chapter Five's general equilibrium model combines the marginal productivity (2.1) and marginal rate of substitution (2.5) equations, together with equations describing the evolution of consumption and capital, in order to simultaneously determine the effects of distortions on consumption, capital, productivity, and labor.

31. Between 2007-Q4 and 2009-Q4, log real GDP declined 0.039 and log labor hours declined 0.083, which means that other inputs increased as long as the elasticity of real GDP with respect to hours is greater than 0.47 (= 39/83), even if that elasticity varies with the amount of hours. In order to conclude that other inputs increased in the nonmanufacturing nonresidential-construction parts of the business sector, the elasticity of real value-added with respect to hours must exceed 0.48 (see the final column of Table 2.2).

32. The new hires tax credit is examined more formally in Chapter Three. The implicit tax accrues on payrolls before the credit goes into effect but is not collected until afterward, which is why it is excluded from the usual measures of labor compensation at the time the implicit tax accrues.

33. If, however, the employer liabilities are associated with employee assets of equal value, the result is not a labor market distortion but rather a change in the composition of employee compensation. For example, if employers expected to incur future health expenses for current employees, but employees valued those health services, the result would be lower cash compensation but a greater willingness to work at a given amount of cash compensation because it would be combined with the expectation of employer-provided health services. The equilibrium amounts of labor and productivity could be unaffected by the anticipated health expenses (Summers 1989).

34. On the third group of causes, it is well known (e.g., Barro and King 1984; Hall 1997) that previous business cycles do not appear to be wealth or intertemporal substitution effects because both labor and consumption decline. The 2008–09 recession is hardly unique in this regard.

35. See also Ohanian (2010), who reports averages for all postwar recessions, with similar conclusions.

36. Employment declined 3 percent from peak to trough. As an upper bound on the composition bias, suppose that the bias was the result of workers exiting the workforce between peak and trough in the amount of 3 percent of peak employment, and whose average wage was one-half of the overall average (according to the Bureau of Labor Statistics 2011c, average hourly earnings in the private sector were $7.44, half of which would be close to the federal minimum wage of $3.35). In this case, the business cycle peak wage would underestimate the average wage of those working in the trough by about 1.5 percent.

37. Despite the 1980s reduction in time worked, the labor supply residual did not fall because (1) productivity fell and (2) consumption per person hardly fell.

38. The labor supply residual for 1981–82 would decline about 0.02 more if real hourly wages were used in the calculation, rather than real GDP per hour, but still much less than the labor supply residual drops shown for the other four recessions.

39. In order to maximize comparability across recessions, hours worked for the 2008–09 recession are measured differently in Figure 2.9 than they are in the rest of the chapter, because the basis for my preferred measure of hours (all employee hours in all private industries) is not available prior to 2003. For the purposes of Figure 2.9 (and Figure 2.8's real GDP and labor compensation per hour series), aggregate hours are the sum of private work hours per person (measured as the all-employees aggregate weekly hours index for the business sector) and aggregate public work hours (estimated as public sector employment times private work hours per private sector employee). Figure 2.9 and Table 2.3 do not adjust for the changing age composition of the population.

40. Although the establishment survey measures jobs, and the household survey measures workers (some workers have more than one job), my establishment and household measures are not different in this regard because I summed hours in the establishment survey and divided by persons, not jobs. With the exception of the civilian employment series shown in Figure 2.1, I take averages from the household surveys, rather than totals, and therefore make no adjustment for the survey's January update of its population controls (U.S. Bureau of Labor Statistics 2011b).

CHAPTER 3

1. A few of these are Elsby, Hobijn and Sahin (2010), Shimer (2010b), Daly et al. (2012) and the studies cited in Council of Economic Advisers (2010a).

2. Mulligan (2008) and Herkenhoff and Ohanian (2011) consider the safety net created by loan discharges. Research on prior business cycles, such as Braun

(1994) and McGrattan (1994) has considered marginal tax rates, especially from income and payroll taxes.

3. The "household budget set" is a good way to visualize the contribution of individual and combined means-tested programs to the reward to working. See Chapters Six and Nine. Two points on the budget set are featured in this chapter's calculation: a full or normal work time point and a point corresponding to the (small) amount of earnings typical of program participants during a month, quarter, or other time interval during which income is measured for the purpose of determining eligibility and benefits.

4. Because the purpose of the book is to understand why people are more frequently unemployed, out of the labor force, or underemployed than they were before the recession, I normalized the generosity index for the remainder group (employed but not underemployed) to be constant, so that the unemployed, out of the labor force, and underemployed are all examined relative to the remainder group.

5. I return to the elderly in Chapter Six but omit them for now because of their small share of the labor market and because of the large amount of government spending on them that, contrary to the program spending examined in this chapter, is not means-tested.

6. Using the 2007 CPS merged outgoing rotation groups, I calculate average hours worked in the reference week among employed heads and spouses less than age sixty-five (persons employed but not at work are not included in this average) using the CPS weights. For every month 2006–2010, I then measure underemployment as the sum of persons not employed in the reference week plus the product of the number employed and 1 minus the ratio of average hours among those at work to the 2007 average noted above, using the same CPS weights. By construction, underemployment is equal to non-employment for 2007 and any other period in which the average hours worked among those at work was the same as in 2007. Otherwise, employed persons also contribute fractionally to underemployment according to hours worked. Given that my purpose is to decompose changes in safety net expenditures on the basis of actual work hours (rather than intended work hours), my underemployment measure is different from Bureau of Labor Statistics measures of labor underutilization.

7. On average between 2006 and 2010, 3.3 percent of regular state UI beneficiaries were aged sixty-five and over (U.S. Department of Labor, various issues); 6.6 percent of SNAP benefits were pro-rated to persons aged sixty-plus (Eslami, Filion, and Strayer 2011; Leftin, Gothro, and Eslami 2010; Wolkwitz and Trippe 2009; Wolkwitz and Leftin 2008); 12.4 percent of SSI benefits were paid out under aged provisions (Social Security Administration 2011); and 21 percent of Medicaid benefits (fiscal years 2009 and 2010 unavailable) were paid to the aged. I assume that the elderly share of Family Assistance, General Assistance, Energy Assistance, and Other is the same as it is for SNAP.

8. Social security, Medicare, education, veterans' benefits, and various medical, retirement, and pension transfers are entirely excluded from Table 3.2 and all of the other calculations in this chapter.

9. The population of nonelderly heads and spouses has a lot of overlap with the population of persons aged twenty-five to sixty-four (a population that can be isolated for the purpose of measuring unemployment insurance participation): only 5 percent of nonelderly heads and spouses are under twenty-five, and 85 percent of persons aged twenty-five to sixty-four are either head or spouse. Unemployment benefit receipt is estimated from the U.S. Department of Labor's reports of persons claiming benefits in state and federal programs. The share of persons under age twenty-five among EB and EUC recipients is assumed to be 55 percent of their share among regular state recipients, because their share (2007–2010 average) of persons unemployed more than twenty-six weeks is 55 percent of their share of persons unemployed no more than twenty-six weeks.

10. Appendix 3.1 gives the index calculation details.

11. For the purposes of this calculation, I assume that, consistent with the law, nobody received unemployment benefits for a week that he or she was employed.

12. Fiscal years begin October 1 in the prior year (e.g., fiscal year 2009 began October 1, 2008). The average household size is 2.2 among SNAP households (Eslami et al. 2011, table A.27) and 2.6 for the entire United States (U.S. Census Bureau 2010). For SNAP purposes, a household is a group of persons purchasing and preparing food together; by that definition, multiple households can share the same living quarters (Food Research and Action Center 2009, 16).

13. Technically, the brochure is called a "TANF/MOE-funded noncash benefit" (Eslami et al. 2011, 4). For example, Connecticut distributes a two-page "Help for People in Need" brochure with links to SNAP and various state safety net programs (U.S. Department of Agriculture, Food and Nutrition Service 2011a). The categorically eligible households need not receive cash benefits from any other welfare program and in some states may have income up to double the federal poverty guideline (Leftin et al. 2010, 56–57). Broad-based categorical eligibility was made possible by a 2002 federal law, but it had been adopted by only twelve states as of January 2007.

14. As a result, more than 95 percent of participating households have monthly income less than or equal to 125 percent of the federal poverty guideline during the months that they are participating (Eslami et al. 2011, table A.3).

15. As of October 2011, at least thirty-eight states plus the District of Columbia had no asset test for determining BBCE (U.S. Department of Agriculture, Food and Nutrition Service 2011a). Three states (Michigan, Nebraska, and Texas) had asset tests that were more lax than SNAP's. The remaining states did not yet confer BBCE. Work requirements for SNAP beneficiaries were dropped between

April 2009 and October 2010. The requirements were also dropped for residents of at least forty-five states and the District of Columbia through at least September 30, 2012 (U.S. Department of Agriculture, Food and Nutrition Service 2011b). Administrative policy changes also increased access to SNAP: potential program participants have increasingly been given the opportunity to apply for benefits on the internet (Eslami et al. 2011, 8), and states' funneling enrollments through the BBCE category eliminated the need to verify applicant asset holdings (U.S. Government Accountability Office 2007). The U.S. Government Accountability Office (2007 4) also points out that, as of late 2006, even states with BBCE had room to further expand the population on whom they confer BBCE.

16. Even without BBCE expansion, the SNAP participation probably would have grown faster than the number of households in poverty because SNAP relaxed work requirements and asset tests and permitted more deductions from income. Moreover, during the period 2007–2011 states created programs to help SNAP households maximize their deductions, as with their dollar-a-year LIHEAP programs (Food Research and Action Center 2009, 10). New York asserts that its LIHEAP program alone increased the state's aggregate SNAP benefits by 6 percent (New York Office of Temporary and Disability Assistance 2009, and U.S. Department of Agriculture, 2012b). But my purpose here is to quantify SNAP participation changes attributable to all eligibility rule changes combined, not to isolate the effect of a specific type of legislation such as BBCE. The Department of Agriculture also found that the food stamp spending increase "is likely attributable to the deterioration of the economy, expansions in SNAP eligibility, and continued outreach efforts" (Leftin et al. 2010, xiii). For this reason, the others cited above, and the fact that SNAP's participation grew so much more than the number of people in poverty while other means-tested programs' participation grew with the population in poverty, it is clear that SNAP eligibility rules underwent significant changes (see also Wolkwitz and Trippe, 2009, 10). Note that the Congressional Budget Office (2012) might appear to conclude otherwise, but it considers only changes in federal legislation, and not state law changes or changes in federal eligibility rules that might have occurred under the 2002 Farm Bill (such as county-by-county waivers from the work requirement that might have created many of the same eligibility changes as the ARRA's nationwide waiver). Moreover, the CBO report was based on a study that had little or no information on categorical eligibility, especially the asset ownership patterns of categorically eligible households.

17. States could exempt up to 15 percent of such persons from the work requirement, or request a waiver for people in areas with an unemployment rate over 10 percent.

18. That is, I assume that adoption of BBCE and other changes in SNAP eligibility rules are responsible for 66 percent of the growth of SNAP household

participation in excess of family (125 percent) poverty growth between fiscal years 2007 and 2010. Appendix 3.1 and Appendix 3.2 have more details and sensitivity analysis.

19. Other forces may have made it more difficult to allow unemployed people to participate in TANF (U.S. Government Accountability Office 2010). The net effect may be that work requirements were relaxed since 2007 because six states (and D.C.) failed to met their work participation rate targets in fiscal year 2009 (U.S. Department of Health and Human Services 2011), as compared to eleven in fiscal year 2007 (U.S. Department of Health and Human Services 2009).

20. To calculate spending per beneficiary, I divide calendar year Medicaid spending (as reported in the government social benefits section of the personal income accounts) by the number of persons enrolled in Medicaid as of June of that year (Henry J. Kaiser Family Foundation 2011b). Sometimes annual spending per beneficiary is measured as the ratio of spending to the number of persons enrolled at any time during the year (Henry J. Kaiser Family Foundation 2011a), in which case the ratio is about $5,000. With the exception of amounts for premiums and copayments (see below), all of the Medicaid statistics reported in this chapter include the Medicaid CHIP program.

21. For example, at $4,000 per beneficiary per year, families with three beneficiaries would receive benefits with an average value (at program cost) of $12,000 per year. Note that private family health insurance, a substitute for Medicaid enrollment, typically costs about $13,000 per year (Crimmel 2010).

22. A few states recently began to require participants to pay regular premiums, make co-payments upon visits to health care providers, or both (Henry J. Kaiser Family Foundation 2011c). The co-payments are small; for example, in 2008 the Wisconsin Medicaid program began collecting co-payments ranging from zero to three dollars from participants with incomes below 200 percent of the poverty level (Dague 2011). The premiums, if any, also increase with beneficiary income (Dague 2011).

23. The poverty rate increased 18 percent between 2007 and 2010, when Medicaid enrollment and inflation-adjusted spending per capita increased 16 percent.

24. The normalization correctly describes the amount of benefits gained as a consequence of not working, relative to working full-time, if zero benefits are received when working full-time. In fact, the median employed nonelderly head or spouse earns too much to participate in employment or means-tested programs. However, the benefit indices constructed in this chapter would not accurately describe the returns to working for low-skilled workers who may be eligible for means-tested benefits even when working full-time. Chapter Six calculates benefit indices for less-skilled workers.

25. I assume that UI and Medicaid benefits are indexed to inflation; unemployment benefits depend on a person's earnings history, and Medicaid provides participants a fixed set of medical goods and services rather than a set dollar amount.

26. Any SNAP household not receiving the minimum benefit has its benefit change dollar-for-dollar with the maximum benefit for their household size, even if their benefit is less than the maximum benefit. About 3 percent of SNAP households receive a minimum benefit, which was increased $4 per month by the 2008 Farm Bill and another $2 by the ARRA. The average household monthly benefit increase from the maximum and minimum benefit provisions of the 2008 Farm Bill and ARRA was therefore $26 and $45, respectively.

27. Note that most Americans—children, practically all of the employed, to name a few—are not receiving unemployment benefits during any given week, so the program's average weekly payment per beneficiary (about $300) is much larger than the program's per capita weekly spending shown in Table 3.4 (about $8 per week in 2010). The table shows per capita amounts in order to compare total spending over time and across programs, adjusting for population growth. Spending shown in the table is for all age groups; the percentages of UI and SNAP spending on nonelderly persons were well above 90 and did not change more than 0.7 percentage point between 2007 and 2010.

28. The ratio is 0.61 in 2007 and 0.72 in 2010. Adjusting the 2007 ratio for the alternative base period rule yields 0.64, and hence a 2007 and 2010 average of 0.68. Four (10.3) percent of unemployed persons age twenty-five to sixty-four had spells already lasting more than ninety-six weeks in 2007 (2010), respectively, which is an average of 7.1 percent. Recall from above that the unemployment claims data do not indicate relationship to head, so I used age twenty-five to sixty-four as a proxy. Farber and Valletta (2011) calculate that the cross-state average maximum UI eligibility, weighted by the number of persons unemployed, has been about ninety-six weeks since the end of 2009.

29. In order to calculate the numerator, I used the fiscal year 2010 SNAP quality control micro datafile prepared by Mathematica Policy Research to identify sample members who were aged eighteen to sixty-four, household head or spouse, and were a SNAP participant or were a non-U.S. citizen who had a dependent in the household who was a SNAP participant. The sample members were projected to the U.S. population (in the average month during each fiscal year) using the file's household weight variable (hwgt). The ratio of the 2007–2010 change in SNAP household heads who are unemployed to the nationwide change is even greater than 0.50, but likely because of program eligibility rule changes rather than an especially high propensity of unemployed to participate in the program.

30. This 0.96 does not imply that 96 percent of the unemployed are enrolled in Medicaid, but rather that on average each head or spouse added to the unemployed adds 0.96 nonelderly persons (including children) to Medicaid enrollment. For example twenty-four unemployed out of one hundred could add a family of four to Medicaid, while the other seventy-six unemployed added none. The value of the Medicaid participation weight ω_j does not affect any of

my estimates of safety net generosity *changes* prior to 2014, because Medicaid eligibility and benefit rules are assumed to be constant prior to 2014 (see also Appendix 3.2).

31. Many people are eligible for Medicaid but do not participate (Aizer 2003), which may suggest that the average eligible person values the program's benefits less than they cost, or that they intend to enroll in the program only if a medical need arises.

32. Appendix 3.2 sketches an explicit model of program participation and suggests that my fixed program weight approach may somewhat understate changes in the log self-reliance rate over time (an important quantity for aggregate labor market analysis).

33. Eslami et al. (2011, table A.2).

34. The average marginal federal income tax rate in 2009 was 21 percent for wage income (National Bureau of Economic Research 2010).

35. Each dollar of UI income can reduce SNAP benefits, but less than dollar-for-dollar (Hanson and Andrews March 2009). The ARRA required that the $25 increase in weekly UI benefits not count against the recipient's Medicaid eligibility (Ross and Parrott 2009).

36. COBRA refers to the Consolidated Omnibus Reconciliation Act, which required "most group health plans to provide a temporary continuation of group health coverage that otherwise might be terminated," and the statute under which laid-off employees have the option to continue on their former employer's health insurance plan (U.S. Department of Labor 2012).

37. Assuming two household members rather than four yields a range of $178 to $1,673, largely because "employee plus one" health insurance costs $9,053 per year rather than $13,027 for an entire family (Crimmel 2010).

38. Ljungqvist (2002) explains why a dollar of layoff costs might not exactly offset a dollar of unemployment insurance benefits in terms of their effects on equilibrium employment.

39. In exchange for funds to make a home purchase or improvement, a homeowner promises in the mortgage agreement to either make his scheduled payments or, at the lender's discretion, pay late fees or surrender ownership of the home.

40. Foote et al (2009, footnote 3). Liebowitz (2009) finds that negative equity was a more important factor than unemployment in causing the foreclosures that occurred in the second half of 2008. Geanakopolos and Koniak (2009) find that foreclosures are "stunningly sensitive" to the amount of home equity. See also First American CoreLogic (2008, 2).

41. A number of states prohibit lenders from holding homeowners liable for the difference between the mortgage amount and funds obtained from a foreclosure sale. Other states technically allow such liabilities, but homeowners can often shield their assets from home loan deficiency judgments. In a few states, homeowners may expect to be liable for the deficiency (Ghent and Kudlyak

2011), but in practice collection of such liabilities may, in effect, involve some of the same means tests noted below.

42. The ratio of housing expenses to income is sometimes called the "debt to income ratio."

43. Through mid-2010, unemployment benefits count as income for the purpose of calculating DTI, with some caveats noted in Chapter Nine. See also Herkenhoff and Ohanian (2011).

44. If not, the modification is said to fail the NPV test.

45. A single-earner household in which that earner went from earning $3,148 to receiving $1,574 in UI would have the same $488 modification amount, but the critical LTV would be 1.29. If an earner were unemployed only part of the year in which earnings were examined for the purposes of modification, then the monthly modification amount would, as a ratio to time unemployed, be the same as shown in the table, but the critical LTV would be closer to 1. Part-year unemployment is an important reason the average actual modification amount is closer to $400 per month (Office of Thrift Supervision, various issues).

46. The prevalence of negative equity is not technically an eligibility rule (although it is necessary for eligibility) and is therefore the one (minor) exception to my description that the overall safety net generosity index constructed below changes only when eligibility or benefit rules change.

47. Trial modifications are given fractional weight 5/60, because a permanent modification reduces payments for sixty months and the average trial modification reduced them about five months (U.S. Department of Treasury 2012).

48. Specifically, anyone with income above the state's median and with monthly income net of necessary expenses more than about $200 is not permitted Chapter 7 (Administrative Office of the U.S. Courts 2011a, 14).

49. The ratio has nonelderly household heads, rather than household heads and spouses, in the numerator and denominator because many nonelderly spouses are out of the labor force for reasons apart from the recession.

50. The interaction term is negligible.

51. The last column is the weighted average of the previous three, using the last row as weights.

52. Ten percent is the assumed difference between (federal, state, and local) personal income taxes paid when working and personal income taxes paid on baseline UI benefits when not working, expressed as a ratio to wages earned when working (see Appendix 3.2 for discussion of additional UI taxes). Appendix 3.4 examines the "Making Work Pay Tax Credit" that was in effect during calendar years 2009 and 2010. Any tax rules that were constant over time only affect the replacement rate level, rather than its changes; Appendix 3.2 presents sensitivity analysis with respect to the replacement rate level. Sales and excise taxes also affect the reward to working, but they can be omitted without affecting the results under the assumptions that (1) their rates are constant over time and

(2) they have a proportional effect on self-reliance rates measured from program benefits and taxes on earnings.

53. Sometimes the replacement rate is defined with respect to lost earnings rather than lost productivity, with the difference being the gap between earnings and productivity due to employer taxes and other employer-side labor market distortions. I use productivity in order to be consistent with the productivity calculations from the previous chapter. See also Chapter Six for an interpretation of the replacement rate in terms of "household budget sets."

54. The median earnings of nonelderly heads and spouses was $727 per week, or $3,148 per month; $3,885 is the result of scaling up monthly earnings by the national accounts ratio of aggregate employee compensation to wages paid, in order to have an estimate of median labor productivity comparable to what I used in the previous chapter. For estimates of replacement rates for persons with productivity different from the median, see Chapter Six.

55. On targeted tax credits, see Sherman (2011). Melvin (2009) explains how "IRS agents were given more flexibility in their collection actions, including the ability to reduce or suspend monthly payments on back taxes so those *hit hard by the financial downturn* are not forced to default on their tax payments" (emphasis added).

56. Chapters Four and Five examine versions of the economic theory in more detail.

57. So far I have omitted employer-side labor distortions that, as noted in Chapter Two, probably changed since 2007. Changes in these distortions would tend to change Figure 3.5's black series, without changing the red one.

58. As a UI beneficiary moves through an unemployment spell, emergency benefits are first classified as tier I, then tier II, etc. (National Employment Law Project 2011). Each tier lasts a number of weeks specified by legislation, which has changed over time.

59. A few states offer an additional seven weeks of extended benefits (for a total of ninety-nine weeks), but this change is not included in my eligibility index.

60. The act allocated $7 billion to states as bonuses for modernizing by the end of 2010-Q3. Assuming that states would be willing to pay another $3 billion to make more of their citizens eligible for UI, the combined payment of $10 billion is 4.7 percent of the total UI benefits ($211 billion) paid nationwide during that period. See also National Employment Law Project (2003b) for estimates of the participation effects of alternative base periods, and note that, contemporaneous with the adoption of alternative base periods, the fraction of persons unemployed one to twenty-six weeks who receive regular state UI benefits increased significantly.

61. According to Rosenbaum (2008), the Congressional Budget Office once estimated that fewer than eighty thousand food stamp participants (well under 1 percent) would be affected by the 2008 Farm Bill's provision to exclude

individual retirement accounts from the SNAP asset test (employer-sponsored accounts such as 401(k) accounts had already been excluded by prior legislation). On the other hand, the Brookings Institution (2007) notes that many people with 401(k) accounts would, under pre-2008-Farm-Bill rules, still find those assets counting against food stamp asset limits when it came time to apply for food stamps because many job separations require that the 401(k) funds be withdrawn or rolled into an individual retirement account. The latter study estimates that "over 7 million Food Stamp households will be immediately affected by a federal exclusion [of retirement accounts]," which was about one-quarter of all food stamp households.

62. An alternative approach could begin with the finding of Daponte, Sanders, and Taylor (1999, table 4) that, in 1994, fourteen households are ineligible on account of assets only for every thirty-two households eligible under both income and asset tests (their sample is from 1994, so if nothing else their estimates are noisy for my purposes because more than ten years passed). Thus, if take-up rates were the same in the two groups, eliminating the asset test would increase log enrollment by 0.36. At least 46 percent of the states (population weighted) eliminated asset tests between fiscal years 2007 and 2010 as they began to confer BBCE, which by itself would be a 0.17 change in nationwide log participation, plus the nationwide effects of relaxed asset tests in the other 54 percent of states.

63. Using the 2005–2007 quality control files, I regressed the state-year ratio of able-bodied nonelderly adult participants without children to able-bodied nonelderly adult participants with children on state fixed effects and the average state unemployment rate for the year and the prior year, and found the unemployment rate coefficient to be zero or negative. If instead the dependent variable were the log of the number of able-bodied nonelderly adult participants with children, then the unemployment rate coefficient would be positive. Thus I expect that unemployment would expand SNAP participation over time but would not have significantly increased the ratio of the two types of adult participants between 2007 and 2010 if the work requirements had remained in place, and that much of the actual increase must be attributed to relaxed work requirements.

64. I also multiply by 0.977 after September 2012, when the current waivers are scheduled to expire.

65. A less conservative approach would divide the two million COBRA beneficiaries by the number of heads and spouses receiving unemployment benefits in 2009, which is less than eight million.

66. Recall that the "other safety net" program weight is based on the propensity of nonemployed people to be ineligible for UI, so for consistency the benefit index should assign program spending only to persons not receiving UI.

67. The number of transactions is from Office of Thrift Supervision (various issues), extrapolated to the industry according to the fraction of mortgages sampled

(0.63). HOPE NOW (2011) reports somewhat more industry transactions, but not a corresponding amount per transaction.

68. A typical modification reduced monthly payments (principal and interest combined) by $400 for a minimum of sixty months. At an annual discount rate of 7 percent, the present value of $400 per month for sixty months is $20,319.

69. For example, to arrive at the 2007 value of $6.9 billion, I begin with the $35.1 billion for 2008, divide by total single family mortgage loan discharges by commercial banks in 2008 ($25.5 billion), and multiply by total single family mortgage loan discharges by commercial banks in 2007 ($5.0 billion). Note that the mortgage discharge amounts in Table 3.3 represent discharges by all mortgage lenders—not just commercial banks—but only for home retention actions (not for foreclosures).

70. The population in the denominator changed its composition in the direction of being more unemployed (receiving more benefits) and less out of the labor force (receiving less benefits).

71. Ratner (2011) finds that about half of regular state unemployment benefits are funded by the former employer. Since 2009-Q1, total unemployment benefit payments have been about double the regular state benefit payments.

72. Prior to the ARRA, half of extended benefits were state funded, which I include in the eligibility index assuming that extended benefits are paid at the end of the unemployment spell (Center on Budget and Policy Priorities 2010).

73. Note that Medicaid, SNAP, SSI, TANF, and a number of other safety net benefits are not taxable by the personal income tax. On the other hand, an income tax itemizer might owe additional personal income tax as the result of having his mortgage interest rate reduced (mortgage amounts forgiven have not been taxable since 2007).

74. Of $131 billion in UI benefits paid in calendar year 2009, the U.S. Internal Revenue Service (2012) reports that $51 billion was reported on taxable personal income tax returns.

75. Versions of the law with tight restrictions on the amount of the credit and the types of new hires counted toward the credit were actually passed by the federal government effective February 2010 through the end of that year (U.S. Department of Treasury 2010b), and by state governments such as California effective January 2009 (State of California Franchise Tax Board 2012) and Illinois effective July 2010 (Manchir 2010).

76. The present value tax cost is not quite 12.4 percent, because part of the tax liability accrues in the future. For example, at a 7 percent annual discount rate, the present value tax cost would be 12.0 percent. More generally, expectation of a payroll expansion tax holiday inflates the expected present value cost of having employees before the holiday by the discounted tax rate times the probability that the pre-holiday payroll is part of a future tax holiday determination of payroll expansion.

77. Lucas (1976) explains how factor demand depends on the anticipation of tax credits. Auerbach and Hines (1988) found that the anticipation of tax credits had real effects on the behavior of U.S. corporations.

78. Extensions of the ARRA's EITC and ACTC provisions in 2011 and 2012 are not included in these amounts.

79. In tax year 2009, the maximum credit was reached at annual earnings of $6,000, $9,000, and $12,600 for families with zero, one, or 2+ children, respectively (IRS publication 596, various issues). Adjusting for inflation, we find these amounts are about $300 greater than they were in 2007.

CHAPTER 4

1. The supply and demand model is sometimes derived from an optimizing or rational choice framework—Chapter Five is an example—but can also be derived from irrational behavior (Becker 1962).

2. Chapters Five and Six also discuss how employment changes for nonelderly heads and spouses (that are directly affected by the expanding safety net) are related to employment changes for other persons.

3. Krueger and Meyer (2002) is a survey of some of the literature.

4. Equivalently, the pretax reservation wage is the ratio of the after-tax reservation wage to the self-reliance rate. If the self-reliance rate fell from, say, 1.0 to 0.5, then the pretax reservation wage would have to double in order for a worker to receive the same reward from working after taxes and subsidies.

5. Holding the consumption change constant at its actual value, we see that the formula for the model's predicted log labor change is

$$\frac{\Delta \ln(1-\tau) + (1/\eta)\Delta \ln N + 0.3\Delta \ln A - \Delta \ln(c/P)}{1/\eta + 0.3}$$

where, as defined in Chapter Two, N is the adult population, A is production inputs other than labor hours, c/P is consumption per capita, η is the wage elasticity of aggregate labor supply (assumed to be one for the purposes of Figure 4.1), and Δ denotes changes from 2007-Q4 to 2009-Q4. $\Delta \ln(1-\tau)$ is the change in the log self-reliance rate.

6. With the 3.0 percent assumption, nonlabor production inputs still appear to increase over those eight quarters, but only 1.4 percent (in the quantity dimension) rather than 6.1 percent.

7. With a labor supply elasticity of 0.75, the total labor market distortion change was −0.198, of which −0.144 is the expanding safety net and −0.054 is "other distortions."

8. As noted above, in theory the consumption change is greater the more the safety net expansion is expected to be permanent. In order to be conservative about the fraction of labor changes explained, I assume that the expansion is more

permanent than temporary, although results would be quite similar (especially at the smaller η values) if two-thirds were replaced with one-third. Chapter Five examines the dynamics of consumption, labor, and the self-reliance rate in more detail. The formula for the simulated changes in log labor per adult shown in Figure 4.2 is

$$\frac{\Delta \ln (1-\tau)+0.1\Delta \ln N(A/N)}{1/\eta+0.767}=\frac{-0.139}{1/\eta+0.767},$$

where η is the wage elasticity of labor supply.

9. The results are hardly sensitive to the assumed labor share. For example, if labor's share were assumed to be one-third rather than 0.3, the impact of that assumption on the shares shown in Figure 4.2 would be less than 1 percentage point (e.g., at $\eta = 0.75$, 0.705 of the actual log labor per capita change is explained, rather than 0.711).

10. For example, Pencavel (1986) is often cited for his finding that the wage elasticity of male weekly work hours is, among men working positive hours during the week, 0.1, but that is only a portion of the aggregate hours response to wages (Browning, Hansen, and Heckman 1999).

11. Another, although probably less important, difference among studies is the type of wage measure used. Some micro studies look at hourly take-home pay, while others use hourly pay net of taxes and subsidies. My model (4.2) features a third measure, the total labor product (the sum of take-home pay, fringe benefits, and employer taxes) minus taxes and subsidies. Because my measure tends to be greater than the other two by additive terms such as fringe benefits, its percentage changes (with respect to a change in safety net benefits) are less than the percentage changes in the other two measures. As a result, any given value for the elasticity of labor supply with respect to one of the other measures implies a somewhat large elasticity of labor supply with respect to my measure. The size of the adjustment depends on the share of fringe benefits in total compensation, which is small enough that I ignore it in order to be (1) clearer about the source of my calibrated elasticities and (2) slightly conservative as to the aggregate labor hours effects of safety net expansions.

12. Chetty et al. (2011) discuss the separate magnitudes of the "intensive" and "extensive" components of the aggregate hours elasticity, but those components have a time frequency, which Chetty et al. leave unspecified. For example, the extensive margin in a time diary study refers to the probability of working positive hours sometime during a particular day. The extensive margin in Hoynes and Schanzenbach (2011) is the probability of working positive hours sometime during a particular calendar year. For what it is worth, the log change in per capita hours among nonelderly household heads and spouses between calendar years 2007 and 2009 can be decomposed into 33 percent extensive margin (positive hours sometime during the calendar year), 25 percent weeks per year, and 42 per-

cent hours per week (the first two margins are measured from the CPS Annual Demographic Files, and the hours per week margin from the CPS-MORG).

13. See, for example, Galí, Gertler, and Lopez-Salido (2007) or Shimer (2010b), who assume a Frisch elasticity of aggregate hours with respect to wages of 1.

14. The Hicksian elasticity (of aggregate hours with respect to wages) range is (0.31,0.61), assuming, as I do in Chapter Five, an elasticity of the marginal rate of substitution with respect to consumption of 1.35. At the Frisch elasticity of 0.75, the Hicksian elasticity is 0.48.

15. In his cross-country examination of the labor supply effects of taxes, Prescott (2004) assumes an elasticity of 3 (specifically, the elasticity of his assumed marginal rate of substitution function with respect to average labor hours is 3 at the U.S. level of hours), or almost triple the elasticity at the top end of my assumed range. A larger elasticity may be appropriate for his purposes because the cross-country marginal tax rate differences he examined had been in place for many years. See also Alesina, Glaeser, and Sacerdote (2005), Davis and Henrekson (2005), and Lindbeck (1995). For the purpose of long-term tax policy analysis, Mankiw and Weinzieri (2006) consider an elasticity range of 0.5 to 1.5, as well as comment on Prescott's assumed value.

16. Meyer (2002) notes that one reason supply behavior might differ among safety net participants is that they are imperfectly informed about available benefits. However, I account for imperfect take-up in my marginal tax rate measures through the program weights; it would be double-counting to also adjust the wage elasticity of labor supply for imperfect take-up.

17. One complexity with this view, however, is that it needs the labor market effects of the financial panic (or other impulse exterior to the labor market) to suddenly appear and then wear off in coincidence with the delayed appearance of labor market effects of the safety net expansions, so that the net result is for the labor market changes to track the safety net expansions (see Figure 1.1).

18. See also Sargent and Ljungqvist (1998).

19. To make this calculation, I used the 2007 CPS MORG weekly earnings distribution among nonelderly heads and spouses at work full-time in the reference week, measured in 2005 dollars and scaled using the CPS weights (the reference week from the twelve monthly surveys were pooled to obtain a representative week for the year). With the distribution cut at $415, its left tail contained 12.5 million full-time employed heads and spouses.

20. The employment effect of the $270 billion safety net expansion is less in the models of Figure 4.1 and Chapter Five because the subsidy programs in those models are not targeted, except that the model programs exclude the elderly and young people.

21. One rough indicator of the combined quit and layoff rates is the ratio of number of people aged twenty-five to sixty-four who (so far) have been unemployed exactly one week, expressed as a ratio to the number of people that age who are

employed (see Shimer 2007 for related measures). According to the monthly Current Population Survey, that ratio was 23 percent greater in 2009, and 8 percent greater in 2010, as compared to 2007.

22. See Heckman and Sedlacek (1985) and other applications of the Roy (1951) model to the choice of whether or not to work in the marketplace.

23. Typically the studies calculate the amount of the labor supply shift and do not attempt to calculate an equilibrium employment effect of that shift, which would require additional information about the effects of labor supply on the equilibrium wage rate.

24. The elasticity is a Frisch elasticity to the extent that the UI expansions did not affect the marginal utility of consumption. All of this assumes that UI extension studies are still informative as to the effect of post-2007 UI on individual behavior. Labor economists such as Katz (2010) and Daly et al. (2012) sometimes point to a secular decline in temporary layoffs as evidence that UI might have a smaller individual-level effect now than it once did. However, this may mean only that the UI recipients now are seeing their offer wages further below their previous wages (because their offer wage does not come from their previous job) than UI recipients in the past did, so that the ratio of the UI benefit to the offer wage is greater now than it was in the past. Also relevant is the Schmieder, von Wachter, and Bender (2012) study finding that individual-level responses to UI extensions (in Germany) are similar during recessions and expansions.

25. Chapter Three's main estimates apply to persons whose weekly earnings would be about $700 if they worked full-time, which is essentially the median weekly earnings among nonelderly household heads and spouses working full-time. UI extensions are even less important, relative to other safety net provisions, for people with less than median earning potential because UI benefits tend to be proportional to earnings potential (see also Chapter Six); yet the other provisions are often dollar amounts that are independent of earnings potential. Because employment changes were disproportionately large among low-skill demographic groups (recall Chapter Two's composition bias analysis), arguably one should scale estimates of the behavioral effects of UI extensions even more than I do in what follows.

26. They report "15 to 40 percent," but those percentages relate to the change in unemployment duration, rather than the change in the propensity to be unemployed. In order to obtain percentages of unemployment changes, I therefore scale down their percentages by a factor of 0.81, which is my estimate (based on the flow rates shown in their figure 6) of the magnitude of the unemployment outflow rate log change (0.69) as a ratio to the sum of the inflow rate log change (0.16) and the magnitude of the outflow rate log change.

27. The BLS reports that the ratio of employment to unemployment in 2009 was 9.8.

28. Before the American Reinvestment and Recovery Act of 2009 (ARRA), half of Extended Benefits and essentially all of Emergency Unemployment Compensation were federally funded. The ARRA also federally funded the other

half of Extended Benefits. State-funded benefits are typically experience-rated, which means that every two dollars of unemployment benefits received create about one dollar of payroll tax liability for the recipient's former employer (Ratner 2011).

29. See also Topel and Welch (1980) and Meyer (2002).

30. To the degree that extensions increase job separations, they will also increase hiring, but the latter is a movement along the labor supply curve rather than a shift of it; we need only the shift for the purpose of calculating a wage elasticity of labor supply.

31. Topel (1983) is the first study. See also Card and Levine (1994) and Ratner (2011).

32. Ratner (2011) finds that about half of regular state unemployment benefits are funded by the former employer. Since 2009-Q1, total unemployment benefit payments have been about double the regular state benefit payments.

33. See also Marinescu (2012), which measures online job search effort during the years 2007–2009 and finds that the median state experienced a 29 percent reduction in online job applications as a consequence of extended benefits.

34. Decomposing 0.27 to 0.54 into "liquidity" and "moral hazard" components is not especially important for the positive question of why work hours fell since 2007, but it would matter for normative analysis of safety net expansions.

35. See Ben-Shalom, Moffitt, and Scholz (2011), who also use Chetty's estimates (2008) to calibrate the UI part of their model of the labor supply effects of the safety net. However, Ben-Shalom et al. and this book differ in several ways: (1) this book's counterfactual is different (2007 safety net rules versus their pre-2005 counterfactual of no safety net), (2) only this book calculates a marginal tax rate for the entire safety net, (3) Ben-Shalom et al. assume that UI has no effect on layoffs or initial unemployment claims, and (4) they approximate "small" labor supply effects of SNAP as literally zero, which is a poor approximation for my purposes, especially for households with replacement rates near 100 percent.

36. In the CPS-MORG sample of nonelderly household heads and spouses pooling fiscal years 2007 and 2010, I regressed weekly work hours (including zeros) on indicator variables for age and an indicator variable for fiscal year 2010. The coefficient on the latter indicator variable was 2.0.

37. The primary purpose of this book is to offer a quantitative explanation for *changes* in labor market behavior. My explanation depends more on the amounts that labor market distortions *changed* over time, and less on the amount of labor market distortions that existed even before the recession. In contrast, the results of this appendix are also sensitive to measures of the amount of labor market distortions that existed even before the recession. A prerecession self-reliance rate of, say, 0.50 rather than the value of 0.40 as shown in Figure 3.6 would result in a significantly greater dollar amount of the distortions created by the safety net rule changes.

CHAPTER 5

1. Kydland and Prescott (1982), McGrattan (1994), Prescott (2002), Cole and Ohanian (2004), Prescott (2004), Mulligan (2010a), Ohanian (2010), and many others; Chapter Seven looks at New Keynesian models.

2. In this sense, my simulation results can be interpreted as an American transition from its 2007 welfare state to a welfare state more like Europe's, as modeled by Prescott (2004).

3. See also Parkin (1988); Hall (1997); Mulligan (2005); Gali, Gertler, and Lopez-Salido (2007); and Chari et al. (2007).

4. The model used in this chapter is closely related to the "real business cycle" (RBC) model with the crucial distinction that the RBC model emphasizes stochastic shocks to the parameter A, whereas this chapter holds A constant. To keep the presentation closer to other presentations of the neoclassical growth model (King, Plosser, and Rebelo 1988), this chapter does not put the $(1-\alpha)$ exponent on the technology parameter A as Chapter Two did. This normalization has no effect on the results because A is held constant.

5. For example, with $\alpha = 0.7$, this upper bound on the intertemporal substitution elasticity σ is 3.3.

6. As a result of these assumptions, the equilibrium relative supply prices of n and m will be constant (and equal to β) and the composition of the workforce will be constant, at values that are independent of technology and public policy parameters. More generally, the composition of the workforce could be affected in either direction by those parameters if the utility function were nonhomothetic or the two types of labor were substitutes in production.

7. A labor distortion or "labor wedge" has also been used to model labor market regulations (Mulligan, 2002, 2005), other market distortions (Galí, Gertler, and Lopez-Salido 2007; Shimer 2009), as well as errors in the specification of the marginal rate of substitution function (Parkin 1988; Hall 1997). This chapter does not attempt to quantify them except perhaps as a residual labor wedge that cannot be attributed to means-tested subsidies.

8. Examples are Blanchard and Gali (2007) and Shimer (2010b).

9. Another functional form commonly used in the real business cycle literature—Cobb-Douglas in consumption and leisure—has constant proportional long-term effects on consumption and *leisure*. I have also obtained numerical paths derived from the Cobb-Douglas consumption-leisure specification (not shown here), and they arguably fit the data well too.

10. To prove this, note that the large quadratic root increases with σ, is 0 at $\sigma = 0$, and is one at $\sigma = (1-\alpha)^{-1}$.

11. They cannot cross. To prove this, suppose not: they cross at (k,c) with $k > k_{ss}$ and the stable arm corresponding to the lesser marginal tax rate crossing from above. The labor-capital ratio N must be greater on the lesser marginal tax rate

arm. From equation (5.9), this means that the stable arm for the smaller distortion is steeper, which is a contradiction.

12. For a formal proof, differentiate $c'(k)$ as shown in equation (5.9) with respect to the distortion τ, holding c and k constant, and note that this derivative is negative.

13. Because I am writing in early 2012, the values for program eligibility and benefit indices beyond January 2012 are my forecasts about the future of safety net program rules.

14. As noted in Chapter Two, anticipated employer health expenditures do not create a labor market distortion if those expenditures confer a benefit to employees of equal value (to them).

15. Chapter Seven presents a simple new Keynesian model in which a safety net contraction drives a wedge between labor productivity and wages. See below and Sbordone (2002) for this and other interpretations of the real unit labor cost variable, which I measure as the deviation of the log of the ratio of the implicit price deflator for personal consumption expenditures to the Bureau of Labor Statistics' measure of unit labor cost for the business sector from a linear trend (fit to quarterly data 1980–2007).

16. The total distortion series from Chapter Two is adjusted for changing population age. See also below on the measurement of actual labor changes.

17. The quarterly overall distortion and log inverse real unit labor cost series are transformed into a monthly series by assigning the quarterly value to the middle month of the quarter, and linearly interpolating the remaining months. As of the time of finalizing this chapter, the data required to calculate the total distortion was available only through mid-2011.

18. The relationship between the residual marginal tax rate τ_r, the safety net marginal tax rate τ_s, and the overall log distortion change Δ_T, and the log gap between productivity and wages Δ_w is $(1-\tau_r)(1-\tau_s)=(1-0.404)^2 e^{\Delta_w - \Delta_T}$ where 0.404 is the safety net marginal tax rate at the end of 2007. When expressing the employer side distortion or total distortion as a marginal tax rate, I used the formula $1 - (1-0.404)e^{-\Delta}$ for $\Delta = \Delta_w$ or Δ_T and then smooth with a five-month centered moving average. Thus, if the safety net marginal tax rate were unchanged and the overall distortions change were zero, then the residual marginal tax rate would also be unchanged at 40.4 percent.

19. In logs, the age adjustments to labor per capita average 0.003, 0.006, 0.009, and 0.012 in 2008–2011, respectively. With some additional complexity, age changes could alternatively be incorporated into the model through time-varying taste parameters, as in Chapter Four's labor market equilibrium analysis of changes in the age distribution. See also Jorgenson et al (2008).

20. For example, δ in the model is not only capital's rate of economic depreciation but also the rate at which capital must be augmented to keep up with population and exogenous technical change (for more on growth models with exogenous trends, see Barro and Sala-i-Martin, 2003).

21. See Appendix 5.1 for further discussion of historical TFP growth, and for sensitivity analysis. The Hodrik-Prescott filter is often used for this purpose, but the filter sometimes has unusual properties at the very end of a time series.

22. Appendix 5.1 explains the numerical simulation method, as well as the sensitivity of results to assumed parameter values.

23. This chapter does not adopt a formal definition of *fit*. In my use of the term, a model fits to the degree that its times series agree with the amount of the changes in the major economic variables and their dynamics since 2007, as compared to competing economic models. A model does not fit if its time series change in the opposite direction, or in economically different amounts, or at economically different times, as the actual series. All of the simulation results are displayed for the reader to apply alternative definitions of fit (see also Hansen and Heckman (1996)).

24. Kydland and Prescott (1982) is an example; I present another example below.

25. As shown in Figure 5.5d, the empirical results are fairly insensitive to the inclusion of housing investment because housing investment is less than one-fifth of total investment. For the same reason, modifying the model to have separate flows of housing and business investment would have little effect on the results. The housing stock, on the other hand, is a large share of the total stock, which is why housing debt can be associated with transfer flows as large as shown in Chapter Nine.

26. Note that the percentages here have the age-adjusted per capita labor decline as a base, whereas the percentages cited in Chapter Four have the unadjusted per capita labor decline as a base.

27. Figure 5.6b's results for the safety net MTR series are in many ways in between the corresponding results shown in Figures 5.6a and 5.6c.

28. Mulligan (2002), Mulligan (2005), and Mulligan (2010a).

29. The act first passed the U.S. House of Representatives in October 2009 (U.S. Government Printing Office 2010).

30. Baker, Bloom, and Davis's index (2011) of economic policy uncertainty jumps up in late 2008 and remains at a higher level. Arellano, Bai, and Kehoe (2011) show how idiosyncratic uncertainty can drive a wedge between the marginal product of labor and the real wage rate.

31. The equilibrium quantities for any period $t \geq 0$ are calculated as the solution $\{c_t, n_t\}$ to the two algebraic equations (5.5) and $c_t = An_t^{\alpha} k_t^{1-\alpha} - I_t$, where I_t is gross investment expenditure at date t and τ_t is set to zero.

32. For the purposes of constructing Figures 5.8a and 5.8b, monthly investment data are measured by assigning quarterly investment rates (as shown in Figure 5.5d's actual series) to the middle month of each quarter, and linearly interpolating the remaining months.

33. Chari, Kehoe, and McGrattan (2007) offer a methodology (not yet applied to this recession) that would account for *all* of the changes during a recession as the

combination of several shocks in the neoclassical growth model. Because their method includes the same labor market condition (5.5) as mine, and the same definition of total factor productivity, we would agree that changes in the marginal tax rate or labor distortion during this recession were substantial and TFP changes minor.

34. See Chapter Four for an extensive discussion of appropriate values for the Frisch wage elasticity of the aggregate supply of labor hours.

35. See, for example, Huff Post Business (2010), Krugman (2011), and Norris (2011).

36. In the model, government consumption and investment are each a perfect substitute for private consumption and investment, respectively, so that, holding marginal tax rates constant, any change in government purchases has no effect on the aggregates. More work is needed to measure the degree to which actual government purchases made by the stimulus law were not substitutes for private purchases and to determine whether the departures from perfect substitution are enough to offset the labor-depressing effects of the law's marginal tax rate provisions.

37. See also the debate (Ramey 2011a) as to whether "the presence of search frictions does not substantially modify the behavior of a business cycle model" (Rogerson and Shimer 2011, 658).

38. Krussel et al (2008) and Shimer (2010a) are two examples of search models with exogenous job separation rates, and sometimes exogenous wage rates.

39. Productivity and leisure preference are normalized so that low marginal tax rate steady state labor and capital are one.

40. Capital and labor income are not separately measured for proprietors, or in the public sector.

41. I measure TFP growth from Q1 to Q1 because capital is measured at the beginning of the year (real GDP, compensation of government employees, and labor hours are therefore measured in the first quarter of the year). For example, 2007 TFP growth is measured from 2007-Q1 to 2008-Q1.

42. Given the assumptions of additive separability over time and the functional form (5.2), $\sigma = 1$ is required for balanced growth (that is, for the wealth and substitution effects on labor of a permanent increase in productivity to exactly offset). However, neither $\sigma = 0.68$ nor $\sigma = 1.35$ is very far from the balanced growth case, and both are therefore consistent with wealth and substitution effects that approximately offset. The assumed value for σ is more important for determining the dynamics of consumption and labor in response to the (partly) temporary marginal tax rate changes that are examined in this chapter.

43. The path in the [k,c] plane approaches the stable arm of the stationary system with long-term marginal tax rate from above, and thereby it crosses that stable arm at least twice.

44. Time T is the calendar time when the marginal tax rate stops changing.

CHAPTER 6

1. Recall that the self-reliance rate is 1 minus the replacement rate, and the replacement rate is the ratio of the effect of not working on net-of-tax benefits received to the amount produced when working.

2. Yet another reason that low- and high-skill workers might experience a different replacement rate change is that they have different rates of eligibility for benefits. A cross-section analysis of program participation would add to our understanding of the cross-sectional patterns of employment changes, but is beyond the scope of this book.

3. For example, in 2007 most states had a cap of less than $400 per week (U.S. Department of Labor 2007, Table 3–5).

4. Family income is not the only eligibility criterion for means-tested programs, because many of the programs also condition eligibility on asset ownership, citizenship, presence of children, and other characteristics. Due to these other eligibility criteria, a sole earner might be ineligible regardless of the amount (if any) she earned from employment, just as a dual earner would. Hereafter, this chapter uses the term "dual earner" to refer to a person who would be ineligible for means-tested programs regardless of her earnings, which usually but not always is someone with a working spouse. "Sole earner" refers to persons who are not dual earners.

5. The exact percentage depends on SNAP's earnings and shelter deductions (Hanson and Andrews March 2009).

6. For simplicity, I assume in this chapter that eligibility for both SNAP and Medicaid ends at the same income threshold regardless of UI eligibility. In reality, the two programs have somewhat different ending points, Medicaid for children ends at a different point than Medicaid for adults, and UI income counts differently than wages (Romich, Simmelink and Holt 2007). Moreover, the dollar amount of the poverty threshold varies with family size, and somewhat by state of residence. For all of these reasons, this chapter's practice of taking the income threshold for poverty program eligibility as a single dollar amount for the entire nation is just an illustrative calculation and should be fine-tuned in future research.

7. The budget set jump at the poverty threshold is known as the "Medicaid notch" because Medicaid eligibility is discrete, rather than phased out with income as with SNAP (Yelowitz 1995).

8. My average slope approach is related to the tax force concept used in Gruber and Wise's analysis of retirement behavior (1999). However, the time dimension of their analysis is a calendar year, whereas mine is roughly a quarter (I say "roughly" because safety net programs vary in terms of the time interval over which they measure earnings for the purposes of determining eligibility and benefits). See also note 12 in Chapter Four.

9. For brevity, the formula (6.1) does not distinguish between home mortgage forgiveness and consumer debt discharges; $727 is what the median nonelderly household head or spouse earned in 2007, converted to 2010 $.

10. The same numerical values are used here as in Chapter Three. Recall that the eligibility indices for the Medicaid and "other" programs are assumed equal to 1 for all months prior to January 2014.

11. For simplicity, I assume that any UI income received by a sole earner SNAP household with zero earnings is offset by deductions, so that its SNAP benefit is the maximum. I calculate the statutory maximum M as a weighted average of the maximum for each household size, weighted by the frequency of that household size in the SNAP program.

12. Holt and Romich (2007) and Kotlikoff and Rapson (2007) show that self-reliance rate *levels* are least for incomes near, but above, FPG.

13. Different self-reliance rate schedules apply to dual earner households in which one of the earners is out of work and the other is low-skill and therefore cannot earn above the poverty line on her own, and to dual earner households in which both husband and wife are simultaneously out of work and whose combined UI benefits are still below the poverty line, but for brevity they are not shown here. This omission is one reason the self-reliance rates shown in Figure 6.3 are not appropriate for calculating national average self-reliance rates. For national averages, see Chapter Three.

14. More precise conclusions cannot be obtained from Figures 6.2 and 6.3 alone, because they are examples for particular demographic groups and simplify the actual phase-out rules for Medicaid and other means-tested programs. Among other things, the federal poverty guideline (FPG) varies by household size, Medicaid eligibility ends at a couple of different income levels relative to FPG, and at a slightly different income level than SNAP eligibility ends.

15. As of 2009, the typical state at least partially offset UI benefits with retirement benefits, other than Social Security (U.S. Department of Labor 2009a). As of 2003, eighteen states used a beneficiary's Social Security income to offset unemployment benefits (National Employment Law Project 2003a). By 2008, it was down to five states (National Employment Law Project 2007). By 2010, it may be down to three states (AARP Illinois 2010).

16. This is the approach I adopt in Chapter Five.

17. See Chapter Seven and the references cited therein. Another factor to consider when analyzing teen labor supply over the business cycle: their labor supply is probably more elastic to wage changes.

18. In the same sample, married women were on average seven months older than the unmarried women.

19. By my calculations, a marital status gap for hours changes among women was also present in the 2001 recession. I am not aware of a study of this gap for prior recessions, except for Arulampalam and Stewart's study (1995) of the United Kingdom, which found slightly longer unemployment duration for married women in 1979.

20. The full-time earnings potential of a person not working full-time is likely less than the average earnings among full-time workers in the same demographic

group, but the level of earnings is less important for my purposes than the differences across groups.

21. I use wide, and full calendar year, sample intervals in order to minimize sampling error and seasonal fluctuations.

22. See also Hoynes and Schanzenbach (2012), who find that employment and hours were reduced, especially among single mothers, when the food stamp program was introduced.

23. As noted below, the elderly and nonelderly are quite different in terms of their work hours changes and their program participation (e.g., old age Social Security benefits can begin at age sixty-two, and Medicare begins at age sixty-five). For the purposes of making cross-sectional comparisons among the nonelderly, I consider only people up to age sixty-one.

24. Hours changes for each of the fourteen groups shown in Figure 6.4 are, as in Table 6.1 below, adjusted for changes over time in the composition of their samples in terms of age, state of residence, and race. Unadjusted hours changes are similar to the adjusted hours changes shown in the figure. Results are also similar if hours changes are adjusted for the industries in which the members of each group were working in 2005–2007, or if the horizontal axis is measured according to hourly (rather than weekly) earnings among full-time workers.

25. Their tendency to earn below FPG is an important reason more than 50 percent of women in these groups had a household member participating in the Medicaid program during the average year 2005–2007, and 37 percent of them had a household member participating in food stamps during the average year 2005–2007.

26. Yelowitz (1995) and Yelowitz (2000) show that, historically, labor supply behavior depends on the federal poverty guideline, as the result of safety net eligibility rules that are tied to it.

27. Because each respondent's log self-reliance rate change is evaluated for a single potential income value y, the change reflects only changes in program rules and not changes in potential income that the respondent may have experienced.

28. In 2006, the federal poverty line for a four-person household was $20,000 per year. Although the dual earner measure excludes means-tested government programs, Figure 6.3 shows that the general shape of its log change is similar to the shape of the sole earner self-reliance rate log changes for incomes above 125 percent of FPG or so, which do reflect the level and changes of the replacement rates for means-tested government programs. Moreover, each unit of dual earner log change is associated with more than one unit of sole earner log change—that is why the sole earner measure is generally steeper in Figure 6.3—and therefore sole earner work hours should increase more than dual earner work hours with each unit log change of the dual earner self-reliance rate.

29. The appendix to this chapter shows the summary statistics for the sample used in Table 6.1.

30. 1.1 is at the top end of the range of wage elasticities of national labor supply considered in this book. However, the national wage elasticity could be different for the elasticity relevant for comparing groups of women because, among other things, women's labor supply is thought to be more wage elastic than men's.

31. Age is included among the independent variables, in addition to its contribution to log potential earnings, because wealth effects on labor supply may have varied across age groups.

32. To put it another way, the gender gap in the residuals from Table 6.1's fourth regression is economically insignificant (0.1 hours per week).

33. Note that a zero change in the self-reliance rate is outside the range of the nonelderly data.

34. The idea that group-specific supply shifts create a positive correlation between hours and wage changes in the cross-section has been emphasized in the literature on the gender wage gap: Becker (1985), Goldin and Katz (2002), Mulligan and Rubinstein (2008), and others.

35. The various assumed supply slopes are 11.6, 21.8, and 31.9, which correspond to wage elasticities of labor supply of 0.4, 0.75, and 1.1.

36. The nationwide average log change in the dual earner self-reliance rate is about 0.12. The average regression coefficient on that log change is about 30 (e.g., take the second column, drop the interaction with married, and estimate among married people only), so even if a single provision contributed 0.03 to that change and a group could be identified that was 100 percent affected by the provision and compared with another group zero percent affected, the expected hours change gap between the two groups would be 0.9, which is a gap that may be statistically difficult to detect with an analysis such as Table 6.1's.

37. On the other hand, workers within a state may be complements for each other, even while workers are substitutes at the national level.

38. The second-highest log migration was 0.025 for Colorado.

39. Persons aged sixty-two to sixty-four are eligible for some elderly programs (such as old age Social Security), but not others (such as Medicare), so I do not allocate them to either group for the purposes of Table 6.2, Table 6.3, or Figure 6.6.

40. Because so many elderly do not work, I did not attempt to quantify their potential earnings and instead use years of schooling as a proxy for how potential earnings might vary among elderly people.

41. The series for seventeen years of schooling (in between four year degree and professional/doctorate) is omitted from Figure 6.6 because the group is too small.

42. Schirle (2008), Blau and Goodstein (2010), and Hurd and Rohwedder (2011) quantify various factors causing average work hours to increase among the elderly.

43. Recall from formulas (6.1) and (6.2) that the program weights and eligibility indices do not vary with potential earnings y. See Mulligan (2012) for an alternative approach.

44. Meyer, Mok and Sullivan (2009) find that, in recent years, more than 30 percent of UI benefits and more than 45 percent of food stamp benefits are not reported in the CPS-ADF. I do not attempt to make an underreporting adjustment.

CHAPTER 7

1. The slack market hypothesis that, as compared to nonrecession years, demand matters more and supply matters less for determining aggregate employment and output at the margin in a recession is sometimes said to be the intellectual basis for Keynesian models of the business cycle (Eggertsson 2010a, 2). However, prior to this recession, other New Keynesian models were used to explain how labor supply shocks would significantly affect employment in the expected direction (Smets and Wouters 2003). It is therefore possible that future work with New Keynesian models might find that the employment effects of marginal tax rate changes like those I measure in Chapter Three are even greater than I have estimated. Galí, Smets, and Wouters (2011) is a New Keynesian model of the 2008–09 recession that does not have safety net programs per se, but one of its eight shocks ("wage markup") resembles a safety net expansion in that it tends to increase unemployment and wages and reduce employment. However, they assume that the wage markup shock's employment effect is minimal for the first year or so, which may be why their procedure does not attribute much unemployment to that shock until 2010.

2. By definition, a dollar's worth of a labor-intensive final good requires more labor for its production than a dollar's worth of a less-labor-intensive good. Presumably less-labor-intensive goods require more capital, or some other input.

3. I do not claim here that government borrowing is "Ricardian equivalent," as in Barro (1974). Perhaps it is true that government borrowing increases consumer spending and reduces investment spending. But the question remains: Are the growing spending categories more or less labor-intensive than the contracting categories?

4. Gruber (1997) and Johnson, Parker, and Souleles (2006) are two studies.

5. Auerbach and Feenberg (2000, 53–54), Orzag (2001), and Cogan et al. (2010, 291) also jump from the observation that unemployment benefits are largely consumed to the conclusion that unemployment benefits stimulate the economy, with no further explanation of how the economic mechanism might work.

6. One can debate whether Medicaid benefits are transfers or government purchases, but Medicaid had no significant expansions between 2007 and 2013. In general, government purchases of items that the beneficiaries would have purchased on their own (if they had the full discretion over the spending of those resources) should be treated as transfers for economic analysis.

7. The ARRA also included so-called tax cuts, for which labor market affects should also be accounted. However, in many cases the tax cuts were more like safety net expansions in that they provided additional resources for people with low incomes, and for this reason they would be expected to reduce aggregate work hours.

8. It is sometimes claimed that the neoclassical growth model holds the employment rate constant, but Hansen (1985) and Mulligan (2001) show otherwise.

9. The poor might do this because they need to cut spending somehow—the safety net does not fully replace the income they lose from not working. The rest of the country might do this, on average, because now they must devote some of their resources to helping pay for the safety net expansion.

10. See also Barro and Grossman (1971). Landais, Pascal, and Saez (2010) also assume that job rationing is more common, and therefore that labor supply matters less, during recessions.

11. If instead the employment-wage tradeoff were not isoelastic, then workers' reservation wages could be "overshifted," so that employment in the distorted market would be more sensitive to supply than it would be in a competitive market (Sumner 1981).

12. Rosen (1972, 338–39) discusses such a model of the minimum wage.

13. By the same reasoning, safety net contractions in a New Keynesian model (with sticky prices but flexible wages) would reduce real wages but not increase labor, and thereby create a gap between labor productivity and the real wage (relative to the gap before the safety net contraction). As noted in Chapters Two and Five, a wedge like this was economically significant in 2010 and 2011 but still many times less than the wedge created by safety net expansions.

14. Mulligan (2011c) presents some of the arguments of this chapter in the context of a New Keynesian model with labor market distortions and slowly adjusting final goods prices.

15. As documented by Hansen and Singleton (1983) and noted by Curdia and Woodford (2010) and Ohanian (2010) in the context of the recent events, the nominal interest rate in the model's consumption Euler equation is not the same as the federal funds rate, and the gap between the two may well have changed during the recession because financial intermediaries were under stress. Mulligan and Threinen (2010) show that the marginal product of capital has never been close to zero, at least since 1930. Nor does the marginal product of capital appear to be limited by any lower bound in the sense that it closely follows the pattern predicted by the model in Chapter Five. All of this casts doubt on approaches such as Eggertsson and Krugman (2011) that assume a tight relationship between consumer spending and the federal funds rate.

16. For a general equilibrium model of labor market seasonals, with similar results, see Mulligan (2011c).

17. The vectors v_t^S and v_t^D and matrix $\Theta(X_t)$ are calculated as:

$$v_t^S \equiv \begin{pmatrix} \alpha_L^S(a_t) + \gamma_L^S(X_t) + \varepsilon_{Lt}^S \\ \alpha_N^S(a_t) + \gamma_N^S(X_t) + \varepsilon_{Nt}^S \end{pmatrix}, \; v_t^D \equiv \begin{pmatrix} \alpha^D(a_t) + \gamma^D(X_t) + \varepsilon_{Lt}^D \\ \alpha^D(a_t) + \gamma^D(X_t) + \varepsilon_{Nt}^D \end{pmatrix}$$

$$I - \theta(X_t) \equiv \begin{pmatrix} \beta_L^S(X_t) & 0 \\ 0 & \beta_N^S(X_t) \end{pmatrix} \left[\begin{pmatrix} \beta_L^S(X_t) & 0 \\ 0 & \beta_N^S(X_t) \end{pmatrix} + \begin{pmatrix} \beta_L^D(X_t) & \eta^D(X_t) - \beta_L^D(X_t) \\ \eta^D(X_t) - \beta_N^D(X_t) & \beta_N^D(X_t) \end{pmatrix} \right]^{-1}$$

The reduced form for wages is $\begin{pmatrix} \ln w_{Lt} \\ \ln w_{Nt} \end{pmatrix} = \begin{pmatrix} \beta_L^S(X_t) & \circ \\ \circ & \beta_N^S(X_t) \end{pmatrix}^{-1} [I - \Theta(X_t)][v_t^D - v_t^S].$

18. Fullerton and Metcalf (2002).

19. Note that I do not put real money balances (M/π) in the utility function in order to abstract from the dynamics of inflation but still obtain the same safety net comparative statics as with the dynamic model (see Mulligan 2011c and the references cited therein for the dynamic version of the model).

20. See also Woodford (2011) on flexible price fiscal policy comparative statics.

CHAPTER 8

1. A couple of papers (Auerbach and Gorodnichenko 2010; Barro and Redlick 2009) examine whether fiscal policy multipliers are greater during recessions, which are indirectly tests of whether labor demand matters more during recessions (Mulligan 2011c).

2. See also Miron (1996, 9) and the labor market indicators shown below.

3. See also an econometric literature on the cyclical sensitivity of seasonality by Krane and Wascher (1999), Christiano and Todd (2002), and Matas-Mir and Osborn (2004).

4. I omit observations from District of Columbia, where seasonal changes, and their business cycle, are much different from the rest of the country due to changes in congressional activity. I also omit observations from Louisiana in 2005 (Hurricane Katrina).

5. The teen summer hours spike is 0.295 (that is, teen weekly per capita hours worked during the summer are 29.5 percent more than their per capita weekly hours worked during April, May, September, and October), which far exceeds the scale used in Figure 8.1.

6. The fraction of people employed changes over the seasons, which means that composition changes contribute to seasonal fluctuations in the average hourly wage among employees. However, the supply and demand interpretation, and not composition bias, explains why (1) the Christmas wage seasonal is so different from the summer wage seasonal, (2) the wage seasonals always have the opposite sign of the unemployment seasonals, and (3) hourly wages fail to increase during the summer even for the twenty-five-to-thirty-four age group for whom the composition has little change.

7. I use the Census Bureau's monthly NSA Retail and Food Service Sales. Before 1992, I use the Census Bureau's discontinued NSA retail sales series. My regression analyses of retail sales include a dummy variable for years before 1992.

8. The CPS survey reference week is the calendar week that includes the twelfth of the month.

9. Mulligan (2011a) reports that results are similar when the NBER recession indicator is replaced with a "standardized unemployment" variable: the seasonally adjusted average percentage of men aged twenty-five to fifty-four who were unemployed during the months September through February, deviated from its 3.9 percent average for nonrecession years.

10. In the slack market model, a recession would be a time when the retail sector could expand without taking resources from other sectors, so aggregate employment would expand more with retail sales during recessions even while *retail* employment per dollar of retail sales had no business cycle.

11. The recession years appear as spikes because most recessions do not include more than one consecutive summers, and the spikes are small because the recession coefficient of –1.70 shown in Table 8.3 is small compared to the non-recession seasonal of 24.7 (both in 100ths of log points).

12. The slack market theory delivers a similar result: a reduction in demand in one sector cannot lower wages in other sectors because wages do not adjust to clear the labor market, and without lower wages the other sectors have no incentives to hire the workers let go by the contracting sector.

13. I obtained quantity indices for residential and nonresidential structures investment from the Bureau of Economic Analysis' NIPA Table 5.3.3 and mid-quarter population from their NIPA Table 2.1. Based on the assumption that building factors would move between the two sectors on roughly a dollar-for-dollar basis, I converted each sector's quantity index series (which were equal to 100 in 2005) to 2005 dollars by multiplying the series by the sector's 2005 nominal investment expenditure from BEA Table 5.3.5 (results are similar if investment is measured as the log of the per capita quantity index, rather than in chained dollars). Male employment rates are used rather than overall employment rates to focus on the business cycle rather than secular changes in the propensity of women to work.

14. Time-to-build and price measurement errors are good reasons to include lagged price terms in the investment regressions.

15. The specifications without housing investment ignore crowding out even before 2008 and thereby grossly underpredict nonresidential investment for 2007-Q4—my procedure of adjusting the constant allows the model to fit 2007-Q4 in order to see whether crowding out is needed to predict the nonresidential investment changes during the recession (that is, since 2007-Q4). The adjustment of the constant for the specification including housing investment is quite small, because that model predicts 2007-Q4 well.

16. See Mulligan (2011c) for similar results from alternative specifications.

17. The July CPI (NSA) for all items was 219.964 and 215.351 in 2008 and 2009, respectively (www.bls.gov/cpi).

18. I hold constant each study's use of "year effects." The fraction of specifications omitting year effects is greater in Burkhauser, Couch, and Wittenberg (2000) than in Even and Macpherson (2010), and it is well known that elasticity point estimates are greater when year effects are omitted (Neumark and Wascher 2008).

19. Among other things, younger people may have better access to family support when not working, whereas persons over age twenty-five may have better access to government subsidies, and these factors could help determine the magnitude of the minimum wage's employment effects.

20. For example, the models of Gali, Lopez-Salido, and Valles (2007), Smets and Wouters (2007), and Christiano, Trabandt, and Walentin (2011) include a Calvo (1983) pricing setup in which output prices, and thereby labor demand, are independent of supply conditions in the short term. Uhlig's model (2007) includes a sticky wage and labor markets for which equilibrium labor usage is independent of labor supply conditions.

CHAPTER 9

1. National and city-level housing price changes in this paragraph are for the Case-Shiller composite home price index.

2. New York Times Editorial Board (2009) and Adler (2009). About one in four homes with mortgages were under water by 2009-Q2 (Levy 2009).

3. Making Home Affordable was originally announced in February 2009 as the Homeowner Affordability and Stability Plan (HASP). The FDIC's initiative was called Streamlined Mortgage Modification.

4. Office of Thrift Supervision (April 18, 2009) and Office of Thrift Supervision (December 6, 2009).

5. Geanakopolos and Koniak (2009) and Congressional Oversight Panel (2009, 81).

6. HUD has another program with a fundamentally different incentive structure (Congressional Oversight Panel 2009, 81). Understandably, very few mortgages have been modified under the HUD program, so consideration of it is omitted from this chapter.

7. Note that "inability to pay" is probably not enough by itself to create a foreclosure (Foote, Gerardi, and Paul 2008, footnote 3), because a homeowner unable to pay but with positive home equity may want to sell his home to pay the loan (and thereby retain his home equity) rather than invite foreclosure. Liebowitz (2009) finds that negative equity was a more important factor than unemployment in causing the foreclosures that occurred in the second half of 2008. Geanakopolos

and Koniak (2009) find that foreclosures are "stunningly sensitive" to the amount of home equity. In any case, the FDIC and Treasury have represented their programs as solutions to foreclosures motivated by negative equity, and not foreclosures that result from unemployment spells (Congressional Oversight Panel 2009, 4). As noted below, the programs consider borrowers with the lowest income to be ineligible for modification.

8. FDIC's early plan said "Modifications would be designed to achieve sustainable payments at a 38 percent debt-to-income ratio of principal, interest, taxes, and insurance." (Federal Deposit Insurance Corporation 2008b). See also U.S. Department of Treasury (2009a, 2–3). The FDIC (2008a, 8) indicates that homeowners' association dues are also included in "housing expenses."

9. FDIC (2009), U.S. Department of Treasury (2009c). Congressional Oversight Panel (2009, 47) explains, "If the NPV of the modification scenario is greater [than the NPV of foreclosure], then the servicer must offer to modify the loan."

10. For a while the FDIC program had $\mu = 38$ percent; HAMP has always been $\mu = 31$ percent.

11. In principle, such modifications could leave payments after year 5 unmodified, although the U.S. Treasury (2009a, 2–3, emphasis added) has said "[the] lower interest rate must be kept in place for five years, after which it could *gradually* be stepped up to the conforming loan rate in place at the time of the modification."

12. A third possibility is that reductions in payments for years 1–5 are at least partially offset by increases in payments after year 5, as with an increase in the loan's amortization period. In this third case, foreclosure incentives after year 5 (and perhaps even as early as year 2) can be increased by modification, and little is done to improve foreclosure incentives in year 1. Perhaps this is why increases in payments after year 5 are rarely used in practice and are rarely advocated even by those who disagree with current foreclosure policies. Following Kahn and Yavas (1994), my chapter does not consider modifications that fail to affect the present value of payments.

13. To the degree that the collateral has a different market value than its value to the lender, H_I should be interpreted as value to the lender for the purpose of these formulas.

14. If, for example, the lender anticipated borrowers to be modified again in year 3, then the appropriate parameter for the NPV test would be R_3 (rather than the R_M and R_5 shown above).

15. HAMP gives loan servicers the option to reduce principal before reducing interest (U.S. Department of Treasury, 2009b, p. 8), but the FDIC's protocol specifies that interest be reduced before principal (FDIC, 2008a).

16. See Appendix 9.1 and Mulligan (2010b) for the more general analysis. Note that a mortgage borrower could be without a job for the entire base year, but still have positive income for the purpose of modification because spousal income,

and often unemployment insurance benefits (Fannie Mae 2010), counts as income for that purpose. In mid-2010, the U.S. Treasury introduced a new modification program for unemployed borrowers, and ceased to count unemployment benefits as income under its HAMP program (Making Home Affordable 2011).

17. To the degree that year 5 modifications automatically create smaller modifications in years later than 5 in order to prevent interest payments from adjusting too quickly, R_5 should be augmented to include the additional terms, and therefore be greater than calculated above. See Appendix 9.2 for marginal tax rates calculated for longer modification horizons, and for principal modifications that can have marginal tax rates of almost 400 percent. In some cases, repeated modifications may be expected, with the next one occurring in less than five years. In this case, the parameters R_5 and R_M in the proposition's MTR formula should be replaced by the present value of a dollar paid in each year from the present until the year prior to the next modification. The marginal tax rate on year zero income could be as small as $\mu R_1/(1 + r_o)$ (about 30 percent) in such cases, but even then the marginal tax rate of $\mu R_5/(1 + r_o)$ applies to income earned in the year prior to the final modification, because of the anticipation that the final modification will be reducing (at least) five years of payments.

18. More recently, the FDIC has used a mix of 31 percent and 38 percent targets (FDIC, 2008a), which results in various marginal income tax rates over the eligible income range. The resulting marginal tax rates can be somewhat less than they are with HAMP, but typically still more than 100 percent.

19. FDIC (2008a, appendix).

20. More generally, the NPV test binds at a minimum income threshold that is strictly greater than zero (Mulligan 2010b), but Figure 9.1 captures the general result that the point W_o strictly dominates many other points on the budget set.

21. Because the mortgage is assumed to be under water, I do not distinguish among foreclosure, "walking away," and "deed in lieu of foreclosure." I refer to all three as "foreclosure" and assume that they result in the payment of deadweight "foreclosure costs." I model foreclosure costs as if they are entirely paid by borrowers. This is just a normalization, achieved by defining the amount of negative equity b to be the par value of the mortgage minus the value of the home to the lender in the case of foreclosure.

22. Moving costs may be expected to decline over time, for example, as family circumstances change. A full dynamic model of the moving decision is beyond the scope of this chapter (Herkenhoff and Ohanian 2011 have such a model), but the moving cost m can be interpreted as an average over the modification horizon, and therefore would be low for a family that expects to soon outgrow its current house.

23. A borrowing constraint would tend to increase the rate at which borrowers discount future cash flows, and create a gap between discount rates for borrower

and lender. Appendix 9.2 offers some quantitative analysis of the former, showing that marginal tax rates are expected to exceed 100 percent even for borrowers who discount much more than 6 percent per year.

24. Despite the lack of prompt compliance with the federal modification guidelines, it is still possible that a significant number of borrowers understand that their income affects their position in a future modification. Even if borrowers were surprised in, say, 2008 that mortgages would be modified according to borrower income, they still had the option to delay their modification until 2009, 2010, or later, and in the meantime supply income in a way that reflected all known costs and benefits, including the benefits of future mortgage modification. A large literature has documented behavioral responses to various means-tested and earnings-tested benefits (Moffitt 2003; Gruber and Wise 1999), and most of those pay benefits on the basis of lagged incomes. For example, the food stamp program has a monthly reporting form in some states (Neighborhood Legal Services Association 2009), and a quarterly reporting form in other states (Legal Services of Northern California 2008), that determines food stamp allotments approximately two or three months later. In public pension programs, beneficiary behavior can affect benefits over a horizon of several years (Gruber and Wise 1999) and benefit reductions pursuant to the earnings test do not occur until the following calendar year (Myers 1993, 211–12). Indeed, the personal income tax itself is many times not settled until April following the calendar year in which income was received.

25. The labor supply model from, for example, Chapter Two is a special case in which $u(c,y;\gamma) = \ln c$ minus a term proportional to $(y/A)^{(\eta+1)/\eta}$, where the constant A is labor productivity and the constant η is the wage elasticity of labor supply.

26. A borrower with characteristics γ has efficient income = $\arg \max_y u\left(a - \dfrac{b}{1+r_o} + y, y; \gamma\right)$.

27. Mirrlees (1971) is the classic paper, which had only heterogeneity in persons' ability to produce income. Here the vector γ can represent that ability, as well as borrower-specific tastes. Moreover, borrowers in this chapter are heterogeneous in yet another dimension: their foreclosure costs.

28. Congressional Oversight Panel (2009, p. 48), and Office of Thrift Supervision (2009a, p. 18).

29. Recall that, under full compliance with the FH modification rule, borrowers respond by earning exactly the minimum income threshold, where the NPV test binds.

30. HAMP also offers modification subsidies, so that in reality lenders likely care about the sum of collections and subsidies.

31. Mulligan (2009a) derives the collection-maximizing modification rule under full compliance by placing some additional structure on the unobserved heterogeneity among borrowers and obtains a closed-form solution for the income profile of collection-maximizing marginal tax rates that is fundamentally different from the profile under FH.

32. Perhaps this is why lenders often do not publish debt forgiveness formulas, and the Treasury itself has been secretive about the NPV test (Congressional Oversight Panel 2009, 47) that determines the minimum collection point.

33. (Congressional Oversight Panel 2009, 71) suggests that the subsidy is about of the same magnitude as the costs of administration and redefault.

34. Sixty-seven percent of nonelderly household heads and spouses owned a home, of which 19 percent had negative equity in fiscal year 2010. On the basis of the amount by which HAMP fell short of its goals, I assumed that 31 percent of negative equity homes would receive modifications.

35. For an underwater mortgage that is modified once, the marginal tax rate is about 131 percent in the year preceding the modification (see above) and is zero in all other years. For the purposes of aggregate analysis, one might consider an appropriately weighted average of 131 percent and zero, which would coincide with the 29 percent cited in the text if 22 percent of all underwater mortgages were in the year prior to its only (or final) modification.

36. To recall the economic interpretation of the remaining symbols, see inequality (9.1) and the surrounding text.

CHAPTER 10

1. Both safety and efficiency measures vary between zero and 1. Safety is zero and efficiency is 1 when the self-reliance rate is 1 (no sharing of the imperfect information risks). Safety is 1 and efficiency is zero when all of the risks are shared.

2. A related argument is that the equity-efficiency tradeoff is fixed, but the optimal balance of equity and efficiency has changed since 2007 because people became more risk-averse, at least temporarily. See Holmstrom and Milgrom (1987, 323) for a risk-aversion comparative static.

3. So far, economists have not suggested that the labor market effects of uncertainty would work through marginal tax rates, but rather that uncertainty discourages firms from undertaking new investment projects or otherwise expanding their payrolls (Bloom et al. 2011).

4. However, to the extent that wage or earnings inequality is an indicator of uncertainty, uncertainty may have not increased significantly since 2007 because those inequality measures have not. Moreover, the VIX is probably not a good indicator of idiosyncratic risk (as opposed to aggregate risk, which depends on whether the volatility of average stock prices derives from redistribution or aggregate shocks), which is featured in my model of the equity-efficiency tradeoff.

5. Holmstrom and Milgrom (1987, 323) give an example, consistent with the model above, in which the elasticity of the optimal self-reliance rate (μ in my notation, α in theirs) with respect to the standard deviation of the shock is equal to $-2(1-\mu)$, which is roughly -1. Thus, an increase in the log of that standard deviation of

about 0.16 would justify a reduction in the log self-reliance rate of 0.16, which is about the reduction I measured in Chapter Three. The same self-reliance rate reduction could also be justified by a 0.32 increase in the log of the coefficient of absolute risk aversion.

6. A zero self-reliance rate (equivalent to a 100 percent marginal tax rate) is not optimal in the model (10.5). To prove this, note that a marginal increase in μ has, in the neighborhood of μ = 0, only a second-order effect on the variance of utility but a first-order effect on mean disposable income (while the marginal disutility of labor is low).

CHAPTER 11

1. I also assume that real consumption per capita would have been constant, rather than falling about 3 percent and rather than following the previous upward trend. The formula for the impact of redistribution on log aggregate labor hours at any point in time is (log self-reliance rate impact—log employer side distortion—log consumption impact) divided by the incidence parameter (0.3 plus the inverse of the labor supply elasticity), plus the minimum wage impact, where "impact" refers to the difference between actual and hypothetical values. The minimum wage impact for 2010 and 2011 is assumed to be −0.005, based on the smaller 1.2 million jobs impact from Chapter Eight and assuming that all of those jobs would have had hours equal to average hours among part-time workers in 2007. Because the minimum wage hikes occurred over time, the calendar year average minimum wage impact is assumed to be −0.003 in 2009, −0.002 in 2008, and 0 in 2007. The employer-side distortion refers to the gap between labor productivity and real wages (see Chapter Five, esp. note 15) and has the characteristics of an employment cost (borne by employers) in addition to current employee compensation.

2. See also Cole and Ohanian (2004) on the Great Depression and lack of recovery.

3. See Becker and Posner (2007) and Neumark and Wascher (2008).

4. See the studies cited in Chapter Four.

5. As for the marginal tax rate series from Chapter Three, the amounts in Figure 11.2 are calculated for a nonelderly household head or spouse with potential earnings equal to the median real earnings among working nonelderly household heads and spouses in 2007. Because base UI benefits tend to be proportional to earnings on the previous job and the other safety net benefits independent of potential earnings, the "increase UI duration" share of real safety net generosity changes for low-skill workers would likely be less than shown in Figure 11.2.

6. This book's marginal tax rate units (shares of total labor compensation) are somewhat different from NBER's units (shares of AGI).

7. See, among others, Hall (2009), Akerlof and Shiller (2010), and Diamond (2010).

8. The safety net expansion might seem to be welfare-improving for the lowest-skill members of the labor force, but a full welfare analysis for that group must also consider the minimum wage hikes.

9. Krueger and Mueller (2011) and the references cited therein document the fact that unemployed people are less happy than employed people, and that unhappiness increases with the duration of unemployment.

Bibliography

AARP Illinois. *The Social Security "Offset" Rule: What Is It and How Could It Affect You?* March 19, 2010. http://www.aarp.org/work/social-security/info-03-2010/the-social-securityoffset.html (accessed November 5, 2011).

Abel, Andrew B., Avinash K. Dixit, Janice C. Eberly, and Robert S. Pindyck. "Options, the Value of Capital, and Investment." *Quarterly Journal of Economics* 11, no. 3 (August 1996): 753–77.

Abraham, Katharine G., and John C. Haltiwanger. "Real Wages and the Business Cycle." *Journal of Economic Literature* 33, no. 3 (September 1995): 1215–64.

Adler, Lynn. "About 12 pct of US Homeowners Late Paying or Foreclosed." reuters.com. May 28, 2009. http://www.reuters.com/article/2009/05/28/usa-housing-foreclosures-idUSN2832609020090528.

Administrative Office of the U.S. Courts. "Bankruptcy Basics." *United States Courts*. November 2011a. http://www.uscourts.gov/Viewer.aspx?doc=/uscourts/FederalCourts/BankruptcyResources/bankbasics2011.pdf (accessed January 9, 2012).

Administrative Office of the U.S. Courts. "Bankruptcy Statistics." *United States Courts*. November 2011b. http://www.uscourts.gov/Statistics/BankruptcyStatistics.aspx (accessed January 9, 2012).

Aiyagari, S. Rao, Lawrence J. Christiano, and Martin Eichenbaum. "The Output Employment, and Interest Rate Effects of Government Consumption." *Journal of Monetary Economics* 30, no. 1 (October 1992): 73–86.

Aizer, Anna. "Low Take-Up in Medicaid: Does Outreach Matter and for Whom?" *American Economic Review* 93, no. 2 (May 2003): 238–41.

Akerlof, George A., and Robert J. Shiller. *Animal Spirits*. Princeton, NJ: Princeton University Press, 2010.

Alesina, Alberto, Edward Glaeser, and Bruce Sacerdote. "Work and Leisure in the United States and Europe: Why So Different?" *NBER Macroeconomics Annual* 20 (2005): 1–64.

Alesina, Alberto F., and Silvia Ardagna. "Large Changes in Fiscal Policy: Taxes Versus Spending." *NBER working paper* no. 15438 (October 2009).

Anderson, Patricia M., and Bruce D. Meyer. "Unemployment Insurance Takeup Rates and the After-tax Value of Benefits." *Quarterly Journal of Economics* 112, no. 3 (August 1997): 913–37.

Arellano, Cristina, Yan Bai, and Patrick Kehoe. "Financial Markets and Fluctuations in Uncertainty." *Federal Reserve Bank of Minneapolis Research Department Staff Report*, January 2011.

Arulampalam, Wiji, and Mark B. Stewart. "The Determinants of Individual Unemployment Durations in an Era of High Unemployment." *Economic Journal* 105, no. 429 (March 1995): 321–32.

Auerbach, Alan J., and Daniel Feenberg. "The Significance of Federal Taxes as Automatic Stabilizers." *Journal of Economic Perspectives* 14, no. 3 (Summer 2000): 37–56.

Auerbach, Alan J., and Yuriy Gorodnichenko. "Measuring the Output Responses to Fiscal Policy." *NBER working paper* no. 16311 (August 2010).

Auerbach, Alan J., and James R. Hines, Jr. "Investment Tax Incentives and Frequent Tax Reforms." *American Economic Review* 78, no. 2 (May 1988): 211–16.

Autor, David H., and Mark G. Duggan. "The Growth in the Social Security Disability Rolls: A Fiscal Crisis Unfolding." *Journal of Economic Perspectives* 20, no. 3 (Summer 2006): 71–96.

Aversa, Jeannine. "Government Plans Massive Citigroup Rescue Effort." *Associated Press*, November 24, 2008.

Baker, Scott R., Nicholas Bloom, and Steven J. Davis. "Measuring Economic Policy Uncertainty." Manuscript, University of Chicago Booth School of Business., October 2011.

Barro, Robert J. "Are Government Bonds Net Wealth?" *Journal of Political Economy* 82, no. 6 (December 1974): 1095–1117.

Barro, Robert J. "The Folly of Subsidizing Unemployment Insurance." *Wall Street Journal* (online, n.p.), August 30, 2010.

Barro, Robert J., and Herschel I. Grossman. "A General Disequilibrium Model of Income and Employment." *American Economic Review* 61, no. 1 (March 1971): 82–93.

Barro, Robert J, and Robert G. King. "Time Separable Preferences and Intertemporal Substitution Models of Business Cycles." *Quarterly Journal of Economics* 99, no. 4 (November 1984): 817–39.

Barro, Robert J, and Charles J. Redlick. "Macroeconomic Effects from Government Purchases and Taxes." *NBER working paper* no. 15369 (September 2009).

Barro, Robert J., and Chaipat Sahasakul. "Measuring the Average Marginal Tax Rate from the Individual Income Tax." *Journal of Business* 56, no. 4 (October 1983): 419–52.

Barro, Robert J., and Xavier Sala-i-Martin. *Economic Growth*. Cambridge, MA: MIT Press, 2003.

Barsky, Robert B., and Jeffrey A. Miron. "The Seasonal Cycle and the Business Cycle." *Journal of Political Economy* 97, no. 3 (June 1989): 503–34.

Becker, Gary S. "Irrational Behavior and Economic Theory." *Journal of Political Economy* 70, no. 1 (February 1962): 1–13.

Becker, Gary S. "Human Capital, Effort, and the Sexual Division of Labor." *Journal of Labor Economics* 3, Part 2 (1985), S33–S58.

Becker, Gary S., and Richard A. Posner. "Paycheck Politics." *Hoover Digest*, no. 2 (April 2007).

Ben-Shalom, Yonatan, Robert A. Moffitt, and John Karl Scholz. "An Assessment of the Effectiveness of Anti-Poverty Programs in the United States." *NBER working paper* no. 17042 (August 2011).

Bernanke, Ben S. "Nonmonetary Effects of the Financial Crisis in the Propagation of the Great Depression." *American Economic Review* 73, no. 3 (June 1983): 257–76.

Bernanke, Ben S., Mark Gertler, and Mark Watson. "Systematic Monetary Policy and the Effects of Oil Price Shocks." *Brookings Papers on Economic Activity* 19, no. 1 (December 1997): 91–157.

Bernstein, Jared, and Isaac Shapiro. *Nine Years of Neglect.* Washington, DC: Economic Policy Institute, 2006.

Bils, Mark J. "Real Wages over the Business Cycle: Evidence from Panel Data." *Journal of Political Economy* 93, no. 4 (August 1985): 666–89.

Bishaw, Alemayehu. "Poverty: 2009 and 2010 American Community Surveys." American Community Survey Briefs. October 2011. http://www.census.gov/prod/2011pubs/acsbr10-01.pdf (accessed January 7, 2011).

Bishaw, Alemayehu, and Suzanne Macartney. "Poverty: 2008 and 2009 American Community Surveys." American Community Survey Briefs. September 2010. http://www.census.gov/prod/2010pubs/acsbr09-1.pdf (accessed January 7, 2011).

Bishaw, Alemayehu, and Trudi J. Renwick. "Poverty: 2007 and 2008 American Community Surveys." American Community Survey Reports. September 2009. http://www.census.gov/prod/2009pubs/acsbr08-1.pdf (accessed January 7, 2011).

Blanchard, Olivier, and Jordi Gali. "Real Wage Rigidities and the New Keynesian Model." *Journal of Money, Credit, and Banking* 39, no. 1, Supp. (February 2007): 35–65.

Blau, David M., and Ryan M. Goodstein. "Can Social Security Explain Trends in Labor Force Participation of Older Men in the United States?" *Journal of Human Resources* 45, no. 2 (March 2010): 328–63.

Blau, Francine D., and Lawrence M. Kahn. "Gender Differences in Pay." *Journal of Economic Perspectives* 14, no. 4 (Autumn 2000): 75–99.

Bloom, Nicholas, Max Floetotto, Nir Jaimovich, Itay Saporta-Eksten, and Stephen Terry. "Really Uncertain Business Cycles." Manuscript, Stanford University, December 2011.

Braun, R. Anton. "Tax Disturbances and Real Economic Activity in the Postwar United States." *Journal of Monetary Economics* 33, no. 3 (June 1994): 441–62.

Brookings Institution. "Increasing Retirement Saving: Clarifying Food Stamp Asset Test Rules." *Retirement Survey Project.* 2007 http://www.brookings.edu/about/projects/retirementsecurity/~/media/projects/retirementsecurity/03_increasing_saving.pdf (accessed May 15, 2012).

Browning, Martin, Lars Peter Hansen, and James J. Heckman. "Micro Data and General Equilibrium Models." In *Handbook of Macroeconomics*, by John B. Taylor and Michael Woodford eds, 543–633. Amsterdam: North-Holland, 1999.

Burkhauser, Richard V., Kenneth A. Couch, and David C. Wittenburg. "A Reassessment of the New Economics of the Minimum Wage Literature with Monthly Data from the Current Population Survey." *Journal of Labor Economics* 18, no. 4 (October 2000): 653–80.

Burtless, Gary. "Why Is Insured Unemployment so Low?" *Brookings Papers on Economic Activity* 1 (1983): 225–49.

Burtless, Gary. "Unemployment Insurance for the Great Recession." Testimony for the Senate Committee on Finance, 2009.

Bush, George W., interview by Charlie Gibson. ABC News. December 1, 2008.

Calvo, Guillermo A. "Staggered Prices in a Utility-maximizing Framework." *Journal of Monetary Economics* 12, no. 3 (September 1983): 383–98.

Campbell, John Y., and John H. Cochrane. "By Force of Habit: A Consumption-Based Explanation of Aggregate Stock Market Behavior." *Journal of Political Economy* 107, no. 2 (April 1999): 205–51.

Card, David, and Phillip B. Levine. "Unemployment Insurance Taxes and the Cyclical and Seasonal Properties of Unemployment." *Journal of Public Economics* 53, no. 1 (January 1994): 1–29.

Center on Budget and Policy Priorities. *Introduction to Unemployment Insurance.* April 16, 2010. http://www.cbpp.org/cms/index.cfm?fa=view&id=1466 (accessed January 8, 2012).

Centers for Medicare and Medicaid Services. *Medicaid Program—General Information.* June 16, 2011. https://www.cms.gov/medicaidgeninfo/ (accessed November 14, 2011).

Chari, V. V., Patrick J. Kehoe, and Ellen R. McGrattan. "Business Cycle Accounting." *Econometrica* 75, no. 3 (April 2007): 781–836.

Chetty, Raj. "Moral Hazard Versus Liquidity and Optimal Unemployment Insurance." *Journal of Political Economy* 116, no. 2 (April 2008): 173–234.

Chetty, Raj, Adam Guren, Day Manoli, and Andrea Weber. "Are Micro and Macro Labor Supply Elasticities Consistent? A Review of Evidence on the Intensive and Extensive Margins." *American Economic Review* 101, no. 2 (May 2011): 1–6.

Chicago Board Options Exchange. "The CBOE Volatility Index—VIX." 2009. http://www.cboe.com/micro/vix/vixwhite.pdf (accessed January 6, 2012).

Christiano, Lawrence J., and Richard M. Todd. "The Conventional Treatment of Seasonality in Business Cycle Analysis: Does It Create Distortions?" *Journal of Monetary Economics* 49, no. 2 (March 2002): 335–65.

Christiano, Lawrence, Martin Eichenbaum, and Sergio Rebelo. "When Is the Government Spending Multiplier Large?" *NBER working paper* no. 15394 (October 2009).

Christiano, Lawrence J., Mathias Trabandt, and Karl Walentin. "Involuntary Unemployment and the Business Cycle." *NBER working paper* no. 15801 (December 2011).

Clarida, Richard, Jordi Galí, and Mark Gertler. "The Science of Monetary Policy: A New Keynesian Perspective." *Journal of Economic Literature* (December 1999): 1661–1707.

Clarida, Richard, Jordi Galí, and Mark Gertler. "Monetary Policy Rules and Macroeconomic Stability: Evidence and Some Theory." *Quarterly Journal of Economics* 115, no. 1 (February 2000): 147–80.

Clark, Kate, Liz Elwart, Sam Hall, and Tommy Winkle. "Retirement Benefits and Unemployment Insurance." Manuscript, University of Wisconsin Madison, Spring 2007.

CNNMoney.com. *How Long Should We Help the Unemployed?* April 23, 2010. http://money.cnn.com/2010/04/23/news/economy/extending_unemployment_benefits/ (accessed January 2, 2012).

Cogan, John F., Tobias Cwik, John B. Taylor, and Volker Wieland. "New Keynesian Versus Old Keynesian Government Spending Multipliers." *Journal of Economic Dynamics and Control* 34, no. 3 (March 2010): 281–95.

Cole, Harold L., and Lee E. Ohanian. "The Great Depression in the United States from a Neoclassical Perspective." *Federal Reserve Bank of Minneapolis Quarterly Review* 23, no. 1 (Winter 1999): 2–24.

Cole, Harold L., and Lee E. Ohanian. "New Deal Policies and the Persistence of the Great Depression: A General Equilibrium Analysis." *Journal of Political Economy* 112, no. 4 (August 2004): 779–816.

Congressional Budget Office. "Estimated Impact of the American Recovery and Reinvestment Act on Employment and Economic Output as of September 2009." Congressional Budget Office. November 2009a. http://www.cbo.gov/ftpdocs/110xx/doc11044/02-23-ARRA.pdf (accessed November 13, 2011).

Congressional Budget Office. "February 10, 2009 Letter to Nancy Pelosi." Congressional Budget Office. February 10, 2009b. http://www.cbo.gov/ftpdocs/99xx/doc9983/hr1Ltr-COBRAenrollment.pdf (accessed February 19, 2012).

Congressional Budget Office. "Social Security Disability Insurance: Participation Trends and Their Fiscal Implications." *Economic and Budget Issue Brief*, July 2010.

Congressional Budget Office. "The Budget and Economic Outlook: Fiscal Years 2012 to 2022." Congressional Budget Office. January 2012a. http://www.cbo.gov/ftpdocs/126xx/doc12699/01-31-2012_Outlook.pdf (accessed February 8, 2012).

Congressional Budget Office. "The Supplemental Nutrition Assistance Program." *Congressional Budget Office.* April 2012b. http://www.cbo.gov/sites/default/files/cbofiles/attachments/04-19-SNAP.pdf (accessed April 20, 2012).

Congressional Oversight Panel. "October Oversight Report: An Assessment of Foreclosure Mitigation Efforts After Six Months." October 2009.

Congressional Oversight Panel. *March Oversight Report: The Final Report of the Congressional Oversight Panel.* Washington, DC: Government Printing Office, 2011.

Connecticut Department of Social Services. "Help for People in Need." Hartford Public Library. 2009. http://www.hartfordinfo.org/issues/wsd/FamiliesandChildren/HelpforPeopleinNeed.pdf.

Council of Economic Advisers. *The Economic Impact of Recent Temporary Unemployment Insurance Extensions.* Executive Office of the President, December 2010a.

Council of Economic Advisers. *Economic Report of the President.* Executive Office of the President, February 2010b.

Crimmel, Beth Levin. "Employer-Sponsored Single, Employee-Plus-One, and Family Health." *Medical Expenditure Panel Survey.* July 2010. http://www.meps.ahrq.gov/mepsweb/data_files/publications/st285/stat285.pdf (accessed November 10, 2011).

Crucini, Mario J., and James Kahn. "Tariffs and Aggregate Economic Activity: Lessons from the Great Depression." *Journal of Monetary Economics* 38, no. 3 (December 1996): 427–67.

CTIA. *Wireless Quick Facts.* 2011. http://www.ctia.org/advocacy/research/index.cfm/aid/10323 (accessed October 24, 2011).

Cullen, Julie Berry, and Jonathan Gruber. "Does Unemployment Insurance Crowd out Spousal Labor Supply?" *Journal of Labor Economics* 18, no. 3 (July 2000): 546–72.

Curdia, Vasco and Michael Woodford. "Credit Spreads and Monetary Policy." *Journal of Money, Credit and Banking* 42, no. 1 (2010): 3–35.

Dague, Laura. "Effects of Medicaid Premiums and Copayments on Insurance Coverage, Utilization, and Health: A Regression Discontinuity Approach." Manuscript (University of Wisconsin, Madison), October 2011.

Daly, Mary, Bart Hobijn, Aysegul Sahin, and Rob Valletta. "A Rising Natural Rate of Unemployment: Transitory or Permanent?" *Journal of Economic Perspectives* forthcoming (2012).

Daponte, Beth Osborne, Seth Sanders, and Lowell Taylor. "Why Do Low-Income Households Not Use Food Stamps? Evidence from an Experiment." *Journal of Human Resources* 34, no. 3 (Summer 1999): 612–28.

Davis, Steven J., and Magnus Henrekson. "Tax Effects on Work Activity, Industry Mix and Shadow Economy Size: Evidence from Rich-Country Comparisons." In *Labour Supply and Incentives to Work in Europe,* by Ramon Gomez-Salvador, Ana

Petrongolo, Barbara Lamo, Melanie Ward and Etienne Wasmer eds., 44–104. Northampton, MA: Edward Elgar, 2005.

de Wolf, Mark, and Katherine Klemmer. "Job Openings, Hires, and Separations Fall During Recession." *Monthly Labor Review* 133, no. 5 (May 2010): 36–44.

Dean, Stacy, Colleen Pawling, and Dottie Rosenbaum. "Implementing New Changes to the Food Stamp Program: A Provision by Provision Analysis of the 2008 Farm Bill." *Center for Budget Policies and Policy Priorities.* July 1, 2008. http://www.cbpp.org/files/7-1-08fa.pdf (accessed January 10, 2012).

Diamond, Douglas W., and Raghuram G. Rajan. "Fear of Fire Sales, Illiquidity Seeking, and Credit Freezes." *Quarterly Journal of Economics* 126, no. 2 (May 2011): 557–91.

Diamond, Peter A. "Unemployment, Vacancies, Wages." Nobel Prize Lecture, December 2010.

Dugas, Christine. "Graduates Saddled with Debt, Student Loans Can't Easily Turn to Bankruptcy." *USA Today*, May 15, 2009.

Dynan, Karen E., and Donald L. Kohn. "The Rise in U.S. Household Indebtedness: Causes and Consequences." *Finance and Economics Discussion Series* (Federal Reserve Board), no. 2007–37 (August 2007).

Eggertsson, Gauti. "What Fiscal Policy Is Effective at Zero Interest Rates?" November 2009.

Eggertsson, Gauti. "A Comment on Casey Mulligan's Test of the Paradox of Toil." Working paper, Federal Reserve Bank, May 2010a.

Eggertsson, Gauti. "The Paradox of Toil." Working paper, Federal Reserve Bank, January 2010b.

Eggertsson, Gauti, and Paul Krugman. "Debt, Deleveraging, and the Liquidity Trap." *Federal Reserve Bank of New York.* February 2011. http://www.newyorkfed.org/research/economists/eggertsson/EggertssonKrugmanWP[1].pdf.

Elsby, Michael W., Bart Hobijn, and Aysegul Sahin. "The Labor Market in the Great Recession." *Brookings Papers on Economic Activity* (Spring 2010): 1–48.

Eslami, Esa, Kai Filion, and Mark Strayer. "Characteristics of Supplemental Nutrition Assistance Program Households: Fiscal Year 2010." *Supplemental Nutrition Assistance Program (SNAP) Studies.* September 2011. http://www.fns.usda.gov/ora/menu/Published/snap/FILES/Participation/2010Characteristics.pdf (accessed November 5, 2011).

Even, William E., and David A. Macpherson. *The Teen Employment Crisis: The Effects of the 2007–2009 Federal Minimum Wage Increases on Teen Employment.* Washington, DC: Employment Policies Institute, 2010.

Even, William E., and David A. Macpherson. *Unequal Harm: Racial Disparities in the Employment Consequences of Minimum Wage Increases.* Washington, DC: Employment Policies Institute, 2011.

Fannie Mae. "Servicing Guide Announcement 09-05R: Home Affordable Modification." eFannieMae.com. February 25, 2010. https://www.efanniemae.

com/sf/guides/ssg/relatedservicinginfo/pdf/hampfaqs.pdf (accessed February 7, 2012).

Farber, Henry S., and Robert Valletta. "Extended Unemployment Insurance and Unemployment Duration in the Great Recession: The U.S. Experience." *Institute for the Study of Labor.* June 23, 2011. http://www.iza.org/conference_files/UnIRe2011/valletta_r3299.pdf (accessed February 19, 2012).

Federal Communications Commission. "15th Mobile Wireless Competition Report." *Commercial Mobile Radio Services (CMRS) Competition Reports.* June 27, 2011. http://hraunfoss.fcc.gov/edocs_public/attachmatch/FCC-11-103A1.pdf (accessed October 24, 2011).

Federal Deposit Insurance Corporation. "FDIC Loan Modification Program." November 2008a.

Federal Deposit Insurance Corporation. *Loan Modification Program for Distressed Indymac Mortgage Loans.* August 20, 2008b. http://www.fdic.gov/news/news/press/2008/pr08067.html.

Federal Deposit Insurance Corporation. *FDIC Loan Modification Program Overview.* March 6, 2009. http://www.fdic.gov/consumers/loans/loanmod/loanmodguide.html.

Federal Reserve Bank of St. Louis. "Series ATAIEALLGCLCRACB." Federal Reserve Economic Data. 2011. http://research.stlouisfed.org/fred2/series/ATAIEALLGCLCRACB (accessed November 26, 2011).

Feldstein, Martin. "Tax Avoidance and the Deadweight Loss of the Income Tax." *Review of Economics and Statistics* 81, no. 4 (November 1999): 674–80.

First American CoreLogic. "Core Mortgage Risk Monitor, Q42008." November 21, 2008. https://www.corelogic.com/documents/Core_Mortgage_Risk_Monitor_Q4_2008.pdf (accessed November 26, 2011).

First American CoreLogic. "Underwater Mortgages on the Rise According to First American CoreLogic Q4 2009 Negative Equity Data." Press release, First American CoreLogic, February 2010.

First American CoreLogic. "CoreLogic Reports Negative Equity Increase in Q4 2011." Press release, First American CoreLogic, March 2012.

Food Research and Action Center. "Heat and Eat: Using Federal Nutrition Programs to Soften Low-Income Households' Food/Fuel Dilemma." *frac.org.* March 2009. http://frac.org/newsite/wp-content/uploads/2009/09/heat_and_eat09.pdf (accessed April 17, 2012).

Food and Research Action Center. *National and State Program Data.* 2011. http://frac.org/reports-and-resources/reports-2/ (accessed November 10, 2011).

Foote, Christopher, Kristopher Gerardi, and Willen Paul. "Negative Equity and Foreclosure: Theory and Evidence." *Journal of Urban Economics* 64 (2008): 345–245.

Foote, Christopher, Kristopher Gerardi, Goette Lorenz, and Willen Paul. "Reducing Foreclosures: No Easy Answers." *NBER working paper,* June 2009: 15063.

Friedman, Milton, and Anna J. Schwartz. *A Monetary History of the United States, 1867–1960*. Princeton, NJ: Princeton University Press, 1963.

Fullerton, Don, and Gilbert E. Metcalf. *Tax Incidence*. Vol. 4, in *Handbook of Public Economics*, by Alan J. Auerbach and Martin Feldstein, eds. Amsterdam: Elsevier, 2002: 1787–1872.

Galí, Jordi. *Unemployment Fluctuations and Stabilization Policies: A New Keynesian Perspective*. Cambridge, MA: MIT Press, 2011.

Galí, Jordi, Mark Gertler, and J. David Lopez-Salido. "Markups, Gaps, and the Welfare Costs of Business Fluctuations." *Review of Economics and Statistics* 89 (February 2007): 44–59.

Galí, Jordi, J. David López-Salido, and Javier Vallés. "Understanding the Effects of Government Spending on Consumption." *Journal of the European Economic Association* 5, no. 1 (March 2007): 227–70.

Galí, Jordi, Frank Smets, and Rafael Wouters. "Unemployment in an Estimated New Keynesian Model." In *NBER Macroeconomics Annual 2011*, edited by Daron Acemoglu and Michael Woodford. Chicago: University of Chicago Press (for NBER), 2011.

Garen, John E. "Executive Compensation and Principal-Agent Theory." *Journal of Political Economy* 102, no. 6 (December 1994): 1175–99.

Geanakopolos, John D., and Susan P. Koniak. "Mortgage Justice Is Blind." *New York Times*, October 2008.

Geanakopolos, John D., and Susan P. Koniak. "Matters of Principal." *New York Times*, March 5, 2009: A31.

Ghent, Andra C., and Marianna Kudlyak. "Recourse and Residential Mortgage Default: Evidence from US States." *Review of Financial Studies* 24, no. 9 (September 2011): 3139–86.

Goldin, Claudia, and Lawrence F. Katz. "The Power of the Pill: Oral Contraceptives and Women's Career and Marriage Decisions." *Journal of Political Economy*, 110 (August 2002), 730–770.

Grochulski, Borys. "Optimal Personal Bankruptcy Design: A Mirrlees Approach." *Richmond Federal Reserve Working paper*, no. 08-5 (September 2008).

Gruber, Jonathan. "The Consumption Smoothing Benefits of Unemployment Insurance." *American Economic Review* 87, no. 1 (March 1997): 192–205.

Gruber, Jonathan, and David A. Wise, eds. *Social Security and Retirement Around the World*. Chicago: University of Chicago Press (for NBER), 1999.

Hall, Robert E. "Macroeconomic Fluctuations and the Allocation of Time." *Journal of Labor Economics* 15, no. 1, Part 2 (January 1997): S223–50.

Hall, Robert E. "Employment Fluctuations with Equilibrium Wage Stickiness." *American Economic Review* 95, no. 1 (March 2005): 50–65.

Hall, Robert E. "Reconciling Cyclical Movements in the Marginal Value of Time and the Marginal Product of Labor." *Journal of Political Economy* 117, no. 2 (April 2009): 281–323.

Han, Song, and Wenli Li. "Fresh Start or Head Start? The Effects of Filing for Personal Bankruptcy on Work Effort." *Journal of Financial Services Research* 31 (2007): 123–52.

Hansen, Gary D. "Indivisible Labor and the Business Cycle." *Journal of Monetary Economics* 16, no. 3 (1985): 309–27.

Hansen, Lars Peter, and James J. Heckman. "The Empirical Foundations of Calibration." *Journal of Economic Perspectives* 10, no. 1 (Winter 1996): 87–104.

Hansen, Lars Peter, and Kenneth J. Singleton. "Stochastic Consumption, Risk Aversion, and the Temporal Behavior of Asset Returns." *Journal of Political Economy* 91, no. 2 (April 1983): 249–65.

Hanson, Kenneth, and Margaret Andrews. *State Variations in the Food Stamp Benefit Reduction Rate for Earnings.* EIB-46, U.S. Department of Agriculture, Economic Research Service, March 2009.

Hausman, Jerry A. "Exact Consumer's Surplus and Deadweight Loss." *American Economic Review* 71, no. 4 (September 1981): 662–76.

Heckman, James J. "Effects of Child-Care Programs on Women's Work Effort." *Journal of Political Economy* 82, no. 2, Part 2 (March 1974): S136–63.

Heckman, James J. "What Has Been Learned About Labor Supply in the Past Twenty Years?" *American Economic Review* 83, no. 2 (May 1993): 116–21.

Heckman, James J., and Guilherme Sedlacek. "Heterogeneity, Aggregation, and Market Wage Functions: An Empirical Model of Self-Selection in the Labor Market." *Journal of Political Economy* 93, no. 6 (December 1985): 1077–1125.

Henry J. Kaiser Family Foundation. *Medicaid Payments per Enrollee, FY 2008.* 2011a. http://www.statehealthfacts.org/comparemaptable.jsp?ind=183&cat=4 (accessed November 14, 2011).

Henry J. Kaiser Family Foundation. *Monthly Medicaid Enrollment.* 2011b. http://www.statehealthfacts.org/comparemaptable.jsp?ind=774&cat=4 (accessed November 14, 2011).

Henry J. Kaiser Family Foundation. *Premium and Copayment Requirements for Children, January 2011.* 2011c. http://www.statehealthfacts.org/comparereport.jsp?rep=85&cat=4 (accessed November 14, 2011).

Herkenhoff, Kyle F., and Lee E. Ohanian. "Labor Market Dysfunction During the Great Recession." *NBER working paper* no. 17313 (August 2011).

Holahan, John, and Irene Headen. *Medicaid Coverage and Spending in Health Reform.* May 2010. http://www.kff.org/healthreform/upload/Medicaid-Coverage-and-Spending-in-Health-Reform-National-and-State-By-State-Results-for-Adults-at-or-Below-133-FPL.pdf (accessed November 29, 2011).

Holmstrom, Bengt, and Paul Milgrom. "Aggregation and Linearity in the Provision of Intertemporal Incentives." *Econometrica* 55, no. 2 (March 1987): 303–28.

Holt, Stephen D., and Jennifer L. Romich. "Marginal Tax Rates Facing Low—and Moderate—Income Workers Who Participate in Means-Tested Transfer Programs." *National Tax Journal* 60, no. 2 (June 2007): 253–77.

HOPE NOW. "Industry Extrapolations and Metrics." www.hopenow.com. September 2011. http://www.hopenow.com/industry-data/HOPE%20NOW%20Data%20Report%20(September)%2011-10-2011.pdf (accessed November 28, 2011).

Hossain, Farhana, Amanda Cox, John McGrath, and Stephan Weitberg. "The Stimulus Plan: How to Spend $787 Billion." *New York Times.* March 2009. http://projects.nytimes.com/44th_president/stimulus (accessed January 15, 2012).

Hoynes, Hilary Williamson, and Diane Whitmore Schanzenbach. "Work Incentives and the Food Stamp Program." *Journal of Public Economics* 96, no. 1–2 (February 2012): 151–62.

Huff Post Business. "Nouriel Roubini: Double-Dip Odds Now Greater Than 40%, GDP To Be 'Pathetically Lousy'." huffingtonpost.com. August 26, 2010. http://www.huffingtonpost.com/2010/08/26/roubini_n_695536.html (accessed February 27, 2012).

Hurd, Michael, and Susann Rohwedder. "Trends in Labor Force Participation: How Much Is Due to Changes in Pensions?" *Journal of Population Ageing* 4, no. 1 (June 2011): 81–96.

Jacob, Brian A., and Jens Ludwig. "The Effects of Housing Assistance on Labor Supply: Evidence from a Voucher Lottery." *American Economic Review* 102, no. 1 (February 2012): 272–304.

Jermann, Urban J., and Vincenzo Quadrini. "Macroeconomic Effects of Financial Shocks." *NBER working paper* no. 15338 (September 2009).

Johnson, David S., Jonathan A. Parker, and Nicholas S. Souleles. "Household Expenditure and the Income Tax Rebates of 2001." *American Economic Review* 96, no. 5 (December 2006): 1589–1610.

Jorgenson, Dale W. "Introduction." In *The Economics of Productivity,* by Dale W. Jorgenson, 9–28. Northampton, MA: Edward Elgar, 2009.

Jorgenson, Dale W., Richard J. Goettle, Mun S. Ho, Daniel T. Slesnick, and Peter J. Wilcoxen. "U.S. Labor Supply and Demand in the Long Run." *Journal of Policy Modeling* 30, no. 4 (July 2008): 603–18.

Jurajda, Štepan, and Frederick J. Tannery. "Unemployment Durations and Extended Unemployment Benefits in Local Labor Markets." *Industrial and Labor Relations Review* 56, no. 2 (January 2003): 324–48.

Kahn, Charles, and Yavas Abdullah. "The Economic Role of Foreclosures." *Journal of Real Estate Finance and Economics* 8 (1994): 35–51.

Katz, Lawrence F. "The Labor Market in the Great Recession: Comment." *Brookings Papers on Economic Activity* (Spring 2010): 49–56.

Katz, Lawrence F., and Kevin M. Murphy. "Changes in Relative Wages, 1963–1987: Supply and Demand Factors." *Quarterly Journal of Economics* 107, no. 1 (February 1992): 35–78.

Keane, Michael, Robert Moffitt, and David Runkle. "Real Wages over the Business Cycle Estimating the Impact of Heterogeneity with Micro Data." *Journal of Political Economy* 96, no. 6 (December 1988): 1232–66.

Keynes, John Maynard. *The General Theory of Employment, Interest and Money.* New Dehli: Atlantic Publishers and Distributors, 2008/1936.

King, Robert G., Charles I. Plosser, and Sergio T. Rebelo. "Production, Growth and Business Cycles: I. The Basic Neoclassical Model." *Journal of Monetary Economics* 21, no. 2 (March 1988): 195–232.

Klerman, Jacob Alex, and Caroline Danielson. "The Transformation of the Supplemental Nutrition Assistance Program." *Journal of Policy Analysis and Management* 30, no. 4 (Fall 2011): 863–88.

Kneebone, Elizabeth. *Economic Recovery and the Earned Income Tax Credit.* Brookings Institution. October 21, 2009.

Kotlikoff, Laurence J., and David Rapson. "Does It Pay, at the Margin, to Work and Save?" In *Tax Policy and the Economy,* edited by James M. Poterba, 83–144. Cambridge, MA: National Bureau of Economic Research, 2007.

Krane, Spencer, and William Wascher. "The Cyclical Sensitivity of Seasonality in U.S. Employment." *Journal of Monetary Economics.* 44, no. 3 (December 1999).

Krueger, Alan B., and Bruce D. Meyer. *Labor Supply Effects of Social Insurance.* Vol. 4, in *Handbook of Public Economics,* edited by Alan J. Auerbach and Martin Feldstein, 2327–92. Amsterdam: Elsevier, 2002.

Krueger, Alan B., and Andreas Mueller. "Job Search, Emotional Well-Being, and Job Finding in a Period of Mass Unemployment: Evidence from High Frequency Longitudinal Data." *Brookings Papers on Economic Activity,* Spring 2011: 1–57.

Krugman, Paul. "The Wrong Worries." *New York Times,* August 5, 2011: A23.

Krussel, Per, Toshihiko Mukoyama, Richard Rogerson, and Aysegül Sahin. "Aggregate Implications of Indivisible Labor, Incomplete Markets, and Labor Market Frictions." *Journal of Monetary Economics* 55, no. 5 (July 2008): 961–79.

Kydland, Finn, and Edward C. Prescott. "Time to Build and Aggregate Fluctuations." *Econometrica* 50, no. 6 (November 1982): 1345–70.

Landais, Camille, Michaillat Pascal, and Emmanuel Saez. "Optimal Unemployment Insurance over the Business Cycle." *NBER working paper* no. 16526 (November 2010).

Leftin, Joshua, Andew Gothro, and Esa Eslami. "Characteristics of Supplemental Nutrition Assistance Program Households: Fiscal Year 2009." *Supplemental Nutrition Assistance Program (SNAP) Studies.* October 2010. http://www.fns.usda.gov/ora/menu/Published/snap/FILES/Participation/2009Characteristics.pdf (accessed November 5, 2011).

Leftin, Joshua, Esa Eslami, and Mark Strayer. "Supplemental Nutrition Assistance Program Participation Rates: Fiscal Year 2002 to Fiscal Year 2009." *Supplemental Nutrition Assistance Program (SNAP) Studies.* August 2011. http://www.fns.usda.gov/ora/menu/Published/SNAP/FILES/Participation/Trends2002-09.pdf (accessed November 5, 2011).

Legal Services of Northern California. *California Guide to the Food Stamp Program:Prospective Quarterly Budgeting.* 2008. http://www.foodstampguide.org/prospective-quarterly-budgeting/.

Levy, Dan. *U.S. Underwater Mortgages May Reach 30 percent, Zillow Says.* August 11, 2009. http://www.bloomberg.com/apps/news?pid=20601103&sid=a2p_zMYkFQFg.

Li, Wenli, and Pierre-Daniel Sarte. "U.S. Consumer Bankruptcy Choice: The Importance of General Equilibrium Effects." *Journal of Monetary Economics* 53, no. 3 (April 2006): 613–31.

Liebowitz, Stan. "New Evidence on the Foreclosure Crisis." *Wall Street Journal,* July 2009: A13.

Lindbeck, Assar. "Welfare State Disincentives with Endogenous Habits and Norms." *Scandinavian Journal of Economics* 97, no. 4 (December 1995): 477–94.

Livshits, Igor, James MacGee, and Michèle Tertilt. "Consumer Bankruptcy: A Fresh Start." *American Economic Review* 97, no. 1 (March 2007): 402–18.

Ljungqvist, Lars. "How Do Lay-off Costs Affect Employment?" *Economic Journal* 112, no. 482 (October 2002): 829–53.

Lower-Basch, Elizabeth. *Hearing on TANF"s Role in Providing Assistance to Struggling Families.* Testimony for the Record, Committee on Ways and Means, Subcommittee on Income Security and Family Support, 2010.

Lucas, Robert E. Jr. "Econometric Policy Evaluation: A Critique." *Carnegie-Rochester Conference Series on Public Policy* 1, no. 1 (January 1976): 19–46.

Lucas, Robert E. Jr. "Bernanke Is the Best Stimulus Right Now." *Wall Street Journal,* December 23, 2008. http://online.wsj.com/article/SB122999959052129273.html.

Making Home Affordable. "Frequently Asked Questions." MakingHomeAffordable.gov. December 23, 2011. http://www.makinghomeaffordable.gov/about-mha/faqs/Pages/default.aspx (accessed February 7, 2012).

Manchir, Michelle. "Quinn Signs Tax Credit for New Hires at Small Businesses." chicagotribune.com. April 13, 2010. http://newsblogs.chicagotribune.com/clout_st/2010/04/quinn-signs-tax-credit-for-new-hires-at-small-businesses.html (accessed March 5, 2012).

Mankiw, N. Gregory, and Matthew Weinzieri. "Dynamic Scoring: A Back-of-the-Envelope Guide." *Journal of Public Economics* 90, no. 8–9 (September 2006): 1415–33.

Marinescu, Ioana. "Online Job Search and Unemployment Insurance During the Great Recession." Manuscript, University of Chicago, May 2012.

Matas-Mir, Antonio, and Denise R. Osborn. "Does Seasonality Change over the Business Cycle? An Investigation Using Monthly Industrial Production." *European Economic Review* 48, no. 6 (December 2004): 1309–32.

Mattingly, Marybeth J., and Kristin E. Smith. "Changes in Wives' Employment When Husbands Stop Working: A Recession-Prosperity Comparison." *Family Relations* 59, no. 4 (October 2010): 343–57.

McCarthy, Kevin E. "Unemployment Compensation Offsets." Office of Legislative Research—Connecticut General Assembly. February 13, 2002. http://www.cga. ct.gov/2002/rpt/2002-R-0188.htm (accessed November 5, 2011).

McGrattan, Ellen R. "The Macroeconomic Effects of Distortionary Taxation." *Journal of Monetary Economics* 33, no. 3 (June 1994): 573–601.

Melvin, Jasmin. *More Americans Wary of Tax Man This Year.* April 14, 2009. http:// www.reuters.com/article/2009/04/14/us-usa-taxes-recession-idUSTRE53D01 M20090414 (accessed November 25, 2011).

Meyer, Bruce D. "Unemployment and Workers' Compensation Programmes: Rationale, Design, Labour Supply and Income Support." *Fiscal Studies* 23, no. 1 (2002): 1–49.

Meyer, Bruce D., Wallace K. C. Mok, and James X. Sullivan. "The Under-Reporting of Transfers in Household Surveys: Its Nature and Consequences." *NBER working paper* no. 15181 (July 2009).

Mian, Atif, and Amir Sufi. "What Explains High Unemployment? The Aggregate Demand Channel." Manuscript, University of Chicago Booth School of Business, November 2011.

Mian, Atif, Kamalesh Rao, and Amir Sufi. "Household Balance Sheets, Consumption, and the Economic Slump." Manuscript, University of Chicago Booth School of Business, November 2011.

Miron, Jeffrey A. *The Economics of Seasonal Cycles.* Cambridge, MA: MIT Press, 1996.

Mirrlees, James A. "An Exploration in the Theory of Optimum Income Taxation." *Review of Economic Studies* 38, no. 114 (April 1971): 175–208.

Moffitt, Robert A., ed. *Means-Tested Transfer Programs in the United States.* Chicago: University of Chicago Press (for NBER), 2003.

Moore, Kevin B., and Michael G. Palumbo. "The Finances of American Households in the Past Three Recessions: Evidence from the Survey of Consumer Finances." *Federal Reserve Board Finance and Economics Discussion Series*, no. 2010–06 (2010).

Morgenson, Gretchen. *Reckless Endangerment: How Outsized Ambition, Greed, and Corruption Led to Economic Armageddon.* New York: Holt, 2011.

Mountford, Andrew, and Harald Uhlig. "What Are the Effects of Fiscal Policy Shocks?" *Journal of Applied Econometrics* 24, no. 6 (2009): 960–92.

Mulligan, Casey B. "Aggregate Implications of Indivisible Labor." *Advances in Macroeconomics* 1, no. 1 (2001): article 4.

Mulligan, Casey B. "A Century of Labor-Leisure Distortions." *NBER working paper* no. 8774 (February 2002).

Mulligan, Casey B. "What Do Aggregate Consumption Euler Equations Say About the Capital Income Tax Burden?" *American Economic Review* 94, no. 2 (May 2004): 166–70.

Mulligan, Casey B. "Public Policies as Specification Errors." *Review of Economic Dynamics* 8, no. 4 (October 2005): 902–26.

Mulligan, Casey B. "A Depressing Scenario: Mortgage Debt Becomes Unemployment Insurance." *NBER working paper* no. 14514 (November 2008).

Mulligan, Casey B. "Means-Tested Mortgage Modification: Homes Saved or Income Destroyed?" *NBER working paper* no. 15821 (August 2009a).

Mulligan, Casey B. "What Caused the Recession of 2008? Hints from Labor Productivity." *NBER working paper* no. 14729 (February 2009b).

Mulligan, Casey B. "Aggregate Implications of Labor Market Distortions: The Recession of 2008–9 and Beyond." *NBER working paper* no. 15681 (January 2010a).

Mulligan, Casey B. "Foreclosures, Enforcement, and Collections Under Federal Mortgage Modification Guidelines." *NBER working paper* no. 15777 (February 2010b).

Mulligan, Casey B. "The Housing Cycle and Prospects for Technical Progress." *NBER working paper* no. 15971 (May 2010c).

Mulligan, Casey B. "Does Labor Supply Matter During a Recession? Evidence from the Seasonal Cycle." George J. Stigler Center Working Paper Series no. 243, 2011a.

Mulligan, Casey B. "Means-Tested Subsidies and Economic Performance Since 2007." *NBER working paper* no. 17445 (September 2011b).

Mulligan, Casey B. "Simple Analytics and Empirics of the Government Spending Multiplier and Other Keynesian Paradoxes." *BE Journal of Macroeconomics* 11, no. 1, Contributions (2011c): article 19.

Mulligan, Casey B. "Recent Marginal Labor Income Tax Rate Changes by Skill and Marital Status." paper prepared for NBER conference on Tax Policy and the Economy. June 2012.

Mulligan, Casey B., and Yona Rubinstein. "Selection, Investment, and Women's Relative Wages over Time." *Quarterly Journal of Economics*, 123, no. 3 (August 2003): 1061–1110.

Mulligan, Casey B., and Luke Threinen. "The Marginal Products of Residential and Non-Residential Capital Through 2009." *NBER working paper* no. 15897 (April 2010).

Murphy, Kevin M., and Robert Topel. "Unemployment and Nonemployment." *American Economic Review* 87, no. 2 (May 1997): 295–300.

Myers, Robert J. *Social Security*. 4th ed. Philadelphia: Pension Research Council, 1993.

National Bureau of Economic Research. *Marginal Tax Rates, Federal Only*. October 15, 2010. http://www.nber.org/~taxsim/marginal-tax-rates/af.html (accessed February 8, 2012).

National Employment Law Project. *Unemployment Insurance and Social Security Retirement Offsets*. December 2003a. http://nelp.3cdn.net/f96d84de63766102b2_8rm6b99ab.pdf (accessed November 5, 2011).

National Employment Law Project. "What Is an 'Alternative Base Period' and Why Does My State Need One?" *National Employment Law Project*. April 2003b. http://www.nelp.org/page/-/UI/abpfactsheet041003.pdf (accessed December 2011).

National Employment Law Project. *Development of State Laws Regarding Social Security Retirement.* November 5, 2007. http://www.nelp.org/page/-/UI/Development_of_social_security_offsets_Nov_2007.pdf (accessed November 2011).

National Employment Law Project. "Recovery Act's Unemployment Insurance Modernization Incentives Produce Bipartisan State Reforms in Eight States in 2010." National Employment Law Project. September 3, 2010. http://nelp.3cdn.net/ebbff6219d7fb6acb4_ksm6bcaec.pdf (accessed November 14, 2011).

National Employment Law Project. "Overview of Unemployment Insurance Federal Extensions." *National Employment Law Project.* July 2011. http://www.nelp.org/page/-/UI/2011/current.extension.law.impact.pdf (accessed January 16, 2012).

Neighborhood Legal Services Association. Food Stamps. July 27, 2009. http://www.nlsa.us/legal_information/benefits/pb7_food_stamps_overview.htm.

Neumann, John von, and Oskar Morgenstern. *Theory of Games and Economics Behavior.* Princeton, NJ: Princeton University Press, 1944.

Neumark, David. "Delay the Minimum Wage Hike." *Wall Street Journal,* June 12, 2009: A15.

Neumark, David, and William L. Wascher. *Minimum Wages.* Cambridge, MA: MIT Press, 2008.

New York Office of Temporary and Disability Assistance. "Governor Paterson Announces Increased Efforts to Ensure That Vulnerable New Yorkers Have Access to Food and Nutritional Supports as State Sees Record High Enrollment in Food Stamp Program." *otda.ny.gov.* January 2, 2009. http://otda.ny.gov/news/2009/2009-01-02.asp (accessed April 21, 2012).

New York Times Editorial Board. "As Foreclosures Surge..." *New York Times,* May 4, 2009: A22.

New York Times Editorial Board. "A Minimum Wage Increase." *New York Times,* March 26, 2011: WK9.

Norris, Floyd. "Time to Say It: Double Dip Recession May Be Happening." *New York Times,* August 5, 2011: B1.

Office of Thrift Supervision. *OCC and OTS Mortgage Metrics Report,* various issues.

Ohanian, Lee E. "The Economic Crisis from a Neoclassical Perspective." *Journal of Economic Perspectives* (Fall 2010): 45–66.

Olson, Mancur. *Power and Prosperity.* Oxford: Oxford University Press, 2000.

Orzag, Peter. "Unemployment Insurance as Economic Stimulus." *Center on Budget and Policy Priorities.* November 15, 2001. http://www.cbpp.org/cms/?fa=view&id=830 (accessed February 10, 2012).

Orzag, Peter. "Tie U.S. Recovery Program to Economic Indicators: Peter Orszag." Bloomberg.com. February 7, 2012. http://www.bloomberg.com/news/2012-02-08/tie-u-s-recovery-program-to-economic-indicators-peter-orszag.html (accessed February 14, 2012).

Parkin, Michael. "A Method for Determining Whether Parameters in Aggregative Models Are Structural." *Carnegie-Rochester Conference Series on Public Policy* 29, no. 1 (January 1988): 215–52.

Pencavel, Joohn. "Labor Supply of Men: A Survey." In *Handbook of Labor Economics*, by Orley Ashenfelter and Richard Layard eds. Amsterdam: North-Holland, 1986.

Prescott, Edward C. "Prosperity and Depression." *American Economic Review* 92, no. 2 (May 2002): 1–15.

Prescott, Edward C. "Why Do Americans Work So Much More Than Europeans?" *Federal Reserve Bank of Minneapolis Quarterly Review*, July 2004: 2–14.

Ramey, Valerie A. "A Brief History of the Real Business Cycle—Search & Matching Literature." February 22, 2011a. http://weber.ucsd.edu/~vramey/research/Search_and_Matching_Lit_History.pdf (accessed February 29, 2012).

Ramey, Valerie A. "Identifying Government Spending Shocks: It's All in the Timing." *Quarterly Journal of Economics* 126, no. 1 (March 2011b): 1–50.

Ratcliffe, Caroline, Signe-Mary McKernan, and Kenneth Finegold. "The Effect of State Food Stamp and TANF Policies on Food Stamp Program Participation." Urban Institute. March 2007. http://www.urban.org/url.cfm?ID=411438 (accessed January 10, 2012).

Ratner, David. "Unemployment Insurance Experience Rating and Labor Market Dynamics." Manuscript, University of Michigan, October 2011.

Rogerson, Richard, and Randall Wright. "Involuntary Unemployment in Economies with Efficient Risk Sharing." *Journal of Monetary Economics* 22, no. 3 (1988): 501–15.

Rogerson, Richard, and Robert Shimer. *Search in Macroeconomic Models of the Labor Market*. Vol. 4, Part A, in *Handbook of Labor Economics*, edited by Orley Ashenfelter and David Card, 619–700. Amsterdam: Elsevier, 2011.

Romer, Christina, and Jared Bernstein. "The Job Impact of the American Recovery and Reinvestment Plan." January 9, 2009.

Romich, Jennifer L., Jennifer Simmelink, and Stephen Holt. "When Working Harder Does Not Pay: Low-Income Working Families, Tax Liabilities, and Benefit Reductions." *Families in Society: The Journal of Contemporary Social Services* 88, no. 3 (2007): 418–26.

Rosen, Harvey S. *Public Finance*. 7th ed. New York: McGraw-Hill, 2005.

Rosen, Sherwin. "Learning and Experience in the Labor Market." *Journal of Human Resources* 7, no. 3 (Summer 1972): 326–42.

Rosen, Sherwin. "Authority, Control, and the Distribution of Earnings." *Bell Journal of Economics* 13 (Autumn 1982): 311–23.

Rosenbaum, Dottie. "Food Stamp Provisions of the Final 2008 Farm Bill." July 1, 2008. http://www.cbpp.org/files/5-23-08fa.pdf (accessed May 15, 2012).

Ross, Donna Cohen, and Sharon Parrott. *Medicaid and CHIP Eligibility Is Protected for Jobless Families That Receive Boost in Unemployment Benefits*. March 20, 2009.

http://www.cbpp.org/cms/index.cfm?fa=view&id=2723 (accessed November 16, 2011).

Rothstein, Jesse. "Unemployment Insurance and Job Search in the Great Recession." *Brookings Papers on Economic Activity* (Fall 2011): 143–210.

Roy, Andrew D. "Some Thoughts on the Distribution of Earnings." *Oxford Economic Papers* 3, no. 2 (June 1951): 134–46.

Rudebusch, Glenn D. "The Fed's Monetary Policy Response to the Current Crisis." Federal Reserve Bank of San Francisco Economic Letter, no. 2009–17 (May 2009).

Sack, Kevin. "Recession Drove Many to Medicaid Last Year." *New York Times*, October 1, 2010: A16.

Sargent, Thomas, and Lars Ljungqvist. "The European Unemployment Dilemma." *Journal of Political Economy* 106, no. 3 (June 1998): 514–50.

Sbordone, Argia M. "Prices and Unit Labor Costs: A New Test of Price Stickiness." *Journal of Monetary Economics* 49, no. 2 (March 2002): 265–92.

Schirle, Tammy. "Why Have the Labor Force Participation Rates of Older Men Increased Since the Mid-1990s?" *Journal of Labor Economics* 26, no. 4 (October 2008): 549–94.

Schmieder, Johannes F., Till von Wachter, and Stefan Bender. "The Effects of Extended Unemployment Insurance over the Business Cycle: Regression Discontinuity Estimates over 20 Years." *Quarterly Journal of Economics* forthcoming (2012).

Sharp, Keith P. "Tests of U.S. Short and Long Interest Rate Seasonality." *Review of Economics and Statistics* 70, no. 1 (February 1988): 177–82.

Sherman, Arloc. "Poverty and Financial Distress Would Have Been Substantially Worse in 2010 Without Government Action, New Census Data Show." *Center on Budget and Policy Priorities*. November 7, 2011. http://www.cbpp.org/files/11-7-11pov.pdf (accessed November 21, 2011).

Shimer, Robert. "Reassessing the Ins and Outs of Unemployment." *NBER working paper* no. 13421, September 2007.

Shimer, Robert. "Convergence in Macroeconomics: The Labor Wedge." *American Economic Journal: Macroeconomics* 1, no. 1 (January 2009): 280–97.

Shimer, Robert. *Labor Markets and Business Cycles*. Princeton, NJ: Princeton University press, 2010a.

Shimer, Robert. "The Labor Market in the Great Recession: Comment." *Brookings Papers on Economic Activity* (Spring 2010b): 57–65.

Smets, Frank, and Raf Wouters. "An Estimated Dynamic Stochastic General Equilibrium Model of the Euro Area." *Journal of the European Economic Association* 1, no. 5 (September 2003): 1123–75.

Smets, Frank, and Rafael Wouters. "Shocks and Frictions in US Business Cycles: A Bayesian DSGE Approach." *American Economic Review* 97, no. 3 (June 2007): 586–606.

Smith, Charles Hugh. *Real Estate: The Worrying Numbers Behind Underwater Homeowners.* August 10, 2010. http://www.dailyfinance.com/2010/08/07/real-estate-underwater-homeowners/ (accessed November 26, 2011).

Smith, Vernon K., Kathleen Gifford, Ellis Eileen, Robin Rudowitz, and Laura Snyder. "Moving Ahead Amid Fiscal Challenges: A Look at Medicaid Spending, Coverage and Policy Trends." *Medicaid/CHIP.* October 2011. http://www.kff.org/medicaid/8248.cfm (accessed November 11, 2011).

Social Security Administration. *Food Stamp Facts.* May 2008. http://ssa.gov/pubs/10101.html (accessed November 12, 2011).

Social Security Administration. *SSI Annual Statistical Report, 2010.* Washington, DC: Office of Research, Evaluation, and Statistics, 2011.

Solon, Gary, Robert Barsky, and Jonathan A. Parker. "Measuring the Cyclicality of Real Wages: How Important Is Composition Bias?" *Quarterly Journal of Economics* 109, no. 1 (February 1994): 1–25.

State of California, Employment Development Department. "California System of Experience Rating." 2010 UI, ETT, and SDI Rates. June 2011a. http://www.edd.ca.gov/payroll_taxes/rates_and_withholding.htm (accessed November 3, 2011).

State of California, Employment Development Department. *Employer Extended Benefit Cost.* 2011b. http://www.edd.ca.gov/unemployment/Employer_Extended_Benefit_Cost.htm (accessed December 6, 2011).

State of California Franchise Tax Board. "New Jobs Credit." http://ca.gov. January 2012. https://www.ftb.ca.gov/businesses/New_Jobs_Credit.shtml (accessed March 5, 2012).

Summers, Lawrence H. "Some Simple Economics of Mandated Benefits." *American Economic Review* 79, no. 2 (May 1989): 177–83.

Sumner, Daniel A. "Measurement of Monopoly Behavior: An Application to the Cigarette Industry." *Journal of Political Economy* 89, no. 5 (October 1981): 1010–19.

Texas Education Agency. *Student Loan Forgiveness for Teachers.* September 2011. http://www.tea.state.tx.us/loan.aspx (accessed November 21, 2011).

Topel, Robert H. "On Layoffs and Unemployment Insurance." *American Economic Review* 73, no. 4 (September 1983): 541–59.

Topel, Robert, and Finis Welch. "Unemployment Insurance: Survey and Extensions." *Economica* 47, no. 187 (August 1980): 351–79.

Townsend, Robert M. "Microcredit and Mechanism Design." *Journal of the European Economic Association* 1, no. 2/3 (April 2003): 468–77.

Trippe, Carole, and Jessica Gillooly. "Non-Cash Categorical Eligibility for SNAP." Mathematica Policy Research. July 23, 2010.

Uhlig, Harald. "Explaining Asset Prices with External Habits and Wage Rigidities in a DSGE Model." *American Economic Review* 97, no. 2 (May 2007): 239–43.

U.S. Bureau of Economic Analysis. "Components of Value Added by Industry as a Percentage of Value Added." April 26, 2011. http://www.bea.gov/industry/

gpotables/gpo_action.cfm?anon=1014136&table_id=27013&format_type=0 (accessed October 24, 2011).

U.S. Bureau of Labor Statistics. "Characteristics of Minimum Wage Workers: 2006." February 28, 2007. http://www.bls.gov/cps/minwage2006.pdf (accessed October 15, 2011).

U.S. Bureau of Labor Statistics. "Characteristics of Minimum Wage Workers: 2007." March 24, 2008. http://www.bls.gov/cps/minwage2007.pdf (accessed October 15, 2011).

U.S. Bureau of Labor Statistics. "Characteristics of Minimum Wage Workers: 2008." Labor Force Statistics from the Current Population Survey. March 11, 2009a. http://www.bls.gov/cps/minwage2008tbls.htm (accessed February 16, 2012).

U.S. Bureau of Labor Statistics. "Employment Characteristics of Families." Economic News Releases. May 27, 2009b. http://www.bls.gov/news.release/archives/famee_05272009.pdf (accessed January 24, 2012).

U.S. Bureau of Labor Statistics. "Characteristics of Minimum Wage Workers: 2009." March 1, 2010a. http://www.bls.gov/cps/minwage2009tbls.htm (accessed October 15, 2011).

U.S. Bureau of Labor Statistics. "Industry Employment and Hours." Labor Productivity and Costs. October 29, 2010b. http://www.bls.gov/lpc/ipr_aphin.xls (accessed October 24, 2011).

U.S. Bureau of Labor Statistics. "BLS series id MPU490017." Major Sector Multifactor Productivity Index. September 23, 2011a. http://www.bls.gov/mfp/ (accessed October 26, 2011).

U.S. Bureau of Labor Statistics. "Employment from the BLS Household and Payroll Surveys: Summary of Recent Trends." Economic News Release: Employment Situation. October 7, 2011b. http://www.bls.gov/web/empsit/ces_cps_trends.pdf (accessed October 25, 2011).

U.S. Bureau of Labor Statistics. "Historical Hours and Earnings, Table B-2." October 2011c. ftp://ftp.bls.gov/pub/suppl/empsit.ceseeb2.txt (accessed October 22, 2011).

U.S. Bureau of Labor Statistics. *Labor Force Statistics from the Current Population Survey.* October 7, 2011d. http://www.bls.gov/cps/(accessed November 3, 2011).

U.S. Census Bureau. 2006 *American Community Survey Table B25096.* 2007. http://factfinder2.census.gov (accessed November 26, 2011).

U.S. Census Bureau. 2005–2009 *American Community Survey 5-Year Estimates.* 2010. http://factfinder.census.gov/servlet/ACSSAFFFacts?_event=&geo_id=01000US&_geoContext=01000US&_street=&_county=&_cityTown=&_state=&_zip=&_lang=en&_sse=on&ActiveGeoDiv=&_useEV=&pctxt=fph&pgsl=010&_submenuId=factsheet_1&ds_name=DEC_2000_SAFF&_ci_nbr=null&qr_ (accessed December 28, 2011).

U.S. Census Bureau. "Information Sector Services." 2009 Service Annual Survey Data. July 12, 2011. http://www2.census.gov/services/sas/data/51/2009_NAICS51.xls (accessed October 24, 2011).

U.S. Department of Agriculture, Food and Nutrition Service. "Broad-Based Categorical Eligibility." *Food and Nutrition Service.* February 25, 2009. http://www.fns.usda.gov/snap/rules/memo/2009/022509.pdf (accessed April 21, 2012).

U.S. Department of Agriculture, Food and Nutrition Service. "Broad-Based Categorical Eligibility." Soft Eligibility Requirements States. October 4, 2011a. http://www.fns.usda.gov/snap/rules/Memo/BBCE.pdf (accessed December 29, 2011).

U.S. Department of Agriculture, Food and Nutrition Service. "Supplemental Nutrition Assistance Program (SNAP)-Able Bodied Adults Without Dependents Waivers for Fiscal Year 2012." *Food and Nutrition Service.* May 3, 2011b. http://www.fns.usda.gov/snap/rules/Memo/PRWORA/abawds/waivers_2012.pdf (accessed April 24, 2012).

U.S. Department of Agriculture, Food and Nutrition Service. "Able-Bodied Adults Without Dependents." *Food and Nutrition Service.* February 16, 2012a. http://www.fns.usda.gov/snap/rules/memo/PRWORA/abawds/abawdspage.htm (accessed April 21, 2012).

U.S. Department of Agriculture, Food and Nutrition Service. "Supplemental Nutrition Assistance Program Benefits, Annual State Level Data." *Food and Nutrition Service.* April 2, 2012b. http://www.fns.usda.gov/pd/17SNAPfyBEN$.htm (accessed April 21, 2012).

U.S. Department of Defense. "Selected Military Compensation Tables Report." U.S. Department of Defense. various. http://prhome.defense.gov/rfm/mpp/Reports.aspx (accessed June 5, 2011).

U.S. Department of Health and Human Services. "Temporary Assistance for Needy Families: Combined TANF and SSP-MOE Work Participation Rates, Fiscal Year 2007." Administration for Children and Families. August 28, 2009. http://www.acf.hhs.gov/programs/ofa/particip/2007/tab1a.htm (accessed February 13, 2012).

U.S. Department of Health and Human Services. "Temporary Assistance for Needy Families: Combined TANF and SSP-MOE Work Participation Rates, Fiscal Year 2009." Administration for Children and Families. May 5, 2011. http://www.acf.hhs.gov/programs/ofa/particip/2009/tab01a.htm (accessed February 13, 2012).

U.S. Department of Labor. "Monetary Entitlements." Comparisons of State Unemployment Laws. 2007. http://workforcesecurity.doleta.gov/unemploy/uilawcompar/2007/comparison2007.asp (accessed November 2, 2011).

U.S. Department of Labor. "Nonmonetary Eligibility." Comparisons of State Unemployment Laws. 2009a. http://workforcesecurity.doleta.gov/unemploy/pdf/uilawcompar/2009/nonmonetary.pdf (accessed November 5, 2011).

U.S. Department of Labor. "Unemployment Insurance Program Letter No.14-09." *Employment and Training Administration.* February 26, 2009b. http://wdr.doleta.gov/directives/corr_doc.cfm?DOCN=2715 (accessed January 18, 2012).

U.S. Department of Labor. *Characteristics of the Insured Unemployed.* 2011a. http://www.ows.doleta.gov/unemploy/chariu.asp (accessed November 2, 2011).

U.S. Department of Labor. "Persons Claiming UI Benefits in Federal Programs." Unemployment Insurance Program Statistics. October 7, 2011b. http://www.ows.doleta.gov/unemploy/docs/persons.xls (accessed October 25, 2011).

U.S. Department of Labor. "Unemployment Compensation: Federal-State Partnership." *Unemployment Insurance Laws.* April 2011c. http://www.ows.doleta.gov/unemploy/pdf/partnership.pdf (accessed October 28, 2011).

U.S. Department of Labor. *Unemployment Insurance Data Summary.* September 6, 2011d. http://www.ows.doleta.gov/unemploy/content/data.asp (accessed November 3, 2011).

U.S. Department of Labor. "Unemployment Laws and Insurance." Chronology of Federal Unemployment Compensation Laws. May 3, 2011e. http://workforcesecurity.doleta.gov/unemploy/pdf/chronfedlaws.pdf (accessed October 28, 2011).

U.S. Department of Labor. "An Employee's Guide to Health Benefits Under COBRA." Employee Benefits Security Administration. January 2012. http://www.dol.gov/ebsa/publications/cobraemployee.html (accessed February 19, 2012).

U.S. Department of Treasury. "Homeowner Affordability and Stability Plan: Executive Summary." February 2009a.

U.S. Department of Treasury. "Homeowner Affordability Modification Program Guidelines." March 2009b.

U.S. Department of Treasury. "Homeowner Affordable Modification Program: Introduction." 2009c.

U.S. Department of Treasury. "COBRA Premium Assistance." Interim Report to Congress, 2010a.

U.S. Department of Treasury. "Estimates of Newly Hired Employees Eligible for the HIRE Act Tax Exemption." treasury.gov. July 12, 2010b. http://www.treasury.gov/resource-center/economic-policy/Documents/HIREAct-Analysis-7-11-2010-FINAL.pdf (accessed March 5, 2012).

U.S. Department of Treasury. "February 2011 Making Home Affordable Program Report." U.S. Department of Treasury. April 1, 2011. http://www.treasury.gov/initiatives/financial-stability/results/MHA-Reports/Documents/Feb%202011%20MHA%20Report%20FINAL_Revised.pdf (accessed January 11, 2012).

U.S. Department of Treasury. "November 2011 Making Home Affordable Program Report." United States Department of Treasury. January 9, 2012. http://www.treasury.gov/initiatives/financial-stability/results/MHA-Reports/Documents/FINAL_Nov%202011%20MHA%20Report.pdf (accessed January 11, 2012).

U.S. Government Accountability Office. *Food Stamp Program.* Report to Congressional Requesters, Washington, DC: United States Government Accountability Office, March 2007.

U.S. Government Accountability Office. *Temporary Assistance for Needy Families.* Report to Congressional Requesters. Washington, DC: U.S. Government Accountability Office, 2010.

U.S. Government Printing Office. "Public Law 111—148—Patient Protection and Affordable Care Act." gpo.gov. 2010. http://www.gpo.gov/fdsys/pkg/PLAW-111publ148/content-detail.html (accessed February 27, 2012).

U.S. Internal Revenue Service. "Schedule M: Making Work Pay Credit." IRS Forms and Publications. December 15, 2010. http://www.irs.gov/pub/irs-pdf/f1040sm.pdf (accessed February 18, 2012).

U.S. Internal Revenue Service. "State to State Migration Data." SOI Tax Stats. December 5, 2011. http://www.irs.gov/taxstats/article/0,id=212702,,00.html (accessed January 20, 2012).

U.S. Internal Revenue Service. "Individual Income Tax Return (Form 1040) Statistics, 2009." irs.gov. January 23, 2012. http://www.irs.gov/taxstats/indtaxstats/article/0,,id=133414,00.html (accessed March 12, 2012).

U.S. Internal Revenue Service. "Publication 596." *IRS Forms and Publications.* Various issues.

Vaughn, Martin. "Payroll Tax Cut: A Short Primer." *Wall Street Journal,* December 7, 2010.

Washington State Employment Security Department. *Emergency Unemployment Compensation.* 2011a. http://www.esd.wa.gov/uibenefits/fileweekly/extension/emergency-unemployment-compensation.php (accessed December 6, 2011).

Washington State Employment Security Department. *Extended Benefits.* 2011b. http://www.esd.wa.gov/uibenefits/fileweekly/extension/extended-benefits-faq.php (accessed December 6, 2011).

White House. *Fact Sheet: The American Jobs Act.* September 8, 2011. http://www.whitehouse.gov/the-press-office/2011/09/08/fact-sheet-american-jobs-act (accessed November 28, 2011).

White, Michelle, and Zhu Ning. "Saving Your Home in Chapter 13 Bankruptcy." *NBER working paper* no. 14179 (July 2008).

Winkler, Hernan. "The Effect of Homeownership on Geographic Mobility and Labor Market Outcomes." Manuscript, University of California Los Angeles, September 2011.

Wolkwitz, Kari, and Joshua Leftin. "Characteristics of Food Stamp Households: Fiscal Year 2007." *Supplemental Nutrition Assistance Program (SNAP) Studies.* September 2008. http://www.fns.usda.gov/ora/MENU/Published/snap/FILES/Participation/2007Characteristics.pdf (accessed November 5, 2011).

Wolkwitz, Kari, and Carole Trippe. "Characteristics of Supplemental Nutrition Assistance Program Households: Fiscal Year 2008." *Supplemental Nutrition Assistance Program (SNAP) Studies.* September 2009. http://www.fns.usda.gov/ora/MENU/Published/snap/FILES/Participation/2008Characteristics.pdf (accessed November 5, 2011).

Woodford, Michael. *Interest and Prices: Foundations of a Theory of Monetary Policy.* Princeton, NJ: Princeton University Press, 2003.

Woodford, Michael. "Simple Analytics of the Government Expenditure Multiplier." *American Economic Journal: Macroeconomics* 3, no. 1 (January 2011): 1–35.

Yelowitz, Aaron S. "The Medicaid Notch, Labor Supply, and Welfare Participation: Evidence from Eligibility Expansions." *Quarterly Journal of Economics* 11, no. 4 (November 1995): 909–39.

Yelowitz, Aaron S. "Evaluating the Effects of Medicaid on Welfare and Work: Evidence from the Past Decade." Employment Policies Institute, 2000. http://epionline.org/studies/yelowitz_12-2000.pdf.

Zandi, Mark. "To Shore up the Recovery, Help Housing." Moody's Analytics. May 25, 2011. http://www.economy.com/mark-zandi/documents/To-Shore-Up-the-Recovery-Help-Housing.pdf (accessed January 11, 2012).

Zedlewski, Sheila. "The Role of Welfare During a Recession." December 2008. http://www.urban.org/UploadedPDF/411809_role_of_welfare.pdf (accessed November 13, 2011).

Zedlewski, Sheila. "What Role Is Welfare Playing in This Period of High Unemployment?" *Unemployment and Recovery Project.* August 2011. http://www.urban.org/UploadedPDF/412378-Role-of-Welfare-in-this-Period-of-High-Unemployment.pdf (accessed November 13, 2011).

Ziliak, James P., Craig Gundersen, and David N. Figlio. "Food Stamp Caseloads over the Business Cycle." *Southern Economic Journal* 69, no. 4 (2003): 903–19.

Index